Teaching
the Literatures
of the American
Civil War

**Modern Language Association of America
Options for Teaching**

For a complete listing of titles,
see the last pages of this book.

Teaching the Literatures of the American Civil War

Edited by
Colleen Glenney Boggs

The Modern Language Association of America
New York   2016

MLA and the MODERN LANGUAGE ASSOCIATION are trademarks owned
by the Modern Language Association of America. For information about obtaining permission to reprint material from MLA book publications, send your
request by mail (see address below) or e-mail (permissions@mla.org).

Library of Congress Cataloging-in-Publication Data

Names: Boggs, Colleen Glenney, editor.
Title: Teaching the literatures of the American Civil War / Edited by Colleen
    Glenney Boggs.
Description: New York : The Modern Language Association of America, 2016. |
    Series: Options for teaching, ISSN 1079-2562 ; 39 | Includes bibliographical
    references and index.
Identifiers: LCCN 2016006382 (print) | LCCN 2016015612 (ebook) |
    ISBN 9781603292757 (cloth : alk. paper) | ISBN 9781603292764 (pbk.) |
    ISBN 9781603292771 (EPUB) | ISBN 9781603292788 (Kindle)
Subjects: LCSH: American literature—19th century—History and criticism. |
    United States—History—Civil War, 1861–1865—Literature and the
    war—Study and teaching (Higher) | United States—History—Civil War,
    1861–1865—Study and teaching (Higher) | United States—History—Civil
    War, 1861–1865—Sources.
Classification: LCC PS217.C58 T433 2016 (print) | LCC PS217.C58 (ebook) |
    DDC 810.9/0040711—dc23
LC record available at https://lccn.loc.gov/2016006382

Options for Teaching 39
ISSN 1079-2562

Cover illustration of the paperback and electronic editions: Saint-Gaudens,
Augustus. *Shaw Memorial.* 1900. Detail. Patinated plaster. US Department of
the Interior, National Park Service, Saint-Gaudens National Historic Site,
Cornish, NH. Image courtesy of the National Gallery of Art, Washington.

Published by The Modern Language Association of America
85 Broad Street, Suite 500, New York, New York 10004-2408
www.mla.org

For Noah and for Liam

Contents

Acknowledgments   xi

Introduction   1
Colleen Glenney Boggs

Part I: Teaching Civil War Literature in Historical Context

Contradictions and Ambivalence: Emerson, Hawthorne,
and the Antebellum Origins of Civil War Literature   23
Larry J. Reynolds

Complicating the Relation between Literature and History:
Slave Participation in Fact and Fiction   33
Tess Chakkalakal

Truth and Consequences: Helping Students Contextualize
the Literary Aftermath of the American Civil War   43
Coleman Hutchison

Teaching Civil War Literature to International Students:
A Case Study from South Korea   53
Wiebke Omnus Klumpenhower

Team-Teaching the Civil War at Historical Sites   58
Darren T. Williamson, Shawn Jones, and William Steele

Part II: Teaching Various Genres

Constituting Communities: Reading the Civil War in Poetry
and Song   71
Faith Barrett

Reading on the (Home) Front: Teaching Soldiers' Dime Novels   81
Allison E. Carey

Letters, Memoranda, and Official Documents: Teaching
Nonfiction Prose   91
Christopher Hager

Approaches to Life Writing: Confederate Women's Diaries
    and the Construction of Ethnic Identity   101
    Dana McMichael

Teaching Civil War Speech; or, Abraham Lincoln's Texts
    in Context   111
    Alex W. Black

Part III: Teaching Specific Topics

The Civil War and Literary Realism   123
    Ian Finseth

Civil War Landscapes   135
    Michael Ziser

Brotherhood in Civil War–Era America   145
    Matthew R. Davis

Poetic Representations of African American Soldiers   156
    Catherine E. Saunders

Women's Roles in Antislavery and Civil War Literature   165
    Jessica DeSpain

"Treasonable Sympathies": Affect and Allegiance
    in the Civil War   174
    Elizabeth Duquette

Part IV: Teaching Materials

Teaching through Primary Source Documents   187
    Julia Stern

Teaching with Images: Synthesizing the Civil War in
    Fact and Fiction   198
    Melissa J. Strong

Recollecting the Civil War through Nineteenth-
    Century Periodicals   211
    Kathleen Diffley

Teaching with Contemporary Anthologies   221
    Timothy Sweet

Teaching with Historical Anthologies   233
    Jess Roberts

Using Digital Archives   243
    Susan M. Ryan

Civil War Literature and First-Year Writing Instruction   255
    Rebecca Entel

Part V: Resources

Reference Guides   267

General Studies   267

Anthologies, Readers, and Document Collections   268

Visual Materials   270

Recommended Print Editions   272

Additional Resources for Specific Authors and Texts   273

Autobiographies and Diaries   275

Dime Novels   278

Special Topics   279

Notes on Contributors   285
Works Cited   289
Index   311

Acknowledgments

My first expression of gratitude goes to the volume contributors. They were delightful to work with throughout this long process. I am grateful to my students at Dartmouth, especially those in my course The Civil War in Literature. Thanks to Dartmouth's Center for the Advancement of Learning and its inaugural director, Thomas Luxon, as well as to the Summer Institute for American Studies; its director, Donald Pease; and my seminar groups.

The MLA shepherded this project from an idea to a proposal to a draft to a book, with careful attention paid at each step of the way. I thank the members of the publications committee, the anonymous reviewers, and my editors, Margit Longbrake, James Hatch, Angela Gibson, Michael Kandel, and Katherine Kim.

I am grateful to come from a family of teachers, and I thank my parents, Paul and Ursula Boggs; my brother, Sean; and my husband, Brian Glenney, for the example they set. Last, never least, I thank my sons, Noah and Liam Glenney. May this volume teach them and others an understanding of war that fosters peace.

Colleen Glenney Boggs

Introduction

When Abraham Lincoln met Harriet Beecher Stowe in 1863, he reportedly greeted her as "the little woman who wrote the book that started this Great War" (Hedrick vii). Lincoln's comment intertwines cultural with historical events, and to this day, *Uncle Tom's Cabin* (1851–52) has almost mythical status as a touchstone for the war. Yet the literature of the conflict has remained both central to and absent from our scholarly and pedagogical approaches to American literary studies. Historians have filled libraries with books on the Civil War, while only a few works, such as *Uncle Tom's Cabin*, have been selected to stand in for the literature of the Civil War. When the curriculum in American literary studies was first designed in the 1940s, the Civil War was implicitly central to the way instructors structured survey classes and anthologies. As Richard Slotkin has noted, the curriculum was organized chronologically, and the Civil War functioned as a dividing line in course titles and period labels ("What Shall" 120). Scholars understood the war as the unfinished business of the American Revolution: it provided a termination point for the early national enterprise, which had failed to resolve the issue of slavery. The Civil War's own unfinished business shaped literature written after the war, giving rise to

1

literary movements such as realism and providing themes such as national reconciliation.

Although the Civil War has taken on a central role in structuring the chronology of the curriculum in American literature, what counts as Civil War literature has been a subject of scholarly disagreement and pedagogical debate. Must an author have had combat experience for his work to count as Civil War literature, or are there other forms of experiencing and witnessing the war that qualify, when recorded? That none of the canonical American authors of the nineteenth century participated as soldiers in the Civil War led Daniel Aaron to refer to it as "the unwritten war." And yet several major writers responded to the war, drawing both on first-hand experiences and on printed source materials. Using a largely auto-biographical format, Walt Whitman recorded his experiences as a nurse in *Specimen Days* (1872), but he also invented war scenes for the poems included in *Drum-Taps* (1865). Louisa May Alcott fictionalized her nursing experiences in *Hospital Sketches* (1863). Even for writers who had little or no direct involvement with the battlefront, the war loomed large in their experience of the war years, and it affected their literary imagination. Drawing mainly on newspaper and magazine accounts of the war action, Herman Melville composed *Battle-Pieces and Aspects of the War* (1866). The war bears a particularly complicated relation to Emily Dickinson. Despite her seeming isolation in Amherst, she was deeply engaged with the war, as Shira Wolosky has argued, and Dickinson's most productive years as a poet fall into that period.

It is now possible to situate major authors in relation to the vast array of literature that was written ad hoc, by people who had no other experience with writing and saw their literary production directly called forth by the war. The rise of cultural studies and the new accessibility of cultural artifacts in the digital age has transformed how we might read and what we might read when it comes to Civil War literature. The archive has not only expanded but also become newly legible because of specific scholarly developments over the past decades. For instance, sustained attention has been paid since the 1980s to sentimental literature and its relevance in the creation of a sense of national belonging and identity. This scholarly attention is making it possible to read Civil War literature in a new way, since that literature is often sentimental and highly stylized, thereby defying modern expectations of an unmediated authenticity in the representation of war.

The questions that emerge from the shifting field of Civil War literature, and that this volume hopes to help teachers address, are as follows: What is the relation of canonical works to the multitude of occasional texts that were penned in response to the war, and how can students understand them in conjunction with each other? Should an approach to war literature reflect the chronology of historical events or focus instead on thematic clusters, generic forms, and theoretical concerns? How do we embrace the pedagogical challenges of introducing students to archival materials that sometimes support, at other times resist, the close reading practices in which they have been trained?

One challenge we face is identifying what the object of study is when we talk about Civil War literature. We may ask of much literature written during the Civil War whether or in what sense it is even about the war. In assessing our object of study, we need to rethink the sway that Whitman's claim has had, that "the real war will never get into the books" (*Complete Poetry* 778). That claim led to three assumptions, which this volume calls into question: one, that the war years did not produce their own literature; two, that the war itself had to await the advent of literary realism to find accurate depiction, for instance in Stephen Crane's *Red Badge of Courage* (1895); three, that books are the proper place to locate Civil War literature. As Alice Fahs's impressively researched monograph *The Imagined Civil War: Popular Literature of the North and South, 1861–1865*, Faith Barrett and Cristanne Miller's anthology of Civil War poetry *"Words for the Hour": A New Anthology of American Civil War Poetry*, and Ian Finseth's genre-crossing anthology *The American Civil War: An Anthology of Essential Writings* demonstrate, the war years produced a vast outpouring of popular literature—that is, of poetry, prose fiction, nonfiction prose, political oratory, personal letters (private and published), magazines, gift books, and scrapbooks. The anthologies also speak to a new interest in making that literature available to a new audience of teachers and students.

What is missing is guidance on how to integrate these materials into existing courses on American literature and on how to approach these materials in new courses that focus on the war. How should we teach this archive of popular works to students schooled in book culture? What are the methodologies for this undertaking? How do we best approach this literature—chronologically, generically, topically, theoretically? As the founders of the American Studies Association's recently formed War and Peace Studies Caucus argue, we need "new directions for teaching and research regarding how issues of violence and conflict intersect with issues ranging from notions of patriotism and nationalism to the role of technology and religion in American life" (*War and Peace Studies Caucus*). This volume provides answers to that call. Its main focus lies on literature written during the war years themselves, but the book also asks the question whether that literature is necessarily war literature.

This volume comes at a particularly important juncture in our national life and our pedagogical practices. The years 2011–15 marked sesquicentennial commemorations and reevaluations of the Civil War, which created a unique opportunity for scholars and students to be in dialogue with each other as well as with a broader public. The commemoration of the war found expression in local events as well as in national media outlets. For instance, the *New York Times* devoted a whole op-ed series, Disunion, to tracking the history of the Civil War as it unfolded. This public interest calls for a broader engagement with pedagogical resources, and vice versa, those pedagogical resources can inform the public conversation as we move beyond this moment of reassessment toward an ongoing and sustained dialogue about the Civil War's significance for American life. The proliferating interest in the Civil War across audiences, disciplines, genres, and media adds urgency to the need for a comprehensive resource focusing on the pedagogy of teaching Civil War literature at colleges and universities.

Because scholarly publications on the Civil War continue to be voluminous and transformative of our knowledge, one might ask why we need yet another book on the topic. First, despite all that's been published on the Civil War, there is no volume like this one, focused on pedagogy. Second, precisely for the reason that so much has been published, guidance on how to turn that scholarship into effective pedagogy is sorely needed. The great number of available materials provides a rigorous context for this volume, but it can also discourage newcomers to the field. Recent anthologies and paperback editions have called attention to the wide range of texts available for study, from canonical forms of literary accomplishment to unfamiliar forms of popular writing. This volume seeks to make accessible a variety of approaches for a range of courses serving students from different backgrounds and at different stages of their education; it seeks to make current remappings of American literary study pedagogically legible.

No volume can cover all that there is to cover when it comes to teaching the Civil War, and we do not attempt to undertake such a Herculean task. Our focus is literature, which remains an understudied field both from the perspective of Civil War scholarship and from the perspective of the teaching curriculum. This volume aims to provide a resource for teachers and at the same time to make a scholarly and pedagogical intervention into how we engage with the Civil War. All too often, Civil War literature has been a research domain, not a teaching resource. By changing that, we hope to build a connection between the vast scholarly field of Civil War studies and a curriculum that has not kept up-to-date with the developments in that field or has ceded them to specific departments without reflecting on their cross-disciplinary implications.

A consideration of literature adds an important dimension to discussions about the Civil War: it reminds us that our relation to the war is itself mediated by time and distance, by documents and archives, and enables us to think about the consequences of that mediation for our own understanding as well as for that of the people alive then. Take the following example. James R. Randall was a college tutor with limited previous writing experience. He wrote the poem "Maryland, My Maryland," which today is the state song of Maryland, in response to a specific event, the firing on civilians by the Sixth Massachusetts Regiment while it marched through Baltimore (M. Andrews 11). Penned in the course of one night, the poem did not just record what happened; it also gave voice to the state's secessionists when it called on them to "Avenge the patriotic gore / That flecked the streets of Baltimore" (Randall 49). The poem fueled anti-Union sentiment and forced Governor Hicks to call the assembly for a vote on secession (McPherson, *Battle Cry* 287). Published in the newspaper *New Orleans Delta* on 26 April 1861 and reprinted in newspapers throughout the region, the poem became a powerful anthem of the Southern cause that readers embraced: Mary Chesnut copied the poem into her diary on 16 January 1862 (*Mary Chesnut's Civil War* 282), and William Galt, a cadet of the Virginia Military Institute, wrote the poem into a wartime notebook.

We tend to think of literature as printed text and to distinguish strictly among different genres, but texts during the Civil War moved freely and with dizzying speed from newspaper accounts into published verses that were copied into private journals, made into song lyrics, turned into parodies, and adapted for the stage. "My Maryland" was set to music and became known as "the Marseillaise of the Confederate cause" (Barrett and Miller 389); Oliver Wendell Holmes reportedly described it as the greatest of all poems produced by the war.[1] It was sung to the melody of the Christmas song "O Tannenbaum," which was also the tune for the popular college song "Lauriger Horatius" (Fahs, *Imagined Civil War* 80). The emotional appeal of literature was not just in the words but also in the melodies that spoke to people's feelings about college friends and family holidays. Yet the poem could quickly reclaim its political meaning and serve as a comment on military events. When Lee's troops marched into Frederick on 6 September 1862, they sang "My Maryland" as a victory tune (McPherson, *Battle Cry* 535). By 11 October 1862, *Harper's Weekly* was publishing accounts of the Battle of Antietam alongside a parody of Randall's poem. Declaring, "Ah me! I've had enough of thee, / Maryland, my Maryland!," the parody combined the humor of sweethearts breaking up with ominous references to the "vengeful ire" pounding the northern war effort ("My Maryland"). We don't often think of the Civil War in relation to humor, and yet literature not only repeated images familiar to readers but also played with them and mingled the silly with the serious. The ease with which literature was adapted and even parodied reflects its generic nature. The poem gained much of its power from appeals to Maryland as a mother figure with a "blush on thy cheek." It asked this personified figure to "gird thy beauteous limbs with steel" and reveal her "peerless chivalry" (Randall 50). As Mark Twain recognized when he blamed Sir Walter Scott for the American Civil War (501), such lines are taken as much from *Ivanhoe*, Scott's vastly popular 1819 novel of medieval England, as they are from newspaper accounts of the war. But the serious political consequences of conventional literary imagery become evident when we consider the following lines: in a stanza that begins, "Dear Mother, burst the tyrant's chain, Maryland!" (Randall 50), the poem also hauntingly includes the line "*Sic semper!*," which anticipates John Wilkes Booth, who shouted, "*Sic semper tyrannis!*," when he shot Abraham Lincoln at Ford's Theatre. Often, literature runs like a conversation through the Civil War—rousing to action one moment, giving rise to parody the next, tying new events to established images, and appealing to feelings as much as to reason.

Civil War literature, then, enables us to ask larger questions about the ways in which representation works on multiple levels. Not only does this volume expose students and teachers to new archives and areas of interest, but it also asks questions about how we should engage with those archives and areas. Many of the essays in this volume generate and interrogate productive tensions between canonical and noncanonical works, between literature as a mark of accomplishment and literature as a broader cultural practice, between history as literary context and literature as historical context, between material culture and its digitized forms. We also ask how our narratives can responsibly tread the difficult territories of a fractured past. What are our responsibilities as teachers in instructing students about past controversies without either replicating them or brushing them aside? Far from becoming paralyzing, these challenges can stimulate a great deal of creative pedagogical work. This book is designed to showcase a range of approaches that have been worked out at different kinds of institutions, mainly in the United States, from community colleges to research universities, and for both traditional and nontraditional students. Our contributors, drawing on early pioneering work as well as on state-of-the-art research, focus their attention on enabling instructors in many fields and at any levels to reflect on the pedagogy of teaching Civil War literature and learn more about others' practices. The volume hopes to offer collaborative, practical, nuts-and-bolts strategies for teaching.

This volume, intending to demonstrate the array of genres, contexts, reading practices, engagements, and pedagogical innovations that literature produces and enables, can only be exemplary, not exhaustive. Any one of the essays and topics discussed here gives rise to other engagements and considerations. The resources section provides suggestions as to the field's larger contours and guidance on how to broaden or deepen the issues represented here. The volume hopes to show how teachers can create innovative combinations and juxtapositions of issues and integrate specific themes into a course.

The case for teaching Civil War literature might be easy to make for special topics courses or seminars and classes that focus on this period of American cultural and political life. But why free up curricular space for Civil War literature in a survey course on American literature? This volume argues for the benefits of teaching more Civil War literature in postsecondary literature courses. Decanonization has meant an expansion of the field of American literature but not of the time to teach it, so the gains and costs of choosing one subject over another must always carefully be weighed as Civil War literature is introduced to a curriculum.

Strategies for Using This Volume

Civil War literature is of interest to scholar-teachers in different departments and programs for the fields of English, African American literature, American studies, history, war and peace studies, comparative literature, composition, women's and gender studies, art history, digital humanities, and media studies. This volume points to the intersections among these different fields and offers instructors insights on how to help students think through the subject's interdisciplinary contexts. The range of topics and methodological approaches is meant to be wide yet cohesive, and the contributors are a mix of established and emerging scholars. The volume aims to be judiciously representative, including northern and southern literatures, African American and women's roles in writing about the conflict, canonical and noncanonical material. We balance long-standing scholarly concerns with specific authors such as Whitman, Hawthorne, and Dickinson as well as with particular modes of writerly and political engagement, such as sentimentality. We consider such new themes as technology, periodical studies, and the international contexts of American literary studies.

To accommodate the diverse interests of teachers of Civil War literature, we offer alternative routes through this volume's contents. Readers who primarily or exclusively teach survey courses may wish to pay special attention to the teaching materials section, which discusses the use of familiar resources in unfamiliar ways and the value of new resources, such as images or digitized periodicals, to supplement or replace previously used materials. Colleagues who teach more specialized courses will want to turn to the suggestions offered in parts 2 and 3, which speak to one another productively—for example, containing suggestions for teaching genre through a cross-generic approach to specific topics. Hopefully each essay will offer both scholarly content and pedagogical guidance, so that a colleague primarily interested in literature's historical contexts might nevertheless read about and benefit from teaching strategies. For seasoned instructors as well as those who have not yet incorporated Civil War literature into their classrooms, the collective insights of the teachers on whose experience this volume draws will provide a sense of the extraordinarily rich opportunities available.

An instructor with little background might want to start with the essays by Larry Reynolds and by Coleman Hutchison, which offer a strong connection between Civil War literature and the more familiar genres of the antebellum and postwar periods. Someone who has taught many of the canonical texts of Civil War literature and wants to find new texts to incorporate might look at the essays by Faith Barrett and by Alex W. Black, which connect familiar genres, such as lyric and inaugural addresses, with other kinds of poetry and speech, and familiar writers, such as Emily Dickinson and Abraham Lincoln, with unfamiliar textual expressions, such as song and oratorical performance. Someone teaching a course on war and peace studies might want to integrate Matthew Davis's discussion of brotherhood or Elizabeth Duquette's analysis of treason into discussions of the effects that war has on family and might even use the framing concepts these essays introduce to set up cross-cultural and transhistoric comparisons of war writings from different regions and eras. An expert in Civil War literature might find Julia Stern's essay helpful for the way it addresses the challenge of turning detailed scholarly knowledge into effective classroom pedagogy. The essays by Wiebke Omnus Klumpenhower and by Melissa Strong reflect on how to engage nontraditional classrooms, and the essays by Timothy Sweet and by Rebecca Entel provide models for how to make the most traditional classrooms (the survey course, the composition class) innovative and exciting for teachers and students alike.

Several of the essays engage with the same texts from very different perspectives. For instance, someone teaching Thomas Wentworth Higginson's Civil War writings will find it useful to compare and contrast how Tess Chakkalakal, Faith Barrett, Christopher Hager, and Alex W. Black engage with his work. Classes reading Louisa May Alcott will want to benefit from the teaching insights provided by Allison Carey, Ian Finseth, Matthew Davis, Jessica DeSpain, Melissa Strong, Kathleen Diffley, Susan Ryan, and Rebecca Entel.

Our volume contributors span a vast range of institutional contexts, courses taught, and relations to their field. Some came to Civil War literature later in already established careers; others built their scholarly and intellectual lives in relation to this field of inquiry from an earlier stage. Some suggest that pedagogy is often about experimentation and risk taking, and they are passing on those experiences to others. The volume understands that one size does not fit all: not all institutions have the same kinds of resources available. Someone who teaches in northern New England might never be able to take students to a Civil War battlefield, but strategies can be adapted for on-site reflection at Civil War monuments. One might discuss the popularity of reenactments, which not only measure the war's centrality in the public consciousness but also provide a useful teaching tool, tying Civil War literature to the materiality and physicality of war.

The volume is divided into five parts:

1. teaching Civil War literature in historical context
2. teaching various genres

3. teaching specific topics
4. teaching materials
5. available resources

Each of these rubrics is as much a subject of inquiry as a category for grouping the essays.[2] They reflect a broad range of approaches to Civil War literature and to the existing and emerging courses in which it is and might be taught.

Recognizing that the Civil War marks a particular moment in American political, cultural, and historical life, part 1 examines how we might approach the relation between fact and fiction, events and literature. Beginning with Larry Reynolds's essay on the antebellum origins of the Civil War, it ties Civil War literature to the more familiar and more frequently taught literature of the so-called American Renaissance and the abolitionist writings of the 1850s and traces continuities and rifts between them. It devotes particular attention to teaching students about the ways in which literary form intersects with the construction of history. Literature helps us understand history as an experience shaped not only by events but also by cultural narratives. Taking the history of African American soldiers' participation in the Civil War for her case study, Tess Chakkalakal provides examples for working through texts that range from fiction to history and are often difficult to classify as either. By contextualizing a variety of narratives with one another, students begin to understand how remembering the Civil War became crucial to postemancipation racial segregation in the South.

Chakkalakal's concern with the commemorative dimensions of the Civil War connects with Coleman Hutchison's asking how we can teach students to understand the ruptures as well as continuities of literary history. Taking Albion Tourgée's "The South as a Field for Fiction" as his point of departure, Hutchison complicates two generally agreed-on literary consequences of the war: the development of American literary realism and of regional literatures. He offers pedagogical approaches and techniques that allow students to read the well-established relations among realism, regionalism, and the Civil War in less absolute and more contingent terms that reveal continuities of the war with the antebellum period. He pays particular attention to the vexed relations between regional and national cultures before, during, and after the conflict.

This interest in the historic locations of culture carries over to the next two essays, which represent careful but very different approaches to the problematic old adage that the past is a foreign country. Literally situating herself in a classroom halfway around the world, Wiebke Omnus Klumpenhower examines how South Korean students, who themselves live in daily fear of a civil war with North Korea, engage with these materials. Her reflections speak to a highly specialized context but also give us all insight into the teaching of international students and the opportunity to reflect on the Civil War's national specificity and transnational relevance. Moreover, her essay addresses strategies for engaging students with little preparation for and limited interest in the subject matter. Klumpenhower's essay demonstrates the ways in which the Civil War enables us to cut against the grain of canonical isolationism by putting the war into a global conversation.

The coauthors of the essay "Team-Teaching the Civil War at Historical Sites" advocate a radically different approach: using location rather than dislocation as a pedagogical resource for inquiring into the relation between history and literature. Shawn Jones, Darren T. Williamson, and William Steele also offer a model for collaborative teaching that suggests how to sequence different pedagogical materials and set them in dialogue with one another across disciplinary divides.

Part 2 is aimed at teachers who wish to examine Civil War literature in genre-based courses or course units. These essays give a general overview of war writing in poetry, prose fiction, nonfiction prose, life writing, and speech. Instead of treating these genres as established and fixed, each essay shows how the Civil War changed and shaped the genre discussed, questions the assumptions behind the organization of genres, and offers opportunities for teaching genre through cross-generic inquiry. Faith Barrett shows how the Civil War prompted an extraordinary outpouring of poetry by men and women from all walks of life. Poems and the closely related genre of popular songs could be circulated cheaply and efficiently in the form of broadsides, pamphlets, or sheet music. Writers used poetry to define a collective we and to trace the relation between that we and the I: in doing so, they also defined the relation of poetry to nation, home, and family. Barrett's essay serves as an introduction to the cultural position of poetry in this era and also suggests some groupings of related texts for further exploration—texts by canonical and popular writers as well as by writers who have less frequently been read in relation to the war: women and African Americans.

Similarly neglected has been a genre that shares poetry's mobility and immediacy, the dime novels aimed at entertaining the troops. These novels present a particular challenge, requiring us to take into account not only the texts but also the readers to whom they were marketed. Publishers created book series expressly for the reading audience of soldiers. Allison Carey explains how students make meaning of these unfamiliar, popular texts and how those texts in turn enable students to develop new perspectives on the more recognizably literary texts they will encounter.

Readers of Civil War fiction and poetry frequently encounter everyday texts that circulate outside the channels of literary and journalistic publication. For instance, Walt Whitman's "Come Up from the Fields Father" revolves around the arrival of a letter. The ubiquitous real-life documents that inspired such works rarely find their way into English courses. Christopher Hager discusses their pedagogical applications in literature classrooms. The everyday workings of bureaucracy can produce texts that transgress publishing's proprieties, casting into relief what literary texts often leave out—as when women divulge intimate details in government affidavits to prove their marital status and thus their eligibility for widows' pensions or when Freedmen's Bureau staff members write down escaped slaves' explicit descriptions of racist and sexual violence. Even General Benjamin Butler's notorious General Order 28 opens new ways of reading how gender and insurgency intersected. Other documents, especially those by semiliterate writers, are idiosyncratic, challenging students to reconstruct, as they read, individual processes of composition. Hager discusses not only the opportunities this body of literature offers but also its challenges: some undergraduates find spare, pro forma writings off-putting or simply boring; English majors accustomed to New Critical close reading can have difficulty engaging with these texts; and students at all levels, if they (consciously or not) define literature in terms of aesthetics or social influence, may question the value of reading rough-hewn writings.

Students may place diaries at the opposite end of the spectrum from official documents and assume that such private composition is removed from the larger political engagements of the war. But Dana McMichael's study makes evident that Confederate women's diaries were deeply engaged with the war and often rhetorically intervened in it. McMichael explores the connection between periodic life writing and the formation of ethnic identity and argues that certain rhetorical moves practiced in Confederate diaries enabled women to actively maintain and build power structures that privileged white Southerners. Through its close examination of key passages in several well-known diaries, the essay explores methods for helping students understand how diarists both incorporate and reshape contemporary sermons, periodicals, and popular literature even as their diaries are used to document a particular version of Confederate history.

For our understanding of the past, we rely on the textual and pictorial archives from an era in which sound recording had not yet been invented. But in the nineteenth century, the spoken word played a significant role in shaping public life. Alex W. Black examines the practices of speech during the Civil War. Instead of focusing on the more formal category of oratory, he considers all genres of oral expression, even texts that were not spoken by their authors but read by someone else, and the printed formats in which they were then and are now experienced. He also surveys the changing critical reception of a speech since the war: how we have come to emphasize Abraham Lincoln's Gettysburg Address and Second Inaugural Address over anything else that Lincoln or others said.

Moving cross-generically to examine specific topics, part 3 shows that Civil War literature was highly repetitive in its use of certain tropes and themes. Each essay takes up a topic of the literature and suggests how to apply a specific methodological or theoretical approach to it. The essays give an introduction to recurring topics in the literature, indicate the variations and complications we see in their repetition, and suggest how different approaches might help us frame our discussions of these topics and texts. The essays link—sometimes explicitly, sometimes implicitly—realism with witnessing, landscape with ecocriticism, brotherhood with citizenship, African American soldiers with critical race theory, women's antislavery activism with gender studies, and treason with affect theory. The links are not meant to be exhaustive: many other pairings may arise from these suggestions. Our volume will hopefully be read less for what it details than for the ideas it offers to instructors as they decide which topics, methodologies, primary and secondary texts, historical and theoretical approaches are appropriate for their students.

Ian Finseth's essay asks what the experience of the Civil War was like and what the strengths and weaknesses are of different representational forms in conveying that experience. The war is often associated with the rise of literary realism in the United States, but that view deserves scrutiny. In the college classroom, realism is a helpful frame of reference if it is construed as a form of critical engagement. Finseth uses photography, battle experience, and race to provide strategies for teaching Civil War literature from the perspective of realism, both presenting close readings of individual authors (Herman Melville, Stephen Crane, Charles Chesnutt) and outlining broader thematic and pedagogical issues.

The environment has often remained in the background even of approaches to literature's realism. The Civil War was a major event in the environmental history of the United States, having enormous repercussions for the way landscapes and ecosystems were represented afterward in literature, photography, and painting. Michael Ziser addresses the racialization of American geography, literary depictions of battlefields, and the memorialized landscapes of war found in photographs and on battle sites.

One way in which memorialization occurred even during the war was through an emphasis on the costs and possibilities of personal and national fraternity. As Matthew R. Davis reveals, the phrase "brother against brother" became a primary way to describe the horrors of civil conflict. Understanding why brotherhood became a preferred means for talking about the ruptured nation is crucial to considerations of American personhood. The language of brotherhood encapsulates the brutality of sustained civil conflict and offers the potential for reconstituting the national family. Davis provides guidance on how to theorize brotherhood's complex meanings and explore its centrality to imagining the Civil War.

Brotherhood's affectionate emphasis on family ties raises the question of how nonwhites and nonmales were incorporated into the war narrative, and the next essays take up that issue. Catherine Saunders shows how a trio of poems addressing African Americans' role in the Civil War offers opportunities for teaching both close reading and the importance of cultural context in interpreting literature. Jessica DeSpain suggests ways to complicate students' understanding of the intersections between race and gender in the Civil War. She develops a classroom unit that uses Thomas Crawford's *Statue of Freedom*, installed atop the capitol dome in 1863, as a framing device for teaching about the complicated circles of influence in which women maneuvered. Elizabeth Duquette takes up an issue often associated with women, sympathetic feeling, but ties it to political frameworks. She shows how we can introduce students to the challenging uses to which Civil War literature put nineteenth-century notions of sympathy. The ability to feel with or for others provided the standard for political and moral affiliation, yet, as the Constitution makes clear, providing aid and comfort to an enemy is a form of treason. Sympathy therefore quickly became a personal and national danger. Students examine the complexities of that transformation by seeing the different responses that allegiance generated in the Confederate States of America and the United States of America.

Part 4 presents different approaches to teaching with a range of primary, secondary, electronic, textual, and visual materials across first-year, survey, specialized, and advanced courses for undergraduate and graduate students. Julia Stern discusses how to teach students trained in book culture methods for archival research: analyzing orthography (the study of penmanship), making sense of census records, or reading personal letters in the context of public events. She provides guidance on interpreting documents as diverse as account books and work rolls for the postwar period, documents from the state courts of South Carolina, trial records, manumission decrees, and reimbursement for a manumitted slave.

Melissa Strong gives suggestions on how to teach an online course and how to help students read images as texts in their own right. Students better understand the relation between the Civil War and cultural memory by researching an image—such as an advertisement or photograph—published between 1861 and 1865 and analyzing it in connection with assigned materials.

Kathleen Diffley continues the inquiry into archives and methodologies for using literary texts. Magazines provide a literary record of the war as it unfolded, challenge us to assess how we construct knowledge, and allow students of the Civil War to trace emerging public memory without neglecting its gaps.

The next two essays provide innovative engagements with a familiar resource, the anthology. Timothy Sweet focuses on contemporary anthologies, whereas Jess Roberts discusses the use of newly available historical anthologies to reflect on the war's construction.

Susan Ryan argues that a digital archive is not a transparent means of access but a pedagogical tool. Because nineteenth-century anthologies and periodicals are now widely available in keyword-searchable databases, they offer an excellent means of teaching digital research methods. When students experiment with keyword search strategies, they discover that nineteenth-century Americans used a vocabulary different from ours when discussing matters of racial difference and civil unrest. As students move among articles, entries, and larger print contexts, they learn how to apply their findings meaningfully. Ryan offers pedagogical tools to help students narrow their research questions and build effective analytic arguments in the digital age.

Rebecca Entel contributes advice on incorporating Civil War literature into first-year writing seminars. In the lessons she outlines, the concern is not with what happened but with how what happened has been
represented—or not represented. Students learn to view literature, and
therefore their own writing, as a rhetorical construct rather than as the
unmediated presentation of content.

Part 5 lists resources that instructors might want to draw on for their
teaching. This material also helps draw together some of the themes explored in this volume. Let me offer an example that is near and dear to
my heart; it involves the transnational turn in American literary studies.
Although my scholarship (*Transnationalism*) and work as an editor for
the book series Edinburgh Critical Studies in Transatlantic Literatures and
Cultures has centrally engaged with the transnational, this exciting and important area seems to have been overlooked in this volume, if one judges
by the contents page. There is no essay dedicated to the transnational
turn, but the transnational is a thematic thread that runs throughout the
volume. Larry Reynolds frames the issue this way:

> [T]he slavery controversy became more and more divisive in the United
> States following the Mexican War and the European Revolutions of
> 1848. Although William Lloyd Garrison and his followers continued
> to argue for nonresistance during most of the 1850s, a number of abo-
> litionists had a change of heart and accepted violence as a viable politi-
> cal means.

This statement beautifully points us toward both the transatlantic and the
transhemispheric. Also, as Duquette points out, "the standard division
of North and South [obscures] the importance of the West during the
conflict." Darren Williamson writes that "Western expansion is a subtheme within the political context of the war, because every time a new
state or territory was added to the Union, the debate over slavery was
rekindled." That debate was not only an internal American affair but also
a "concern to Europeans, who technically stayed out of the conflict but
had great interest in its outcome." Williamson and his colleagues teach
this transnational dimension to students by exploring what Mark Twain
called the "Sir Walter disease" (501)—that is, the connection between
southern culture and English aristocrats. Since Paul Gilroy's ground-
breaking *The Black Atlantic* (1993), scholarship has uncovered specifically the ways in which issues of race, national belonging, and transnational diaspora get worked out in these contexts. Catherine Saunders

explains how the black regiment raises "questions about the relation between established cultural tropes and representations of African American soldiers" by echoing the era's most popular war poem, Tennyson's
"Charge of the Light Brigade." This textual pairing "allows discussion
of intertextuality and of the transatlantic nature of nineteenth-century
Anglo-American culture."

Allison Carey provides one example of how something as seemingly
mundane as the comparison of a text's different editions and its publication history can reveal the fascinating politics and complicated possibilities
of the transatlantic print sphere. She writes that Metta Victor's

> American introduction to *Maum Guinea* contains a paragraph, absent
> from the British version, that disavows any abolitionist intent in the
> book and frames it as purely escape fiction. . . . Victor didn't need
> this disavowal for the British audience: in its London publication, the
> book was unabashedly an abolitionist text, intended to sway the British
> against the Confederacy through an indictment of the slave system.

DeSpain points out that British writers such as Fanny Kemble crucially intervened in the debates over slavery and abolition and emphasizes the importance of teaching students that women's views were far from uniform.
She reads pamphlets with her students that teach them "how women's
narratives were refigured for different political ends. The Ladies' London Emancipation Society pamphlet provides students with an example
of how women's labor in Britain became metaphorically linked to slave
labor in the United States." Such textual circulations also unsettle literary
and historical teleologies, as Coleman Hutchison reveals in his discussion
of contingencies.

The transnational turn, then, is an explicit theme throughout this volume as well as a methodology and pedagogy for approaching Civil War
literature. For that matter, this volume goes further than most work on
the transnational turn in that it includes essays on teaching outside the
traditional American classroom, in South Korea (Klumpenhower's essay).
The transnational turn is aimed at unsettling geographies—note the recent
recovery of the Mexican American war's importance and the new scholarly focus on southern areas that extend beyond the states that formed
the Confederacy. This approach provides us with new perspectives on the
Civil War.

Another example of how to use the resources section of this volume
may be useful: the postwar writings of María Amparo Ruiz de Burton

would make a fruitful pairing with and offer valuable provocation to notions of southern identity and gender, offering a productive dialogue for instance with the Confederate women's diaries that McMichael discusses in her essay. Ways for us to place pressure on these readings—and ways that these readings place pressure on us—are discussed throughout the volume.

Given that Civil War literature forces us to move away from a canon toward an archive, how do we make good decisions about the content, contours, and pedagogies of our courses? I offer an example of an integrated approach in the student-centered classroom. For an advanced seminar, I gave my students an assignment that consisted of several stages and targeted different kinds of analysis and different learning styles. They had to develop their own research project for their final paper, use primary materials, and discuss them in relation to existing scholarship on Civil War literature. They had to decide what the archive would be for their project, on the basis of the scholarly readings we did for class and additional research in secondary materials. The paper had to develop a coherent, nuanced, and informed argument about the materials selected.

The class met with the director of our special collections library and with the college archivist for an introduction to the materials housed there and for a discussion of research methodologies. Students were then required to go into the special collections library each week and call up at least three items for examination. The purpose of this exercise was exploratory: to give students familiarity with the different materials in special collections and to enable them to develop their own interests. I asked them to share their notes with me, so that we could discuss emerging research ideas.

I then asked students to develop display case proposals and to present those to the class. I asked them to imagine how they would use one of the display cases in our library to present their research: which items would they include, how would they label them, and what would they want visitors to learn from the presentation? This assignment enabled students to create a narrative thread for the different items they viewed in the first assignment and also to engage in visual thinking. They had to write up a short proposal detailing the aims and objective of their display case. We discussed these proposals in class, first developing criteria for assessing their merits and then using those criteria to vote on the proposals. The students who won the most votes were given the opportunity to curate one of our display cases. The range of projects that the students developed was exciting to us all: "Female Spies," "Representations of Home and Domesticity," "Case Study of a New Hampshire Soldier," "Experience of Doctors and Nurses," "Dartmouth during the War," "Soldiers and Deserters," "Southern Perspectives on the Civil War."

The next challenge was for students to translate this archive, and their knowledge of scholarship on the topic they researched, into a textual and scholarly argument. The other writing assignments for the course had been geared toward that end, targeting especially how to engage critically with scholarly and theoretical arguments. Working across different registers of representation in terms of the materials that students selected prepared them to think through different contexts of narrative display and analytic rigor, to create arguments about their findings, and to relate their arguments to existing scholarly discourse. This assignment lent transparency to the production of scholarly knowledge and enabled students to participate in that dialogue.

My example reflects the larger aims of this volume: while each essay highlights a specific concern and particular practice, many of the suggestions here will gain force by being put in relation to one another. Our contributors offer their pedagogical expertise as an open-ended invitation for instructors to experiment with a range of strategies and resources.

Notes

A few paragraphs of this essay, from "Randall was a college tutor . . ." to ". . . appealing to feelings as much as to reason," are taken from my essay "A War of Words."

1. M. Andrews quotes Douglas Stader on Holmes's attitude (32).

2. In the comments that follow, I draw from the abstracts and essays provided by the contributors.

Part I

Teaching Civil War Literature in Historical Context

Larry J. Reynolds

Contradictions and Ambivalence: Emerson, Hawthorne, and the Antebellum Origins of Civil War Literature

In a special topics course on political violence and the American Renaissance, which I have taught at both the undergraduate and graduate level, I use works by Ralph Waldo Emerson and Nathaniel Hawthorne to explore the ways the two authors approached the topic of warfare and to illuminate how their perspectives altered when civil war broke out. Because the course focuses on intellectual history rather than literary analyses, the assigned readings are mostly noncanonical. We read Emerson's "Concord Hymn" (1836), his lecture "War" (1838), his 1844 Antislavery Address, one of his speeches about John Brown (1859), and his "Dedication of the Soldiers' Monument in Concord" (1867). We read Hawthorne's "The Old Manse" (1846), excerpts from his letters about the Civil War, his unpublished romance "Septimius Felton" (c. 1861), and his *Atlantic Monthly* essay "Chiefly about War-Matters by a Peaceable Man" (1862). These readings allow students to discover how Emerson's arguments supporting pacifistic idealism were transformed into justifications of violence and warfare, until Emerson could claim that "war ennobles the age" (*Complete Works* 10: 257). Hawthorne, on the other hand, tried to remain committed to peace while acquiring the suspicion that pacifism may constitute treason during wartime. My goals as we study these works is to advance students' understanding of the challenging ideas and events these authors struggled with as the impending crisis led to war, and I encourage students to think more critically about war in their present world.

Throughout the course, I have students give oral reports on such topics as the "Concord Fight" of 19 April 1775, the Haitian Revolution of 1791, the 1854 remission of Anthony Burns, the 1856 beating of Senator Charles Sumner, the 1856 Pottawatomie massacre in "Bleeding Kansas," and John Brown's raid on Harpers Ferry in 1859, all of which provide contexts that illuminate the readings and the rising tide of violence that preceded the Civil War. The reports are fifteen-to-twenty-minute *Power-Point* presentations based on research drawn from scholarly books and articles and incorporating relevant images or video clips. Brief Q&As follow the presentations. Students submit their reports electronically along with bibliographies of their written and visual sources.

Although I prefer to use open-ended questions to elicit class discussion and provoke critical thinking, I begin the course with popular received knowledge. I show a clip from Ken Burns's documentary television series *The Civil War*, in particular the scene titled "The Meteor," from episode 1, which features John Brown and ends with a series of quotations about his death by hanging after his failed raid on Harpers Ferry. The film's narrator relates that Emerson at this time compared Brown to Christ, while Hawthorne asserted that "nobody was ever more justly hanged." I ask students to keep in mind that the clear dichotomy Burns uses for dramatic effect has a complicated background, which we will explore during the semester. Our readings, I tell them, are intended to reveal the wavering trace of each author's attitude with regard to violence and warfare.

Background

Since students assume the abolition of slavery can be viewed with moral clarity, I try to challenge this assumption by introducing them to the keen awareness within antebellum American society of the horrors of the Haitian Revolution of 1791, which provided terrifying images for those who were convinced of the cause-and-effect relation between abolitionist exhortation and slave violence. Students tend to regard abolitionists as heroic moral leaders of their age; however, I point out that for a number of years abolitionists were viewed as dangerous fanatics in the United States, even by those, such as Emerson, who would later join their ranks. We review the number of forms the antislavery movement initially took—colonization, philosophical abolitionism, and gradually staged emancipation—but focus on the immediate and unqualified emancipation advocated by William Lloyd Garrison and his followers, because it galvanized public attention, inspired the most violent reactions, and eventually dominated the field of antislavery thought.[1] Even many progressive supporters of the antislavery movement feared the consequences of immediate emancipation, especially the prospects of a race war in the South and of large numbers of ex-slaves joining northern society and its labor force.

In addition to having a student report on the Haitian Revolution, I show two videos that do an excellent job of dramatizing the paranoia and anger that arose among white Americans as a result of abolitionist rhetoric and slave uprisings: part 1 of *The Abolitionists*, directed by Rob Rapley, and *Nat Turner: A Troublesome Property*, directed by Charles Burnett. Along with these viewings, I have students read Thomas Gray's *The Confessions of Nat Turner* (1831). These three works provide compelling evidence of the turmoil generated by the slavery issue and bring into question the effectiveness of Garrisonians' impassioned rhetoric and Turner's bloody slave insurrection. I encourage students to consider why nonresistance and violence competed as solutions to the problem of slavery in the antebellum period. In what respect was Turner justified in leading an uprising that killed some sixty white men, women, and children and eventually led to the deaths of countless blacks at the hands of revengeful whites? Should he be regarded as an insane religious fanatic or a heroic black liberator? The video about Turner contains proponents of both views. As a supplemental reading, I distribute to students a speech Frederick Douglass delivered in 1857, in which he argued that the rebellion of the slaves in San Domingo against their French masters led to the peaceful emancipation of slaves in the British West Indies and that "Virginia was never nearer emancipation than when General Turner kindled the fires of insurrection at Southampton" ("West India Emancipation" 368).

Eric J. Sundquist has echoed Douglass by pointing out that in the wake of Turner's rebellion, "the Virginia House of Delegates undertook the most serious debate in its history on the question of slave emancipation" (9–10). I have students read Sundquist's classic essay "Slavery, Revolution, and the American Renaissance," because it illuminates the relations among the Haitian Revolution, Turner's failed rebellion, and the American revolutionary tradition. Sundquist does an excellent job of sensitizing students to the notion that slavery generated a growing pressure within antebellum national ideology that finally exploded into war. For

Emerson and other abolitionists, the Civil War finally instantiated the principle of liberty that the "first Revolution" failed to do, because the founders "over-looked the moral law, and winked at a practical exception to the Bill of Rights they had drawn up" (*Complete Works* 11: 351–52).

Emerson

Near the beginning of his career, Emerson celebrated the American Revolution, especially its beginning in Concord, Massachusetts. I have students analyze his perspective in his "Concord Hymn," written to commemorate the fight between British troops and American provincials at the North Bridge in Concord on 19 April 1775. In the poem, Emerson writes that the "embattled farmers" who "fired the shot heard round the world" chose "to die, or leave their children free" ("Hymn"). After the Civil War, he would say they were resisting "offensive usurpations, offensive taxes of the British Parliament" (*Complete Works* 11: 352). I ask students to compare the two motives that Emerson sets out and to speculate on why he altered his views. The discussion provides a good opportunity to examine the rhetorical importance of occasion and audience.

To provide a context for "Concord Hymn," I have a student give a historical account of what happened that day in 1775 and assign John McWilliams's essay "Lexington, Concord, and the 'Hinge of the Future,'" which describes the five successive states of commemorating the historical incident and its literary recreations. One of the important points that McWilliams makes is that the incident and its representations "seem to have been inseparable from the beginning" (3). This observation often leads to a theoretical discussion about the textuality of history, which picks up on points raised by Turner's so-called "confessions." The issue of how to access the truth of the past is one often unfamiliar to students. To complicate the issue more, I show a photograph of the grave of the two British soldiers buried near the old North Bridge and ask students to consider these visual and apparently material results of the shots "heard round the world," which go unmentioned in Emerson's poem. I also ask whether it is patriotism when armed civilians fire upon and kill regular troops. Do uniforms matter?

A year after the 1837 celebration in Concord (it was delayed a year), Emerson delivered a lecture titled "War" before the American Peace Society, in which he argued that war is "on its last legs" (*Complete Works* 11: 161) because of the progress of civilization. When students read this little-known lecture, I ask them to look closely at how Emerson's transcendentalism informs the antiwar argument. Those students who have previously read his book *Nature* or early essays such as "The American Scholar" and "Self-Reliance" recognize the emphasis he places on the power of the enlightened individual, able to change the world in response to divinity acting through the soul. I ask students to discern the pivot point in the lecture, where Emerson turns from viewing war as fratricide committed by savage and juvenile tribes to a vision of "universal peace" constructed by men of "love, honor, and truth." In this lecture, he imagines a "Congress of Nations" and defends the peace doctrine by arguing that whenever it is "embraced by a nation, we may be assured it will not be one that invites injury; but one, on the contrary, which has a friend in the bottom of the heart of every man, even of the violent and the base" (169). Class discussion soon revolves around the impracticality of this vision and around the suspicion that military might, not moral elevation, keeps nations from harm. In response to his assertion that "the increase of civility has abolished the use of poison and of torture" (158), students make the obvious point that 175 years later, this statement remains wishful thinking.

As Emerson was drawn into the antislavery movement, he maintained a transcendentalist approach to the problem but revealed a glimpse of an alternative way to solve it. When students read his "Address on the Emancipation of the Negroes in the British West Indies," I ask them to discern his argument. The essay praises the British abolitionists and their peacefully staged emancipation in the West Indies, yet it also celebrates "the arrival in the world of such men as Toussaint, and the Haytian Heroes," for "the might and the right are here: here is the anti-slave: here is man: and if you have man, black or white is an insignificance. The intellect, —that is miraculous!" (*Emerson's Antislavery Writings* 31). His admiration for those Haitians who fought one of the bloodiest and most successful revolutions known to mankind follows his praise for the "touching" moderation displayed by the freed Negroes in the British West Indies, which "brings tears to the eyes" (18). The apparent contradiction can lead to an engaging discussion of the relation between Emerson's activism and his idealism.[2]

Although some scholars have argued that the lecture shows Emerson joining the abolitionist movement, I ask students to distinguish his ideas from those of reformers such as Garrison. What does it mean when Emerson says, "[I]deas only save races. . . . I say to you, you must save yourself, black or white, man or woman; other help is none" (31)? Also, how does one interpret his conclusion where he says, "[T]he genius of the Saxon race, friendly to liberty; the enterprise, the very muscular vigor of this nation, are inconsistent with slavery" (33)? Students are often struck not only by the emphasis on intellect in the address but also by its race consciousness. This observation provides a good opportunity to emphasize that hatred of slavery did not necessarily mean respect for blacks or even for abolitionists. I share Emerson's journal entries in which he calls abolitionists "an altogether odious set of people" (*Journals* 9: 120) and declares, "It is better to hold the negro race an inch under water than an inch over. . . . You cannot preserve races beyond their term" (10: 357). The latter entry, informed by racialist pseudo-science, can lead to a discussion of Emerson's belief that "most of the great results of history are brought about by discreditable means" (*Complete Works* 6: 256).

Drawing upon my own research, I point out to students that the slavery controversy became more and more divisive in the United States after the Mexican War and the European revolutions of 1848 (see Reynolds 18–33). Although Garrison and his followers continued to argue for nonresistance during most of the 1850s, a number of abolitionists had a change of heart and accepted violence as a viable political means. We discuss how the Compromise of 1850, which made slavery a national, as opposed to regional, abomination, outraged New Englanders, for the Fugitive Slave Act made them complicit in helping capture runaway slaves. The arrest of the fugitive slave Anthony Burns in Boston in 1854 by southern slave hunters caused a violent confrontation—I have a student report on that event. The Boston Vigilance Committee held an excited protest meeting in Faneuil Hall, and a mob of abolitionists battered down the courthouse door in an unsuccessful attempt to rescue Burns, killing a volunteer guard in the process. I ask students whether they view this killing as righteous, as Frederick Douglass, Henry David Thoreau, and others did.

Student oral reports on the beating of Charles Sumner in the United States Senate, the Pottawatomie Massacre in Bleeding Kansas, and the Harpers Ferry raid show the rising tide of violence in the United States during the second half of the 1850s. I also assign a transcript of the speech John Brown gave in Concord in March 1857. In it, Brown makes no mention of his killing five proslavery settlers at Pottawatomie Creek; rather, he presents himself and his sons as victims of Missouri Ruffians and the United States government. At one point he holds up a trace chain and declares, "Here is the chain with which one of my sons, John J., was confined after the *cruelty, sufferings, & anxiety he underwent* had rendered him a Maniac. *Yes a Maniac*" (83). We discuss Brown's rhetorical skills and probe how and why Emerson and others in New England found him so worthy of admiration. We then read "A Meeting to Aid John Brown's Family," the speech Emerson gave on 18 November 1859, after Harpers Ferry, in which he declares that "John Brown was an idealist. He believed in his ideas to that extent, that he existed to put them all into action. He did not believe in moral suasion;—he believed in putting the thing through" (*Emerson's Antislavery Writings* 119). What is the "thing," I ask students, and what does it mean to "put it through"? In what sense was Brown like Christ, given Emerson's description of him as "that new saint . . . who, if he shall suffer, will make the gallows like the cross" (*Complete Works* 7: 427)?

Hawthorne

Emerson's celebratory "Concord Hymn" lends itself to comparison with Hawthorne's "Old Manse," where a different story about 19 April 1775 is told. In this preface, Hawthorne relates that when the fight at the North Bridge occurred, a young boy, chopping wood at the back door of the Manse, heard the noise of the battle, which was only some hundred yards away, ran over to the scene, found a wounded British soldier lying on the ground, and struck him on the head with his ax, splitting open his skull. Hawthorne writes that, "as an intellectual and moral exercise," he has thought about the boy's later life and wondered if "his soul was tortured by the blood-stain, contracted, as it had been, before the long custom of war had robbed human life of its sanctity, and while it still seemed murderous to slay a brother man" (*Centenary Edition* 10: 9–10). Hawthorne, whose chief subject was human sin, assumes the boy felt guilty about what he had done, but I ask students if this is a reasonable assumption. Do all those who kill in war experience guilt? Does group participation alter psychology? What about all the farmers and colonists who shot and killed British soldiers that day on the road back to Boston? Were they guilty savages, as the British claimed, or proud sons of liberty?

Throughout his career, Hawthorne criticized those who claimed knowledge of God's will, for he thought they, like his Puritan ancestors, could do more harm than good. In 1857 he responded to an abolitionist pamphlet by Elizabeth Peabody, his sister-in-law, by telling her that "vengeance and beneficence are things that God claims for Himself. His instruments have no consciousness of His purpose; if they imagine they have, it is a pretty sure token that they are *not* His instruments" (18: 116). I ask students to consider how Hawthorne could know this. What distinguishes his intuition of God's will from Emerson's or Brown's?

Given his tendency to avoid absolutes, it is not surprising that Hawthorne viewed the Civil War from multiple perspectives. In one of his letters that we read in class, he tells a friend in England:

> The Southern man will say, We fight for state rights, liberty, and independence. The middle and Western states–man will avow that he fights for the Union; whilst our Northern and Eastern man will swear that, from the beginning, his only idea was liberty to the Blacks, and the annihilation of slavery. All are thoroughly in earnest, and all pray for the blessing of Heaven to rest upon the enterprise. (387)

I ask students, What is the effect of such a perspective? How does it become offensive?

Soon after the Civil War began, Hawthorne started writing a new romance, "Septimius Felton," and by setting it in Concord in 1775 at the beginning of the American Revolution, he was able to draw upon his own ambivalence about the war fever surrounding him. As the protagonist's townspeople prepare for battle, he writes, "Oh, high, heroic, tremulous juncture, when man felt himself almost an angel, on the verge of doing deeds that outwardly look so fiendish; oh, strange rapture of the coming battle. We know something of that time now" (13: 17). After the skirmish at the North Bridge, the romance describes the retreat of the British troops as the colonists shoot at them from behind trees and walls. When Hawthorne's scholarly protagonist-observer sees one redcoat stagger and fall, he shudders, because this patriotic violence "was so like murder that he really could not tell the difference." Revealing his own sense of uncertainty, Hawthorne writes, "[H]ow strange, how strange it is, this deep, wild passion that nature has implanted in us, to be the death of our fellow-creatures and which coexists at the same time with horror" (24). Is it truly "nature," I ask students, that leads to killing? What role do systems of values and beliefs play?

Hawthorne has Septimius succumb to the "Demon of War" by killing a British soldier in a face-to-face confrontation on the hillside behind his house, acquiring a burden of guilt as a result (37). Meanwhile, the protagonist's earnest neighbor goes off to war, returns a hero, and shames the scholar by telling him, "This is not a generation for study, and the making of books; that may come by and by. This great fight has need of all men to carry it on, in one way or another; and no man will do well, even for himself, who tries to avoid his share in it" (116). A key question that Hawthorne's narrative raises is whether a detached intellectual can be as politically effective as a soldier willing to risk his or her life for a cause. One of my graduate students once answered yes by pointing to the example of Karl Marx at work on the Communist Manifesto. Hawthorne and his protagonist, however, appear to have answered no, for Septimius becomes increasingly depressed and seeks a tree on which to hang himself, while Hawthorne abruptly abandons his manuscript and never goes back to it.

His "Chiefly about War-Matters" begins with the statement, "I magnanimously considered that there is a kind of treason in insulating one's self from the universal fear and sorrow, and thinking one's idle thoughts in the dread time of civil war." He says he "determined to look a little more closely at matters, with my own eyes" (23: 404), and tells of his trip to Alexandria, Fort Ellsworh, Harpers Ferry, Fortress Monroe, Manassas, and Washington, DC. He describes seeing General McClellan reviewing the troops, fugitive slaves making their way north, war profiteers, and President Lincoln. He signed the article "A Peaceable Man," adding footnotes as "Editor" criticizing his own views, anticipating readers who he knew would find them outrageous. I ask students if they realized that the notes were Hawthorne's, and usually about half the class say they did. The notes challenge a number of Hawthorne's political statements, including his observation that war is juvenile and barbaric: "Set men face to face, with weapons in their hands, and they are as ready to slaughter one another now, after playing at peace and good will for so many years, as in the rudest ages, that never heard of peace societies. . . . It is so odd, when we measure our advances from barbarism, and find ourselves just here" (421). Such a statement, which echoes Emerson's "War," obviously impugns the militancy of both North and South at the time, and Hawthorne's compassion for those rebel soldiers imprisoned in the Union fort at Harpers Ferry also calls the fighting into question. Hawthorne describes these men as "simple, bumpkin-like fellows, dressed in homespun clothes, with faces singularly vacant of meaning," adding, "It is my belief that not a single bumpkin of them all . . . had the remotest comprehension of what they had been fighting for, or how they had deserved to be shut up in that dreary hole." His "Editor" declares, "We should be sorry to cast a doubt on the Peaceable Man's loyalty, but he will allow us to say that we consider him premature in his kindly feelings towards traitors and sympathizers with treason" (429). Many readers agreed with the "Editor" and denounced Hawthorne as unpatriotic and slandered him as treasonous. I ask students to consider whose perspective they agree with. Does a soldier's ignorance relieve him or her of personal responsibility? To what extent are we complicit with the group to which we belong?

Hawthorne, who died in 1864, ended his career ambivalent about the war effort. In an insightful posthumous review, Edward Dicey, the young English journalist who spent weeks with him near the end of his life, pointed out that Hawthorne loved the North but could not hate the South, adding, "It was curious to me at that time to see how universal this conviction of the justice of the war was amongst the American people" (245). Emerson, who lived until 1882, was one of those who expressed this conviction most strongly, using terms reminiscent of his Puritan forebears. In his 1867 address he asserts, "Every principle is a war-note. When the rights of man are recited under any old government, every one of them is a declaration of war. War civilizes, rearranges the population, distributing by ideas, —the innovators on one side, the antiquaries on the other. It opens the eyes wider" (*Complete Works* 11: 353). Obviously, Emerson has come far from his view that fighting and warfare are juvenile and barbaric, but, as one of my students pointed out, perhaps he has merely replaced the concept of an earlier stage of civilization with his current concept of the South: "The armies mustered in the North were as much missionaries to the mind of the country as they were carriers of material force, and had the vast advantage of carrying whither they marched a higher civilization." As for the common people of the South, he claims that they, "rich or poor, were the narrowest and most conceited of mankind, as arrogant as the negroes on the Gambia River" (355). As a class we discuss the degree of imperialism found in Emerson's comments.

At my university in Texas, Emerson's sense of righteousness strikes most of my students as less congenial than Hawthorne's ambivalence; nevertheless, the struggle of both writers to come to terms with slavery and the war effort provides a sense of how difficult it was for these well-known authors to maintain their commitment to the types of literature that had led to their fame. Idealism and guilt had become outdated themes. As Hawthorne said of his friend in November 1861, "Emerson is breathing slaughter, like the rest of us; and it is really wonderful how all sorts of theoretical nonsense . . . vanish in the strong atmosphere which we now inhale" (*Centenary Edition* 18: 422).

Notes

1. A narrative of this development can be found in Elkins 175–93.

2. For excellent studies of this topic, see Packer; Gougeon; Von Frank; Capper and Wright; and Garvey.

Tess Chakkalakal

Complicating the Relation between Literature and History: Slave Participation in Fact and Fiction

The 1989 film *Glory* brought considerable attention to the story of the Fifty-Fourth Massachusetts Volunteer Infantry. Based, in part, upon the letters of Robert Gould Shaw and the 1973 book *Lay This Laurel*, by Richard Benson and Lincoln Kirstein, *Glory* celebrates the role abolitionists, former slaves, and free blacks played in the Civil War. Though Shaw emerges as the film's hero, it is the black troops—played by Denzel Washington (Private Trip), Andre Braugher (Thomas Searles), and Morgan Freeman (Captain John Rawlins)—whom *Glory* celebrates. Unlike the role of Shaw, played by Matthew Broderick, the black characters are not based on actual historical figures but drawn instead from historical imagination.

What is the relation between the imagined historical narrative and the real historical narrative? Is it possible to distinguish between the two? While *Glory* and more recent efforts to uncover the real story of the Civil War have brought into sharper focus the significance of the role played by former slaves, we still need to grapple with the ways in which fictional representations of black soldiers have shaped and even distorted our understanding of the war. *Glory* concludes with the statement, "President Lincoln credited slave-soldiers with turning the tide of the war." Should we accept this statement as true? Did "slave-soldiers" turn the tide of the war? Would the Union have lost without their participation? Possibly. There is no accurate way of measuring their contribution. But the image of slaves fighting for their freedom is powerful. It was this image—perhaps more than their actual participation—that turned the Civil War into a war for freedom. Where did this image come from? It was produced largely by Civil War literature (rather than history), and tracing its origins helps our students understand how literary representations of "slave-soldiers" did, in fact, turn the tide of the war.

In my undergraduate course Literature of the Civil War Era, I devote several sessions to exploring works of nineteenth-century literature that present the history of the black troops: the role they played in the war and in constructing a northern narrative about the victory of the Union. Complicating the Civil War thus serves as a metaphor for presenting it from many different perspectives; such a multifaceted approach is essential to evaluating and interpreting the ways in which this story, once singular, is told today. As teachers of literature, we need to recall the political contexts out of which Civil War accounts originally arose and how they and sectional prejudices were transformed by art and literature, as Ralph Ellison reminds us, "into something deeper and more meaningful than its surface violence" (xvii). For Ellison in the mid-twentieth century, the story of the Fifty-Fourth Massachusetts Negro Regiment, as imagined by Augustus Saint-Gaudens's monument, provides an ideal image of black-and-white fraternity so essential to his novel *Invisible Man*.

For nineteenth-century American authors, the story of the black troops served a different, but related, function: to give the Civil War a purpose after the South surrendered in 1865, a purpose that was nowhere in sight when the war began four years earlier. In particular, by presenting white and black stories about black troops side by side, we can show our students the role literature played in creating a history of the Civil War that helps us come to terms with, perhaps even justify, the vast number of dead, which was, as Drew Gilpin Faust recently reminds us, its primary result (xiii). This essay invites students and instructors to consider a deceptively simple question: What role did slavery, and slaves, play in the Civil War? Answering that question gives us profound insights into how historical fact and historical fiction intersect and inform our understanding or understandings of the Civil War.

To this end, I would encourage instructors to highlight the connections between four nineteenth-century works of Civil War literature that are rarely read together: Thomas Wentworth Higginson's *Army Life in a*

Black Regiment (1869) and William Wells Brown's *The Negro in the American Rebellion: His Heroism and Fidelity* (1867); Anna E. Dickinson's *What Answer?* (1868) and Frances E. W. Harper's better-known novel *Iola Leroy; or, Shadows Uplifted* (1892). Higginson's and Brown's texts are explicitly histories of the black troops, while Dickinson's and Harper's texts, speaking primarily though not exclusively to female audiences, are fictional accounts of particular black soldiers. Though the generic differences among these four narratives allow readers to view the war and the role black troops played in it from multiple perspectives, the similarities among the narratives are striking. Taken together, they show students the role individual authors played in placing former slaves and free blacks at the center of the Civil War. The story of the black troops remains a vital aspect of histories of the Civil War. The texts I consider here enable students to understand the ways in which literature has influenced, even shaped, the historical record.

The role of slave labor in the Civil War was, as historians have long recognized, a crucial aspect of both the political and military campaigns. Slave labor enabled an astonishing eighty percent conscription rate among the Confederacy's white male population. Yet this resource proved unreliable. Over time, slaves became increasingly identified with the Union campaign when emancipation was embraced as its purpose. Frederick Douglass had predicted this development in 1861: "The American people and the Government at Washington may refuse to recognize it for a time, but the 'inexorable logic of events' will force it upon them in the end; that the war now being waged in this land is a war for and against slavery" (*Douglass' Monthly*).

On 1 January 1863, Lincoln signed the Emancipation Proclamation, a measure that resulted in a major escalation of what had been a limited conflict. Ulysses S. Grant called it "the heaviest blow yet given the Confederacy" (*Papers* 195). In all, over 180,000 blacks served in the Union army. Nearly 40,000 were killed as a result of their participation in the war. The number of black men who fought and died in the war is even more remarkable when we consider how little is actually known about the men who served, their lives and deaths, and even what became of them following their service.[1]

Though Douglass has been heralded by historians as crucial in the effort to recruit black men to serve in the Union army, no text provides as detailed and yet as vexed an account of the former slaves who enlisted to fight as does Higginson's *Army Life*. Two reasons why Higginson's account of black soldiers has received less attention by historians are its inherent contradictions and its decidedly literary features. *Army Life* is riddled with sweeping generalizations of black men, whom Higginson admires for their "capacity of honor and fidelity" while marveling at "the childish nature of this people" (37). He provides the names and backstories of several black soldiers that help support assertions that might otherwise be attributed to the author's Romantic and racialist tendencies.

Higginson was an abolitionist and commander of the First South Carolina Volunteers, and his perspective of the war, and of the black troops, reflects both his political bias and position. The scholar who has done the most valuable work on Higginson's life and work, Christopher Looby, has emphasized the literary rather than the historical quality of his writings about camp life. Branding Higginson as "a literary colonel," Looby highlights his ambition in writing *Army Life*: to provide readers with "real and vivid" access to the mission he undertook and the experience he underwent (5). Looby's introduction emphasizes Higginson's unique role in the war. Though a white commanding officer, Higginson saw himself as "cast altogether with the black troops." Though cast with them, he was not, as he repeatedly states throughout the text, one of them. "Camp-life," he explains, "was a wonderfully strange sensation to almost all volunteer officers, and mine lay among eight hundred men suddenly transformed from slaves into soldiers, and representing a race affectionate, enthusiastic, grotesque, and dramatic beyond all others" (3).

Higginson's role in the war may have been, as Looby suggests, primarily literary, but Higginson was also a colonel in the army who fought in the Civil War. Rather than separate his experience from his writing, I invite my students to consider ways in which we might understand how the one speaks to the other: just as Higginson's experiences were shaped by his narrative, so, too, were his experiences of the war shaped by literature. Whereas today we tend to separate fact and fiction, experience and representation, I help my students understand how for nineteenth-century writers the two often went together.

Viewed from the perspective of students (and twentieth-century critics, most notably Edmund Wilson), Higginson's experience of the war and his relationship with the black troops can be easily dismissed as racist, colonialist, and arrogant. These assessments of Higginson's work are difficult obstacles to overcome in the classroom. Some students try to counter them with an apology. As one student insisted, "Higginson was a product of his time! We can't judge him by the terms we use today!" Instead of closing off debate, I actively encourage students to examine how Higginson's experiences of the war were shaped by his prior political and aesthetic commitments.

Though written primarily in the form of a diary that simply records what Higginson did and saw during the seventeen months he served as commander of the First South Carolina Voluntary Infantry, this diary includes an account of his particular form of abolitionism as well as an account of the books he read both during and before his wartime experiences. I require students to use the Penguin edition (Army Life) because it includes an appendix of his other writings and a brief introduction placing his work in the political-cultural context in which it was written. This supplementary material provides students with a better sense of Higginson's politics. It is important for students to interrogate the diary form, to read the diary as a literary genre regulated by a set of conventions. This genre is important to our more general understanding of Civil War literature.

No other writer of the period provides students with such an unequivocal defense of the form: "There is nothing like a diary for freshness,—at least so I think,—and I shall keep to the diary through the days of camp-life, and throw the later experience into another form" (4). The other form Higginson chose to narrate his experiences of the war was the personal essay, and in it he makes plain his argument concerning the centrality of his troops to providing the war with its proper cause. His brief "Conclusion" to *Army Life* constitutes the text's most controversial chapter. It is here that he lays out the purpose of his narrative:

> But the peculiar privilege of associating with an outcast race, of training it to defend its rights, and to perform its duties, this was our especial meed. The vacillating policy of the Government sometimes filled other officers with doubt and shame; until the negro had justice, they were but defending liberty with one hand and crushing it with the other. From this inconsistency, we were free. (206)

I have students compose a response to this conclusion. How were Higginson and his fellow commanders free from inconsistency? What were the material consequences of his work with the black troops? Leaving his personal approach to recording the history of the black troops, I have students turn to Brown's narrative, which is based, in his words, on "historical research" (*Negro* v) and which picks up on several themes introduced by Higginson.

Extending the political work of Higginson's diaries into the post–Civil War era, Brown, a former Kentucky slave and novelist, penned *Clotel; or, The President's Daughter: A Narrative of Slave Life in the United States*, the first novel by an African American, in 1853, and published *The Negro in the American Rebellion: His Heroism and His Fidelity* (1867), the first military history of African Americans, a work that is generally ignored by scholars today. John David Smith's introduction to the 2003 edition provides a fine overview of the role Brown's text plays in African American historiography. The work was well received in its own time, reviewed by major newspapers and journals and seen as a necessary recognition of the rights of freemen. In *The Negro in the American Rebellion*, Brown presented the earliest assessment of the contributions of African Americans in the Civil War. Like Higginson, he emphasizes the black soldier's "heroism and fidelity," but by "collecting facts connected with the rebellion" instead of through personal observation. After reading *Army Life*, students will find Brown's use of Higginson of particular interest. I have them look closely at the passages from Higginson that Brown incorporates into his history to understand the connection between these texts and authors. Like Higginson, Brown remained unforgiving toward Lincoln's administration and extolled slave rebels such as Denmark Vesey and Nat Turner. Higginson was among the first to write a history of Turner's insurrection in 1861. But Brown, having never joined the army, provides no personal account of the war. Instead, he offers a secondhand account largely based upon his reading of "newspaper correspondents" and his conversation with "officers and privates of several of the colored regiments" (xliii).

"The gallantry and loyalty of the blacks during the Rebellion is a matter of history," he wrote proudly, "and volumes might be written upon that subject" (178). He condemns slavery, documents anti-Negro sentiment among Southerners and white Northerners, champions the role of the United States Colored Troops, interprets the war as a struggle for blacks to attain social equality, and assails those who oppressed blacks after Appomattox. Brown believed passionately that the almost 180,000 African Americans who fought in the Union army should share equally in the civil rights and liberties that white Americans enjoyed. Through his history of the black troops, he sought to recognize publicly the contribution of African Americans to the nation's Constitution in order to ensure that they no longer be "deceived" out of their rights (5). Above all, he gave faces and names to the otherwise anonymous mass of black troops—by employing literary figures and conventions in a work that purported to be based on facts.

Brown's extensive quotations from newspapers of the period as well as from works by Higginson and other authorities can be wearisome for undergraduates. His tendency to quote other authors, with or without proper citation, is the subject of lively debate among critics today (see Sanborne). What is the value of his method of documentation? What are its costs? Though his historical account of black soldiers opens with the "Revolutionary War and 1812," our reading begins with chapter 8, "The Union and Slavery Both to Be Preserved" and concludes with chapter 40, "Fall of the Confederacy, and Death of President Lincoln." These chapters dealing specifically with the Civil War offer students a bird's-eye perspective of the black troops that broadens yet in many ways supports Higginson's personal view of the war by lending it the authority of an exceptionally well-read and eloquent former slave.

From these explicitly historical and male accounts of the black troops we move to two novels by women: one white, Dickinson, the other black, Harper. Like Brown, neither Dickinson nor Harper participated directly in the Civil War, but both made the story of the black troops central to their novels. There are obvious differences between Dickinson's *What Answer?* and Harper's *Iola Leroy*, but I ask students to consider the similarities instead. Both novels are written in the mode of romance and center on a mulatta heroine. Though Dickinson's and Harper's heroines are shaped by familiar sentimental conventions, embedded within both novels is a decidedly unconventional historical narrative, that of the black troops, through which the novels' politics can be clearly discerned. Our reading considers the interplay between the novels' literary and historical plots. Whereas Higginson and Brown are committed to including the black troops in the historical narrative of the Civil War and the nation more generally, Dickinson's and Harper's fictional renderings of the black troops teaches readers what to feel about the black troops. Both novelists celebrate the tremendous sacrifice of black soldiers who fought bravely though without the recompense of the white soldiers.

What Answer? first appeared in the fall of 1868. At the heart of the novel is a love story between a wealthy white businessman and a free African American woman. Between the pages of that melodramatic love story is the story of the heroic but failed attempt of the Fifty-Fourth Massachusetts Negro Regiment to capture Fort Wagner. The novel's purpose, as Dickinson so eloquently puts it, is "to write in glowing characters the record of their deeds" (243).

Dickinson came as close as was possible for a woman of her time to being a politician. Though unable to cast a vote herself, she was hired by the Republican Party to campaign on its behalf in the 1863 and 1864 elections. She was later invited to speak in the hall of the House of Representatives, the first woman ever to do so. Though she was generally sympathetic to the Republican Party's platform, her personal politics concentrated on the rights of women and African Americans. Her novel exemplifies the ways in which literature can be a passionate voice for the right to vote that women and African Americans were denied at the time.

Though the novel centers on a fictional romance between the light-skinned Francesca Ercildoune and the wealthy young New Yorker Willie Surrey, Dickinson insists in the concluding note that "every scene in this book is copied from life, and that the incidents of battle and camp are part of the history of the great context." Like Brown, she makes a point of revealing her sources and underlining their reliability:

> From the *New York Tribune* and the *Providence Journal* were taken the accounts of the finding of Hunt, the coming of the slaves into a South Carolina camp, and the voluntary carrying, by black men, ere they were enlisted, of a schooner into the fight at Newbern. Than these two papers, none were considered more reliable and trustworthy in their war record. (313)

In other words, the scenes of war and the draft riots depicted are true, despite the far-fetched love story, making the novel more history than literature. What are the stakes of such a claim? How are students to read this novel when its author insists that she has "necessarily used a somewhat free pencil, but the main incident of each [scene] has been faithfully preserved" (314)?

By having students pay close attention to the novel's form, we can begin to understand the role that sentiment plays in recording the history of the Civil War and the role that the slaves played in the war. Chapters 15 and 16 provide detailed descriptions of particular slaves who assisted Union soldiers. Though the story of Fort Wagner is ostensibly told through the perspective of one of her minor white characters, Dickinson departs from the plot of her novel to narrate the events at Fort Wagner and the activities of "the famous Fifty-Fourth" without the intrusion of any of her characters. She narrates the story as if she were present at the attack:

The evening, or rather the afternoon, was a lurid and sultry one. Great masses of clouds, heavy and black, were piled in the western sky, fringed here and there by an angry red, and torn by vivid streams of lightning. Not a breath of wind shook the leaves or stirred the high, rank grass by the water-side; a portentous and awful stillness filled the air,—the stillness felt by nature before a devastating storm. Quiet, with the like awful and portentous calm, the black regiment, headed by its young, fair-haired, knightly colonel, marched to its destined place and action. (241)

While Dickinson emphasizes the "knightly colonel," Harper uses the story of the famous Fifty-Fourth to glorify the black troops rather than Shaw: "After Colonel Shaw led his charge at Fort Wagner, and died in the conflict, he got bravely over his prejudices. . . . I suppose any white soldier would rather have his black substitute receive the bullets than himself" (*Iola Leroy* 43). Shaw is no hero here. Indeed, Harper holds all whites to task for their "prejudices." And it is against such prejudices that her novel of the Civil War and its aftermath is directed. We begin our reading of the novel by dwelling on its introduction, in which William Still reveals his "doubts" about Harper's "story." He admits that he prefers a history by Harper, given that there is "no other woman, white or colored, anywhere, who has come so intimately in contact with the colored people in the South as Harper" (5). Intimate contact with the "colored people" made her a suitable representative of the colored troops.

Harper's depiction of the colored troops revolves around the character of Robert Johnson, with which the novel opens. Having been "reared by his mistress as a favorite slave," Robert escapes from slavery as "a contraband of war." Prior to the introduction of the novel's heroine, he occupies a central role in the novel's plot. Equipped "with his intelligence, courage, and prompt obedience, he rose from the ranks and became lieutenant of a colored company" (43). Though his status in the novel is eventually eclipsed by the more conventional love story of the tragic mulatta heroine, we focus on Harper's portrayal of this slave-soldier.

Robert Johnson, not Colonel Shaw, is the leader of the colored troops Harper presents in her novel. Robert tells us "the truth," though it is not based on history, about the colored troops: "To silence a battery, to capture a flag, to take a fortification, they will rush into the jaws of death" (44). He provides eyewitness accounts of colored soldiers and their exceptional bravery; they, unlike their white counterparts, are willing to go above and beyond the call of duty. Through Harper's Robert, black soldiers become symbols of unequivocal American patriotism, and it is an image that is captured by the film *Glory*. By introducing Robert in this romance, Harper shows readers the glory of the colored troops. He is not the only black soldier in the novel; there is also Tom Anderson, who dies saving the lives of his fellow men, and Iola's brother, Harry, who joins a colored regiment upon discovering that his mother was a slave. Like his Uncle Robert, Harry turns "his back upon his chances of promotion" to join the colored troops (127). Both men are not only American patriots; they are also, paradoxically, loyal to their race. I draw students' attention to the paradoxes of this romance, which concludes with a black marriage, a happy reunion of former slaves and their progeny in the reconstructed South. Through a close reading of Harper's fictional black heroes, we come to understand that, without men like them, white war heroes like General Grant and Colonel Shaw would have been lost.

By comparing and contrasting Dickinson and Harper's fictional histories, students begin to understand the formal differences between the writing of an American history and the writing of an African American history. While both rely on the story of the black troops to persuade their audiences to grant black men voting rights and provide former slaves and their descendants with a decent education, Dickinson's and Harper's novels diverge sharply in their visions of a United States of America after the abolition of slavery. Our reading of these fictions with Brown's and Higginson's nonfictions allows students to understand the role these literary accounts of the black troops play in the "new birth of freedom" Lincoln declared on 19 November 1863 at Gettysburg (*Gettysburg Address*).

Note

1. Students will find of considerable interest the online resource offered by the Freedmen and Southern Society Project. The project's Web site addresses this absence in the historical record by providing online access to thousands of documents that convey "with first-person immediacy" the experiences of black soldiers and liberated slaves during and after the Civil War (www.freedmen.umd.edu).

Coleman Hutchison

Truth and Consequences: Helping Students Contextualize the Literary Aftermath of the American Civil War

In an often quoted 1888 essay, Albion W. Tourgée—novelist, Civil War veteran, and ardent advocate for color-blind justice—made one of the first cases for the literary importance of the American Civil War. Tourgée saw scattered amid the ruins of Richmond the seeds of a vigorous national literature: "The history of literature shows that it is those who were cradled amid the smoke of battle, the sons and daughters of heroes yet red with slaughter, the inheritors of national woe or racial degradation, who have given utterance to the loftiest strains of genius." We must look, he argued, to the "children of soldiers and of slaves to advance American literature" (413). As useful as Tourgée's essay is, it tells an all too familiar story about triumphant literary nationalism in the wake of this so-called war between brothers. *Pace* Tourgée, how can we help students appreciate the literary consequences of the Civil War without offering a teleological or exceptionalistic account of the conflict? That is, how can we teach the literatures of the American Civil War in a way that allows for the messiness and provisionality of literary history?

Much of the best recent work in American literary studies has touted such messiness and provisionality. For instance, Robert S. Levine challenges scholars to "restore a sense of the contingency to the literary history of the

United States consistent with the contingency of the nation itself" (5). Similarly, critics like Wai Chee Dimock and Lloyd Pratt call into question the temporal logics that grant the category of nineteenth-century American literature a sense of coherence. Most germane for my purposes, Christopher Hager and Cody Marrs rail against the widespread tendency to frame American literary history as a "series of before-after narratives that pivot on the Civil War's interruption" (266). While Hager and Marrs are quick to acknowledge that the Civil War "most certainly transformed the U.S. and its cultural productions" (261)—that it was indeed a rupture—they also want us to see the conflict as a "catalyst for accrual and extension" (266): "In certain respects, the war is less an endpoint than a crucial link in the raucous, irregular unfolding of literary forms, practices, and careers across the nineteenth century, many of which commence long before 1861 and continue long after 1865" (260–61).

Contingencies, temporal extensions, and irregular unfoldings: it is one thing to espouse these literary-historical features in a scholarly essay or monograph; it is quite another to bring them into the classroom. Put simply, messiness and provisionality are notoriously difficult concepts for undergraduates, who often hunger for clean and absolute historical narratives. As per usual, the challenge lies in squaring students' desire for iterable knowledge with an instructor's sense of intellectual responsibility.

This essay argues that the literature of the American Civil War offers students an uncommon opportunity to study both the ruptures and the continuities of literary history. A sustained study of Civil War texts offers a middle way of sorts, a pedagogical space between the messy and the clean, between the provisional and the absolute. I advocate a pedagogy that has students contextualize individual texts before comparing them transhistorically. This process gives students (and instructors) the comfort of those "before-after narratives" while allowing for the discomforting complications that define American literary history.

A dialectic of comfort and discomfort is a mainstay in two courses I regularly teach at the University of Texas at Austin: a standard survey of post–Civil War American literature and an upper-division seminar entitled Literature, Cultural Memory, and the American Civil War. Not surprisingly, my opening lectures and our early discussions in the survey focus on the world the war made; I then return to the Civil War again and again throughout the term. The seminar on Civil War memory considers the conflict in relation to the ways literary and cultural texts have remembered and rewritten it over time. Focusing on five periods of American cultural memory—the immediate postwar period, the 1890s, 1930s, 1960s, and 1990s—the course asks, How did subsequent generations narrate the causes and effects of the war? How do contemporary events affect the way a given generation reads and rewrites the war? What agendas are brought to bear on representations of this fierce and bloody conflict? In both courses, the Civil War emerges as a recurrent, even dominant theme in American literature. Indeed, I have to be careful in both settings not to make all American literature seem like a function of the Civil War.

Drawing on my experiences teaching these two courses, I reexamine in this essay two widely agreed-upon literary consequences of the war: the development of American literary realism and more complicated postwar relations between regional and national literatures. As a result of these consequences, many scholars see the Civil War as initiating a new literary history—or, at the very least, a new chapter in literary history. I do not dispute the veracity of such claims; these are indeed important literary consequences of the conflict. Instead, I offer pedagogical approaches and techniques that allow students to read the well-established relations among realism, regionalism, and the American Civil War in less absolute and more contingent terms.

Realism

It is a truth universally acknowledged that the Civil War helped bring about something called American literary realism.[1] Since nearly the end of Reconstruction, literary critics and historians have consistently argued that the war and its aftermath either encouraged or demanded more accurate modes of literary description and that postwar readers were, in turn, increasingly eager consumers of realist texts. As early as 1879, Henry James could claim that the "great convulsion" had "left a different tone from the tone it found, and one may say that the Civil War marks an era in the history of the American mind. It introduced into the national consciousness a certain sense of proportion and relation, of the world being a more complicated place than it had hitherto seemed, the future more treacherous, success more difficult." James would go on to prognosticate, à la Tourgée, about the future character of American literature: "At the rate at which things are going, it is obvious that good Americans will be more numerous than ever; but the good American, in days to come, will be a more critical person than his complacent and confident grandfather." To James's mind, the Civil War had forced that "good American" to eat "of the tree of knowledge" (144). The postwar world was, then, postlapsarian, and the new American writer would need to adjust accordingly—with wandering steps and slow, as it were. Realism, James avers, might provide one way out of Eden.

James's rich and provocative prose teaches exceedingly well. Here is the Master making a bold claim about an epistemic shift in American intellectual life—and doing so in biblical terms, no less. Presented without context, this statement seems like an ideal before-after narrative about the Civil War. Students can cite it as evidence or use it as an epigraph for an essay. Yet, as I often remind them, context is key. This familiar quotation comes from James's idiosyncratic study of Nathaniel Hawthorne. Published some fifteen years after Hawthorne's death as part of the series Morley's English Men of Letters, James's *Hawthorne* is an anxious and engaging text.

Throughout this slim volume "Henry James, Jr.," reads—or perhaps willfully misreads—Hawthorne in realist terms. On at least three occasions he states flatly his case: "It cannot be too often repeated that Hawthorne was not a realist" (124). And yet his opening pages also acknowledge the protorealist effects of Hawthorne's fiction:

> I have alluded to the absence in Hawthorne of that quality of realism which is now so much in fashion . . . and yet I think I am not fanciful in saying that he testifies to the sentiments of the society in which he flourished almost as pertinently . . . as Balzac and some of his descendants—MM. Flaubert and Zola—testify to the manners and morals of the French people. He was not a man with a literary theory; he was guiltless of a system, and I am not sure that he had ever heard of Realism, this remarkable compound having (although it was invented some time earlier) come into general use only since his death. He had certainly not proposed to himself to give an account of the social idiosyncrasies of his fellow-citizens, for his touch on such points is always light and vague, he has none of the apparatus of an historian, and his shadowy style of portraiture never suggests a rigid standard of accuracy. Nevertheless he virtually offers the most vivid reflection of New England life that has found its way into literature. . . . Hawthorne's work savours thoroughly of the local soil—it is redolent of the social system in which he had his being. (4–5)

Even absent "a rigid standard of accuracy," Hawthorne managed to capture something fundamental about his time and place.

I often teach these characteristically long passages in tandem. Read contrapuntally, they force my students to see that if American literary realism was indeed a consequence of the Civil War, then the causality therein was complex. In turn, James's comments on Hawthorne's realistic effects reveal American literary realism's dual debts to romance (Hawthorne's favored mode) and European literature (e.g., Balzac, Flaubert, and Zola). By James's own parenthetical admission, American literary realism may have begun its great career after Hawthorne's death in 1864, but it had a long foreground elsewhere. Finally, the dynamics of attraction and repulsion that characterize James's at times bewildering criticisms of Hawthorne are immensely helpful in getting students to think about the strange ways of literary influence. Here, then, is some of that messiness and provisionality.

The example of American literary realism bears out well the process of accrual and extension that Hager and Marrs posit. Among other things, the genre's "raucous, irregular unfolding" clearly predates the Civil War. Nonetheless, most historians of the genre seem reluctant to dub any bellum or antebellum text as realist. Tellingly, many follow Edmund Wilson's lead and cite John W. De Forest's *Miss Ravenel's Conversion from Secession to Loyalty* (1867) as an urtext or "precursor of realism in American fiction" (670). The novel, which De Forest wrote partially from notes he had taken while serving as a captain in the Union army, was lauded by contemporary reviewers for its detailed and unflinching representations of army life. Two of those reviewers, James and William Dean Howells, would go on to become leading lights of American literary realism. James praised De Forest's "excellent descriptions of campaigning in the terrible swamps and forests of Louisiana," while Howells called *Miss Ravenel's Conversion* "the first novel to treat the war really and artistically" (qtd. in Scharnhorst xxii–xxiii). Three decades later, Howells—echoing James's assessment of Hawthorne—would deem it not just "the best novel suggested by the civil war" but also "of an advanced realism, before realism was known by name" (qtd. in E. Wilson 697).

Teaching *Miss Ravenel's Conversion* as a realist novel *avant la lettre* partially answers Hager and Marrs's call to action by pushing the origin date for American literary realism ever closer to the rupture of 1861–65. The novel also teaches like a dream. Students in my Civil War memory course routinely praise its readability and "romance of reunion" plot (see Silber, esp. 110–11). In turn, I enjoy teaching the novel's heady mixture of domestic, sentimental, and protorealist conventions. But what if there were an even earlier Civil War novel of advanced realism, one that also offered detailed and unflinching representations of army life? How would such a text help unsettle the before-after narrative of American literary realism? Augusta Jane Evans's 1864 novel *Macaria; or, Altars of Sacrifice* is just such a text.

By 1861, Evans was already a hugely popular novelist. With the outbreak of the war, she remade herself as a would-be Confederate historian, political theorist, and military strategist. She corresponded with Civil War luminaries like General P. T. G. Beauregard and the Confederate congressman J. L. M. Curry, discussing the progress of the war with them in bald terms. Her wartime novel bears the mark of that contact; it also speaks resoundingly to her total investment in the Confederate cause. As I have argued elsewhere (Hutchison, *Apples* 79–80), Evans was likely at work on the novel when the Civil War broke out. (Its opening chapters are largely sentimental and domestic and make no mention of rising sectional tension.) I conjecture that she then radically revised her manuscript to incorporate the conflict. Such a ripped-from-the-headlines composition—one might think of Edmund Wilson's dismissal of Melville's "versified journalism" (479)—gives the later chapters of the novel an urgent and evocative aspect. More to the point, Evans's descriptions of battle also pioneer a fierce realism, one that challenges students to think about the boundaries of both genre and gender (see Hutchison, *Apples* 63–98).

Indeed, Evans's description of the First Battle of Bull Run (or First Manassas, the name used by Confederate forces) is among the most graphic contemporary accounts of the war. Here is a representative passage: "Hideous was the spectacle presented—dead and dying, friend and foe, huddled in indiscriminate ruin, weltering in blood and shivering in the agonies of dissolution; blackened headless trunks and fragments of limbs—ghastly sights and sounds of woe, filling the scene of combat" (148). Wilson claimed that the war scenes in *Miss Ravenel's Conversion* were "the first of their kind in fiction in English" (685). And yet scenes like this hold up very well in a comparison with De Forest's. I often excerpt passages from *Macaria* and then ask my upper-division students to blindly date them. The resulting dates are usually dead wrong. As my students point out, Evans's description sounds like something out of Ambrose Bierce, Stephen Crane, or even Tim O'Brien. They are a bit bemused to find out that the passage was written during the war—and by a Confederate woman, no less.

A comparative exercise like this forces students to rethink a number of assumptions about both the character of women's writing and when realism happens. In the subsequent lecture, I take pains to then represent Evans's steadfast adherence to a "rigid standard of accuracy." For instance, on 17 March 1863, Evans wrote to General Beauregard himself to corroborate several facts in her description of the First Battle of Bull Run. After apologizing at some length for disturbing the general during the ongoing siege on Charleston, she cuts to the chase: "I am extremely desirous to know that I am *entirely accurate* in all my statements relative to the Battle" (qtd. in Hutchison, *Apples* 83). Such a concern for accuracy and detail—not to mention the ability to employ a military luminary as her fact-checker—says a great deal about her desire for factual precision if not her nascent realism.

This fiercely partisan novel makes a superb pedagogical counterpoint to the better-known *Miss Ravenel's Conversion*. Like De Forest's novel, *Macaria* has at its center a bizarre love triangle; however, the movement of Evans's novel runs counter to that of *Miss Ravenel's Conversion*—from loyalty to secession and beyond. Thus, *Macaria* can help represent the Confederacy on Civil War literature syllabi, which tend to be Union-centric. The presence of Confederate texts on syllabi underscores, in turn, those contingencies of literary history and nationalism. After all, when Evans was writing *Macaria*, the outcome of the Civil War was far from determined.

Even though they represent different sides of the conflict, these two novels share a great deal in common at the level of genre. Both offer a similarly heady mixture of domestic, sentimental, and protorealist conventions. When confronted with such hybridity, students begin to see genre as a question rather than an answer. In my classes, *Macaria* emerges as a messy, in medias res urtext for American literary realism—one written, importantly, from a southern perspective. Needless to say, such a framing significantly muddies those clean and absolute historical lines and generic boundaries that students seem to want.

Regionalism

Like American literary realism, American regionalism is often dated after the American Civil War. This chronology should come as little surprise, given that regionalism is often treated as a subgenre of realism. In a famous articulation, Richard Brodhead claims that the genre's "great public flowering began with the northern victory in the Civil War, in other words with the forcible repression of sectional autonomy in favor of national union and the legal supplanting of the locally variant by national norms of citizenly rights" (119). His floricultural language can be usefully brought into the classroom. After all, the seeds for that "great public flowering" were planted long before the American Civil War.

In introducing regionalism, I often excerpt portions of Brodhead's chapter "The Reading of Regions" and assign them alongside Amy Kaplan's excellent essay "Nation, Region, and Empire." These texts teach very well together, in no small part because they both make broad, sympathetic historical claims. With their respective before-after narratives in place, I am then able to reintroduce a sense of contingency and provisionality. For instance, one of my favorite assignments has students look for protoregionalist (i.e., antebellum) texts in online periodical archives. Although the *American Periodicals Series* and twin *Making of America* sites are treasure troves, students can get easily overwhelmed. For that reason, I usually choose one or two periodical titles and ask them to read around for literary representations of place. Once they have found an apt story or poem, they do some basic research on the author or periodical and then share their findings either in a presentation or through our online learning management system.

The *Southern Literary Messenger* is a particularly rich resource for this assignment, since the seeds of regionalism are everywhere on its pages. Based in Richmond, Virginia, the *Messenger* was the South's most important and longest running literary magazine. It was published continuously from 1834 to 1864—a period that witnessed not only increasing sectional tensions but also fiery debates about the prospect of a national literature. Although its politics often lived up to its regional title, the magazine featured a surprisingly far-flung set of authors. Among its many contributors were Thomas Bailey Aldrich, John Esten Cooke, Sarah Josepha Hale, Paul Hamilton Hayne, Caroline Hentz, Sidney Lanier, Augustus Baldwin Longstreet, Lydia H. Sigourney, William Gilmore Simms, John R. Thompson, Henry Timrod, and Nathaniel Beverly Tucker. The *Messenger's* best-known contributor, Edgar Allan Poe, even spent a tumultuous year as the magazine's editor. Suffice it to say, each issue of the *Southern Literary Messenger* offers students the opportunity to read regionalist literary productions in a regional literary periodical.[2]

An assignment like this highlights the diverse nature of regional writing before the Civil War—before, that is, the so-called "great public flowering" of the genre. By suggesting continuities that bridge the rupture of the Civil War, the assignment also encourages student to see regional writing for what it is: an ongoing, vibrant, and constitutive part of American literary history. Once students are able to connect antebellum writers like A. B. Longstreet and Caroline Lee Hentz to postwar regionalists like Mark Twain and Kate Chopin, it is only a matter of time before they start reading Sarah Orne Jewett, Charles W. Chesnutt, Hamlin Garland, and Mary Austin alongside latter-day regionalists like Flannery O'Connor, Oscar Casares, Randall Kenan, and Jon Raymond.

Regionalism is a critical category that allows for no small amount of historical drift. This drift is in keeping with the genre's ambivalent relation to history—a feature that I always hammer home in my classes. Brodhead argues that the genre's "public function was not just to mourn lost cultures but to purvey a certain story of contemporary cultures and of the relations among them" (121). And indeed, regionalist text after regionalist text figures those relations. However, Brodhead's reliance on a before-after narrative unduly limits the purview of the genre. For instance, my students often comment on the artificial or clumsy historical frame narratives of Chesnutt's *Conjure Tales.* They also wonder aloud about Chopin's manipulations of narrative time in stories like "Ma'ame Pélagie" and "A Lady of Bayou St. John." And as they compare regionalist texts transhistorically—for instance, we often examine in tandem Paul Laurence Dunbar's, Robert Lowell's, and Natasha Trethewey's representations of African American soldiers in the Civil War—my students begin to see the complexity of those mourning and purveying functions. In discussing all these texts, I try to help my students see how regionalist writing draws the past and the present, lost and contemporary cultures, into a more dynamic conversation than Brodhead's influential argument allows.

I also try to return them to a moment when this purportedly backward-looking genre seemed to be the future of American literature. One way to do this is through Brodhead and Kaplan's arguments that regionalism projected an image of triumphant, reunified nationhood in the wake of the war. A more inductive way is to assign forward-looking contemporary accounts of the genre, such as Tourgée's prognostications about the twinned futures of southern and American literatures. I teach his "The South as a Field for Fiction" nearly every semester. Its length and evocative rhetoric make the essay both accessible and compelling to students, who often become enamored of Tourgée's frank discussions of race and rich figurative language. Students also seem to enjoy teasing out the paradox at the heart of the essay. While Tourgée has great faith in "the unparalleled richness of Southern life . . . as a field for fictitious narrative," he argues that its fecundity is a function of past squalor and ruin (406). Again, it is "national woe or racial degradation" that will feed this genius crop.

In his final sentence, Tourgée is explicit about the concatenation of a traumatic past (i.e., slavery, Civil War, and Reconstruction), a chaotic present (i.e., 1888), and an unknowable future (i.e., the twentieth century and beyond). He predicts:

> Because of the exceeding woefulness of a not too recent past, therefore, and the abiding horror of unavoidable conditions which are the sad inheritance of the present, we may confidently look for the children of soldiers and of slaves to advance American literature to the very front rank of that immortal procession whose song is the eternal refrain of remembered agony, before the birthhour of the twentieth century shall strike (413).

As the semester proceeds, my students take glee in cataloging the ways that Tourgée's predictions proved both wrong and right. (Tourgée seems to have overstated the case when they are reading Stephen Crane, but when they get to Faulkner. . . .) And I take pleasure in the fact that my students are once again thinking about literary historical contingency and provisionality.

Like all expressions of literary nationalism, Tourgée's essay reveals nothing so much as a writer struggling to make sense of his own historical moment. As Levine reminds us, literary history is at its best when it attends to such intimate struggles. Among many other things, they help to establish "a more vital sense of connection between the past and the present by making it clear that what we share with the past is a chaotic, even anarchic, sense of possibility that demands responsible choices and actions" (13). Such a sense of connection and possibility is, I hasten to add, at stake in every pedagogical encounter.

Notes

1. For representative arguments, see E. Wilson; Aaron; Menand; and Fuller. Phillip J. Barrish's excellent *Cambridge Introduction to American Literary Realism* is especially good on the Civil War as a social and historical context for the genre (see esp. 23–25, 32–35).

2. The entire run of the *Messenger* is available at the University of Michigan's *Making of America* site.

Wiebke Omnus Klumpenhower

Teaching Civil War Literature to International Students: A Case Study from South Korea

At a university in South Korea, I faced the challenge of communicating British and American literatures to students who are culturally quite far removed from the West. This essay relates and analyzes my experience teaching the literatures of the American Civil War in a class entitled The History of American Literature, a standard survey course. The teaching approach suggested here is comparative, based on an attempt to build a bridge between America and my South Korean students. My goals were to make students aware of the possibility of a larger literary and cultural conversation and specifically to encourage them to value American literature, as unfamiliar as it may be, in its own right. The methodology I propose has something to offer teachers in contexts beyond the South Korean. First, it should help those who are teaching abroad or in an ESL setting. Second, more generally, my analysis of student motivation may be of interest to anyone who is confronted with students' struggles to relate to a given subject matter. Third, this discussion of teaching the American Civil War in South Korea may suggest ways of placing this national conflict into a larger, global conversation.

The Challenge

The Department of English Language and Literature offers two sections of The History of American Literature every fall semester, and usually both are taught in Korean. I taught a section of this course in the English language four times, once during each of the fall semesters I spent in South Korea, between 2009 and 2013. The concept of having foreign professors teach content courses in English, as opposed to skill-based language courses like composition and conversation, was relatively new at this university and others like it. Students have a deep desire to learn English and to study and experience contemporary Western consumer culture, so they flock to language courses taught by native speakers, who are professors from English-speaking countries. The students consider the more recently established content courses taught by a foreigner in the English department as yet another opportunity to study the English language and to be exposed to a foreign culture through a native speaker. Their interest is more in improving their English language skills for international business than in studying the course content. Their expectations of an English degree are usually more practical than academic, and most have had little or no prior educational training in the analysis of literature.

An additional difficulty is that students gain most of their knowledge of American culture from popular television shows and therefore have almost no grasp of American history. Many have never visited the United States, and so the past of the United States is a country doubly foreign to them. Moreover, that South Korean society remains highly homogenous makes it harder for students to understand the kinds of racial and ethnic diversity they encounter in their studies of the history and literatures of the American Civil War.

In an anonymous survey of forty-nine students in my class, ninety-six percent said that they had had no knowledge of the Civil War before they enrolled. They also said overwhelmingly that most of what they know about American literature and history they learned in this class. Because of my students' limited command of the English language and the absence of any background knowledge, I came to use teaching materials created for American middle school students to provide my own students with information on different authors and literary periods. I gave detailed *PowerPoint* presentations to go along with those materials. I assigned excerpts from literary works to be read at home and often reread the same texts with my students in class to clarify vocabulary and comprehension questions. Despite these efforts, it was difficult to get my students to engage with American history and literature in general and with the literatures of the Civil War specifically. At times their lack of preparation and lack of engagement seemed insurmountable obstacles.

Attempts at Finding a Solution

The thought of focusing on similarities between South Korea and the United States in my teaching occurred to me because of a campus visit of Hyun In-taek, the minister of unification, whose talk drew on the similarities between South Korea and Germany, my native country. I witnessed my students attending talks like this and becoming passionately involved in the discussion, asking me questions about the situation in Germany because they were able to relate it to their lives in South Korea. Their excitement made me realize that it might help my teaching to draw on the obvious, though certainly superficial, similarities between Korea's division into north and south and the American Civil War. Approaching a topic comparatively to bridge cultural differences may be useful, even when there are not that many similarities, in overcoming the sense of alienation students so often feel when they simply cannot relate to the material that is being taught. Moreover, highlighting similarities when discussing literary texts might enable students to appreciate the differences as well, to see familiar things in a new light, and to understand, for the first time, a historical event or literary work.

When students were asked in the survey whether they thought considering the Korean War and the division of Korea helped them understand the American Civil War, seventy-one percent replied that it did—the others stated that the two conflicts were too different politically and historically to be compared. The students who felt that comparison was helpful elaborated on shared issues of division, belonging, and identity. In class, I attempted to build on these common issues to encourage my students to consider the possibility of a dialogue between American and Korean history and literature. I told them that I had no intention of glossing over the differences between these two conflicts but that there were many benefits that could be found in the dialogue made possible by a comparative approach.

Relating the Division of Korea to the American Civil War

In the Korean War and the American Civil War, we see a period of oppression of individuals just before the division, and we see a war within a nation, brother against brother. Underscoring a few basic similarities opened students' minds to literature. I introduced the Civil War by reminding my students of their own past and present as a nation, and I encouraged them to explore the differences and connections by comparatively reading the literatures of both countries. This approach may be taken also with ESL students, who are unfamiliar with the literatures of the target language.

At first my students were completely unable to relate to the horrors of slavery in the United States. Alluding to the Japanese occupation of Korea, which occurred just before the Korean War and continues to be a topic of conversation, helped open their minds to this subject. When I taught *The Narrative of the Life of Frederick Douglass, an American Slave, Written by Himself* (1845), I began by speaking about the Korean experience under Japanese colonialism, where Koreans were exploited as workers, starved, made to study Japanese and forbidden to speak their own language, and forced to give up Korean surnames and instead use Japanese ones (Wright 84). My students became very personally involved, and thinking about this recent history allowed them to look beyond their racial preconceptions and consider the experience of American slaves. The example of Koreans' having to give up their names led to Frederick Douglass's name changes and what they meant to him (2090). I also focused on the issue of limited education for the enslaved and oppression through language: that the Koreans were not allowed to speak their own language during Japanese occupation but forced to learn the language of the oppressor was not unlike the way American slaves were not allowed to learn how to read and write (2056). The reasons behind these policies are similar: to avoid rebellion and insurrection; to belittle, limit, and retrain the individual; to undermine the identity of the individual.

I then asked my students to study the Civil War in greater depth, to look into specific literary works and see how their own literary tradition might relate to that of America. I challenged them to do some research on their own, to take advantage of their unique position as native speakers of Korean to find Korean works that might relate to the books we would discuss in class. Harriet Beecher Stowe's *Uncle Tom's Cabin* (1852), which, legend has it, Abraham Lincoln called "the book that made this great war [i.e., the American Civil War]" (Weaver xi), was particularly hard for my students to understand because of its subtleties involving racial prejudice and abolitionism. It often helped them to find a Korean work that dealt with similar concerns and then compare the two on the level of theme and genre. This approach gave them a more nuanced appreciation of the differences as well. My students arrived at insights that impressed me as a non-Korean, showing me American literature in a different light.

One of my students, Woo Min-hee, wrote a comparison of *Uncle Tom's Cabin* and a short story by Kim Dong-in, an early-twentieth-century South Korean author. "Bare Hills" (1932) tells of oppression set in Manchuria during the Japanese occupation of Korea just before the division of the country (7 [note from Myoung-Hee Hong, the story's translator]). Through her insightful analysis, the student arrived at a deeper understanding of both texts. She concluded that both Stowe and Kim were not strong enough in their criticism—Stowe of American slavery and Kim of the Japanese occupation. She also noted the weaknesses of certain characters.

The comparison between the American Civil War and the Japanese occupation of Korea and the literatures that emerged from them can take us only so far as teachers. Eventually a more subtle engagement with history and culture is needed when a literary work is discussed. If my students do not consider American literature on its own merits and in its own context, their understanding remains superficial. In my experience, the successful students were the ones who became truly interested in Civil War literatures and who used the Korean conflict as a contrast to highlight the subtle dynamics of the war that tore America apart. In their literary analyses, they were able to establish a dialogue between the two cultures, a dialogue that led to insights into each historical event that would not have been possible otherwise.

The American Civil War benefits from being seen not in isolation but rather as part of a larger, global conversation. It is one civil war among many. Although it is not part of Korean literature, analyses of similarities and differences between conflicts prompt conversation, as happened in my classroom in South Korea. Treating literature comparatively challenges the ways in which we view our own history and literary tradition.

Darren T. Williamson, Shawn Jones, and William Steele

Team-Teaching the Civil War at Historical Sites

Although the American Civil War touched nearly all aspects of the lives of the people who experienced it, contemporary educators at every level often reduce its teaching to a rigidly compartmentalized approach. They deal separately with various disciplines—history, literature, politics, theology, and economics—as though each exists in a vacuum. While discussing this frustration in developing Civil War Literature, a course at Cascade College, we developed a cross-disciplinary approach to this subject. We proposed taking a page from the international studies program, in which students travel to sites of historical and cultural importance and learn a variety of approaches to the subject matters related to those places. That variety extends to the pedagogies themselves and notably includes an experiential element for students enrolled in this program.

Our solution to dissolving the perceived barriers among disciplines in the academy resulted in a travel course that was team-taught by us, professors from the religion, history, and English departments. This course was offered as a senior-level elective in each of these fields. Collectively, the class met once a week for three hours. We discussed texts from a common reading list, including material that explicitly addressed the approaches each discipline takes when studying the Civil War. Outside class, the students met with the professor from the discipline for which they were getting credit, to choose a topic for their final paper and tailor the research to their academic field. The most appealing aspect of the class, however, for the students and professors alike, was a week-long travel component that took place during spring break. This experiential portion of the class allowed the students to visit places selected to tie in with the various readings across the three disciplines. One of the greatest challenges in designing the course was maximizing our travel time, providing the students with opportunities to explore a variety of locations related to key participants, witnesses, and pivotal events in the war. Travel sites included Harpers Ferry, West Virginia; Manassas, Virginia; Sharpsburg, Maryland; Washington, DC; and Gettysburg, Pennsylvania.

Itinerary

Because most of our students had never been to a Civil War site, we used the first day of our trip to visit the National Civil War Museum in Harrisburg, Pennsylvania. Providing equal space to the northern, southern, and slave experiences, the museum visit helped students understand the complexities of the political and social climate of the middle nineteenth century beyond the scope of what our limited class time was able to provide. Although the tour was self-guided, the faculty members spent time with all the students at some point, asking them to consider how each of the three areas was presented, the types of information that were included, and how effectively the various exhibits addressed specific fields of study. During the transit time between sites, professors debriefed students about the museum—how the exhibits and artifacts either clarified aspects of the war we had already explored or raised questions that we had not discussed.

By using Gettysburg as a base camp, our group was able to take the second day to travel to Harpers Ferry, where we discussed John Brown's raid on the federal arsenal and the significance of the raid to the war's beginning. Students explored the exhibits related to Brown and the abolitionist movement by reading accounts from newspapers of the time paired with those exhibits. Their puzzled reaction to Brown provided an opportunity for us to discuss the variety of approaches to abolition current in the antebellum period. While students agreed with Brown's fundamental opposition to slavery, his fanaticism and apocalyptic approach to ending slavery made Brown a far from sympathetic figure. Ironically, the visit to

Harpers Ferry helped everyone realize why his raid was so shocking to Southerners and why even staunch abolitionists were uncomfortable with the presence of the likes of Brown in their cause. Students saw that opposing slavery before the war was not as simple as it might seem. The rest of the second day was spent in Sharpsburg, where we toured the battlefield and Dunker Church, tying this visit to the theology of the region in 1862. Our discussions about Sharpsburg led us to the importance of the battle there in Lincoln's Emancipation Proclamation. As we connected this battle to Lincoln's historic and bold executive decision, students began to better grasp the complex issues related to slavery and the Civil War.

The next two days were spent covering the Battle of Gettysburg and locations we had read about in our collective texts. Specific attention was given to Seminary Ridge, Devil's Den and Little Round Top, the Wheatfield, Cemetery Ridge, and the location of Pickett's Charge. The letters and diaries we read before leaving campus set the stage for this part of the trip, allowing students to immerse themselves in what the period was like for soldiers and civilians.

The two remaining days were spent in Washington, where we toured Ford's Theatre and Arlington National Cemetery, both showing how America has chosen to remember iconic figures such as Lincoln and hundreds of thousands of casualties from the war. Before our travel, we briefly discussed the ways in which battlefields and other historic sites commemorate events. In particular, we explored how monuments and memorials pay tribute to individuals and groups of soldiers at Gettysburg, and we noted the shift in recent years to reclaim and restore parts of the battlefield to better illustrate what the sites were like during the war. These discussions exposed the class to the political issues behind establishing such memorials and how memorials shape our modern understanding of history.

Though a significant number of the primary texts changed between the two years we offered this class, one text remained constant to our pedagogical approach to teaching the war through three academic lenses: *Two Witnesses at Gettysburg: The Personal Accounts of Whitelaw Reid and A. J. L. Fremantle*, edited by Gary W. Gallagher. The role of Whitelaw Reid as the Washington correspondent for the Cincinnati *Gazette* gave him the opportunity to showcase his personal interest in military history, while A. J. L. Fremantle's diary provides a glimpse of his time observing Lee's army in the summer of 1863. The class lectures and discussions preceding the trip dealt with the political, economic, social, and religious histories from the American Revolution to the Civil War, but the trip itself showcased the primary sources written by those who fought and observed the war, specifically the battle at Gettysburg. In this essay, each discipline's approach to these accounts is explained, and examples are given of how the travel component enhanced the students' understanding of and appreciation for the subject matter.

Religion (by Shawn Jones)

Presuppositions shape one's views of current events and history; therefore, as we prepared and led our students in this course, we expended considerable time and effort to have them read primary material. We wanted them to immerse themselves in the different ways people in the 1860s thought about the conflict. From a religious perspective, we did not need to look far to see how most of the nation's leaders and the era's most influential public statements and texts were guided by the belief that God (Providence) was active in history and in many ways was directing the outcomes of life, particularly the events of the Civil War.

Religious beliefs significantly influenced the start of the Civil War. John Brown stated during a church gathering in Ohio, "Here, before God in the presence of these witnesses, I consecrate my life to the destruction of slavery" (Ward, Burns, and Burns 4). Having the students stand inside the engine house on the site where Brown was captured helped them imagine the event that many believe sparked the Civil War.

Throughout our trip, students attempted to view these scenes through the eyes of the witnesses. Seeing the sites at Little Round Top that Reid describes shaped each student's historical understanding. Reid, as he reflects on the possible battles in Gettysburg, states, "The week, it would seem, must bring a battle; two days may do it. Our fates depend on no *one* battle now; but if a good Providence shall at last turn the scale in our favor, it will be a sorrier day for rebeldom than defeat of theirs on any field has hitherto proved" (Gallagher 4).

The terrain itself at Gettysburg illustrated how both sides in the conflict interpreted the role of Providence. On the higher ground, which the North held, it was easier to agree with their position that Providence was on the side of the northern army. Students could see that Seminary Ridge and other low-lying positions were no advantage to the rebels. However, understanding the mind-set of the southern army too was important. Robert E. Lee, being a man of ardent faith, stated upon taking command of the army of Virginia, "May God direct all for our good" (Ward, Burns, and Burns 42). Our students knew that Lee believed in Providence and that this belief influenced his decisions. The armies on Cemetery Ridge and Seminary Ridge, on Gettysburg's third day, both felt that God was on their side.

We had the students walk following Pickett's Charge across the field that lay between the ridges. This quiet march allowed them to reflect upon not only the battlefield movements but also the convictions of the soldiers who engaged in this battle. Later in the day, at sunset, after imagining all the events of the battle, we went to the Peace Light Memorial, where students thought about the lives of those we had studied: Lee, Meade, Longstreet, Chamberlain, and many others. We considered their feelings and convictions. Since Cascade College is a Christian, liberal arts institution, we had the freedom to ask students to consider how religious thinking affects their own lives. Earlier in the week, we stood where President Lincoln, in his Gettysburg Address, stated that those who had died on these fields at Gettysburg had given "their last full measure" ("Address"). Building on Lincoln's immortal words and on our travel experiences and academic study, we asked the students to reflect on their own lives and how they would be remembered.

After several days of digesting the events at Gettysburg, we were able to give our students a sense of the "crisis" that Mark Noll addresses in his *The Civil War as a Theological Crisis.* To illustrate the conflicting witnesses of Providence, Noll uses the sermons of John H. Rice, a southern preacher, and Daniel Alexander Payne, a northern preacher (5, 6). Both preached with the full conviction that God would act in support of their cause. Students were also assigned several additional sermons to show the conflicting views of Providence and what Noll calls the "shallowness of providential reasoning" (6).

Until the students had a chance to walk these hallowed grounds, it seemed that our instruction on Providence would not be effective. Limited to a textbook experience, they could not walk in the footsteps of Gettysburg's witnesses. Now they too became witnesses, not only to the Civil War but also to Providence.

English (by William Steele)

On 3 October 1888, Joshua Lawrence Chamberlain, commander of the Twentieth Maine a quarter century earlier, helped dedicate a monument to his men and their role in the Battle of Gettysburg. In what has become one of the most repeated lines related to the war, Chamberlain articulated an obvious connection among the battle, the men who fought there, and the generations of people he knew would be affected by the outcome:

> In great deeds something abides. On great fields something stays. Forms change and pass; bodies disappear; but spirits linger, to consecrate ground for the vision-place of souls. And reverent men and women from afar, and generations that know us not and that we know not of, heart-drawn to see where and by whom great things were suffered and done for them, shall come to this deathless field to ponder and dream . . ." (D. Smith 278)

We read this passage together while standing along the Twentieth Maine's line on Little Round Top, noting Chamberlain's prophetic message that recognized people like us would come to that place "to ponder and dream," connecting the generations together into a sphere that poets like Walt Whitman had, not long before, introduced to American readers.

While the class used both popular and scholarly sources from the twentieth century to set the backdrop for the history and theology portions of the class, most of the literature we covered was in the form of primary documents: letters, diaries, journals, battle reports, newspaper accounts, sermons, and poetry and prose written by those who witnessed the war's events. These selections included speakers and writings, both canonical and noncanonical, from all three disciplines. The discussions related to each text focused on such aspects as authorial intent and literary context. The Reid and Fremantle texts, for example, were written for different audiences and with different purposes—Reid's purpose was to reconstruct the battle for readers, Fremantle's was more personal, to remember the war. Reid, who was a correspondent since the war's beginnings, gives an incomplete account of Gettysburg because he arrived after fighting had ended on the first day; therefore he "relied on testimony from various participants to construct his narrative of the opening phase of action" (Gallagher xi). Fremantle, on the other hand, lacks the minute details afforded by Reid, but the Englishman gave our class personal observations of officers about whom he wrote in his 1864 journal *Three Months in the Southern States, April–June 1863*. Read separately, they are a fragmented and incomplete view of the war; taken together, however, the movements and decisions from both sides are more clearly understood and demonstrate the war's complexities.

Although most students were not familiar with Reid or Fremantle before this class, all had either heard of or read works by other writers from the period. Our discussions on these canonical writers gave some insight into how they dealt with the conflict in their works and how these works may have been interpreted by readers of the day.

History (by Darren T. Williamson)

In many ways, historians are supposed to be jacks of all trades, dabbling in nearly every discipline to aid in crafting a legitimate narrative of the past. The great thing about working with religion and English experts in this class was that I could focus on the political context of the war and the issues of causation and interpretation.

For the political context, I tried to provide the general setting for the Civil War by addressing how slavery and constitutional issues contributed to the outbreak of the conflict. We spent two class periods working through the issue of slavery in the years between the American Revolution and the Civil War, beginning with the compromise of 1820 through the election of an antislavery president in 1860. I showed students the wide spectrum of convictions, from radical abolitionists like John Brown and William Lloyd Garrison to the southern argument for slavery that emerged after the Nat Turner revolt and the Denmark Vesey insurrection. While on-site at battlegrounds, we encountered epitaphs, memorials, and other testimonials that fit into the broad continuum of viewpoints.

Concerning constitutional issues, we tried to help students realize that, second to the founding of the nation, the debate over the constitutionality of secession was the most important moment for political philosophy in American history. Different conceptions of union, nullification, states' rights, and freedom were all up for grabs during this period and ultimately could not be reconciled. Songs like "Battle Cry of Freedom," which was fervently sung by both sides, demonstrated to students that fundamental issues of liberty contributed to the ferocity of combat, especially among Southerners who felt violated by the northern invader. Western expansion is a subtheme within the political context of the war, because every time a new state or territory was added to the Union, the debate over slavery was rekindled, like a simmering ember just waiting for a fresh breath of life.

We also presented the Civil War in international contexts. The theme of unification and centralization playing out in the German states and in Italy was ironically threatened by southern secession. As the greatest conflict of the period, the war was of concern to Europeans, who technically stayed out of the conflict but had great interest in its outcome. We mentioned the affinity between southern culture and English aristocrats, and Fremantle's sympathetic description of the southern officer corps helped bring this point to light. His wry description of the comical clothing of a German officer serving in the Confederate army highlighted the international dimension of the conflict (Gallagher 103). The day at Antietam illustrated the carnage of nineteenth-century combat in the world and the way in which one battle could change the nature and even the outcome of the war, for with that victory and Lincoln's subsequent refocusing of the war as one against slavery, the conflict took on the characteristic of a moral crusade, and therefore England and France would not intervene on the side of the Confederacy.

The primary source material was essential as we considered causation. We ranked the causes of the Civil War by using analogy and posing what-if scenarios. What would have happened if the war had broken out in 1850, when the compromise over California was reached? Would the outcome have been different? Students began to realize that single-cause explanations of historical events were reductionist and did not do justice to the variety of factors that shaped history. The primary source material sometimes confirmed the class's conclusions and at other times challenged them. For example, students arguing that the war was to free the slaves found it hard to square that view with letters from Union soldiers expressing no concern for the slaves but only for the Union.

We asked if we should then understand the Civil War as a mere clash between stakeholders in a political system. Reading aloud Lincoln's Gettysburg Address in the very cemetery in which it was delivered created a sense of sacred meaning that the war evoked in many who lived through it and in many interpreters since. Lincoln's desire that "these dead shall not have died in vain" ("Address") is an attempt to give the war a higher purpose and meaning. Through his reference to the Declaration of Independence ("four score and seven years ago"), Lincoln began the historical interpretation of the war as a fight over liberty and equality, not over the Constitution with its dense legal nuances. Later, while standing at the Lincoln Memorial, we encountered Lincoln's ultimate interpretation of history: the opinion that the war was God's judgment upon the nation for tolerating slavery. At our daily debriefings, we talked about whether or not we should assign some grand meaning to history or simply learn from past events and avoid making the mistakes of our predecessors.

Assessments, Challenges, and Observations

One could argue that these lessons could have been learned through the more traditional means of classroom instruction alone, but we doubt seriously that the lessons would have been learned as *well*. Engaging in the sights, sounds, and smells of the battlefield impressed upon us all the themes and import of the war in ways that will not be soon forgotten. Our academic experience included opportunities for individual and group reflection. That students were allowed time to explore alone many of the sites we visited provided introspection that later helped create rich group discussions.

Although in situ teaching may often conjure images of reenactments—that is, watching others recreate battles or events related to the war—our approach was to give students the opportunity to connect the assigned primary readings to specific locations on the battlefields we visited. Allowing the students to cover Pickett's Charge on foot or to stand along Antietam's Bloody Lane put their readings into a more tangible spatial context and often satisfied curiosity of what the places looked like and how they fit into the larger geography of each battle. We were certainly not the first to conceive of this benefit to students of the Civil War, but our approach does confirm the vision of Ed Bearss, a former chief historian for the National Park Service: "You can't describe a battlefield unless you walk it" (qtd. in Storey).

Both in situ teaching and reenactment share the belief that a physical connection to historical sites can lead to a more meaningful understanding of the people and events being studied. The benefit of our approach, however, is that students could engage actively with the material while walking the sites instead of passively watching others reenact the events. This type of connection between students and texts requires a thoughtful selection of primary readings: a text should be chosen to go with a concrete space that, during a group visit, contextualizes it.

Students were required to keep a travel journal and use it to reflect on each day's excursions and discussion, to pose questions, or to make notes related to their final paper. Most students were diligent in the trip's early stages but found it difficult to stay current with their entries as the trip progressed. These journals were submitted on the return trip, and the instructors read them in preparation for debriefing the students.

Each professor graded the papers from the students within his academic field; the one-on-one meetings mentioned earlier allowed whatever research or content issues arose to be addressed. Following the final exam, the professors met to discuss each student's participation. We discussed the quality and frequency of participation in class discussion before assigning the numeric albeit largely subjective grade.

Though our initial foray into team-teaching a travel course proved successful, the course was not without its share of challenges, the most significant being how to assess the students' work when some of the material was completed for one discipline while other work was done as a group. The faculty members decided that each professor would begin each class he taught with a quiz designed to assess the students' comprehension of the material. The exams were written and graded by all three instructors to ensure parity among the three content areas. Each professor contributed questions for the final exam; the exam was then graded by all three, each professor grading his portion. While students were all required to complete questions related to identifying relevant names, places, dates, and terms, the essay sections allowed them to demonstrate a deeper knowledge within their chosen subject areas. Unfortunately, the quality of work diminished following the trip, because students found it difficult to focus on the content with the anticipation of travel gone.

Though the class responded positively to our approach, the most beneficial learning that took place may have been that of the professors. In the years after this first experiment, we continually revised our pedagogy to address concerns and challenges. In this collaborative approach, each of us not only taught within his area of expertise but also learned from the others as they taught. Each professor regularly contributed to class discussion, something students later said they appreciated as it allowed them to see that these materials were not so easily compartmentalized within the academy.

In what has become one of the most iconic quotation from the war, Walt Whitman wrote, "Future years will never know the seething hell and the black infernal background of countless minor scenes and interiors, (not the official surface-courteousness of the Generals, not the few great battles) of the Secession war; and it is best they should not—the real war will never get in the books" (qtd. in Price). Knowing the names, time line, and locations related to the Civil War is certainly important to understanding the literature written during the war; however, as we discovered, only by following in the footsteps of those who wrote that material can we more fully understand the magnitude of that "seething hell."

Part II

Teaching Various Genres

Faith Barrett

Constituting Communities: Reading the Civil War in Poetry and Song

"Mine eyes have seen the glory of the coming of the Lord," writes Julia Ward Howe in her "Battle Hymn of the Republic." The poem opens with a first-person prophetic speaker, one who sees God's intervention in support of the Union. The final verse of the song builds to a dramatic climax that forges the collective "we" of Union supporters: "As he died to make men holy, let us die to make men free." When Edmund Wilson dismisses the poetry of the Civil War as "versified journalism," he does so in part because he sees too frequent expression of the patriotic "we" and too little of the introspective "I" (479, 487).[1] Yet a closer examination of Howe's work and that of other Civil War poets reveals that the national "we" and the personal "I" are not binary opposites in this era. Rather they are related positions on a continuous spectrum of potential stances. For Howe, as for many poets of this period, the process of articulating the relation between these positions was fraught with conflicting allegiances.

The Civil War prompted an extraordinary outpouring of poetry by women and men from all walks of life. These writers used poetry to define that "we" and to trace the relation between the "we" and the "I": in doing so, they also defined their relation to nation, region, and family, constructs that were all reshaped by the war. Quickly printed and distributed, poems and the closely related genre of popular songs could be circulated cheaply and efficiently in the form of broadsides, pamphlets, or sheet music. Historians note that the Civil War was one of the first conflicts in which the telegraph, the railroad, and the photograph influenced the course of battles. Poetry was well-suited to keep up with the rapid pace of events on battlefields and in Washington and Richmond. If it was not the genre of instantaneity, it was certainly the genre of contemporaneity in this era. In ways both large and small, poetry fueled the American Civil War.

In presenting this material to students, it is helpful to focus on three larger questions. First, where and how did American readers encounter poetry? Second, who wrote poetry, and why did they choose this genre? And third, how did poems work not only to represent but also to shape the ideologies of the Civil War? My essay offers some responses to these questions and also suggests some groupings of related texts for more detailed exploration of them in the classroom. Working with Civil War poetry compels us to reconsider the term *lyric*, examining the ways it is both limiting and anachronistic when applied to this material. Twentieth-century scholars often understood *lyric* to mean a first-person poem expressing a private emotional experience, but in the nineteenth century the term was used far more expansively, generally in reference to poems in which musical qualities dominated.[2] As this inclusive definition suggests, *poetry* in the nineteenth century was itself an extraordinarily inclusive term, embracing songs, ballads, hymns, topical and political pieces, philosophical meditations, doggerel, and comic verse, as well as poems that more readily fit twentieth-century understandings of the lyric poem. In nineteenth-century print contexts, the terms *poem* and *song* were often used interchangeably, a slippage that underlined the importance of oral circulation for these texts. In reading a group of Civil War–era poems then, I argue that poetry offered writers the possibility of experimenting with a broad range of pronoun positions, a range that is too complex and too varied to be adequately described by the term *lyric*. This breadth of experimentation underlines how capacious the category of poetry was throughout this era.

Nineteenth-century American readers encountered poetry every day: poems appeared in newspapers and magazines, and their widespread appearance in periodicals underlines the strong connection between poetry and politics in this era. Central to the pedagogy of literacy, poetry was routinely memorized in classrooms. Nineteenth-century Americans also encountered poetry at social gatherings and lectures, at celebrations for departing and returning soldiers, and in military hospitals and encampments. In these settings, Americans heard poems read aloud, performed, and sung. The hand-in-glove relation between poetry and popular song contributed to the speed with which poems could be written, printed, and circulated.

Given the wide-ranging exposure of the public to poetry, it's not surprising that many Americans tried their hand at writing verse—penning a Valentine for a sweetheart, a birthday message for a friend, or a wartime remembrance for a family member. The centrality of poetry in the schoolroom coincided with an increase in the number of magazines and newspapers being published, growth that was fueled by new technologies for printing and distribution. In the North, Midwest, and West, leading magazines and papers saw rapid increases in their subscriptions both before and during the war. Southern magazines enjoyed great popularity among white Southerners during the war, but shortages of paper and more limited access to print technologies kept these publications from seeing dramatic growth.[3] The general increase in magazine readership coincided with a greater interest in poetry, as both writers and readers recognized its versatility. When Wilson dismisses the poetry of the war as "versified journalism," he misreads poetry's cultural position. During the Civil War, Americans on both sides of the conflict believed that poetry could play a crucial role in shaping the future of the Union, the Confederacy, and the United States.

Howe's "Battle Hymn" offers a striking example of a piece that not only reflected but also influenced wartime ideologies. In view of its continuing presence in the twenty-first century, "Battle Hymn" is a strong candidate for inclusion in a Civil War–focused course. Considering the contexts in which the piece circulated can give students a sense of how permeable the boundary is between poem and song in this era: the piece first appeared in the prestigious *Atlantic Monthly* in February 1862, but it began to circulate as a song sheet soon thereafter and quickly became a favorite with Union troops. Reading "Battle Hymn" in relation to its antecedents makes clear the extent to which poets of this period often wrote in direct response to their contemporaries. On a visit to Washington, DC, in November 1861, Howe and a group of friends had ridden out of the city to watch a review of Union troops, but the review had to be canceled when Confederate forces threatened Union positions. Caught among the Union soldiers headed back into town, Howe and her friends sang "John Brown's Body" to the cheers of the soldiers marching near them. James

Freeman Clarke, a friend who was among Howe's party, urged her to write better words for the popular tune. The next day, she awoke before dawn in the Willard Hotel and scrawled out the verses in the darkness of her room.[4] Though she had published her first volume of poetry eight years earlier, the success of "Battle Hymn" brought her national recognition for the first time.

A particularly productive grouping might be to read Howe's "Battle Hymn" in relation to "John Brown's Body," some of Brown's letters, and the camp meeting song on which "John Brown's Body" was based. Reading Howe's "Reminiscences" would also enrich this conversation. Analyzing these texts comparatively, students could look for similarities and differences between and among the songs, as well as echoes of Brown's language in Howe's lyrics. Howe modeled her "Battle Hymn" on the soldier's song, but "John Brown's Body" was in turn a response to an earlier song, "Say Brother Will You Meet Us," which was sung at evangelical camp meetings. Students may also want to consider the vexed composition history of "John Brown's Body." Music historians have suggested that the song was written not in praise of the abolitionist John Brown but rather in joking reference to a Massachusetts soldier who also had that common name (see Browne 181–99; see also Stutler). This interpretation makes sense of the song's gallows humor: while the abolitionist will live on—as a martyr or traitor—the foot soldier of the same name may well "moulder" in an unmarked grave. Comparing Howe's song with "John Brown's Body," a reader can see why her less graphic and less explicitly abolitionist poem had a broader cultural reach than the soldier's marching song. Moreover, situating "Battle Hymn" in this group of texts makes clear the extent to which she layered her personal voice onto earlier voices and drew rhetorical power from the soldiers, from John Brown, and from the camp meeting singers.

Whereas Howe earned recognition for her career-making "Battle Hymn," Emily Dickinson, a contemporary, preferred not to see her work in print. Still, her astonishing productivity during the war years indicates that the conflict prompted a strong response in her: after R. W. Franklin's dating of the manuscripts, she wrote more than nine hundred poems between 1861 and 1865, a staggering rate of productivity. Although scholars have only recently begun to recognize her as a poet who responded to the war, current criticism now reads her convincingly in this context.[5] Comparing her work with Howe's offers a fuller picture of women poets' responses to the war; it also offers a new angle on this high-canonical poet's work.

Situating Dickinson's poems in relation to other writers of the period makes clear the extent to which Dickinson, like Howe, was talking back to her contemporaries. There are at least two dozen Dickinson poems that could be read in the context of the Civil War, but "My Life had stood—a Loaded Gun—" is a particularly sound choice. Much anthologized and much analyzed, "My Life had stood—a Loaded Gun—" was frequently read in the late twentieth century as the narrative of a woman's loss of identity through marriage. In this reading, the female speaker feels a mixture of tenderness and repressed rage in relation to the "Owner" or "Master" whose identity overpowers her own. Bound to her "Master" by affection but also by the power imbalance of the relationship, the speaker is caught in a position of subservience that only partially contains her anger. Another approach, closely related to this feminist reading, situates the poem in the context of slavery, considering the complex mix of emotions that the speaker feels for her "Owner" and "Master." It's a testament to Dickinson's remarkable gifts as a writer that the poem can be read not only in relation to women's rights and slavery but also in relation to the Civil War. If we consider the poem as a response to war's violence, we can see that it offers a first-person account of a soldier's pleasure in military camaraderie, the new identity the soldier gains when he joins up, and the deep affection he feels for the officer whom he serves. Perhaps most strikingly, this reading suggests the rush of adrenaline the soldier feels as he goes into combat:

> And do I smile, such cordial light
> Opon the Valley glow—
> It is as a Vesuvian face
> Had let it's pleasure through—   (F 764)[6]

Reading the poem in relation to Dickinson's letters from this period suggests that Dickinson was responding to the experience of young soldiers from Amherst, including Frazar Stearns, who was a close friend of her brother, Austin. Connecting the poem to the letters of Elisha Hunt Rhodes, a Union soldier; the poetry of Obadiah Ethelbert Baker, another Union soldier; and the accounts of the soldier's experience offered by James McPherson (*For Cause*) and Reid Mitchell will stimulate students' interpretations, as will an examination of some of the many photographs of soldiers posing with their comrades in arms. Moving beyond the limits of Dickinson's personal I, "My Life had stood—a Loaded Gun—" uses the first person to articulate the excitement, pleasures, and aspirations of the young soldier at war.

As Dickinson's war poems make clear, it is not only writers with direct experience of combat who write powerfully about soldiers. Another writer who offers a fascinating angle on soldiers' views of the war is George Moses Horton, a black poet. Born into slavery in North Carolina, Horton is also a good candidate for inclusion in a Civil War–focused course because of his remarkable life story and because he offers a southern black perspective on the conflict. As a young man working on a farm near Chapel Hill, he began to make weekend trips to town, where he sold fruit, ran errands for the young male students, and wrote love poems made to order for the young women they were courting. So successful was he at writing these poems that he was able to persuade his master to let him hire his own time: from his twenties until the outbreak of the war, Horton mainly lived in Chapel Hill, publishing two collections of poems during these years. Although he had hoped to use the money he made from his first book to buy his freedom, he was not emancipated until the Union army arrived in North Carolina in April 1865. Befriended by soldiers of the Ninth Michigan Cavalry, Horton, who was now in his late sixties, traveled with them in the summer of 1865, once again supporting himself by writing love poems made to order, this time for the wives and sweethearts of Union soldiers. During the months when he was on the march, he completed a third collection of poems, *Naked Genius*.[7] In the year after the war's end, he moved north, to Philadelphia.[8]

The volume that Horton published just after the war is an eclectic collection, including elegies for Union generals, elegies for Lincoln, laments for war's devastation, criticisms of white southern pride, upbeat marching songs for Union soldiers, songs imagining a reconciliation between northern and southern veterans, temperance poems, laments for an unhappy marriage, animal fables, and comic pieces. The first wave of scholars who approached Horton's work dismissed it as derivative, but more recently scholars have begun to attend to his extraordinary skill at reaching and pleasing white audiences from both the South and the North. This recent scholarship considers the strategies of indirection, humor, masking, and irony that Horton uses to express ideas that could never be expressed directly by an enslaved black man.

Horton's work as a poet is so varied that a group of his poems, not one, should be examined in the classroom. A Civil War–focused group that would offer many possibilities for discussion might include "The Southern Refugee," "Jefferson in a Tight Place," and "Weep." In "The Southern Refugee," Horton uses the postures of southern Romanticism to express the melancholy emotions of both blacks and whites displaced in the aftermath of the war. Because the voice might be that of a black refugee, Horton here offers a pointed rejoinder to Dan Emmett's minstrel song "I Wish I Was in Dixie's Land," which presents a caricature of a black speaker who looks back with longing at the South he has left behind. While Emmett's blackface speaker reiterates his longing to return to the "land ob cotton" in every chorus, Horton's speaker insists that he will find emotional resolution by leaving his southern home:

> I trust I soon shall dry the tear
>> And leave forever hence to roam,
> Far from a residence so dear,
>> The place of beauty—my native home.   (124)

In "The Southern Refugee," Horton lends dignity and emotional complexity to the experience of blacks who headed north at the war's end. Analysis of "Dixie," of photograph portraits of black soldiers, and of selections from Thomas Wentworth Higginson's *Army Life in a Black Regiment* would complement the study of this and other Horton poems. Higginson's reflections on black refugees and on southern black musical culture would be particularly relevant to readings of Horton. Another fine complement to this discussion would be Frederick Douglass's description of slaves singing at the end of chapter 2 of his *Narrative*.

"Jefferson in a Tight Place: The Fox Is Caught" shows Horton working in a satiric vein, drawing on the language of animal fables to represent Jefferson Davis's flight from his Union pursuers after the war ended. Classroom discussion of this poem would be enriched by analysis of political cartoons of the time depicting Davis's attempt to escape capture. Reading the poem in relation to cartoons underlines the cultural importance of humorous poetry in this period. Although twenty-first-century print media still publish political cartoons, we no longer look to poetry to provide this kind of commentary. The poem also offers an example of the newly emancipated poet's exercising rhetorical power over the leader of the Confederacy, a man who had devoted his life to protecting the rights of white slaveholders.

Finally in the poem "Weep," Horton mourns the war's devastation and fears for the future of the still deeply divided nation. His extraordinary position as a southern black poet allows him to express emotions rarely seen in the poetry of this period. Comparing his work with that of the freeborn black poet Frances Ellen Watkins Harper would be productive—

for example, students might compare and contrast their activist stances. Though Horton includes a number of poems in *Naked Genius* that celebrate the end of slavery, "Weep" laments the terrible price paid by both North and South. While the poem indicts the overweening pride of the Confederacy, it also expresses grave doubts about the reconciliation of North and South. Throughout *Naked Genius*, Horton adapts the postures of white southern Romanticism to give voice to the experience of black Southerners; his work could thus also be read in relation to that of white southern Romantics such as Henry Timrod and William Gilmore Simms.

Reading the white southern Romantic poets who supported the Confederacy can help students understand how poetry shaped the Confederacy's agrarian ideologies. In the South, as in the North, poets played an important role in clarifying the nation's political goals. Known as the "poet laureate of the Confederacy," Henry Timrod wrote poems celebrating the birth of Confederacy ("Ethnogenesis") and the cotton that was seen as central to the new nation's success ("The Cotton Boll"); he also wrote both calls to arms ("A Cry to Arms") and laments for the war dead ("The Unknown Dead") (Barrett and Miller 311–30). Two decades older than Timrod, William Gilmore Simms was already an acclaimed poet, novelist, and editor when the war broke out, well known for his paeans to the southern natural world ("Song of the South" [Barrett and Miller 35–36]). Both men were left impoverished and in poor health in the war's aftermath, though Simms lived long enough to edit the influential anthology *War Poetry of the South* (1866) and to write poems that would help found the Lost Cause myth of the Confederacy ("Ay De Mi, Alhama!" [Barrett and Miller 188–89]). Reading Timrod's and Simms's pastoral poetry in relation to Horton's, a student can grapple with the ways that the two white poets erase the slave labor on which the southern agricultural bounty depended, representing the South as an edenic haven from northern industry.

If Horton revises white southern Romanticism to articulate the sorrows and longings of black Southerners, Herman Melville uses Romantic stances to lament the ravages of modern warfare. Though better known as a novelist, Melville published a volume of Civil War poems in 1866, in the hope that it would achieve the popular success that had mostly eluded him as a prose writer. He was disappointed, but his *Battle-Pieces and Aspects of the War* offers twenty-first-century readers a valuable lens on American poetry in a state of transition: *Battle-Pieces* looks back with longing toward the consolations of the nationalist "we," even as it also warns that nationalist poetry can drive nations to the violence of war. The volume includes both ringing songs of praise for sunken Union ships and spare fragmented poems that recoil from the slaughter on battlefields. These poems reach back to the early nineteenth century even as they also reach forward into the twentieth.

The two most widely anthologized poems from this collection, "The Portent" and "Shiloh," are both good choices for classroom discussion; both can be read in relation to battlefield photography, the topographical maps of battlefields that appeared in newspapers and magazines, popular songs of the era (including "John Brown's Body" and "The Drummer Boy of Shiloh"), photographs of John Brown and of child soldiers, and the many journalistic sources Melville drew on from Frank Moore's *The Rebellion Record*. However, focusing only on the spare protomodernist compression of Melville's poems like these two wrenches the volume out of its nineteenth-century context and distorts the range of his aesthetic commitments in this collection. With their ringing musical refrains, poems like "The Cumberland" and "Sheridan's Ride" reach for a broader postwar audience. Moreover, each of these poems can be read alongside a poem on the same topic by a more popular poet of this era: Henry Wadsworth Longfellow's "Cumberland" and Thomas Buchanan Read's "Sheridan's Ride."

A poem that shows Melville reaching both backward and forward aesthetically is "An Uninscribed Monument on one of the Battle-Fields of the Wilderness." In this poem, he responds to the epitaphs of the English Romantics but also to the intense cultural focus on monument making and commemoration after the Civil War. The poem could be read in connection with Lincoln's Gettysburg Address, the photography of George Barnard and of Alexander Gardner, and John Trowbridge's essays for the *Atlantic Monthly* describing his tours of battlefield sites ("The Field of Gettsyburg" and "The Wilderness"). Readers will likely note the strong contrast between Trowbridge's casually conversational tone in these essays and the ways that Melville uses understatement and linguistic compression. "An Uninscribed Monument," like the Gettysburg Address, paradoxically uses language to enjoin its readers to silence. Through a speaker who is either dead (a fallen soldier) or inanimate (his tombstone), the poem suggests that language is inadequate to the task of representing war's horrors and that modern warfare has destroyed any possible vantage point for the lyric "I."

As the volume's title already makes clear, Melville's allegiances in *Battle-Pieces and Aspects of the War* are painfully divided: these poems express both a nostalgic faith in the powers of a nationalist voice and a profound skepticism about the possibility that poetry will reunite the nation. The term *aspects*, drawn from visual culture and from the panoramic landscape in particular, points to a proliferation of vantage points, acknowledging that Melville's speakers will assume a range of distinct stances in relation to the conflict. Echoing the divided loyalties of his poetic contemporaries, Melville foretells the changes to come in modernist poetry, where aesthetic unities and patriotic pieties alike will be disrupted by the disintegration of the lyric speaker as the moral center of the poem. *Battle-Pieces* also foregrounds shifts in allegiances and thus in pronoun positions that are evident across a broad range of Civil War–era poetry: this range includes many conflicting collectives for "we," many different "I's," but also a fracturing of the "I" that leaves no solid ground on which a unified poetic speaker might stand. The Civil War brought profound changes to American poetry; still more important, however, the proliferation of pronoun positions in this poetry helped change the way Americans understood the nations of the Union, the Confederacy, and the United States.

Notes

I am grateful to Megan Ward and Colleen Boggs for their helpful responses to earlier versions of this essay.

1. Wilson uses the phrase to dismiss Melville's *Battle-Pieces* in particular, but he applies the same criticism to Civil War poetry as a whole.

2. For analysis of the poor fit between twentieth-century definitions of *lyric* and nineteenth-century poetry writing practices, see V. Jackson. For analysis of nineteenth-century understandings of *lyric*, see Miller 19–48.

3. For discussion of the growth of periodical readership during the war, see Fahs, *Imagined Civil War* (esp. ch. 1).

4. For Howe's account of her composition of "Battle Hymn," see her "Reminiscences" 706–08.

5. See, for example, Wolosky; Lee; St. Armand; Hutchison, "'Eastern Exiles'"; Miller (ch. 6); Bergland; Richards; Friedlander; and my own study, *To Fight Aloud Is Very Brave*, chapter 4.

6. I cite the poem according to the number Franklin assigns to it.

7. For biographical information on Horton, see Sherman; L. Jackson.

8. See Pitts's account of Horton's life after Horton left the South.

Allison E. Carey

Reading on the (Home) Front: Teaching Soldiers' Dime Novels

Although most students are well acquainted with the genre of the novel and the mode of fiction, it would be surprising if they were familiar with dime novels. Hugely popular in the United States from their 1860 inception until their decline at the end of the nineteenth century, dime novels (and their British counterpart, the penny dreadfuls) are little remembered today, even in revisionist anthologies of American literature. Dime novels largely grew out of serialized fiction, with episodic stories that emphasized last-minute escapes and tearjerker plot devices; they were "linked to melodrama in language, plot, and characterization" (Fahs, *Imagined Civil War* 227). Publishers took advantage of innovations in printing and of new postal rates when they packaged such fiction into small paperbound books sized to fit into a pocket and priced to be affordable (typically ranging from a nickel to twenty cents, even if described as costing a dime). They were available by mail order, "at newsdealers' stalls, railway stations, and even saloons" in urban areas, and through door-to-door "subscription canvassers" for rural readers (229, 4). Although later regarded as being primarily boys' books, dime novels actually attracted a diverse readership of both men and women of varying ages, social classes, and—in the North—ethnicities.[1] Dime novels were popular and widely read in the

South, but "there were relatively few sensational stories and novels published in the South during the war," given the "shortages in paper, ink, printing presses, and personnel" (251, 5).

Because dime novels were "the first real escape literature for men" (Kaser 95), publishers aggressively marketed these books to Civil War soldiers. Beadle and Adams, the New York firm that first packaged and sold sensational fiction as dime novels, saw a sales opportunity: "In their leisure moments the soldiers craved cheap and exciting reading. Beadle bundled it like bales of hay and sent it to them in carloads. And, in their rate of increase, the carloads kept step with the expanding armies" (Harvey 40). An 1889 article in *Banner Weekly* reminisced about the novels' popularity, noting that they "were the soldier's solace and comfort in camp and campaign, and contributed, in a wonderful degree, to ameliorate the trials and sufferings of army life—as every yet living member of the Grand Army will attest" (qtd. in Johannsen, *House* [Web] 39). My students are usually taken aback by this image of army camps filled with voracious readers, and also by the high United States literacy rates at the war's beginning: David Kaser describes male literacy rates in 1861 as over 90% in the northern states and about 70% among the free male population of the Confederacy (3). Books and newspapers were sold in camp by traveling news agents, mailed to soldiers by families or through subscriptions, and even traded between enemy soldiers across picket lines with surprising frequency (78–84).

Savvy dime novel publishers like Beadle and Adams aimed their offerings—after April 1861—to a reading public preoccupied by secession, war, slavery, and what it meant to be an American. A number of publishers founded dime novel series designed expressly for the reading audience of soldiers, including Dawley's Camp and Fireside Library, Beadle's American Tales, and James Redpath's Books for the Camp Fires. Advertisements emphasized their value to soldiers, noting that "[o]ur soldier boys will find them just the thing to beguile an otherwise tedious hour" (Redpath qtd. in McKivigan 87). Although some books addressed the war—for example, American Tales featured sensational fictionalized accounts of the siege of Vicksburg and Sherman's March to the Sea—many dime novels were escapist adventures, like another of this series, *The Oronoco Chief; or, The Fortunes of a Diamond Locket: A Story of Adventure in South America* (Johannsen 127–30).[2] Although intended for soldiers and popular with them, these series were crafted for customers on the home front as well. In newspaper ads, Redpath called his series "just the books to read to the soldiers [and] equally adapted to home fires" (qtd. in McKivigan 87), and Dawley's 1864 ad in *Harper's Weekly* urged readers, "Buy it—Read it— Then send it to a friend in the Army" ("Dawley's Camp").

In my experience, students deeply engage with sensational dime novels, identifying strongly with the main characters and becoming immersed in the plot. It is particularly interesting to watch students become furious with the main characters for their poor choices, more impassioned than I have ever seen them about Hester Prynne or Jay Gatsby. The value of dime novels, however, extends far beyond students' emotional engagement; the novels contribute to their intellectual development. Indeed, my students have claimed that dime novels helped them understand social phenomena—like nineteenth-century racial prejudice—more deeply, as if the melodrama allows them to internalize the characters' struggles. Studying these dime novels can give them a glimpse into the preoccupations and pastimes of Civil War civilians and soldiers alike, without the filtering vision of a historian or a practiced orator.

A good way to begin an undergraduate unit on Civil War dime novels is to have students skim a few, ideally in print format but if need be online. Thanks to the mass production of dime novels and to the obsessive habits of their twentieth-century collectors, many libraries have been able to acquire large collections of dime novels and have digitized their offerings for public use. Stanford University's *Dime Novels and Penny Dreadfuls* site offers a narrative history and time line of the novels, over two thousand cover images, and full texts from a selection of Stanford's more than eight thousand titles (http://web.stanford.edu/dept/SUL/library/prod/depts/dp/pennies/home.html). The Library of Congress's *Dime Novels* primarily features covers from its collection (www.loc.gov/exhibits/treasures/tri015.html). Examining the covers of such fare as *Crack Skull Bob No. 5; Keetsea, Queen of the Plains;* and *Prison Pen; or, Dead Line at Andersonville,* students get a fine introduction to the sensationalism of dime novels and to their popular topics: frontier adventure, detective stories, and tales loosely based on historical events. At Northern Illinois University's *House of Beadle & Adams Online* (www.ulib.niu.edu/badndp/contents2.html), students can access a digitized version of the premier bibliography about the dime novel publisher. Finally, many individual titles are available through *Google Books, Archive.org, Project Gutenberg,* and similar open-access archiving sites. Such resources allow students—and instructors—to pursue their own interests in these collections and to do (limited) archival research.

I recommend teaching a selected pair of dime novels, one from Beadle and Adams (1861) and the other from Redpath's Books for the Camp Fires series (1864). The Beadle book, *Maum Guinea, and Her Plantation "Children"; or, Holiday-Week on a Louisiana Estate: A Slave Romance*, by Metta V. Victor, is not technically from a soldiers' series; its December 1861 publication predated any such series. But it was "the novel most likely to be found in the backpacks of Union—and Confederate—soldiers and in the parlors and pockets of readers in both North America and Europe in the early days of the war" (Castagna). The novel from Redpath's series is William Wells Brown's *Clotelle: A Tale of the Southern States*; its 1853 original version is considered to be one of the first novels by an African American writer. *Maum Guinea* chronicles the parallel courtships of a white couple and an enslaved couple from neighboring Louisiana plantations; Maum Guinea, surrogate mother to all the novel's slaves, helps the enslaved couple escape after the virginal, fair-skinned Rose is sold to be a rich man's concubine. *Clotelle* follows the sexual exploitation and abuse of three generations of enslaved women, culminating in the escape and happy marriage of the title character. These novels would pair well in a course on Civil War literature, on the novel, or on nineteenth-century American literature. They present an instructive contrast in literary style, authorial intention, and literary prestige: Beadle's offerings were typically more sensational (and less reputable), while Redpath founded his series "to supply military readers with works of superior literary merit at the same price as the dime novels" (McKivigan 86) and asserted in an 1864 advertisement that it was "of a much higher class than the dime publications now in the market" ("Books"). These two novels, despite having been crafted for different readers, share key traits: both depict the plight of southern slaves by employing tropes of sentimental fiction, both were crafted to arouse abolitionist fervor, and both made a significant impact—one social, the other literary.

Although reading both *Clotelle* and *Maum Guinea* in full might be feasible—the 1864 *Clotelle* is only 104 pages, and *Maum Guinea*'s episodic structure makes it very readable—I realize that few instructors have the flexibility to insert two full novels into their course. I suggest that they select a chapter or two from each novel, depending on which issues or themes resonate with the rest of the course.[3] One powerful point of comparison—to which my students have reacted strongly—is the two novels' very different treatments of race: *Maum Guinea*'s is based on nineteenth-century pseudoscientific theories, whereas *Clotelle* depicts race as a merely cosmetic matter. Another effective approach is to use these two novels to explore the nineteenth-century tradition of sentimental fiction. Both authors, Victor and Brown, employ sentimental tropes (also characteristic of abolitionist literature) such as scenes of family separation and of threats to the sexual purity of a tragic mulatta character. Finally, these texts allow an instructor to address the malleable boundary between high art and low art, by tracing their political and literary influences and their very different fates in the marketplace and canon.

In any discussion of images of race in nineteenth-century literature, I begin by introducing my students to Samuel George Morton's *Crania Americana* (1839), a phrenology-based interpretation of racial difference that helped shape debates on race in America. After I download the text and project it in class, my students and I spend a few minutes simply skimming through it, and I watch their growing amazement at Morton's theory of polygenesis (the idea that God simultaneously created several different races) and his assertions that race determines personality, intellect, work habits, and sexual mores. Then I call students' attention to such pronouncements as, "The Negroes are proverbially fond of their amusements, in which they engage with great exuberance of spirit" (87), and "In disposition the negro is joyous, flexible, and indolent; while the many nations which compose this race present a singular diversity of intellectual character, of which the far extreme is the lowest grade of humanity" (7). In contrast, we note that the Caucasian race "is distinguished for the facility with which it attains the highest intellectual endowments" (5). For my students, such stereotypes of people's intellect and character, based solely on the shape of their skull or the pigment of their skin, are prima facie evidence of racism and of a proslavery stance.

Imagine their surprise when they encounter in *Maum Guinea* nearly identical pronouncements about race. Victor employs every imaginable race-based stereotype and describes whites and blacks as having distinct (and fixed) temperaments. Chapter 4, "Christmas," is an especially rich, concentrated repository of them. The narrator ascribes to the slaves' "African blood" their natural sense of rhythm and melody and then notes that the slaves adore a bonfire because it is "especially delightful to these dark children of the sun, who loved both the heat and the light" (36). Although patronizing, the book portrays these people as innately sweet and harmless:

> Grotesque, wild, uncouth, like the creatures themselves, was their mirth; but it was sunny as the sky, beaming with good-humor, broad and pleasant, good to look at—not a touch of malice, not a sign of

quarreling, not a case of downright drunkenness. Oblivious to the scars
of the past and the toils of the future, these children of the sun basked
in the pleasure of the present. (39)

This emphasis on the slaves' lack of malice and obliviousness "to the scars
of the past" is crucial to a narrative in which an entire chapter ("Sophy's
Story") is dedicated to an insider's account of Nat Turner's rebellion, including a detailed description of the throat-slitting murder of ten-year-old
white Miss Katie.

In contrast, *Clotelle* depicts racial difference as simply an issue of
skin pigmentation. A pointed example occurs in chapter 5, "The Young
Mother," when white riverboat passengers (the boat is also transporting
slaves to the New Orleans market) see "among the new lot of slaves a
woman so white as to not be distinguishable from the other white women
on board," carrying "a child so white that no one would suppose a drop
of African blood flowed through its blue veins." Seeing this woman enslaved makes the white passengers fear for Anglo-Saxons, since everyone
"that saw her felt that slavery in the Southern States was not confined to
the negro" and "now felt that if whites were to become its victims, it was
time at least that some security should be thrown around the Anglo-Saxon
to save him from this servile and degraded position." The attitudes that
Brown attributes to the white spectators represent a crucial slippage in the
prevailing American definition of race. By the one-drop rule, if the Young
Mother, with her "almost snow-white forehead" and "mild blue eyes," has
"a drop of African blood," she is not considered white under the law, yet
the spectators think of her as white.

A sentimental scene like this one—in which the reader is encouraged
to feel along with the spectators as "the hearts of the passers-by grew
softer, while gazing upon that young mother as she pressed sweet kisses on
the sad, smiling lips of the infant that lay in her lap"— introduces students
to the importance of sentimentalism in abolitionist rhetoric. P. Gabrielle
Foreman describes as "sentimental abolition" this "heightened connection between abolition and what is too often considered the separate
sphere of sentimentality" (150). Both *Clotelle* and *Maum Guinea* make
their antislavery cases through affective scenes: the threat to sexual virtue
and the separation of mother and child. *Maum Guinea* contains numerous
scenes of mother-child separation, mother and child watching each other
be whipped, and sexual threats to girls so innocent that they cannot comprehend the danger to them. *Clotelle* employs similar tropes but is a more

measured and restrained work, written not only to illuminate the evils of slavery but also to demonstrate the humanity of the title character and the author himself.

The plot of *Maum Guinea* is filled with scenes of violence and sexual threat, even though the novel is set on plantations that are ostensibly peaceful, having humane masters. During the Christmas week setting of the novel, enslaved characters take turns telling tales, specifically "'bout w'ere we cum from, w'en we's little, or w'en we had anodder massa" (27). As the various characters tell their tales, the reader encounters violence, exploitation, and inhumanity of every degree. In chapter 7, Sophy describes the sale of her two sons (ages two and six), her husband's being burned alive for participating in Nat Turner's rebellion, and herself being tortured for information about the rebellion (85–99). Another character echoes that tale of a whole family lost, saying, "[W]'at's the use o' wife or chil'ren, w'en you don' know w'en dey may be took away. I's had a husband, and four chil'ren, but I hain't one now" (54).

If an instructor is looking for only one chapter from *Maum Guinea* to illustrate both the novel's sentimental appeal and its sociopolitical criticism, chapter 3, "Johnson's Story," will serve. Johnson is the first character to tell his story (his memories of childhood) in the Christmas exchange of stories, and his tale sets the tone for others to follow in its overt appeal to sentiment and its subtle indictment of whites' private actions and political inaction. We learn of the sexual exploitation of a fifteen-year-old slave, Johnson's mother, by a Virginia congressman who was her owner (and thus Johnson's father). We follow Johnson's detailed accounts of his mother's physical and emotional abuse by the congressman's wife and then of the beatings Johnson endured as a five-year-old at his mistress's hands. The most poignant part of his story describes his mother's attempt to lead herself and her eleven-year-old son to freedom. They become lost in the snowy woods and wander for days: "[A]nd one night she sung and sung so sweet to me, dat I stop crying and fell 'sleep, t'inking of de angels, and de next mornin', when I woke up, my mudder was dead" (31). His description of crying beside his mother's frozen body seems tailor-made to evoke the sympathies of a reader. Moreover, the evocation of the dead mother resonates with a wartime literary tradition in which "longings for home, but especially for mother, were part of a shared popular literary culture both north and south" (Fahs, *Imagined Civil War* 106). In this chapter, Victor links her text not only to that "widespread maternalist culture" (105) but also to the wartime literary tradition that highlighted "the tremendous cost borne by discrete individuals in [the war's] cause" (12). Surely contemporary readers—both on the home front and in army camps—could have seen Johnson's plight as analogous to their own wartime suffering, from physical deprivation to separation from home and family.

Remaining unspoken in Johnson's story, amid the sentiment and the forthright indictment of the evil "missus," is any criticism of Johnson's father, the Virginia congressman who "could make a speech as smart as anybody in the city of Washington" (28) yet whose neglect enabled the abuse of his son. This congressman who fathers slave children brings to mind another Virginia statesman: Thomas Jefferson, who was notably absent from the 1864 publication of *Clotelle*. Brown's novel, when originally published in 1853, was entitled *Clotel; or, The President's Daughter*, in direct reference to "the well-known rumor that one of [Thomas] Jefferson's slave daughters had been sold at auction for $1000" (A. Davis ix). By the time of *Clotelle*'s 1864 release, this accusation of Jefferson had been reframed: Clotelle is the great-granddaughter of an American senator and the daughter of a Virginia congressman. Did Brown choose to soften his criticism of a founding father to help soldiers rally around the flag and "kindle . . . their zeal in the cause of universal emancipation" (Redpath's note at end of *Clotelle*)? This question usually provokes lively student discussion of Brown's choice, and the Virginia statesmen and fathers of slaves in both novels allow students to explore the Jefferson-Hemings relationship and recent DNA testing of their descendants (see duCille).

In looking further at Brown's and Victor's rhetorical choices and their attempts to sway readers, an instructor could use *Maum Guinea* and *Clotelle* to prompt student discussion of literary popularity versus prestige and the shifting boundaries between high and low art. The contrast between the novels' original receptions and long-term endurance is striking. *Maum Guinea* was a best seller (over a hundred thousand copies in the United States, tens of thousands in Britain), credited with "creating pro-Union sentiment in the British Isles" (Castagna) and reportedly declared by Abraham Lincoln to be "as absorbing as *Uncle Tom's Cabin*" (see Harvey 38–40; Castagna; Simmons). Yet today it is largely forgotten except in histories of the war. *Clotelle*, on the other hand, found little contemporary popularity or acclaim, either in its original publication (Farrison 228) or in Redpath's series: "Redpath's was not a successful series; of the promised first five titles, only Alcott's and Brown's were published" (W. Brown, *Clotelle* [ed. Mulvey]). Yet today *Clotelle* is anthologized, analyzed in scholarly works, and presented as a digital edition that captures "the multidimensionality the novel has always possessed but could never make fully legible within the confines of the printed page" (Cohen 749). Today scholars write of *Maum Guinea*, not *Clotelle*, that "the novel's vision ensured that it would not outlive its first popularity" (Castagna).

It is through this immense popularity of *Maum Guinea* that instructors could call students' attention to the flexible distinctions between high and low art. Alice Fahs notes, "The high-low dichotomy . . . is often retroactively applied to mid-nineteenth-century culture in ways that readers, writers, and publishers would not have recognized at the time" (*Imagined Civil War* 3). However, when Redpath created his series for soldiers and advertised it as "of a much higher class than the dime publications now in the market," he referred to the stigma that dime fiction carried, a stigma that led one soldiers' aid organization to ban the distribution of "all yellow-covered literature" (qtd. in Kaser 104)—yellow covers being the hallmark of Beadle and other dime publications. (Redpath bound his own dime books in green, presumably to distinguish them from their yellow-covered cousins.) Despite the popularity of dime fiction among soldiers, some of them referred to their reading selections as "trashy" (35) in letters home. One Tennessee soldier "recalled that 'miserable,' 'worthless' novels 'were sold by the thousand. . . . Beadle's novels, novelettes and other detestable works were received with popular favor'" (Fahs, *Imagined Civil War* 229). Another soldier even hesitated to confess this reading crime to his journal: "[R]eading a horrid *Mercury* novel. . . . I am ashamed to make even this private confession, but 'tis done" (Kaser 35). Students are often amused to realize that they are reading such shameful works in English class.

Finally, instructors may wish students to consider how Victor used that shameful stigma to her rhetorical advantage, hiding her abolitionist intent behind the novel's sensational face. Her American introduction to *Maum Guinea* contains a paragraph, absent from the British version, that disavows any abolitionist intent in the book and frames it as purely escape fiction: "'Maum Guinea' has not been written to subserve any special social or political purpose. . . . If the moralist or economist should find in it any thing to challenge his or her attention, it will be for the reason that the book is a picture of slave-life as it is in its natural as well as in some of its exceptional phases" (iv). Victor didn't need this disavowal for the British audience: in its London publication, the book was unabashedly an abolitionist text, intended to sway the British against the Confederacy through an indictment of the slave system. However, for American audiences, Victor needed to be more circumspect in her allegiances. Thus, "Victor's genius in creating a book that confirmed the Union antislavery position and at the same time included nonthreatening recapitulation of current stereotypes" (Castagna) allowed it to become a favorite of Union and Confederate soldiers alike. She retains the popular racial stereotypes found in Morton's *Crania Americana* and even uses the trope of slaves who are so happy that they refuse to run away. Although she situates these racist chestnuts in an abolitionist text that "had a powerful influence in aid of the Union cause" (Harvey 43), the text's contradictions have led some scholars to argue that *Maum Guinea* suffers from "schizophrenic generic identity—a proslavery/antislavery 'romance of fact'" (Stokes 57). This scholarly divide highlights the surprising nuance dime novels can bring to classrooms focused on the literature of the Civil War. These inexpensive paperbacks reveal depths of complexity when one delves beneath the yellow covers.

Notes

1. On the readership of dime novels, see Denning.

2. A complete list of all ninety-three titles in the American Tales series can be found at *House of Beadle & Adams Online*. Six of the nineteen novels published before the end of the war are available in full text at www.archive.org.

3. *Maum Guinea* was released simultaneously in the United States and Great Britain; copies are available through *Google Books* (scanned from the original copy in the Harvard Library) and *Google Play* (also scanned, apparently from Oxford University's Bodleian Library). *Clotelle* may be downloaded in many formats (including Kindle) from www.gutenberg.org. An authoritative scholarly digital edition comparing all four versions of Brown's work is available for subscribing libraries through www.upress.virginia.edu/rotunda.

Christopher Hager

Letters, Memoranda, and Official Documents: Teaching Nonfiction Prose

Published literature represents only a portion of the outpouring of written expression occasioned by the Civil War. Private letters—as many as 180,000 per day, by some estimates—flowed through the postal system between soldiers and the folks back home (Henkin 137). Official correspondence, telegraphed as well as handwritten, oiled the gears of an unprecedented military mobilization. In contraband camps and freedmen's schools, an array of often idiosyncratic texts issued from the pens of former slaves as they ventured into literacy. Petitions filled government officials' desks, and reports and affidavits swelled the files of a growing federal bureaucracy.

This vast corpus may sound mundane, a matter for historians only, and far afield from the realm of literature. But readers of Civil War–era fiction and poetry need reflect only a moment to realize that everyday writings loomed large in Americans' experiences of the war and in the cultural imagination of the time. With striking frequency in the imaginative literature of the war, one encounters figures of ordinary texts circulating outside the channels of literary and journalistic publication. "Come Up from the Fields Father," from Walt Whitman's *Drum-Taps* (1865), revolves around the arrival of a letter: "Open the envelope quickly, / O this is not our son's writing, yet his name is sign'd, / O a strange hand writes for our dear son, O stricken mother's soul!" (436–37). Spy melodramas such as Nora Perry's "Mrs F.'s Waiting Maid" (1867) turn on the maps and military dispatches purloined behind enemy lines. Rebecca Harding Davis's work in the 1860s brims with telling scraps of manuscript. The illiterate Ellen ("Ellen" [1865]) traverses the countryside in search of her brother's regiment with the help of written directions pinned to her basket. The friendship between Joe Scofield and David Gaunt ("David Gaunt" [1862]) is sealed by words inscribed on a bible's flyleaf. Crucial junctures in the plot of *Waiting for the Verdict* (1867) hinge on "a fine slip of paper" (30), a "slip of yellow parchment" (255), and "the back of an old letter, on which were scrawled some numbers" (262)—the last a military scouting report. In Herman Melville's *Battle-Pieces* (1866), "Donelson" centers on broadsides posted in the center of town, "Washed by the storm till the paper grew / Every shade of a streaky blue" (Robillard 64). When the list of a battle's casualties arrives, the women of the town "snatched the damp paper," where

> The death-list like a river flows
> Down the pale sheet,
> And there the whelming waters meet. (75–76)

In Melville's image of type flowing down a wet page and merging with mourners' tears, we find a poignant reminder of the emotional gravity of quotidian documents. What today is the stuff of microfilm then was the stuff of grief.

The ubiquitous written records that inspired such images constitute one of the most voluminous literatures of the Civil War, but they rarely appear in English courses. This essay considers why they haven't and why they should, suggesting along the way some places literature professors can find them and some ways students can learn from them.

Suppose that one's aims in teaching literature, and the literature of the Civil War in particular, include exposing students to the dramatic changes unfolding during the mid–nineteenth century; helping them understand the role of representation in making and remaking culture, history, and ideology; teaching them to appreciate the contingencies of individual perspectives and the modulations of discourse; challenging them to question received ideas about the Civil War's meaning and legacy; and making sure they appreciate the gravity of emancipation and its costs in battle. What better place to turn than the collected writings of Garland H. White?

White was born a slave in Virginia and later sold down to Georgia. When his new owner, Robert Toombs, was elected to the United States Senate, White was taken to Washington, DC, as Toombs's house servant. A few years before his fiercely secessionist enslaver left the Senate to become secretary of state for the Confederate States of America, White escaped to Canada and established himself as a minister of the African Methodist Episcopal Church. When the Civil War broke out, he returned to the United States to serve the Union cause. Though not fully literate, he wrote letters to high-ranking officials in Washington, including Lincoln's secretary of state, William Seward, whom White knew from his days receiving senators at Toombs's Washington home. White traveled first to Ohio, then to Indiana, working throughout the summer and fall of 1863 as a recruiter for various African American regiments. He joined one of those regiments, the Twenty-Eighth United States Colored Troops, departed with it for the eastern front, and became its chaplain—and thus one of fourteen black men to achieve the only officer rank open to them. He served in the siege of Petersburg, Virginia, and was present at the horrific Battle of the Crater. He was in the column of black soldiers who led the way into Richmond on 4 April 1865. In the streets of the fallen Confederate capital, Abraham Lincoln's tall hat visible above crowds of jubilant African Americans, White was reunited with his mother, whom he had not seen in twenty years. After the war, he moved to North Carolina, and during the later years of Reconstruction he ran for Congress—as a Democrat.[1]

White's is one of untold thousands of fascinating and instructive Civil War–era stories that is largely unknown because the individual who lived it was not a diarist or autobiographer. White had no formal education— "[P]lease excuse my bad writing as I never went to school a day in my life," he wrote in an 1862 letter to Secretary of War Edwin Stanton; "I learnd what little I know by the hardest"—and only a few letters to the editor were ever published under his name. Nevertheless, his was a literary life. In texts as different as private letters to white politicians, dispatches to a black newspaper, and bureaucratic reports for the War Department, White described battle, professed religion, constructed autobiographical narratives, and made arguments about war tactics, racial politics, and Reconstruction. In his varied acts of writing, he reckoned with pivotal events of the war. He tried to correct press reports of the Battle of the Crater with an eyewitness account. He movingly recounted his reunion with his mother in the streets of Richmond. He mourned Lincoln in a letter addressed to Seward as Seward lay abed recovering from his own attempted assassination. This modest but stunningly rich corpus tracks startling change in White's literacy and self-image; in his and the nation's outlook on black military service and black suffrage; in ideologies of the war and black citizenship.

White's writings thus are pertinent to the canon of Civil War history and its interpretive problems, all from the surprising and too often inaccessible angle of a former slave's vision and all providing a kind of laboratory for students' literary study. Understanding the Civil War through the writings of White requires close reading in parallax view, since his rhetorical and political formulations shift as he addresses himself to different audiences—a black newspaper, white politicians, the War Department. For the pages of the *Christian Recorder* (and possibly with the benefit of an editor's intervention), White could wax eloquent about the cause of freedom and the valor of black servicemen, who had "left our wives and little ones to follow the stars and stripes . . . with a determination never to turn back until it should be proclaimed from Washington that the flag of the Union waved over a nation of freemen" ("Interesting Letter"). Confidentially to Seward, he could display a crude and startling prejudice against men fresh out of slavery, whom he called "stupit creatures," idle "like the ox," and undeserving of the sacrifices of "white & colored men from the north" ("Black Chaplain"). White's racial politics, and the very meaning of emancipation and the war, are tough to pin down. In these nonfiction writings, contingency is ever at the fore.

What makes White's writings interesting is also what makes them unlikely to appear in classrooms: owing precisely to the kaleidoscopic range of his voices and audiences, his writings ended up in scattered archives. Altogether they comprise barely more than two dozen discrete texts; a handful are preserved in the printed pages of the *Christian Recorder*, and the rest are dispersed among repositories in three states and the District of Columbia, including many different record groups in the National Archives. As the case of Garland White illustrates, inaccessibility is the simple reason that unpublished everyday writings, no matter how revealing, have tended not to figure as Civil War literature.

Thankfully, materials that not long ago existed only in archives have become more available. Through the painstaking work of scholars and editors, manuscripts have been transcribed and published. The Freedmen and Southern Society Project, for instance, has published six volumes of *Freedom: A Documentary History of Emancipation* and is still going. Transcriptions of several of White's letters have been published there and in Edwin S. Redkey's *A Grand Army of Black Men*. Special collections libraries have scanned and digitized significant portions of their Civil War–era holdings, making widely available not only transcriptions but also high-quality images of manuscripts and newspapers. Subscribers to *Accessible Archives* can view all White's dispatches to the *Christian Recorder*, as well as everything else printed there and in numerous other contemporary periodicals. Other online resources abound, from the *Official Records of the War of the Rebellion*—the massive, 128-volume compendium of military orders, reports, and correspondence originally published in the late nineteenth century—to digitized manuscripts now available through numerous research libraries' Web sites.

However abundant and available, everyday prose still faces obstacles on its way into literature classrooms. Edited collections of historical documents do not necessarily cater to the concerns of English courses. Digital materials come in such overwhelming volume that one scarcely knows how to begin identifying a manageable subset of texts one might wish to teach. Finding suggestive text does not automatically make it teachable. In White's case, an individual letter does not raise the interesting questions that his whole corpus does, and any one text's significance can be hard for students to glean in isolation. Knowing where to find the everyday prose of the Civil War era is only the first step. Massive amounts of material must be filtered, and documents must be situated in a coherent textual landscape.

Although finding everyday texts, selecting them, and incorporating them into a syllabus are laborious tasks, that labor can be shared. With guidance, students can venture into online databases, or compendious documentary editions on library reserve, and take upon themselves some of the practical burden and also—a pedagogical benefit—the authority to choose and interpret material. Thomas Newkirk argues that students are done a disservice if they discuss only texts that their professors are well prepared to teach: "If students never see skilled readers confused, never see them puzzled by a word choice, never see how an interpretation is revised in subsequent readings—it is logical for them to believe that *their* difficulty comes from a lack of reading ability" (135). Guide students to a particular digital archive and let them pluck out texts however they wish. When those writings enter the classroom, students and professor alike must work to understand them from scratch. The experience of doing modest primary-source research and trying to make sense of unpublished writings will make students more aware of the contextual equipment they need to understand a text.

For an assignment in one of my classes, I asked students to pick any day in 1862 (their birthday, for instance), find an artifact of that date, and present it to the class. I pointed them to the *Civil War Day by Day* blog of the University of North Carolina's Wilson Special Collections Library. One student located a digitized holograph letter by a Confederate soldier, which he framed for the class as a fact-based (as opposed to fictional) text: an authentic, firsthand account of the Battle of Seven Pines. His classmates raised questions about the author, recipient, and subject of the letter. Thus prompted to do very basic additional research (in which he was aided by the astute curatorship of the blog), the student quickly discovered, and reported back to the class, that in the central element of its reportage the letter was erroneous.[2] Written to perform "the sad duty of confirming the intelligence you already have per telegraph of the fall in battle in the afternoon of the 31st ulto. of your brother," the Confederate general James Johnston Pettigrew, the letter describes in considerable detail the circumstances under which the general was shot and the reasons his body could not be recovered (L. Young). "Permit me now, my dear Sir," the deceased general's aide-de-camp concludes, "to mingle my tears with yours over the loss of one of the best and most gifted of men. I know that your grief must be great."

To my student's surprise, General Pettigrew's wounds were not fatal, as the aide-de-camp believed. The Confederates had been unable to remove his body from the battlefield, and Union forces took him prisoner. Pettigrew's family and comrades shared "the universal opinion that he had been slain" for nearly a week before northern newspaper reports of General Pettigrew's capture began to filter south (Pettigrew). What had seemed to be a text about grief and memorialization—"All who knew the General unite in sorrow at the loss the country has met with" (L. Young)—became a text demonstrating the fog of war; a study in the uncertainty of frontline communication; and, in this student's interpretation, a sign that, particularly for the South, the war had turned grief and memorialization into a kind of reflex. The archive itself—as readily as the modest amount of published literature one can include in a semester-long course—showed the real-time creation, contestation, and recreation of the meanings of the war.

Even without digging into archives and parsing manuscripts, teachers of Civil War literature can use the iceberg tip of everyday prose—well-known textual records of wartime events—to enrich students' understanding of the period's culture. Letters and official documents, when paired with

works of fiction or poetry, can seem equally artful, ambiguous, and provocative. There is something of a tradition of denigrating Civil War literature as prosaic. William Dean Howells, in his 1867 review of *Battle-Pieces*,
described Melville's poetry as filled with "parenthetic bulletin boards"
(qtd. in Renker 106), and Edmund Wilson, about a century later, called
Battle-Pieces "versified journalism" (479). Meanwhile, such prosaic texts
as newspaper dispatches, newsy letters to the folks at home, and decrees of
military regulation could be strikingly oblique and susceptible to different
interpretations. Take, for instance, General Benjamin Butler's notorious
General Order Number 28, not only a well-known episode in the history
of the war but also a fascinating, almost gnomic text. Students to whom
I have taught Butler's order respond to it somewhat as they respond to
poems by Hart Crane or Ezra Pound: they are not sure what it means:

> As the officers and soldiers of the United States have been subject to
> repeated insults from the women (calling themselves ladies) of New
> Orleans in return for the most scrupulous non-interference and cour-
> tesy on our part, it is ordered that hereafter when any female shall by
> word, gesture, or movement insult or show contempt for any officer or
> soldier of the United States she shall be regarded and held liable to be
> treated as a woman of the town plying her avocation. (Butler 426)

The first stumbling block is that most students miss the innuendo that in
Butler's time was lost on no one: for "woman of the town," read "prostitute." Even when that matter is cleared up, though, more questions than
answers arise. What does it mean to be "regarded and held liable to be
treated as" a prostitute? Butler contended it meant that women could be
apprehended and detained in the same jail cell as prostitutes—a demeaning
enough prospect in a lady's eyes, Butler calculated, to deter the offend-
ing behavior. But many Southerners and some outraged observers abroad
believed that Butler was giving his men license to rape southern women.
Butler, unscrupulous, perhaps did not mind if that construction was put
on his order, so long as the deterrent effect was achieved (see Long).
   New Orleans women's provocations had escalated to include, it was
alleged, dumping chamber pots from second-story windows onto the
heads of soldiers below, and Butler feared it was only a matter of time
before a Union soldier retaliated violently. The tricky task of peacefully
occupying a fallen enemy city depended on getting the women of the city
to desist in their protests. From the occasion for the order, then, open out
a broader set of questions to be explored both within and without the text

of the order, questions about ideals of womanhood in the mid–nineteenth century, about tensions between women's agency and propriety (which Butler tries to exploit with his parenthetical "calling themselves ladies"), and about the meaning of the war itself. Sensing the outrage created by this short text, students begin to consider that residents of New Orleans might well have viewed northern soldiers as foreign invaders.

Despite the northern bias that prevails at a New England liberal arts college, I have found that discussing Butler's order draws forth from my undergraduates some sympathy with the women of New Orleans and even a little admiration for their audacity. Female students have wondered aloud what they would have done in the same position. Where works of fiction that thematize domestic womanhood sometimes strike students as remote, the real-world conflict conjured by this military decree excites a kind of imagined participation in that conflict. Butler's order enlivened my students' engagement with a more commonly assigned literary work: the diary of Kate Stone, the twenty-year-old daughter of a wealthy planter upriver from New Orleans in Madison Parish. Less than a month after the passage of the Confederate Conscription Act, Stone inveighed against "the shirking stay-at-homes" and cursed the "coward souls" of these "fire-side braves" (103, 110). Awakened by Butler's order to the drama of New Orleans women's insurgency—to questions of gender and power in a society whose prevailing dynamics had been altered by both the departure of southern men and the arrival of northern ones—my class had sharp eyes out for Stone's sometimes startling reappraisals of masculinity.

In teaching nonfiction prose, it can be eye-opening to let neglected archives themselves reorient our perspective on the war—to consider, for instance, bureaucracy as an expressive medium. Just as Kathleen Diffley's work on periodicals has transformed our understanding of literary circulation during the Civil War (*Where My Heart*), largely untapped bureaucratic archives can reveal channels of creation outside the realm of publication.

The Civil War often is understood as the dawn of modernity in the United States, and the wartime proliferation of prosaic writing reveals in incipient form the bureaucracy and mass media associated with twentieth-century life. For countless people, including soldiers of all races and their families, the war brought state power into unprecedented proximity. During the transition from slavery to freedom, southern blacks especially came into close contact with the authority of the federal government, chiefly through the Freedmen's Bureau and the Pension Bureau. The affidavits, depositions, and transcribed interviews that swelled government files during and after the war form a peculiar and fascinating genre, characterized by a blending of voices, barely visible negotiations between interviewer and interviewee, and occasional moments of startling bluntness and revelation. Many such texts are readily available in a useful volume edited by Elizabeth A. Regosin and Donald R. Shaffer, *Voices of Emancipation: Understanding Slavery, the Civil War, and Reconstruction through the U.S. Pension Bureau Files.*

Freed people met their new government in federal agents—mainly white men from the North, many of whom were quite prejudiced. Even if deeply concerned with the plight of slaves, government officials most often arrived in the South steeped in Victorian propriety and relatively ignorant of the realities of slavery. Pension Bureau agents, tasked in the years after the war with authorizing widow's pensions, often found it difficult to determine whether a given woman had or had not been married to a deceased black soldier. Accustomed to look for licenses and certificates, they instead discovered tangled and complex personal histories. Freed people's experiences included consensual but unrecognized marriages broken up by sale; forced marriages for a slave owner's convenience; casual liaisons between men and women who "took up" with each other but didn't want to forge a deep emotional bond only to have it severed by an owner; and countless other apparent deviations from the accepted definition of marriage. Black Southerners had to explain not just their personal histories but also whole cultures of survival under slavery.[3]

From fraught but promising encounters with federal bureaucracy leap stories the like of which one would never otherwise hear in a nineteenth-century woman's voice. In the late summer of 1866, a Georgia woman named Rhoda Ann Childs appeared at a Freedmen's Bureau office and swore the following statement about what happened when a group of white men came to her house looking for her husband, a former Union soldier:

> They then Seized me and took me Some distance from the house, where they "bucked" me down across a log, Stripped my clothes over my head, one of the men Standing astride my neck, and beat me across my posterior, two men holding my legs. In this manner I was beaten until they were tired. . . . Then I was thrown upon the ground on my back, one of the men Stood upon my breast, while two others took hold of my feet and stretched My limbs as far apart as they could, while the man Standing upon my breast applied the Strap to my private parts

until fatigued into stopping, and I was more dead than alive. Then a
man, Supposed to be an ex-confederate Soldier, as he was on crutches,
fell upon me and ravished me. During the whipping one of the men
ran his pistol into me, and Said he had a hell of a mind to pull the trig-
ger, and Swore they ought to Shoot me, as my husband had been in
the "God damned Yankee army," and Swore they meant to kill every
black Son-of-a-bitch they could find that had ever fought against them.
(Berlin et al. 807)[4]

The issues such a text raises for teachers of Civil War literature are legion:
not just that this brutality ought to be revealed, that students need to
know it is part of the Civil War, and not just that this text, written down
by a white man listening to a black woman's unrecoverable spoken words,
dramatizes problems of discursive authority that literature students should
confront, but also that to find the unspeakable spoken informs all the
lacunae in literary works we more regularly teach. The powerful motif of
inexpressibility in the usual literature of the war years—from Whitman's
"the real war will never get in the books" (*Poetry* 802) to Harriet Jacobs's
"I cannot tell how much I suffered" (774) to Thomas Wentworth Higginson's musing, as he labors to recall a scene of the war, "How weak
is imagination, how cold is memory" (Army Life 130)—resonates most
fully in tension with the immediacy and force of expression in ordinary
writings.

Notes

1. For a full account of White's life and writings, see Hager, ch. 6.

2. See the eight-letter sequence at http://www.lib.unc.edu/blogs/civilwar/
index.php/tag/peter/.

3. On the pension system and African American marital histories, see Regosin
and Shaffer, ch. 4.

4. For more on postwar violence against African Americans, see Rosen.

Dana McMichael

Approaches to Life Writing: Confederate Women's Diaries and the Construction of Ethnic Identity

Several years ago, I sat around the seminar table with my fellow PhD candidates, listening with incredulity as a classmate complained to the professor, "But, what about all of the *good* slave owners?" For the past ten weeks, we had slogged our way through the literature of the antebellum South, encountering Thomas Jefferson's *Notes on the State of Virginia* (1785) and William Gilmore Simms's *The Yemassee* (1844) alongside Frederick Douglass's *Narrative of the Life of Fredrick Douglass, An American Slave* (1845) and Harriet Jacobs's *Incidents in the Life of a Slave Girl* (1861). We had thrown in Harriett Beecher Stowe's *Uncle Tom's Cabin* (1852) for good measure. We repeatedly grieved over the brutality and hypocrisy of those Southerners who benefited from institutionalized slavery, and we noted, dismayed, the complicity of multitudes of enlightened Northerners who allowed slavery to continue through their unwillingness to rock the political, religious, or at times familial boat. So our classmate's question astounded us. We were angry that this extended, hateful, ugly oppression had been allowed to take root and flourish in our nation and that this violence formed our joint heritage. We abhorred the greed. Some in the room identified personally with those enslaved peoples; some, to their shame, knew that their ancestors were slaveholders. None of us wanted to consider the possibility that those who owned slaves might also have a story to tell. Perhaps our reluctance to hear their stories grew from our fear that we might feel again that bitter hatred, or might recognize ourselves in their unbounded capacity for self-deception, or might be forced to concede that America had not progressed as far as we wanted to believe along the path toward human dignity and mutual respect.

Because prejudice can so easily hide, it is important in our American literature classrooms for our students to read both sides of the story: to hear from the slaveholder as well as the slave. This is not an easy pill to swallow, for us as teachers or for our students. We risk reopening old wounds in our racially and ethnically diverse classrooms. We risk perpetuating harmful attitudes. Despite these challenges, giving voice to those with whom we profoundly disagree allows us the opportunity to explore several important questions with our students: How do we craft a full, nuanced picture of the historical past? How do we engage in civil discourse with those whom we oppose? How can intelligent, well-intentioned, or sincerely religious people participate in—and at times actively promote—racial prejudice and brutality? And how can we recognize such attitudes or actions today?

Few bodies of literature give us more direct access to these crucial questions than the life writings of Confederate women.[1] For students used to consuming history through the coherent narratives of history textbooks or the History Channel, reading a mid-nineteenth-century diary can prove a daunting task. Providing them with theoretical and historical context can smooth the way. What basic tools do our students need to decode Civil War diaries? Diaries are a form of autobiography, and students need to be reminded that although autobiographies share characteristics with historical writing, they are more properly understood as literature. The key characteristic that places autobiography in that category is the careful crafting of the text. By engaging in a brief exercise, students can easily recognize the shaping of the persona required in autobiographical writing.

Ask your students to write a paragraph describing last weekend to their roommate, another addressed to their English teacher, and another addressed to their parents. After they read their paragraphs out loud in groups of three to five, ask them to comment on the differences they heard in the three versions of their classmates' narratives, encouraging them to note specific details that were included or omitted, to identify the distinct tone in each, to comment on variations in vocabulary or grammar, and to determine whether any specific action is required of each audience.

The discussion should foreground how writers shape lived experience to fit a perceived rhetorical situation and how our careful attention to the details of autobiographical texts can yield insights. Finally, ask students to write a brief reflection on the exercise, speculating on how they presented the self to each audience and why they chose that particular persona.

This exercise enables students to experience firsthand observations made by literary scholars such as Margo Culley and James Olney, who argue that "all diarists are involved in a process . . . of selecting ideas to create a persona" (Culley 12) and making the past "coherent in the recall of memory" (Olney 37). Harriet Blodgett observes that diaries are works of "literature subjectively interpreting life" (5) that rely on many of the same literary tropes and strategies that students encounter in fiction (6–8). Often these tropes serve not only to influence the writers' perception of the past but also to shape their own and their readers' perceptions and attitudes (Fothergill 41). Culley argues that the "diary shapes the life lived as well as the reverse" (14; see also Kagle and Gramegna 42). These theorists contend that a diarist actively creates a narrative thread and a persona in the pages of the diary, which in turn influences the diarist's future actions, thoughts, and perceptions.

Despite this interaction between diary and diarist, teachers should remind students that, as in other forms of autobiography, the author needs to be separated from the persona or self created in the text.[2] Students frequently perceive diaries as less crafted, less guarded, and thus more authentic representations of the self—the fact that diarists record events as they happen supports this impression. But even when diarists record events immediately, they still reconstruct conversations and incidents, not infrequently reshaping them to more accurately reflect reality as they see it. If writers take liberties with factual details, is the truthfulness of their text invalidated? Teachers can help students frame this thorny question by referring them back to the autobiographical writing exercise earlier described, by engaging them in discussion over the type of truth represented by phrases such as "I haven't slept in weeks," or by pointing them to a well-known yet widely debated event or statement, such as Bill Clinton's comment while on the campaign trail in 1992 that he "experimented with marijuana a time or two" but "didn't inhale" (Ifill). Examples such as these help raise the awareness of students of the expectations they bring to autobiographical statements or texts. This discussion also provides opportunities to introduce them to a short theoretical text, such as an excerpt from Sidonie Smith and Julia Watson's *Reading Autobiography: A*

Guide for Interpreting Life Narratives. Smith and Watson pose a question that troubles many students: "How do we know whether and when a narrator is telling the truth or lying? And what difference would that difference make?" The authors respond by asking what readers expect: "Are we expecting fidelity to the facts of their biographies, to lived experience, to self-understanding, to the historical moment, to social community, to prevailing beliefs about diverse identities, to the norms of autobiography as a literary genre itself?" (15). Raising these questions invites students to examine with us the challenges of accessing truth through literary texts.

Although some theorists argue that autobiographers exercise complete sovereignty over their texts and thus the question of truth is misplaced, most students understand autobiography to refer to the phenomenal world in a way qualitatively different from the way that fiction refers to it.[3] Generally, students approach life writing expecting to encounter the real story about the writer, the writer's contemporaries, and the writer's context, and that expectation gives weight to the reading experience and encourages them to ask different questions. While studying Civil War diaries gives us an opportunity to showcase theory at work as we help students navigate these unfamiliar, sometimes peculiar texts, we should not overlook their natural curiosity. Who were these women? Why, in a time of crisis, did they take time to write diaries? Why did so many of them write? How did they feel about the war? And how did they justify owning slaves?

Before delving into the diaries, students will benefit from some historical context to complement the literary theory. Encourage them to research the author and share their findings with the class. When and where did the diarist live? What do we know about her family, her education, and her community's involvement in the Civil War? Is there a photograph or painting of her? Students should also be reminded that these diaries are primary documents (as opposed to a historian's secondhand account) and so give readers access to information from which historians can draw interpretations. Some of our students' conclusions from reading the diaries will confirm received historical knowledge; others might contradict it.

For example, many students believe that the typical southern belle was willfully ignorant of southern politics, an image nurtured by Scarlett O'Hara's iconic flounce on Tara's front steps while pouting "Fiddle-dee-dee!" to the news of the secession (*Gone*) and by fine scholarly works such as *The Tradition of Women's Autobiography: From Antiquity to the Present,* in which Estelle Jelinek argues that Confederate women "focused their attention on other matters than the war itself and rarely even mentioned its political implications. Instead, most concentrated on the difficulties of maintaining a semblance of domestic life while under siege" (86). Although Jelinek does concede that Mary Chesnut's famous diary provides "a deviation from the usual apolitical accounts by women" (87), broad reading in southern women's Civil War diaries uncovers a different story, making Chesnut's political engagement more the norm than the fictional Scarlett O'Hara's disdain for politics. The Civil War functions as a pervasive backdrop to all Confederate women's diaries, and the diarists comment frequently on the war's progress, following the careers of favorite officers, the movement of troops, the violent engagement of armies, and, of course, the well-being of brothers, fathers, and lovers. While these women certainly write about the difficulties of securing cornmeal, thread, and seed, these domestic struggles are framed as a necessary and significant aspect of the political struggle, one more way that women contribute to the cause. Leading our students to discuss the many ways that today's largely urban, industrial, technological society differs from a preindustrial, agricultural society can help them discover the sometimes surprising intersection of the public and private spheres in these Confederate diaries.[4] As our students recognize fissures between their own study of primary texts and the analysis of some secondary sources, they will feel empowered to read more carefully and critically.

With this brief foundation in personal writing, theory, and history, our students should be ready to begin reading an assigned diary.[5] What can the study of Confederate women's diaries reveal about the way these women formed their own ethnic identity and understood the ethnicity of others? My study of more than two dozen diaries demonstrates widespread, repeated linguistic patterns that enable ethnic bias. Locating these patterns will help our students understand how the diarists use language to both build and maintain power structures that privilege upper-class, white Southerners.

A widespread and easily recognizable pattern in the diaries is how these Confederate women actively ignore the slaves' presence. They refuse to acknowledge similarities between their emotions and motivations and those of their slaves, and, further, they strip agency from the slaves through textual elision. Recognizing elision can prove challenging for our students, but we can aid them by having them watch a short clip from a familiar depiction of the antebellum South, such as *Gone with the Wind* or *North and South*, then by discussing the physical location of the slaves in relation to the slaveholders: the slaves are always in the background.

Although diarists will note disruptions to their daily routines caused by unruly slaves, most frequently they do not mention the constant physical presence of slaves. When a slave is mentioned, *servant* is used, a word that is more neutral, muting the power dynamic of the master-slave relationship and allowing the diarist to imagine herself as a beneficent employer interacting with her employees, analogous to the relationships found in middle- and upper-class northern, British, or Continental families. Often a slave's work is depicted as accomplished through an unseen agent or as done by the diarist, leading inattentive readers to see the slave as a physical extension of the slaveholder, not—as Susan Friedman urges—"a fully rendered Other" (44). For example, Eliza Andrews records that "a buggy drove up" (98) or that all her "preparations were made [for the party], even the bows of ribbon pinned on my undersleeves" (71). Such entries obscure the identity of the worker by using grammatical constructions that remove the actor from the sentence, granting agency to the speaker rather than to the slave who actually performed the work. This removal of the slave's presence from the diary testifies profoundly to the slaveholder's refusal to acknowledge the slave's humanity: the diarist perceives the slave as a tool.

A more subtle, yet no less troubling, pattern is ambiguity when reference is made to slavery, an ambivalence that most charitably could be assigned to a lack of self-awareness, though at times it seems purposefully deceptive. Chesnut's diary provides many entries that will intrigue our students and feed rich classroom discussion, but perhaps none more than this frequently quoted 18 March 1861 passage: "I wonder if it be a sin to think slavery a curse to any land. Sumner said not one word of this hated institution which is not true. Men & women are punished when their masters & mistresses are brutes & not when they do wrong" (*Private Mary Chesnut* 42). C. Vann Woodward, the editor of Chesnut's diary, argues that this statement may stand as "the strongest indictment of slavery ever written by a Southerner" (xv) and urges readers to acknowledge that Chesnut's "abhorrence of slavery and her welcome of its abolition were quite genuine and most extraordinary in her time and place" (xvi). We need to remind our students not to apply twenty-first-century standards of racial sensitivity to mid-nineteenth-century texts, but Chesnut's complaint deserves closer scrutiny. The remainder of the 18 March passage clearly identifies the particular aspect of slavery that Chesnut finds so abhorrent:

> We live surrounded by prostitutes. An abandoned woman is sent out
> of any decent house elsewhere. Who thinks any worse of a Negro or

Mulatto woman for being a thing we can't name. God forgive us, but ours is a monstrous system & wrong & iniquity. Perhaps the rest of the world is as bad. This only I see: like the patriarchs of old our men live all in one house with their wives & their concubines, & the Mulattoes one sees in every family exactly resemble the white children—& every lady tells you who is the father of all the Mulatto children in every body's household, but those in her own, she seems to think drop from the clouds or pretends so to think—

This passage strongly indicts the institution of slavery and the southern men, such as her father-in-law, who eagerly exploit their sexual access to slaves;[6] however, it also reveals ambivalence toward the very women that slavery victimizes. Chesnut excuses southern men as "no worse than men every where," reasoning that "the lower their mistresses, the more degraded they must be" (42). Her diary repeatedly demonstrates her unflinching enjoyment of the privileged lifestyle produced by slave labor even as she cringes at the sexual exploitation and violence inherent in institutionalized slavery. Ultimately, she refuses to blame rich white Southerners for slavery's evils. By the end of this entry, she has reversed her position, effectually absolving her lecherous countrymen and her self-deluded countrywomen from guilt by bemoaning the fact that while her white countrywomen are "as pure as angels," they are "surrounded by another race who are—the social evil!" (43). Chesnut does express outrage at the sexual abuse seemingly encouraged by southern laws that treated human beings as chattel, but she also condemns slave women for their voracious sexual appetites. Students guided toward careful consideration of her logic will uncover these ambivalent ethnic attitudes that mask deep-seated prejudice.

Surprisingly, many of the Confederate women who seek to obscure the presence of slaves in their diaries utilize the rhetoric of slavery to describe their own experiences during the Civil War. For instance, near the war's end, Kate Stone, a refugee, writes, "*Conquered, Submission, Subjugation* are words that burn into my heart. . . . Another month and our Confederacy will be a Nation no longer, but we will be slaves, yes slaves, of the Yankee Government" (339–40). Students might be tempted to connect these diarists with other nineteenth-century women, such as Lydia Maria Child or Angelina Grimké, who believed that in a "patriarchal America where slavery was institutionalized, all women were in a sense slaves" (Yellin, *Women* 78). However, Elizabeth Fox-Genovese, a historian, reminds us that classifying southern women as fervent opponents of southern institutions "encourage[s] the view that privileged southern women were alienated from their own society and were feminists in much the same sense as were the northern advocates of women's rights" (47). Slaves did not view their mistresses as "oppressed sisters" (48), and slave-holders such as Chesnut or Stone enjoyed the advantages of slavery far too much to lobby for abolition. Why, then, did some diarists describe themselves as slaves? Ask your students to speculate, and lead them to discuss the political and moral implications of appropriating another ethnic group's experience. These diarists' use of the rhetoric of slavery powerfully renders the depth of their feelings; simultaneously, applying this language to their own situations weakens its ability to depict the suffering of the millions in literal slavery.

Finally, all these diarists share the belief that the act of writing confers power and that, conversely, those who do not write are powerless. Many of our students will have a nodding acquaintance with the nineteenth-century cult of true womanhood or the "angel in the house" metaphor, both of which link essential womanhood with "piety, purity, submissiveness and domesticity" (Welter 21). In these diaries, the ideal Confederate lady remains pious and pure; however, she no longer aspires to the image of a sheltered magnolia blossom. Instead, she embraces the northern epithet of *rebel*, picturing herself as actively participating in the war through a variety of aggressive actions, not the least of which is recording the local and national history through her diary. These women figured their very diaries as weapons. Each prizes her literary skill and expresses awareness that spoken and written discourse is inherently powerful. Even more than secreting pistols and waving flags, these diarists join the Confederacy's struggle through the books that record their daily thoughts. Sarah Morgan's editor observes that "keeping the diary is also, Sarah at one point confesses, an act of defiance, proof 'to my own satisfaction that I am no coward'" (East xxviii). Calling her diary a "book full of Treason" (184), Morgan eagerly documents her rebellion, an attitude found in many Confederate women's diaries, in which long sections are devoted to detailing the war's precipitating causes and the escalation of undeserved hostilities. Culley notes that during the eighteenth and first half of the nineteenth century, American "women diarists in particular wrote as family and community historians" (4), documenting a particular version of history that privileged their own religious and ethnic group. This observation seems particularly applicable to the diary of Eliza Andrews, which she describes as a "history of each day' (211), or to the diary of Emma Holmes, which opens with a lengthy summary of the "great political changes" that have occurred during the past months (1). For these women who face the terrors of war, the ability to read and write marks an inviolate treasure. Refusing to be silenced, they preserve a powerful autonomy despite the superior force of the Union army.

Perhaps the value they place on their literacy makes their depiction of the men and women they owned even more problematic. Many students will be familiar with Jefferson's controversial remarks in *Notes on the State of Virginia*, where he voices the widely held belief that despite centuries of contact with European arts and sciences, the African has remained dull and witless: not one could be "found capable of tracing and comprehending the investigations of Euclid" (146), and even the poetry of the prodigy Phyllis Wheatley is "below the dignity of criticism" (147). In his explosive *Appeal to the Coloured Citizens of the World* (1829), David Walker responds to Jefferson's argument, pleading with fellow African Americans to study broadly, for when "coloured people . . . acquire learning in this country, [it] makes tyrants quake and tremble on their sandy foundation" (31). Douglass also identifies forced illiteracy as "the white man's power to enslave the black man" (*Narrative* 29), a claim repeated in dozens of slave narratives.[7] These and other works provide context for our students, for whom the antebellum laws prohibiting literacy in slaves seem bizarre; they help students reflect on the historical record and see whose voices made it in and whose voices were kept out. Literacy indeed wields power and validates humanity, a dynamics that both slave and slaveholder understood.[8]

This brief treatment certainly does not do justice to the complexity and range of Confederate women's diaries; however, highlighting some of the mechanisms through which these women inscribed ethnic difference could help students grapple with the complex racial and ethnic biases of nineteenth-century America and with the inherent power texts have to shape reality. Recognizing these rhetorical patterns—and others that students will uncover in their study—could aid students in understanding how the production of texts can strengthen, and at times even create, ethnic boundaries and hierarchies that seem rooted in some natural (and thus unchangeable) order. I believe that many of the deep prejudices that these diarists held were hidden from them, and this blindness should give us pause: perhaps current texts, even our own writing, contain similar ethnic biases.

Notes

This essay draws on my book *How Confederate Women Created New Self-Identities as the Civil War Progressed*.

1. More than two dozen diaries penned by Confederate women have been published, and many unpublished diaries are housed in libraries, historical societies, and private collections. This essay specifically treats dated periodic writing, not retrospective journals or fictional recreations.

2. Louis Renza's "Veto of the Imagination" explores the nuances of the relationship between the writer of an autobiographical text and the persona created in that text. Renza argues that "autobiography is the writer's de facto attempt to elucidate his present rather than his past" (271). Michel Foucault's "What Is an Author?" argues that authorship is culturally constructed, an important argument when one considers the type of truth presented in autobiography.

3. Paul John Eakin comments on what we learned from the furor surrounding James Frey's *A Million Little Pieces*: "[W]e can write about our lives in a memoir as we like, but we can't expect to be read as we like . . . and in case of autobiography, telling the truth is the cardinal rule" (21).

4. As students encounter these nineteenth-century women's voices firsthand, they may also discover that certain texts overturn the popular wilting magnolia image of antebellum womanhood and that these texts complicate readings that dismiss all slaveholders as religious hypocrites.

5. Undergraduate students will find particularly accessible Mary Chesnut's *The Private Mary Chesnut: The Unpublished Civil War Diaries* (1984), Emma LeConte's *When the World Ended: The Diary of Emma LeConte* (1987), and Lucy Buck's *Shadows on My Heart: The Civil War Diary of Lucy Rebecca Buck of Virginia* (2012).

6. Woodward and Muhlenfeld note that when Chesnut considers the "brood of children fathered upon a slave woman" by her father-in-law, her husband's ancestral home becomes a "horrid nightmare" (Chesnut, *Private Mary Chesnut* xi).

7. Many slave narratives explore the connection between literacy and power: among others, Harriet Jacobs's *Incidents in the Life of a Slave Girl*, Peter Bruner's *A Slave's Adventure toward Freedom: Not Fiction but the True Story of a Struggle*, and Mattie Jackson's *The Story of Mattie J. Jackson: Her Parentage, Experience of Eighteen Years in Slavery, Incidents during the War, Her Escape from Slavery: A True Story*.

8. In *Pedagogy of the Oppressed*, Paulo Freire persuasively argues that literacy can be wielded as a powerful weapon of oppression. When those in power "decree the ignorance" of another group, they necessarily define themselves as "those who know or were born to know" and "others as alien entities." The words of this powerful class "come to be the 'true' words, which [they] impose or attempt to impose on others: the oppressed, whose words have been stolen from them. Those who steal the words of others develop a deep doubt in the abilities of the others and consider them incompetent" (129). Further, Sidonie Smith notes that in nineteenth-century America, where "writing [was seen] as the evidentiary scene of reason, absence of written language signified absence of full humanity" (35).

Alex W. Black

Teaching Civil War Speech; or, Abraham Lincoln's Texts in Context

In the Second Inaugural Address, Abraham Lincoln reported that from 1861 to 1865, "public declarations have been constantly called forth [from the White House] on every point and phase of the great contest" (*Collected Works* 8: 332). We regularly only teach two of those declarations, without reference to the calls that occasioned them. This essay has two complementary goals: to detail Lincoln's writing practice and to situate Lincoln in the cultures of speech of which he was a part.[1] I begin with an overview of the speech writing produced during the war, then discuss how speech writing changed with the war. I end with extended treatments of two of Lincoln's speeches. I suggest that we look at them in context, with the calls that elicited them, and in the events in which they were articulated. Lincoln has been portrayed as the representative of nineteenth-century speech making. I demonstrate that although he was not representative, neither was he exceptional.

Phonography was not invented until the decade after the war's close. No matter what form a speech took, the print format was a principal way that it was encountered during the war. It is the only way we can access it now. Lincoln affirmed that the First Inaugural Address was a recapitulation of views that have "all the while existed, and been open

111

to . . . inspection." They are "found in nearly all the published speeches of him who now addresses you" (4: 262). He repeats verbatim part of a speech he gave three years before, in a debate he had with Stephen A. Douglas in the lead-up to the 1858 United States Senate election. That speech, in turn, defended another "printed speech" that Lincoln gave four years before it, shortly after the passage of Douglas's 1854 Kansas-Nebraska Act (3: 14). The First Inaugural Address, of course, would be printed and reprinted. Speech cycled through voice and print, often at the same time. This was by no means a new phenomenon, but the efficiency of circulating speech was boosted by the technological and human power of the Union.

The realization of a speech as print was not a one-way process. A text could also be realized as a speech. The annual message to Congress was the nineteenth-century equivalent of the State of the Union address, only it was written, not spoken. At least not spoken by the president. A congressional clerk read it out to Congress, or congressmen read it in its published form. Article 2, section 3, of the United States Constitution states that the president "shall from time to time give to Congress information of the State of the Union and recommend to their consideration such measures as he shall judge necessary and expedient." The Constitution does not specify when or how the message is to be communicated. In December 1862, Lincoln called what he wrote "a paper addressed to the Congress of the nation by the Chief Magistrate of the nation" (6: 536).

The difficulty in differentiating between speech and text is not limited to the annual message. One of Lincoln's most famous public letters demonstrates the difficulty. Lincoln had been invited to speak at a rally in Illinois in the fall of 1863. He could not attend, so he sent along a letter to one of his supporters with the request that it be read aloud: "You are one of the best public readers. I have but one suggestion. Read it very slowly" (6: 414). The letter's use of the second-person pronoun shifts from the singular sense, when Lincoln addresses his supporter, to the plural sense, when he addresses those to whom his supporter reads the letter: "There are those who are dissatisfied with me. To such I would say: You desire peace; and you blame me that we do not have it" (406). The plural sense is maintained throughout the remainder of the letter. Lincoln did not speak the words, though they were written to be, and were, spoken.

While there is no shortage of published speech from the Civil War era, there is a lack of definitive texts. Stenographers were not always present, and, even when they were, they were not always accurate in their reports. One Illinois newspaper printed the first words of the Gettysburg Address as "Ninety years ago our fathers formed a government" (qtd. in Boritt 265). The Associated Press reporter at Gettysburg consulted Lincoln's manuscript for his account; Lincoln would later revise the address by consulting newspaper accounts of it (7: 23). There was no standard way to record text: some documented audience reaction—it may be hard to imagine that listeners applauded the Gettysburg Address, but they did—and others did not (Wills 261). And not all voices were recorded equally. The fortunate problem with the Gettysburg Address is that we have too many versions of it. Other speakers went unpublished or were at least not publicized to the same extent as Lincoln. There is a tendency now to associate political speech only with politicians. The Library of America's two-volume collection *American Speeches* contains seven speeches from the Civil War, all of them by elected officials: five by Lincoln and one each by Jefferson Davis and Alexander Stephens, who were the president and vice president of the Confederate States of America.

Just as we neglect the diversity of speakers when we emphasize the work of a few, we overlook the variety of speeches when we focus on only a few of their works. *The Norton Anthology of American Literature* (ed. Levine and Krupat) includes two speeches from 1861–65, both of them by Lincoln: the Gettysburg and the Second Inaugural Addresses. Gary Wills may exaggerate when he claims that the speech made by Edward Everett, the keynote speaker at the dedication of the Gettysburg National Cemetery, "was made obsolete within a half-hour of the time when it was spoken," but he has a point when he argues that "all modern political prose descends from the Gettysburg Address" (148). Wills's comments say more about our tastes than about those of nineteenth-century audiences.

There were different expectations for what Everett and Lincoln did. Rather than treat Everett's speech in depth, critics usually refer to the differing lengths of the speeches as evidence that his was inferior. Lincoln spoke for three minutes, Everett for three hours. Such a remark dismisses the speech that was much more in line with mid-century practice. Everett, who delivered the "oration," was expected to be long and learned (qtd. in Boritt 234). Lincoln was capable of speaking for hours: the Cooper Union speech was erudite and, to us, interminable. At Gettysburg, he was asked to give "a few appropriate remarks" (qtd. in Wills 25). And so he did. The difference between the two was a matter of form, not content. Lincoln set the scene at Gettysburg with deixis rather than description: "We are met on a great battle-field of that war. We have come to dedicate a portion of that field, as a final resting place for those who here gave their lives that that nation might live" (7: 23). Everett's treatment of the same scene is exhaustive in comparison:

> We have assembled, friends, fellow-citizens, at the invitation of the Executive of the great central State of Pennsylvania, seconded by the Governors of seventeen other loyal States of the Union, to pay the last tribute of respect to the brave men who, in the hard-fought battles of the first, second, and third days of July last, laid down their lives for the country on these hillsides and the plains before us, and whose remains have been gathered into the cemetery which we consecrate this day. (qtd. in Boritt 209)

The substance of this statement differs little from Lincoln's "We have assembled . . . to pay the last tribute of respect to the brave men who . . . laid down their lives for the country." Lincoln did not invent the plain style of speech, nor did he work only in that mode. But he was aware of the occasions when detail was unnecessary. In the Second Inaugural Address, he recognized that there was "less occasion for an extended address" in 1865 than there was in 1861. In those four years, he had made so many speeches that "little that is new could be presented" (8: 332). He can rise above the occasion that he defined in the First Inaugural Address as "in compliance" with the Constitution, in other words, because he had had so many other occasions to speak "in detail." His most famous speeches are not focused on what Ralph Waldo Emerson, in a discussion of Lincoln's writing, calls "the superficial." They are, instead, preoccupied with "grand human principles" (qtd. in Finseth, *American Civil War* 255). All speeches are occasional, but these still manage to be timeless. They are more easily abstracted from their contexts. In the century and a half since Lincoln spoke at Gettysburg, a process has occurred through which many genres of speech have been reduced to the address. Following Virginia Jackson's account of the way that the lyric has come to stand in for all poetry, we could call this process *addressification*. Lincoln himself was a part of this process. The Gettysburg Address was not an "address" until he gave it that title in the final copy he made (7: 22).

Today, Lincoln's speeches are read in excerpt or in the monumentalized form of the Lincoln Memorial. A comparison of the multiple drafts that survive can remind us of when the Gettysburg Address was a living document and not carved in marble. Five manuscript copies of the address are extant, and many more copies exist in newspaper reports. The manuscript revisions include Lincoln's commemorating "those who here gave their lives" in the final draft rather than "those who died here" in the first (7: 23). Both are acts of sacrifice, but the later version suggests a greater willingness to make it. The first draft has no mention of "the unfinished work which they who fought here have thus far so nobly advanced." Like "those who here gave their lives," this added phrase provides a stronger recognition of what they did. Both drafts stress that we "be here dedicated to the great task remaining before us," but the last one connects this "great task" to that "unfinished work." The first two drafts omit "under God," though all accounts suggest that Lincoln used the words in his delivery. The Associated Press report of the event states that he closed the address with the hope that government "of the people, by the people, and for the people, shall not perish from the earth" (qtd. in Boritt 279–80). The inclusion of the conjunction "and" detracts from the balance of Lincoln's phrasing, in which no prepositional phrase is given grammatical priority. The form of government Lincoln avows is equally "of the people, by the people, for the people."

The Gettysburg Address has had a long life in quotation. A comparison of the texts and contexts of Lincoln and his respondents can reveal as much about their time as his. You could examine any of the many citations of Lincoln's most celebrated speech. In my courses, I choose one of the earliest. At the dedication of the National Monument at Gettysburg in 1869, Bayard Taylor read a poem that revised Lincoln's speech (qtd. in Barrett and Miller 194–95). Taylor opens the poem by admitting that he cannot dedicate the monument, not because "the brave men, living and dead, who struggled here, have consecrated it, far above our poor power to add or detract," as Lincoln put it, but because Lincoln has already done it, in his address and in his death: "What voice may fitly break / The silence, doubly hallowed, left by him?" (lines 4–5). The voice, Taylor tells us, is Lincoln's: "We can but bow the head, with eyes grown dim, / And, as a Nation's litany, repeat / The phrase his martyrdom hath made complete" (6–8). That phrase is the last two sentences of the Gettysburg Address, which Taylor renders into iambic pentameter. The demands of the verse form require Taylor to make changes to Lincoln's diction and syntax for the sake of rhythm and rhyme:

Lincoln, "Gettysburg Address"	Taylor, "Gettysburg Ode"
It is for us the living rather to be dedicated here to the unfinished work which they who fought here have thus far so nobly advanced.	Let us, the Living, rather dedicate Ourselves to the unfinished work, which they Thus far advanced so nobly on its way, And saved the periled State!
It is rather for us to be here dedicated to the great task remaining before us—that from these honored dead we take increased devotion to that cause for which they gave the last full measure of devotion—that we here highly resolve that these dead shall not have died in vain,	Let us, upon this field where they, the brave, Their last full measure of devotion gave, Highly resolve they have not died in vain!—
that this nation under God shall have a new birth of freedom, and that government of the people, by the people, for the people shall not perish from the earth.	That, under God, the Nation's later birth Of freedom, and the people's gain Of their own Sovereignty, shall never wane And perish from the circle of the earth!

Taylor changes Lincoln's sentence from the declarative to the imperative mood. With that change is the sense that it is not possible to speak with the same authority as Lincoln. It is unclear, reading Taylor, what the tasks and goals of this ceremony are and to what extent they have already been completed. Just as "And saved the periled state!" finishes the rhyme that started three sentences before, it also seems to finish the work that the soldiers started. What other work is there to do now, if the work they were doing was to save the state only and not a form of government? Taylor resolves that we should "highly resolve they have not died in vain!," but he does not say, as Lincoln did, how we should do so. Taylor's shift in verb tense from the future perfect tense ("shall not have died") to the present perfect ("have not died") gives the impression that their deaths have already been justified. For Lincoln, the time was yet to come; for Taylor, that process began before, and continued through, his poem.

What is perhaps the most consequential of Lincoln's writings is the least commented on from a literary standpoint. The Emancipation Proclamation may seem the furthest thing from literature that Lincoln ever wrote. Richard Hofstadter said it had "all the moral grandeur of a bill of lading" (169). It has all the aesthetic grandeur of one, too. Frederick Douglass summed up our continued discomfort with the form and the content of the Emancipation Proclamation: "It was not a proclamation of 'liberty throughout all the land, unto all the inhabitants thereof,' such as we had hoped it would be. . . . It only abolished slavery where it did not exist, and left it intact where it did exist" (*Autobiographies* 792).

A comparison of the preliminary Emancipation Proclamation and the final Emancipation Proclamation shows the administration's changes in policy as well as a shift in how Lincoln imagined emancipation would occur. One hundred days passed between the publication of the two documents. Between 22 September 1862 and 1 January 1863, Lincoln abandoned the policies of compensating slave owners for their lost property and colonizing the freed people to Africa or the Caribbean. He also adopted the policy of enlisting free and freed men of color in the army and navy.[2] The preliminary Emancipation Proclamation cited congressional acts that recognized the conditions under which actual liberation occurred: slaves escaped to Union lines or were overtaken by advancing Union troops (5: 435). In omitting these citations, the final Emancipation Proclamation assumed the power to liberate by fiat (6: 29). That is, Lincoln was making the argument that only the commander in chief could effect emancipation. The final proclamation reflects that belief in its form, as the president is the only agent. Emancipation does—or, in the exceptions listed, does not—happen for the reason that the president says so.

Like the annual messages and the public letters, the Emancipation Proclamation was written to be read out loud, and it was. You could look at its recitation at celebrations at home—at the meeting in Boston's Music Hall at which Emerson recited his "Boston Hymn," for example (Barrett and Miller 105–07)—or abroad. In my courses, I choose one of the places it took effect. One celebration in particular highlights the efforts of those who had been agitating for emancipation much longer than Lincoln: enslaved people and their allies in the abolitionist movement. There was a celebration on 1 January 1863 among the First South Carolina Volunteers, the first regiment in what would become the United States Colored Troops. They were based on the Sea Islands, off the coast of South Carolina and Georgia, an area that Union troops had occupied since November 1861. The freedom of the men, women, and children who lived there, abandoned by their owners when the Union navy arrived, had been secured by the Second Confiscation Act of July 1862, a congressional act Lincoln had cited in the preliminary Emancipation Proclamation.[3] The commanding officer of the whole region, General David Hunter, had enlisted freedmen in an earlier regiment. He had also issued an order of general emancipation for the whole Department of the South, which included South Carolina, Georgia, and Florida. Both of Hunter's acts were unauthorized and countermanded by the president. As well as troops from the North, there was also a group of volunteers, the self-nominated Gideonites, that accompanied them to act as superintendents and teachers on the plantations. Both soldiers and civilians published newspapers, sent letters, kept diaries, and wrote memoirs, many of which are now available online. By reading them together we can start to comprehend a single instance of what Lincoln called "the great event of the nineteenth century" (qtd. in Guelzo 66).

Susie King Taylor, a freed African American woman who taught in a freedmen's school, wrote in her memoir that New Year's Day "was a glorious day for us all, and we enjoyed every minute of it" (18). In his journal, Thomas Wentworth Higginson, the regiment's colonel and Emily Dickinson's preceptor, summarized the event: "The services began" with "a prayer by our chaplain" (*Complete Civil War Journal* 76–77). The "President's proclamation [was] read"—the preliminary Emancipation Proclamation; the final one would not arrive in South Carolina for another week (83–84). The regiment's colors "were presented to me," then,

> just as I took & waved the flag, . . . there suddenly arose, close beside the platform, a strong but rather cracked & elderly male voice, into which two women's voices immediately blended, singing as if by an impulse that can no more be quenched than the morning note of the song sparrow—the hymn "My country 'tis of thee." (76–77)

One Gideonite remembered that the voice—which may have been a woman's—"was very sweet and low" and that "gradually other voices about her joined in and it began to spread up to the platform, till Colonel Higginson turned and said, 'Leave it to them,' when the negroes sang it to the end" (Pearson 130). Seth Rogers, the regiment's surgeon, recalled that the freedpeople "sang it so touchingly that every one was thrilled beyond measure" (340). After this unexpected interruption, Higginson spoke, "receiving the flags & then gave them into the hands of two noble looking black men, as color guard, & they spoke, very effectively, Prince Rivers & Robert Sutton" (*Complete Civil War Journal* 77–78).[4] Higginson did not record what they said, but *The Free South*, a newspaper that had just begun publication in Beaufort, did. Sergeant Rivers charged,

"Brother Soldiers! one request I make to you now, for the first and last time. When, on the battle-field, you see me fall under this flag, bury me, *hide me*, but let this flag still float before the eyes of all." Corporal Sutton reminded them, "We shall march, fellow soldiers, under a captain that never lost a battle,—under the 'Captain of our Salvation,' our Captain Jesus Christ!" Higginson noted that Frances Dana Barker Gage, a feminist and abolitionist reformer who served as a superintendent, "spoke to the women very sensibly" (*Complete Civil War Journal* 77–78). None of the journalists recorded what Frances Dana Barker Gage said that day. Charlotte Forten Grimké, the free African American poet who taught in a freedmen's school, remembered another occasion on which Gage "made a beautiful appeal to the mothers, urging them not to keep back their sons from the war fearing they might be killed but to send them forth willingly and gladly as she had done hers, to fight for liberty" (405–06). Read together, these speeches and songs help us see, as Douglass saw, in the Emancipation Proclamation's "spirit a life and power far beyond its letter" (*Autobiographies* 792). It was not an event that occurred at one time and place and through the effort of one person. Its significance and success depended on the actions of people whom traditional studies of wartime oratory have tended to overlook.

My approach to the Gettysburg Address was to look at it through time. My approach to the Emancipation Proclamation was to look at it in its own time. You could take either approach with either text. For example, you could read the Gettysburg Address as part of the "Programme of Arrangements and Order of Exercises" at Gettysburg on 19 November 1863 (qtd. in Boritt 234). Or you could read the Emancipation Proclamation as it was paraphrased on the first Juneteenth by General Gordon Granger in Galveston, Texas in 1865: "The people of Texas are informed that, in accordance with a proclamation from the Executive of the United States, all slaves are free" (qtd. in Wiggins 62). Or you could do both at the same time, as Ivy G. Wilson does when he observes that Martin Luther King, Jr., "essentially transposed the latent poetic impulse of 'The Gettysburg Address' onto the colorless prose of the Emancipation Proclamation edict" when he opened his "I Have a Dream" speech at the March on Washington for Jobs and Freedom, "Five score years ago, a great American, in whose symbolic shadow we stand today, signed the Emancipation Proclamation" (17–18).

Notes

1. I use "speech" instead of "oratory," because "oratory" closes off a discussion of less formal, formulaic speeches.

2. For more on the history of Emancipation Proclamation, see Guelzo.

3. For more on the history of the First and Second South Carolina Volunteer Regiments, see Ash.

4. Laura M. Towne, who opened the first school for the freed people, missed her ferry, so she arrived after the presentation of the colors and the song (98).

Part III

Teaching Specific Topics

Ian Finseth

The Civil War and Literary Realism

It has become a critical truism that the Civil War was indispensable to the rise of American literary realism—that the conflict could be adequately represented only by a kind of writing that moved beyond the conventions of prewar Romanticism and grappled squarely with the war's brutalities and complexities. But like all truisms, this one deserves close attention and, in the very spirit of realism, some measure of skepticism. For literary trends move in complex ways, accelerating, eddying, backsliding, and overlapping, and while the postbellum literary scene may have been dominated by writers who valued, or claimed to value, factual accuracy and a direct confrontation with the world as it is, the nature of realism, its relation to the war, and even its generic coherence are far from self-evident. We do well to bear in mind the observation of David Shi that although Romanticism "suffered numerous blows as a result of the Civil War . . . [,] none proved fatal" and that realism "experienced its own triumphs and setbacks amid the fratricidal struggle" (45). It is also the case that realism practiced its own evasions, often sidling away from direct portrayal of the conflict (as in Mark Twain's *The Connecticut Yankee in King Arthur's Court* or Henry James's *The Bostonians*), and that it grew out of an intimate dialectic with romance, which it both depended on, existentially, as a contrary term and incorporated, promiscuously, into its stylistic surfaces, narrative structures, and thematic maneuverings.[1] The Civil War did not so much produce literary realism as provide a set of conditions in which a variety of writers (and visual artists) grappled with the meanings of large-scale bloodletting and the questions of whether, why, and how to represent it.

In the college classroom, the war's relation to realism is an inevitable and quite fruitful problem to investigate. Both undergraduates and graduate students can generate knowledge about the development of late-nineteenth-century American literature and, more specifically, about the slippages or tensions among different kinds of realism, along with what might be considered unrealistic modes of representation. In a broader sense, students can achieve a better understanding of how literary movements develop and about the intractable difficulties in determining how the real is to be both lived and represented.

In my own experience teaching Civil War literature and culture, what I have found most useful is not so much to pursue some final, all-inclusive definition of *realism*, or to thoroughly explain how the war gave rise to realism, as to identify the complexities of the problem and to explore the interpretive possibilities they present. Also, since the theme of realism, in one form or another, runs throughout a whole semester, I introduce the topic early, treating it not as a discrete unit but as a conceptual framework and set of reading practices that are more or less productive depending on the primary materials.

In broaching the subject, I find it helpful to distinguish the self-conscious literary movement of realism, which arose in the United States only in the late 1870s and 1880s under the guidance of cultural dons such as William Dean Howells and Henry James, from a more capacious, flexible notion of realism as a mode of representation reflecting a certain worldview or orientation toward experience. Instead of plunging into the swirling waters of scholarship on realism (at least in the undergraduate classroom),[2] I pose a series of open-ended questions of students that frame the problem and begin to reveal how difficult it is to define that worldview or orientation: "What does it mean to be 'realistic'? What are the obstacles to being realistic? Is being realistic a good thing?" These questions can then become more focused: "If we grant, for the sake of argument, that the Civil War encouraged the development of American literary realism, why would that be so? Can you imagine other ways in which literature might engage with large-scale violence? What do you suspect are the representational strengths and weaknesses of literary realism?"

The study of realism and the Civil War can go in many different directions. For purposes of illustration, I have organized the discussion here around three important (though by no means comprehensive) topics—photography, the experience of war, and race.

For many people in the late nineteenth century, photography represented a standard of representational immediacy and authenticity that literature could only hope to achieve. Photography was also, of course, a central medium through which Americans experienced—and continue to experience—the Civil War. Students usually come to this discussion with a pretty good sense of the documentary importance of war photography and its centrality to the historical record, but not always with a clear understanding of how reality is transmuted as it passes into the domain of photographic representation. I therefore draw them toward a recognition of how these images do not simply reflect but also re-create reality, or even intervene in history dynamically, because photographs can inform public attitudes and political decision making. Pedagogically, it works well to move from an initial discussion of how a particular image seems to provide immediate access to the real to an introduction of such interpretive problems as artistic control, scene manipulation, and decontextualization.

There are any number of Civil War photographs that can form the basis of conversation, from landscape views and images of the dead to formal portraits and everyday camp scenes, each of which presents certain aspects of the reality of the war. (The best online repository of these images is available through the Library of Congress's *American Memory* project [http://memory.loc.gov/ammem/index.html].) Depending on the particular needs or emphasis of a discussion, various photographic styles can be brought into conversation with such matters as literary representations of landscape, the cultural values and practices surrounding domesticity, or nineteenth-century views of masculinity. To prime discussion, I have had undergraduate students write short essays on how a specific photograph might participate in constructing the meanings of the war. Graduate students can be asked to develop readings that draw in the work of scholars such as Alan Trachtenberg, Mary Warner Marien, Jay Ruby, or John Tagg.

The realism of photography is easily attributed to its power to shock: its capacity to force an unwelcome truth on the sensibilities of the viewer. Since today's students can be difficult to shock, and yet since I want to evoke a powerful emotional reaction, I often display an image that many of them find both disturbing, in its own right, and surprising, given the limitations of how American history is taught. It shows an unidentified Union soldier recovered from Andersonville Prison in Georgia and photographed, probably in 1864, at the United States General Hospital in Annapolis, Maryland (www.loc.gov/pictures/item/2013645513/). Horribly emaciated, expressionless, and profoundly vulnerable, this man resembles the skeletal figures more commonly associated with Buchenwald or Dachau. When this photograph is shown, silence falls on the room and the level of discomfort palpably rises—a reaction seeming to confirm the conclusion of *Harper's Weekly* that such images "are fearful to look upon; but they are not fancy sketches from descriptions; they are photographs from life, or rather from death in life, and a thousand-fold more impressively than any description they tell the terrible truth" ("Rebel Cruelty").

Once students have had a chance to absorb the image, they typically have a great deal to say about it, and discussion can be built around a number of very fruitful questions: What do we feel when viewing this image? What do we do with those feelings? Do our emotions have political significance? Is it possible or desirable to move beyond an emotional reaction and take a more critical view of what the photograph represents? What conclusions can we draw from this image? What is the intention behind it? This last question opens onto the history surrounding such photographs, which involves efforts by the federal government, particularly the Congressional Joint Committee on the Conduct of the War, to investigate and document a variety of military matters, including the treatment of prisoners by the South. The history can get complicated—but usefully so, since it ultimately works to highlight the comparative simplicity of the photograph.

There are several critical themes I try to draw out of this discussion. One is that, while the photograph of the Andersonville survivor may present reality forcefully—as *Harper's* emphasized in contrasting the image's emotional power with mere "description"—it presents but a fragment. The circumstances of this man's life, after all, go well beyond what can be depicted in a single photograph, so we need to be wary of or alert to the ways in which a photograph abstracts its subject from a larger biographical or historical context, potentially distorting or simplifying that subject's meaning. By the same token, this man's experience is not necessarily representative of the experience of prisoners generally at Andersonville, despite the fact that congressional Republicans considered such photographs visual proof of "rebel cruelty." The point here is that a photograph like this does not merely record the real but also exists in a dialectical and dynamic relation to it. Finally, I move to the difficult question of what happens when our initial shock subsides, as it inevitably does. John Berger has written that this dispersal of the sense of shock can result in a feeling of "moral inadequacy" and that, in consequence, "the issue of the war which has caused that moment is effectively depoliticised. The picture becomes evidence of the general human condition. It accuses nobody and everybody" (44). This passage, which can be displayed alongside Susan Sontag's parallel argument that either compassion for suffering is "translated into action" or "one starts to get bored, cynical, apathetic" (101), tends to generate lively discussion. Students, I have found, are eager to discuss this moral problem, particularly since it sheds light not only on Civil War realism but also on our modern culture of the image.

Similar issues can drive the discussion of another, more familiar genre of Civil War photography: images of the battlefield dead, which have often been taken as bringing the reality of the war forcefully home to American civilians—and which continue to exert a powerful influence on how we understand the war. Students will quickly pick up on how these images deromanticize death, in contrast with both the ethos of much antebellum sentimental literature (the death of Little Eva in *Uncle Tom's Cabin* can be adduced as an archetype) and the vogue of Victorian postmortem photography (two or three examples of which will make the point abundantly clear). From there the conversation can turn to how images of the dead were not simply spontaneous, authentic documents of the real but also the artifacts of conscious artistry, as evidenced by the careful composition of a shot (e.g., Timothy O'Sullivan's *A Harvest of Death*), the repositioning of bodies (e.g., John Reekie's *A Burial Party, Cold Harbor, Virginia*), and the imposition of meaning through captioning (as Alexander Gardner did throughout *Gardner's Photographic Sketch Book of the War*).

In formulating essay topics, exam questions, or in-class activities regarding photography, I usually gravitate toward two central themes. The first concerns the visual strategies of text—that is, an author's efforts to approximate the immediacy and psychological impact of photography. The second involves the patterning of meaning across a series of photographs; here, the aim is to assess how images direct, constrain, or liberate the viewer's possible responses. In both cases, there is a basic interpretive question to be addressed: Where do the real and the imaginative meet, and how are they related?

If photography promises the real but always recasts it, we find in postbellum American literature a concern with how best to represent a war of such magnitude, both in its internal characteristics and in its impact on soldiers and civilians alike. Prominent literary realists from Mark Twain to Kate Chopin, along with a great number of minor writers in poetry and prose, and a legion of memoirists and amateur historians, developed their own distinctive strategies, in a variety of works, for capturing the military, social, and psychological dimensions of the war. It is impossible, therefore, to specify definitively what literary realism looked like in relation to the war. Hamlin Garland's "The Return of a Private," Ulysses S. Grant's *Memoirs*, Elizabeth Stuart Phelps's *The Gates Ajar*, and Walt Whitman's "The Wound-Dresser"—to take just four examples—are all realistic, each in its own way and in the way of its particular genre, and yet they all are quite different. Accordingly, I suggest to students that although realism is commonly associated with an emphasis on detail, a concern with ordinary people, and a desire to confront unpleasant truths, it is not very productive to try to align a particular work with some extrinsic definition of the genre. What matters, rather, is how the writers themselves grappled with the challenge of representing war and how that grappling manifests in text.

Both in the classroom and in students' written work, this approach requires two levels of analysis: first, close attention to the strategies, devices, and moves by which authors sought to render the war; second, an exploration of authors' characteristic skepticism toward the ability of words or images to render the war. The questions I pose to students, for essays and discussion, are intended to open up a range of interpretive possibilities regarding works as diverse as Loreta J. Velazquez's *The Woman in Battle* (1876), Samuel Watkins's *Co. Aytch* (1882), and Walt Whitman's *Specimen Days* (1882): In what sense can the representational techniques of the text be considered realist? What cultural work does this realism undertake, and what psychological or social needs does it address? How does the text imagine the relation between the external world and the inner or private self?

An excellent if counterintuitive place to start is with a comparison of Henry Wadsworth Longfellow's "The Cumberland" (1862) and Herman Melville's "A Utilitarian View of the Monitor's Fight" (1866). Both poems treat of the symbolically if not militarily very significant 1862 naval battle in which the Confederate ironclad *Virginia* (née *Merrimack*) sank the wood-sided *Cumberland* before being driven off by the Union ironclad *Monitor*. The factual details of the encounter are quickly sketched—and not the main point in any case, except insofar as they constitute the reality to which both authors respond. The main point is the difference in poetic stance between Longfellow's heroically pitched, narrative encomium to the "brave hearts" and "gallant" captain of the *Cumberland* (lines 43 and 27, resp.) and Melville's austere, angular commentary on the battle's deeper implications for the history of war and the problem of how to represent war. What class discussion can draw out is not simply that Melville's poem is more realistic but also that it ruminates more deeply on its own relation to reality and on the question of how art must adapt to changing historical conditions. This attitudinal difference, which students can readily discern, aptly illustrates the pressure that a Romantic conception of war began to face in the 1860s, and it provides a useful frame of reference for subsequent discussions of literary realism.

More specifically, Melville's comment, in "A Utilitarian View," that "warriors / Are now but operatives" (lines 27–28) serves as an ideal reference point for prose accounts of the war that focus on the experience of the soldiers or are narratively focalized through a soldier's perspective. The most fruitful texts, in my experience, are those that thematize the dynamic between romance and realism, in a number of possible ways: by tracing the loss of innocence or the sloughing off of social myths and conventionalities; by interrogating the relation between violence and maturity, both psychological and national; by exploring the necessary adjustments that people and cultures make when confronted by the shocking force of the unexpected. While these themes also inform much literature of the Civil War home front, from James's "The Story of a Year" to Chopin's "A Wizard from Gettysburg," I focus here on the "warriors" and "operatives" who experienced the violence of the war most directly.

A baseline for one kind of realist writing about battle can be established by having students read one or two of the accounts published, for example, in *Battles and Leaders of the Civil War* (1887–88). These will quickly be identified as objective or historical accounts, and discussion can just as quickly develop around the problem of what is left out or suppressed in such writing. Students will hopefully come to see that the great strength of imaginative literature, by contrast, lies in its ability to disclose the moral, emotional, and experiential complexity of the individual's participation in history.

In *Miss Ravenel's Conversion from Secession to Loyalty* (1867), often considered one of the first realist novels of the war, John William De Forest gives primacy to the marriage plot, but his depictions of battle advance the novel's larger investigation of experience and worldliness. In a discernible shift from the heroic mode that characterized much earlier war writing, the battle passages are notable for their fidelity to detail, their emphasis on individual perception and point of view, and their awareness of complexity. They suggest that De Forest is marking out a new kind of war writing—to call it protorealistic is teleological but convenient—that highlights the importance of individual perspective and the difficulty of clear perception in a situation of apparent chaos. Significantly, De Forest's representation of the fog of war contrasts with a larger pattern in the novel whereby the complexities of military and political life are handled with clear-eyed forthrightness and with an awareness (also realist in spirit) that "[w]ar in the long run is pretty much a matter of arithmetical calculation" (24). Since *Miss Ravenel's Conversion* is quite long, these scenes can be taught in excerpted form, or, if the novel is assigned in its entirety, students can begin tracing connections between battle experience and a broader theme of conversion—one in which the characters, and the country, are by the force of war brought about to a new way of seeing things, ostensibly to a more worldly maturity. "What like a bullet can undeceive!" wrote Melville in "Shiloh," and what makes De Forest's novel so interesting is that it thematizes a variety of forms of undeception, presenting this loss of innocence as a sad but necessary aspect of attaining a realistic view of the world.

Stephen Crane's *The Red Badge of Courage* (1895) pairs exquisitely with *Miss Ravenel's Conversion* because it deepens and complicates the latter's representational logic. Like De Forest, Crane is drawn to the fog of war, but he is more self-conscious in his impressionism and more philosophical in his treatment of the irreducibly subjective nature of reality and of how knowledge is informed by perception, which in turn is informed by various cultural scripts, including that of heroism. A variety of possible questions can help students open up these issues for themselves: In what ways is this a realist novel? Where and why does it depart from realism? What are Crane's strategies for representing combat? What is accomplished by abstracting the narrative so relentlessly from its historical context?

Beyond its representations of battle, *The Red Badge of Courage* displays a rare sophistication in how it explores the relation between maturity and myth. At the beginning, young Henry Fleming chafes under the domestic constraints of life at home with his mother and imagines the war in "large pictures extravagant in color, lurid with breathless deeds" (*Great Short Works* 5)—in Melville's terms, he longs to be a warrior rather than an operative. The sensitive reader is primed, therefore, to expect a coming-of-age story in which Fleming will leave behind, on the killing fields, both the cultural scripts and the petulance of his youth as he grows into an honest and manly realism. Yet Crane's genius is to show that that expectation is itself a cultural script and that Fleming, by the end, has simply traded one set of "gospels" (97) for another. Marching away from the battle, he "knew that he would no more quail before his guides wherever they should point. He had been to touch the great death, and found that, after all, it was but the great death. He was a man" (98). That may be true, depending on how we take the word "man," but Fleming is certainly an operative, a cog in the war machine, and this machine, Crane suggests, thrives on a particular kind of false consciousness, on obscuring the real.

Effective writing assignments abound: for example, contrasting a combatant's first-person account of a battle with that of a literary noncombatant, on the basis of both style and ideology; explaining the perceptual, emotional, and moral nuances of a text's representation of battle or its aftermath; considering the ways in which a text may direct attention away from battle itself and toward surrogate forms of social conflict.

The question of race, finally, deserves serious attention in any course on Civil War literature, given its ethical and social urgency, then and now. Realism represents a helpful conceptual framework precisely because race was the subject of such pernicious mythmaking throughout the nineteenth century and because so much of the energy of politically progressive American literature, by both whites and blacks, was aimed at illuminating the individual experiential realities of racial identity. Yet racial myths are tenacious things, and one of the important problems that a course on the Civil War can investigate is how the imaginative fictions of race can infiltrate even the most seemingly impartial literary work.

These dynamics, of course, were in place before the Civil War began, and for that reason we can trace the origins of American realism to antislavery and African American literature, which sought to expose the true situation of blacks in the United States. The question arises, then, how the war affected this strain of realism. There is no simple answer, as Gene Jarrett, Augusta Rohrbach, Kenneth Warren, Henry B. Wonham, and others have demonstrated, but class discussion can bring forward certain key themes: the contrast between caricature and characterization; the competing impulses toward incorporating African Americans into the body politic and toward excluding them; the shift away from an immediate political crisis toward a grinding cultural conflict; the ways in which race, though an imaginative construct, possessed very real psychological force and had very real consequences.

These issues can be most fruitfully and efficiently explored in short fiction, partly because the form allows for both the descriptive power of novels and the thematic focus of poetry, while also foregrounding a protagonist's moment of transformative insight. It is interesting to explore why the epiphanies or pivotal revelations in stories that focus on race tend to be more expansive, startling, and dramatic—even if morally problematic—than the constricted, ambiguous ways in which war stories often conclude. More broadly, class discussion can center on several fundamental questions: In what ways do these texts show race to be a fiction? In what ways do they show it to be real? How does the shadow of the Civil War fall over the characters and events of the story? Students in my classes also examine the complexities of race and the Civil War in their written work—I usually pose the question in terms of how authors handled (or mishandled) racial myths in their representation of the war experience and of the culture that the war helped produce. The range of primary texts is virtually limitless, from Sarah Emma Edmonds's *Nurse and Spy in the Union Army* (1865) and Mattie Jackson's *The Story of Mattie L. Jackson* (1866) to Mark Twain's "A True Story, Repeated Word for Word As I Heard It" (1874) and the poetry of Paul Laurence Dunbar.

Rebecca Harding Davis's "John Lamar" (1862) and Louisa May Alcott's "My Contraband" (1863, 1869) make for a superb pairing, not only because both authors are associated with the rise of realism but also because the stories illustrate how, during the war itself, two progressive white women sought, with mixed results, to think through the state of race relations in the United States. Both stories struggle to represent black male interiority; both imagine black-on-white violence; and both show how a personal crisis encapsulates a larger social conflict. Confronting students with the question of how the authors' or narrators' subject positions affect their representation of race should lead to energetic discussion—and since students instinctively gravitate toward the concept of plausibility as a representational standard, they tend to have strong opinions about whether the stories are racially realistic. Of particular interest are the texts' highly problematic endings: in "John Lamar," a former slave's murderous vengeance seems to prefigure a divine reckoning for the nation, while "My Contraband" closes with a pointedly, even jarringly, sentimental image of the dying man's final moments: "in the drawing of a breath my contraband found wife and home, eternal liberty and God" ([Hospital Sketches] 197). In discussing what these endings accomplish, whether they are convincing, and what they leave open, an important insight to develop is that each story seems to have trouble arriving at an outcome that balances justice and reconciliation. This trouble, instead of simply reflecting a failure of authorial imagination, actually points up the difficulty of achieving a satisfying narrative resolution at a historical moment when the very foundations under American society were shifting. In their departures from stylistic realism, then, these and other stories can be seen to reflect some deeper, intractable reality.

Stories about race in America are inevitably concerned with the involutions of past and future—that is, with history. The entanglements of race snare all the characters in one way or another, but particularly the African American characters, whose lives are routinely circumscribed or distorted by personal, genealogical, and national histories. The challenge for realism, then, was twofold: both to represent postbellum African American life in its various complexities—economic, psychological, material, social—and to convey how that present emerged from the past in identifiable, intelligible ways, ways that did not violate a commonsense view of historical cause and effect, even if they might offend a reader's sense of justice or fair play, of the "moral stream of the universe" (Parker 71), or of other supposed teleologies of history.

Few authors were as perceptive in their treatment of racial history, or as alert to its tragic dimensions, as Charles Chesnutt, who throughout his fiction limned what the Civil War signally failed to achieve in the realm of American racial thought and human rights. His story "Cicely's Dream" (1899), which tells of an impossible romance between an amnesiac Union veteran and a young African American woman, is especially relevant because it so poignantly thematizes the distance between what can be imagined in life and what can be attained. Simply asking students whether "Cicely's Dream" is realistic can open up surprising lines of analysis. On the one hand, the story displays the hallmarks of realist fiction: the dialect, the attention to detail and the textures of social situations, the interest in regular people. On the other, in its melodramatic love plot (girl finds wounded boy, boy has amnesia, girl and boy fall in love, girl loses boy when his former sweetheart shows up and jogs his memory), the story follows the surrealistic logic of a nightmare. In this melodrama, the problem of race stands forth in tragic vividness. Sans memory, the wounded veteran is a figure of racial innocence, with "the blank unconsciousness of an infant," and Cicely can write upon him as though on a tabula rasa, teaching him, for example, "her own negro English" until "his speech was an echo of [her] own" (177). But the improbability of this romantic arc is matched by the improbability of the fiancée's fateful appearance in the town and the narrative, which thus seems to be entering the precincts of naturalism or even allegory, and Chesnutt's final comment that Cicely's dream of love "had been one of the kind that go by contraries" makes the point with icy detachment (187). In the final analysis, the story suggests, with tragic weight, that neither the past nor the racial codes of society can be unwritten, or written over, and so the contrary dream of interracial romance gives way to the harsh waking reality of the color line. The war, in Chesnutt's vision, accomplished much, but it left the prospect of inter-racial love in the domain of romance.

Both the traumas and the breakthroughs of the Civil War prompted a rethinking of the relation between individual experience and history and of the responsibilities of the artist in representing the reality of war. This rethinking is one of the war's paramount bequests to the modern world, and it can be reconstructed, to some extent, by considering how literary figures wrestled with the challenge of articulating, and thereby helping construct, the truths of the war and its impact on people. *Realism* is simply a term for one form that this challenge took, and if we retain a sense of its ductility and provisionality, it represents a perpetually vital hermeneutic for the study of Civil War literature.

Notes

1. Particularly incisive on this point is Limon, esp. chs. 2 and 3.
2. Recent works that may be helpful to graduate students are Connery; Glazener; Limon; Shi; and G. Thompson.

Michael Ziser

Civil War Landscapes

Just before dawn on 30 July 1864, former coal miners serving in the Forty-Eighth Pennsylvania Volunteers detonated four tons of gunpowder in a horizontal mineshaft that had been painstakingly dug twenty feet beneath the Confederate entrenchments outside Petersburg, Virginia. The explosion flung the earth and all upon it—vegetation, fortifications, horses, and soldiers—high into the air and created a massive pit into which infantrymen, many of them United States Colored Troops, charged to engage the disoriented enemy. The ensuing Battle of the Crater became a cauldron combining many of the geographic and environmental elements of the larger conflict—including the racialization of regional identity, the weaponization of the earth, and the sanctification of place through violence—during the eight hours of brutal fighting and the subsequent period of atrocities.[1] General Grant called it the "the saddest affair I have witnessed in this war" (Eicher 723), a new landscape of war for a new environmental era.

A mere month before that bloodbath, in the lull between the devastating Overland Campaign in the Wilderness of Spotsylvania and the siege of Petersburg, President Lincoln had signed into law the Yosemite Grant, extending preliminary protections to the Yosemite cleft and the Mariposa

Grove, which together would eventually become the core of the second National Park of the United States ("Act"). Frederick Law Olmsted, the eminent journalist and landscape architect, made the connection between these two kinds of landscapes—one the scene of fratricide on an epic scale, the other designed to bind up the wounds of the American body politic—in his report to Congress in support of funds for the new park:

> It is a fact of much significance with reference to the temper and spirit which ruled loyal people of the United States during the war of the great rebellion, that a livelier susceptibility to the influence of art was apparent, and greater progress in the manifestations of artistic talent was made, than in any similar period before in the history of the coun-try. . . . It was during one of the darkest hours, before Sherman had be-gun the march upon Atlanta or Grant his terrible movement through the Wilderness, when the paintings of Bierstadt and the photographs of Watkins, both productions of the War time, had given to the people on the Atlantic some idea of the sublimity of the Yo Semite, and of the stateliness of the neighboring Sequoia grove, that consideration was first given to the danger that such scenes might become private property and through the false taste, the caprice or requirements of some industrial speculation of their holders, their value to posterity be injured. ("Preliminary Report" 488–89)[2]

These two moments from the summer of 1864 form part of a larger nar-rative that includes the Homestead Act and the Pacific Railway Act of 1862 (both had long been held up in Congress but finally passed in the absence of habitual southern opposition). The legislative actions suggest the war's massive repercussions—sometimes direct and deliberate, some-times oblique and accidental—for the environmental history of the United States, a story currently being fleshed out by a new wave of American environmental historians. With environmental and political changes came shifts in the way landscapes and ecosystems were represented in literature, photography, and painting. For students in advanced courses on mid-nineteenth-century American cultural history, on the literature of the Civil War (or of war in general), or on American literature and the environment, the reshaping of the American sense of place under the pressure of war offers a productive way to approach a wide range of issues often covered in such syllabi. This essay aims to make some of this material more visible to literary scholars, who may wish to assign some of it as either primary text or contextual background. In recognition of the fact that instructors rarely have the opportunity to spend an entire term exploring the many dimensions of the landscapes of war, a few subunits that might be spliced into literature courses are offered.

Geography, Environmental History, and Sectional Politics

One can approach the Civil War as a culmination of regional tensions rooted in diverging economic systems that were themselves influenced by underlying environmental and agricultural conditions. For a course in American environmental and cultural history, some background readings that discuss the large-scale trends that bear on the general differences among the North, South, and West (as internally diverse as those regions were) can be helpful. A set of readings on New England, the plantation South, and Appalachia can give students a sense of regional distinctiveness as well as provide a preview of the terrain over which the war will later be fought.

Drawing on distinctions first put to paper in colonial travel accounts, revolutionary-era and antebellum writers began to schematize and detail regional differences. J. Hector St. John de Crèvecœur's conviction that "men are like plants: the goodness and flavour of the fruit proceeds from the peculiar soil and exposition in which they grow" (letter 3) is particularly useful as an introduction to the stereotyping of southern and northern climates and temperaments, especially if it is followed with his two examples, Nantucket and Martha's Vineyard (letters 4–8) and Charles-Town (Charleston, South Carolina; letter 9). Letter 9 in particular contains memorable scenes of the interpenetration of the social practices of slavery and the southern landscape. The more narrowly naturalistic accounts of snakes and birds in letter 10 can also be discussed as an allegory of looming sectional and racial conflict. A useful writing assignment at this early point in the course might ask students to reflect on the ways that creatures and places are being conscripted into evidence of deep cultural and political differences among regions.

A strategy to approach this geographic material more systematically is to contrast scholarly work on the lowland South—Jack Kirby's chapter "Plantation Traditions," for example, in *Mockingbird Song*, or Mark Fiege or Walter Johnson on cotton—with similar work on Appalachia (D. Davis) and New England (Conforti; Ryden). Students might be asked at this point to summarize the ways in which different physical environments produce different horizons of possibility for people in different sections of the country and to speculate about how these differences might give rise to disparate ideological approaches to questions of nature and subsistence. Is geography really destiny, as so many in the nineteenth century asserted? A complicating factor here is the increasing regional divergence in infrastructure during the run-up to and prosecution of the war. To understand better how major features of the environment were being changed then, students might wish to consult the relevant sections on internal improvements in Daniel Walker Howe's history of the Jacksonian period (211–84).

Literary and journalistic texts from the period that exemplify and complicate these secondary overviews are crucial supplements here. There is an abundance of critical description by northern journalists: Olmsted's *The Cotton Kingdom*, an abridgment and revision of three earlier volumes collecting his reports from several journeys to the South in the mid-1850s, provides a wealth of excerptible material and can stand as a fair approximation of elite Union opinion about the southern landscape at the outset of the war. Instructors may wish to assign a few pages from each of Olmsted's geographically organized chapters or include the introductory essay and long chapter on Virginia as representative of his attitudes toward the people and places of the South, including his notable impatience with its labor inefficiency, substandard infrastructure, and absence of the signs of capital accumulation. Asking students to draw out Olmsted's unstated assumptions about these subjects can lead to a productive conversation about how landscape was the object of moral discourse even before it was consecrated with the blood of fallen soldiers. Slavery of course was the subtext of many such accounts, and to get a sense of the range of contemporary feelings on it a class might read excerpts from writers like Charles Lyell, a British geologist who published two less polemical book-length accounts of his travels in North America about a decade earlier (*Travels* and *Second Visit*—the second of which contains somewhat bolder criticisms of slaveholding society), or George Perkins Marsh, the first systematic American commentator on large-scale environmental degradation, who touches hardly at all on slavery in his *Man and Nature* (and its later revision). The kidnapping and enslavement of Solomon Northup, detailed in an as-told-to memoir *Twelve Years a Slave* (1853), recently made into a motion picture (2013), offers a detailed tour of the South through northern eyes under circumstances radically different from those experienced by these free white writers (183).

Before discussion of the agricultural landscape became irredeemably partisan, frank discussion of the consequences of plantation monocropping (tobacco or cotton) could be found in the research and writing of Southerners like Edmund Ruffin—later an extreme Confederate fire-eater who sometimes claimed to be personally responsible for the start of the Civil War and who committed suicide after Appomattox (see his 1832 *Essay on Calcareous Manures*). Although much less focused on the landscape of the region, the writings of George FitzHugh, an aggressive proslavery propagandist, reinterpret southern scenes of inefficiency and disorder as indices of the South's freedom from the oppressive northern system of wage slavery (see esp. ch. 1 of his *Cannibals All!; or, Slaves without Masters* [1857]). Hinton Rowan Helper, the white supremacist Southerner who nevertheless argued that slavery was destroying the South for whites outside the planter elites, provides a third view of the political-economic situation of the two regions. While perhaps too drily historical for all but the most advanced course, chapter 1 ("Comparison of the Free and the Slave States") in Helper's *The Impending Crisis* (1857) paints a dramatic picture of the South as a landscape deprived of the fruits of modern civilization by its dependence on slavery. The coda to *The Impending Crisis* reinforces Olmsted's argument about the connection between aesthetic advancement and the demise of slavery in terms that recall older discourses of climate and culture: "Mental activity—force—enterprise—are requisite to the creation of literature. Slavery tends to sluggishness—imbecility— inertia. . . . *Literature and liberty are inseparable; the one can never have a vigorous existence without being wedded to the other*" (254, 256).

No single southern equivalent of Olmsted reported on the northern landscape, but John Hope Franklin has collected a range of early southern reportage on the North in his *A Southern Odyssey*. Short journalistic travelogues appeared with some frequency in *The Southern Literary Messenger* and *De Bow's Review*, and guidebooks aimed at Southerners touring the North emerged after Gideon Minor Davison's pioneering 1822 *The Fashionable Tour* (for other examples of this genre, see Dwight; Myer). The comic literary potential of the southern tourist was first exploited in popular culture by William Tappan Thompson, a northern transplant to Georgia who first gained a modicum of fame with magazine tales told through the eyes of Joseph Jones, an affable, ill-educated, smalltime slaveholder and officer in the Pinedale, Georgia, militia. In 1848, Thompson published *Major Jones's Sketches of Travel*, a collection of epistolary reports derived from a fictional tour from "Pinedale" to "Quebeck."

Landscapes of Slavery

The literature of slavery, which grew rapidly in size and influence from the 1830s onward (particularly with the popularity of slave narratives and plantation novels set in southern locales), offers a wealth of environmental detail. Northup has already been mentioned, but the full archive of this material extends through virtually the entire corpus of slave narrative, early fiction, and abolitionist journalism and poetry (see Finseth, *Shades*, for the most thorough overview). The specter of slave rebellion haunted the landscapes of the Haitian Revolution (the smoke billowing over destroyed plantation houses), Nat Turner's rebellion (the blood-smeared leaves in his prophetic vision), the climax of Frederick Douglass's first autobiography (involving a talismanic root, unruly oxen, and a fistfight in the woods), and Harriet Beecher Stowe's richly drawn locations of slavery (the Kentucky-Ohio border, New Orleans, rural Louisiana, and Carolina's Great Dismal Swamp). The literary record is arguably the best archive for discovering the deep geographic and environmental knowledge possessed by enslaved people in the South, as the plots of slave narratives and of fictions like Martin Delany's *Blake* trace out African American networks of knowledge and mobility that went largely unrecorded elsewhere. If any of these works are assigned, students can be asked to attend to the overwhelming sense of the landscape as something haunted by the people who lived in it.

The power of landscape was mobilized in less direct ways by a variety of northern abolitionist writers. Henry David Thoreau's furious polemic against the Compromise of 1850, "Slavery in Massachusetts," converts the guilty political parties into dung beetles and rotting corpses before finding a form of consolation in the spotless bloom of the water lily, nature's promise to convert even the worst forms of moral decay into beauty and purpose. The great antislavery poet John Greenleaf Whittier, while generally offering a diffuse sense of the South as a place, has moments in which locographic description fuses with moral denunciation. "The Panorama" (1856) presents a double vision of twentieth-century America, one in which the western lands have been annexed as free states, and another in which they have been filled with southern slaveholders fleeing their exhausted soils:

> The moving canvas shows
> A slave plantation's slovenly repose,
> Where, in rude cabins rotting midst their weeds,
> The human chattel eats, and sleeps, and breeds;
> And, held a brute, in practice, as in law,
> Becomes in fact the thing he's taken for.

Herman Melville inscribed the arrival of abolition in the heavens themselves, calling John Brown "the meteor of the war" whose appearance announced the decisive end of slavery (*Battle-Pieces* [1866] xii) that earlier, in his metaphysical romance *Mardi*, Melville had deferred, like Hawthorne, to the indefinite future (ch. 58).

The ideological activation of landscape was not confined to the abolitionists. The tradition of plantation literature, often called anti-Tom literature after it grew in the aftermath of Stowe's novel, was launched by John Pendleton Kennedy's *Swallow Barn* (1832), a mildly antislavery set of sketches that nevertheless casts the aristocratic South in the best possible light. The landscape is depicted as a bucolic paradise, with self-conscious allusions to the classical pastoral tradition. Such flattering scenes are frequently to be found in the historical novels that William Gilmore Simms published from the 1830s, culminating in his explicit anti-Tom novel *The Sword and the Distaff* (1852; see also Hentz's *The Planter's Northern Bride*). Although such texts are rarely taught to undergraduates in their entirety, it can be useful to excerpt them to give students a richer context for the reformist literature that is more frequently focused on.

Battlescapes

Once the fighting began in earnest, there was a marked shift away from the large-scale ideologization of region toward an intensive focus on the microlandscapes of individual military campaigns and battles. It is on this smaller stage that nonhuman actors play their most prominent roles: the meanders in the Mississippi River that invited and resisted Union attempts to cut strategic canals; the cave-dwelling bats of the South, whose copious guano was a key ingredient in Confederate gunpowder; the mosquitoes that conveyed malaria and yellow fever to susceptible Union troops; the glanders epidemic that contributed (along with deliberate Union destruction) to the deaths of more than a million southern horses and mules; the trees felled to make *abates*, chevaux-de-frise, and railroad sleepers; et cetera (Bell; L. Brady; Fiege; Nelson; Sachs). Megan Kate Nelson's chapter "Battle Logs"—on the fate of the forests plundered for lumber to build roads and fortifications—delves deeply into one such aspect of the war and includes many arresting illustrations from wartime newspapers, magazines, and anthologies (103–59). Thick descriptions of the field of battle are surprisingly hard to find in the literature of the 1860s, with the exception of John De Forest's *Miss Ravenel's Conversion from Secession to Loyalty* (1867), the memoirs of General Sherman and of General Grant, a smattering of magazine pieces (see Diffley, *To Live*), and a host of later reconstructions.

In the category of reconstructions are eyewitness accounts published many years after the fact, most notably Ambrose Bierce's personal account "What I Saw of Shiloh" and the fictionalized versions found in his *Tales of Soldiers and Civilians* (1891); pure fictionalizations like Stephen Crane's impressionistic novella *The Red Badge of Courage*; military reconstructions like Michael Shaara's *The Killer Angels* (1974); and historical fictions like Margaret Mitchell's *Gone with the Wind* (1936) and Charles Frazier's *Cold Mountain* (1997), a novel that perhaps more than any work in this tradition seeks to thematize the environmental alongside the military and romantic. A further-flung fictional meditation on the war is Cormac McCarthy's projection of Civil War carnage onto the postbellum Southwest, *Blood Meridian* (1992), a regional transference that can be traced back to María Ruiz de Burton's *Who Would Have Thought It?* (1872). The Civil War's modern flavor may be responsible for its unexpected appearance in early science fiction, most notably Jules Verne's *The Mysterious Island* (1874; which involves a group of escaped Union soldiers and engineers) and Edgar Rice Burroughs's Barsoom series of pulp novels involving the Martian adventures of a former Confederate soldier named John Carter. Asking students for other echoes of wartime literature in contemporary television, film, and video games helps drive home the point that the Civil War still flows through our culture in the form of genre conventions and quiet allusions.

Memorialization on the Land

As historical reconstructions, the texts discussed above must be presented to students not as transparent renderings of Civil War experience but as complex revisions of history that are in conversation with their historical contexts, be it the hagiography of Grant after his 1885 death that prompted Bierce's stories, the transformations in sexual politics behind *Gone with the Wind*, or the rise and extension of environmentalism in the new South that shows up in *Cold Mountain*. Where landscape and environment are concerned, a large part of the story begins with the very real devastation of the South and the subsequent transformation of this environmental trauma into a resource for the mythology of the lost cause. A little-studied novel, William Henry Peck's *The M'Donalds; or, The Ashes of Southern Homes: A Tale of Sherman's March* (1867) presents a fictionalized picture of the *chevauchées* (organized military raiding parties) that were an official part of Union strategy (see L. Brady):

"Sir," said Mrs. Jasper, in a tone of deep despair, and addressing the leader, "you spoke of loading your wagons. For Heaven's sake, as you are a man, and I trust a Christian, I beg you, I pray you not to carry off the few bushels of corn and wheat which my own poor hands have made. Look at these five innocent children, and be merciful!"

"Must have every bushel—live off the country—that's the ticket," replied Flaskill. "If you and your rebel brood suffer, go curse Jeff. Davis and them as put you into it."

Perceiving that the leader was a hard-hearted wretch, incapable of feeling pity, the disconsolate mother appealed to the troopers, almost kneeling to them, to spare at least a few bushels of her scanty store of grain.

But she might as well have appealed to the wind. They gave her no heed, unless a curse or a scoff. She stood bare-headed in her yard, and with streaming eyes and sinking heart beheld her hogs and poultry shot down by bearded men in blue; saw her only cow slaughtered and cut up, and the pieces tossed into a wagon; saw all her corn and wheat ruthlessly swept away and heaped into the wagon; saw her weeping children clinging to her poor homespun dress, their little hearts terrified by the scene; saw in the future rain, storm, bleak winter, starvation rushing down upon her and those helpless ones, and there in her desecrated home, upon the bare earth, she knelt and lifted her hard-worked and plundered hands to Heaven and prayed that a curse, bitter and scathing, might fall upon those who robbed the widow and her orphans. (119–20)

As David Blight argues in his magisterial *Race and Reunion*, accounts like Peck's are part of a larger shift in which the sectional and racial divisions that fueled the war were transformed into visions of white solidarity (see also Simms, *Sack*). The wounded landscape itself, rendered an ideological blank canvas, became an emblem for this sentimental postbellum reconciliation between northern and southern whites, and students may find it interesting to trace several postwar developments that further illustrate the conversion of what were highly charged and racialized landscapes into sites of generalized white supremacy.

One of these sites is the history of landscape-scale memorials and the rituals of commemoration that arose alongside them, culminating with the establishment of Memorial Day. Local cemetery associations took charge of many of the major battlefields of the war almost immediately, but it was not until the 1890s that the battlefields (beginning with Chickamauga, Shiloh, Gettysburg, and Vicksburg) were nationalized and eventually placed, with Yellowstone and Yosemite, under the protection of the

National Park Service (Linenthal). Many books of photography invite the viewer to compare the images of the nineteenth-century battlefields with the carefully curated parks of today (Frassanito, *Antietam, Early Photography*, and *Gettysburg*; Muench and Ballard) or with the blighted suburban landscapes that did not fall under park protection (Huddleston). The preservation of these sites made possible the complex performative tradition of Civil War reenactment, described in detail and with sympathetic intelligence in Tony Horwitz's *Confederates in the Attic*. The differences between the official national monuments and the unofficial one at Stone Mountain, Georgia, a massive bas-relief tribute to the Confederates Stonewall Jackson, Robert E. Lee, and Jefferson Davis that was conceived and begun by Gutzom Borglum, a Klan sympathizer and the eventual sculptor of Mount Rushmore, make for an interesting discussion (see Freeman).

The role of the environment in the racialized reunification of the North and South reached even into obscure corners of science and culture. Cyril Hopkins's *The Story of the Soil* (1911), for instance, is a polemic by a practicing soil scientist about proper agronomic practices loosely cloaked as a romance that turns on the relationship between a northern soil scientist and a southern belle whom he saves from rape at the hands of two black men. More familiar to literary scholars are stories by Charles Chesnutt that expose the continuing exploitation of southern soils and farm laborers at the hands of carpetbagging Northerners (*Conjure Woman*). By turning the tables on the moralizing of the North, Chesnutt can help students get some needed critical distance from the oversimplified contrast between pro- and antislavery whites that naturally develops when they study the earlier part of the century.

The last third of the nineteenth century witnessed an enormous consolidation of environmentalism in terms both of public sentiment and of public policy. Though not often remarked in the commentary of the time, much of this change was ushered in by events leading up to, during, and immediately after the Civil War. Perhaps the keenest question with which to grapple in the classroom is the degree to which the American environmental tradition is haunted by the slavery, carnage, and exclusionary reverence in the history of its central object, the land.

Notes

1. Richard Slotkin's *No Quarter* is the best of the many books on the battle.

2. In the Giant Forest, a preserve of giant sequoia trees in Sequoia National Park south of Yosemite, the largest individual specimens are named after the Union Generals Sherman and Grant.

Matthew R. Davis

Brotherhood in Civil War–Era America

During the Civil War, countless songs sung by both the Union and Confederate armies portrayed the conflict as fraternal. Some of these songs wish for the safe return of a brother ("Bring My Brother Back to Me"); others encourage brothers to continue the fight ("Hasten Brothers to the Battle"). Sometimes news is sought from the front ("Brother Tell Me of the Battle") or the fallen are mourned ("Farewell Dearest Brother"). At the close of the war, songs plead for inclusion ("We Know That We Were Rebels; or, Why Can We Not Be Brothers") or welcome back former rebels ("Wayward Brothers!"). In these songs, a few themes predominate: the loss of a brother is devastating, what one desires most in the face of national instability is some piece of reassuring news, and a war fought brother against brother is particularly heart-wrenching. Although many songs utilize brotherhood literally—asking that mothers, brothers, and sisters be comforted—others invoke brotherhood symbolically to stand for the American national family. While students recognize and embrace brotherhood as a central conceptual frame for engaging the Civil War, it is important to push them to understand its deeper and frequently conflicted meanings.

It has become commonplace to memorialize the Civil War as having pitted brother against brother, a characterization that encapsulates the themes of loss, suffering, and war's inhumanity. Take, for example, the sketch "Brother against Brother" from Frank Moore's 1867 edited collection *Anecdotes, Poetry, and Incidents of the War: North and South, 1860–1865*: it centers on a poor Philadelphia father of four boys. Before the war, the two older brothers relocated to New Orleans, where they became successful in business, with the eldest planning to bring up the "youngling of the flock" in his trade. During the Civil War, the two younger brothers fight in the front lines at the battle of Fredericksburg, where both are killed. When a rebel soldier approaches the body of his dead enemy and turns it over, "to his horror [he] beheld the corpse of his younger brother." Having killed his own brother, the rebel soldier "made his way into the Union lines and is now . . . a hopeless maniac" (132). The anecdote concludes by highlighting the tragedy of a Civil War fought fraternally: "Unless the remaining rebel brother survive, the family are now extinct. The father died of a broken heart, and was buried last Sunday" (133). This story's account of fraternal violence demonstrates brotherhood's central role in depicting the horrors and losses of the American Civil War.

The great challenge in teaching brotherhood as a Civil War concern is that although most people think that they know what is meant by *brotherhood*, conflicting definitions of the term and ambiguity about its meaning and scope prevail, both literally and figuratively. When one introduces a unit on brotherhood and the Civil War in a larger survey of American literature, a quick question of the class as to its definition typically elicits a few answers: consanguineous, affinal, or voluntary. In the story and songs related above, most invocations of brotherhood are literal—real, biological brothers brought into conflict with each other; however, in many of these same works, *brotherhood* can also function figuratively, bringing together Northerners and Southerners as brothers in spirit. Follow-up questions will quickly dismantle this oversimplification: Does brotherhood as a universal category include women? men of other races? Which is more real to a Klansman, the blood oath that links him to his fellow Klansmen or his shared biology with African Americans? Brotherhoods that are neither fully biological nor fully imaginary, such as the relationship of brothers-in-law, complicate matters further. Brotherhood also conveys a sense of belonging while simultaneously providing a means of exclusion, as the decades following the Civil War have been described as a "Golden Age of fraternity," when both the Ku Klux Klan and Prince Hall Freemasons (the African American tradition of freemasonry largely derided by white masons) structured themselves along imaginary blood ties (Harwood 623).

Brotherhood most often is used to call on the sympathetic bonds of love and affection that one imagines come from kinship, but it never fully escapes its associations with violence and exclusion—beginning with Cain and Abel and continuing through the practices of the Klan. Further, consanguineous brotherhoods that cross racial lines are often dismissed as inauthentic. *Brotherhood* is typically invoked to signal equality among those recognized as brothers; however, that brotherhoods are sometimes narrowly circumscribed—to biological brothers, to biological brothers of the same race, or to brothers-in-law of the same race, class, or creed—shows that they can foreclose equality and foster exclusion. This complication, often overlooked, is obvious when one considers that *brotherhood*, even when used to include all humanity, remains an exclusionary gendered term.

Asking students to imagine brotherhood as a broad spectrum that spans not just from consanguineous to affinal but also from love to hate and from equal to exclusionary illuminates the term's variety of meanings and associations. One way to develop this taxonomy is to ask students to reflect on what the Bible tells us of brotherhood (contrasting the Old and New Testaments) and to imagine how both the Ku Klux Klan and abolitionists could see themselves as Christians united in brotherhood. Thus, whenever Civil War–era literature invokes brotherhood, one must remain cognizant of brotherhood's many possible meanings. Brotherhood always brings with it notions of sameness (being of one blood), equality (Josiah Wedgwood's "Am I Not a Man and a Brother?"), and the possibility of violence (brother against brother), sometimes simultaneously. To illustrate these divergent associations, this essay explores a cluster of works that highlights the deployments of brotherhood in the literature of the American Civil War: Louisa May Alcott's 1863 sketch "My Contraband," Edward H. Dixon's 1868 *The Terrible Mysteries of the Ku-Klux-Klan*, and Thomas Dixon's 1905 *The Clansman*. These texts enable students to see firsthand the possibilities inherent in brotherhood, both inclusive and exclusionary, as well as the inescapable role played by violence. Additionally, they demonstrate how the Civil War's terrible toll on the nation was fraternal and how further attention to brotherhood's many meanings deepens our understanding of this era.

Alcott's "My Contraband"

Widely anthologized, Louisa May Alcott's "My Contraband" was originally published in the November 1863 edition of the *Atlantic Monthly* under the title "The Brothers" and was based on her experiences at Union Hotel Hospital in Washington, DC. Most editions of the story utilize Alcott's preferred title of "My Contraband,"[1] emphasizing Nurse Dane's illicit desire for Robert Dane and marking the story, as the *Norton Anthology of American Literature* does, as being "about interracial sexuality" ([Baym] 1734).[2] In introducing this text, I share this publication history and ask my students to consider how the title used shapes the reading. By foregrounding the original title, we focus on how the story marks the violence of the Civil War as fraternal, dramatizes the legal and social obstacles to recognizing brotherhood across racial lines, and suggests the difficulty of establishing an alternative brotherhood divorced from its violent and unequal tendencies.

The most dramatic moment in Alcott's narrative comes not when Nurse Dane awakes to discover that Bob, her "contraband for a servant," has shut fast the window to the room where she attends to a dying rebel soldier in the hope of "let[ting] the lord take him," but rather when Bob admits that he did so because "[h]e's my brother" ([*Alternative Alcott*] 75, 83). From this point forward, Alcott's story highlights the complicated roles played by brotherhood in the Civil War era. I ask students how each character defines brotherhood and to note also how those definitions shift over the course of the narrative. The reading that follows is offered as the basis for a class discussion that might follow.

Nurse Dane, on hearing Bob's reasons for wanting to see the rebel soldier die, believes that reminding Bob of his consanguineous brotherly bonds might turn him from his deadly plan: "Oh, no! remember he is your brother," she pleads. Bob's response, "I'm not likely to forgit dat," reveals that what for Nurse Dane is an appeal to one's humanity to forgive a brother instead points to the crime of enslaving one's own kin (83). When it is later revealed that Master Ned (or Captain Fairfax) "always hated" Bob because he "looked so like old Marster," Bob makes it clear that it is the combination of the biological connection between masters and slaves and the denial of the rights of the slaves as individuals that makes brotherhood more complicated and contested than usually imagined (84). Nurse Dane's recognition of Bob and Ned's shared fraternity fails precisely because brotherhood, in the context of slavery, partakes of the violence, brutality, and exclusion of a system that does not recognize the rights of brothers possessing black blood.

When Bob reveals that he hopes to discover the fate of his wife, Lucy, and tells Nurse Dane that Ned "took her" from him, she abandons her appeal to fraternal benevolence or Christian brotherhood:

> In that instant every thought of fear was swallowed up in burning indignation for the wrong, and a perfect passion of pity for the desperate man so tempted to avenge an injury for which there seemed no redress but this. He was no longer slave or contraband, no drop of black blood marred him in my sight.

Her recognition of brotherhood's potential for violence and betrayal is complete when she "hated him as only a woman thinking of a sister woman's wrong could hate" and when she refuses to stir when the "captain moaned again, and faintly whispered 'Air!'" (84). In the discussion, students should pay attention to how brotherhood has shifted and how sisterhood is both similar to and different from it. Brotherhood can include women—the Christian brotherhood of man—but can also exclude them (e.g., the Fraternal Order of Elks). Sisterhood never includes men and therefore does not possess the same power of appearing to be universal while retaining raced, gendered, and classed divisions.

During Nurse Dane's long night negotiating with Bob to allow her to treat Ned, brotherhood figures in the blood bond between the brothers and in her shifting conceptions of brotherhood's divergent meanings. When she promises that Bob will find Lucy "here or in the beautiful hereafter, where there is no black or white, no master and no slave," she references brotherhood's more positive associations with inclusion and equality (86–87). She traverses the full spectrum of brotherly relations from love ("he is your brother") to hate (her refusal to stir and aid the suffering soldier) and from consanguineous and unequal to universal and egalitarian.

When Nurse Dane and her contraband are reunited at the end of the story, Bob is now "Robert Dane," a combination of the name she initially preferred to call him and her surname (90). This renaming signals his acceptance of interracial, nonbiological ties over the violent, coercive, and exclusionary brotherhood shared with his half brother and former master. More noteworthy is that Robert Dane is mortally wounded by the brother he previously allowed to live. Ned also dies in the confrontation, avenged by "the dark freeman" Sarah Elbert describes as Robert's "newest brother" (Alcott 91; Elbert xliv). Alcott's "My Contraband" has moved away from both a broadly inclusive Christian model of brotherhood and a strictly literal definition of it to one that allows for far more flexibility. The conclusion privileges the voluntary, affective, and egalitarian aims of brotherhood that signal her embrace of brotherhood's most positive associations. Yet "My Contraband" never forgets that brotherhood is also violent and exclusive.

Given its engagement with both the full spectrum of brotherly relations and its recognition of violence's central role, Alcott's "My Contraband" allows for a well-rounded discussion of brotherhood in Civil War–era America. The work is also effective when paired (or contrasted) with more limited visions of brotherhood such as those proffered in fictions about the violent and exclusive fraternal practices of the Ku Klux Klan.

Edward Dixon's *The Terrible Mysteries of the Ku-Klux-Klan*

Ridiculous in its sensationalism and blatant in its exploitation of the Ku Klux Klan's notoriety, Edward H. Dixon's 1868 *The Terrible Mysteries of the Ku-Klux-Klan* is nevertheless notable in its depiction of the Civil War's disruption of American brotherhood and therefore useful in the classroom for exploring brotherhood's more troubling deployments. In Dixon's wild imaginings, the initiation rituals of the Ku Klux Klan utilize the false promise of aiding consanguineous brothers and enact the violent exclusion of African Americans to promote a brotherhood that is voluntary yet paradoxically still blood-based. As such, the novel challenges more optimistic and inclusive visions of brotherhood.

Little information exists regarding the original publication of *Terrible Mysteries*. According to the frontispiece of the 1970 republication, the novel was originally credited to Scalpel, M. D., a pseudonym frequently adopted by Dixon. Although currently out of print, the work is short enough to be made available, electronically or by photocopy, either the whole work or just the pivotal initiation scene (34–54). Wyn Craig Wade's view that Dixon was cashing in on a popular subject matter ("the confessions of a former Klansman . . . was nothing more than a cheap thriller in which Klansmen were portrayed as modern-day sorcerers who made pacts with the devil" [52]) is in keeping with how the Klan itself became attached to "knives, paint, pills, a circus act, and a 'Ku Klux Smoking Tobacco'" as well as associated with a "Ku Klux" juvenile baseball team, a theatrical burlesque called "Ku Klux Klan," and a musical piece titled "Kuklux Midnight's Roll Call" (Trelease 60). The Ku Klux Klan's popularity and notoriety as a secret fraternal organization make it clear that brotherhood infused many areas of American life in the Civil War era, as a rhetorical trope to promote not only American unity but also violent exclusion and division.

Tom, a pretended business traveler from Boston, visits an unnamed southern town. He is later revealed to be a spy for William H. Seward, tasked with monitoring the "negro lodges of the League" (E. Dixon 38). His real purpose for being in the South speaks to the novel's intimate concern with what kinds of fraternal associations are permissible. Because the Union League operated as "a secret society with oaths, ritual, and closed meetings" and was therefore "both a fraternal organization like the Grange and a branch of the Republican party" (Trelease xxix), Tom's presence indicates the unease surrounding black men who are fraternally bound to one another and meeting in secret. Tom thus becomes a candidate for Klan membership, and the remainder of the novel traces his transformation into a "perfect brother of the Klan" (E. Dixon 49).

Alone, seated at a bar, Tom hears two distinct voices call "Brother!": on his right speaks "the voice of my twin-born, who died in the front on Shiloh's awful day," on the left speaks "my little boy brother, starved to death in the prison-pens of Andersonville" (18). The trauma of the war is literalized in the ghostly materialization of both. His first inclination is to avenge his brothers, but their response shifts his focus from the consanguineous to a broader national conception of brotherhood: shaking their heads, they suggest, "Your living brothers in the South need your care" (19). When these two voices later are revealed as imposters employed by the Red Death to lure Tom, brotherhood's ability to both associate and dissociate from consanguinity comes to light. He admits that he fought in the Union army not for love of the Negro but for money and further asserts that he hates the Negro for making him "fight his Southern brother," espousing a national confraternity of white citizens that excludes African Americans (39). Brotherhood is thus a source of tragedy (the deaths of Tom's biological brothers), a threat (the Union League as a quasi-fraternal organization of armed black men; the Klan), and malleable in its inclusiveness (Tom's "living brothers in the South").

The most dramatic invocation of brotherhood's complicated meanings for the Ku Klux Klan emerges as Tom finds himself before the White Arch Death, who asserts, "We are a secret band . . . sworn by bonds thou couldst not understand to keep our secret safe—yea, even by blood, if need be" (23). The complicated interplay of brotherhood, affinity, and violence are linked, as "even by blood" promises quasi-consanguineous ties while also anticipating the initiation ritual's violent conclusion, suggesting the ends to which the Klan is willing to go to secure white hegemony (54). Remarkably, the blood that cements Tom's status as a member comes not from himself or from other members but from the slain bodies of sacrificial African Americans. Dixon's account of Klan initiation rituals offers a powerful counter to Alcott's more unifying vision of American brotherhood, but its intensely racist and violent focus presents new challenges. In teaching any literature about the Ku Klux Klan, I find it helpful to caution students ("Before you read Dixon, I want to warn you that what you are about to read is both terribly racist and horrifically violent . . .") and to acknowledge both my own and their discomfort with these texts' depictions. I remind them that any discussion of brotherhood must recognize all its aspects to provide an accurate accounting of its power during this time period. It might be more comfortable and reassuring to remember—or, rather, misremember—the Civil War as a brief family squabble that was resolved by the unifying power of national confraternity, but we must also acknowledge that any promised fraternal alliance likely depends on exclusion and violence.

It is in the final stages of the Klan's initiation ritual that the full spectrum of brotherhood comes into focus. Tom progresses from "brother thou mayest be" to "brother thou art" through his disavowal of service to the Union army, his expressed hatred for African Americans, his imagined brotherhood with the South, and his endorsement of bloody retribution directed toward African Americans (42, 46). Most disturbing is that Klan brotherhood depends not just on the exclusion of African Americans but also on their bloody sacrifice. When Tom signs his oath to the Klan, he does so not with his own blood (as one might expect in any other ritual of blood brotherhood) but with a sword that has been plunged "deep into the bowels of the negro baby" (48). To cement his status as a brother of the Klan, he engages in the "bloody kiss of Ku," where he kisses "the bloated, frothy tongue" of a Negro man's "ghastly severed head" (48–49). At the conclusion of the ceremony, he drinks the mingled blood of the slain African American man and two murdered babies, in this way securing his ties to the Klan.

It is important that the created bond disavows any possibility of interracial fraternity, such as that between Ned and Robert or even between Nurse Dane and Robert in Alcott's story. Dixon's tale reveals anxieties surrounding the actual blood ties that link men as brothers while it imagines an alternative and violent means for fostering a quasi-blood brotherhood that excludes African Americans. Paired with a progressive vision of brotherhood's possibilities, such as that provided in many of the songs that emerged out of the Civil War or in Alcott's story, Dixon's exclusionary, violent, and racist novel helps students recognize brotherhood's divergent meanings in Civil War–era America.

Thomas Dixon's *The Clansman*

Like Edward H. Dixon's *The Terrible Mysteries of the Ku-Klux-Klan*, Thomas Dixon's better-known and more widely available *The Clansman* can serve as a useful (and less graphically violent) counter-narrative to national rhetoric of the Civil War as a fraternal squabble. Of the three works discussed in this essay, Dixon's novel reached the widest audience, both through its impressive print runs and through its transformation into America's first blockbuster motion picture, D. W. Griffith's *The Birth of a Nation* (1915).[3]

The novel deals with brotherhood's violent ties to the Civil War, opening with Elsie Stoneman's tending to the wounded Confederate soldier Ben Cameron, who himself has lost his "first brother" in a war that has been "one long horror" (20). Throughout the novel, the two families become inextricably linked. Though much that binds them initially is their animosity toward each other (a useful reminder that brotherhood spans love and hate), the novel displaces the hostility between Northerners and Southerners onto African Americans, who are depicted as lazy, vengeful, and rapacious. *The Clansman*, then, much like Edward Dixon's novel, posits violence against African Americans as the basis for white fraternity, because they are presented as obstacles to the national interest: "There can be no such thing as restoring this Union to its basis of fraternal peace with armed negroes, wearing the uniform of this Nation, tramping over the South" (45). By the end of the novel, through the machinations of the Klan and a thorough reworking of brotherhood, the Camerons and Stonemans come to stand for the reconstituted American national family.

Dixon effects this transformation through tropes of brotherhood. Early on, it is revealed that Ben Cameron and Phil Stoneman "were as much alike as twins"; later, their connection is revealed as stronger because of their shared Scotch heritage, which makes them "brethren of a common race" (8, 293). Margaret Cameron is enamored of Phil before their first meeting because she has heard that he is "as Ben's twin brother" (281–82). Ben begins "to feel closer than a brother" to Phil (225). Later, he even tells him, "you're the kind of man I'd like to have for a brother" (337). Dixon concludes with the twin-like brothers, one from the North and one from the South, each engaged to the other's sister, thus promising to become very real brothers-in-law, literalizing and authorizing the brotherhood of these former enemies.

That Dixon's imagined American nation also excludes African Americans should not be surprising and emerges through the novel's gross characterizations of African Americans: Gus is a rapist who drives Marion to suicide; the mixed-race Silas Lynch forces Reconstruction on the South, and Lydia Brown, Austin Stoneman's housekeeper, is revealed to be the "yellow vampire" responsible for all his misdeeds (371). Dixon's nation also emerges as white through its esteem of Ben and Phil as fellow Klansmen who avenge Marion's death and prevent the African American vote in the election that concludes the novel. Discussion or screening of *The Birth of a Nation* can be productive here, as the film manipulates sympathy and identification in its viewers, encouraging them to identify with the plights of the Cameron and Stoneman families while projecting African Americans as obstacles to national unity. Indeed, the film's powerful manipulation of tropes of brotherhood contributed to the reestablishment of the Ku Klux Klan in the early twentieth century, because screenings of the film were utilized to recruit new adherents to the Klan's exclusionary and violent brotherhood.

As demonstrated in the Civil War song sheets that began this essay, the Civil War is most often remembered as traumatically fraternal, having pitted brother against brother. In literature that engages brotherhood in and around the Civil War, however, brotherhood is reconfigured as neither universal nor strictly consanguineous in the project of making the American nation white. Although brotherhood in its most expansive and inclusive forms can signal equality, kinlike affinity, and adherence to a common goal, it is never fully free from violence or exclusion. Benedict Anderson's observation that we have been encouraged "to remember/forget the hostilities of 1861–65 as a great 'civil' war between 'brothers' rather than between—as they briefly were—two sovereign nation-states" might be modified to note that brotherhood's many conflicting associations have been similarly forgotten (201). Students pushed to grapple with brotherhood's many contested possibilities are better able to understand Civil War–era America and recognize our nation's difficult and unfinished project of crafting unity out of diversity, achieving equality for all.

Notes

1. The title "The Brothers" was proposed by her Atlantic editor, James Fields. Alcott briefly utilized the title "My Contraband; or, the Brothers" in the 1869 revised publication of *Hospital Sketches and Camp and Fireside Stories*.

2. The *Heath Anthology of American Literature* echoes this assessment, suggesting that this and other stories that came out of Alcott's hospital experiences "tacitly supported inter-racial marriage" (Butos).

3. Given the many similarities between Dixon's text and *The Birth of a Nation*, another alternative for teaching this work would be to screen clips from the film alongside any of the other works discussed.

Catherine E. Saunders

Poetic Representations of African American Soldiers

One hundred and fifty years after the American Civil War, and another fifty after the major civil rights landmarks of the twentieth century, many students come to the classroom with a simplistic understanding: the North, they often believe, fought not only for the preservation of the Union but also for the end of the slavery (and, by extension, for racial equality), while the South fought for the preservation of both slavery and racial inequality. Despite periodic references in popular culture (including the movies *Glory* and *Lincoln*), students tend to be unaware of debates in the North over the inclusion of African American soldiers in the conflict or of the complex interconnections among ideas about race, freedom, equality, and citizenship that those debates reveal.

The three occasional poems discussed in this chapter—Alice Cary's "Song for Our Soldiers,"[1] Benjamin Clark's "Be Joyful!,"[2] and George Henry Boker's "The Black Regiment"[3]—offer an opportunity for building deeper cultural understanding of the tensions between many Union supporters' embrace of freedom as an ideal and their often unthinking invocation of racial stereotypes and hierarchies. The poems are suitable for study in a variety of courses, from introductory and advanced literature to composition and history. "Song for Our Soldiers" and "Be Joyful!" rely on basic poetic devices such as rhyme and repetition, making them easy for novices to analyze, but are nevertheless representative of differing cultural attitudes surrounding slavery, emancipation, and African Americans' role in the fight. "The Black Regiment" makes more sophisticated use of both poetic form and language, offering opportunities for more advanced literary analysis, while also raising questions about the relation between established cultural tropes and representations of African American soldiers. In addition, it can be read alongside Alfred Lord Tennyson's "Charge of the Light Brigade," a combination that allows discussion of intertextuality and of the transatlantic nature of nineteenth-century Anglo-American culture.

On first reading, students tend to focus on the similarities between Cary's and Clark's poems: both are simple compositions, imagined as songs articulating a group's common purpose, and both associate the Union cause with freedom for the enslaved. However, when invited to enumerate the actors in each poem and describe what those actors are doing, students begin to notice a crucial absence in Cary's poem: although African Americans are present in both texts, black soldiers appear only in Clark's. In Cary's poem, the soldier-speakers and "Union-loving black men / True and loyal black men" (lines 14, 15, 34, 35) are imagined as distinct groups, with no suggestion that former slaves could become soldiers. The refrain "let 'em run away!" highlights this division: running away from a master can be seen as an act of rebellion, but running away from a battle is customarily seen as an act of cowardice, one that some supporters of the Union feared African American soldiers would commit. In the scenario Cary's poem describes, white soldiers are liberators, while black men (and presumably women) are not even self-liberators; they "run away" only after Union soldiers, who are assumed to be white, have cleared the way by "[breaking] . . . [striking] . . . [knocking] off their chains" (17–19, 37–39).

In contrast, Clark employs a first-person plural voice that is explicitly African American. Despite its hopeful title and refrain, "Be Joyful!" reflects a darker, more nuanced understanding of the war, its goals, and the possible outcomes for African Americans. The first line's recollection of rejection of African American volunteers "two years gone by" is a measure of how much progress toward full participation in the nation's life African Americans have made in a short time, and, in classroom discussion, provides crucial historical context for both poems. At the same time, this line suggests the fragility of that progress. Students will better grasp the uncertain situation in which Clark is writing if they are asked to work their way through the poem as a whole, and especially through the complex syntax of stanza 4, with its multiple conditionals ("and victory shall be won . . . if we're true and brave . . . be what we will" [lines 32, 36, 37]), looking for all the possible answers to the stanza's opening question: "What, then, shall our status be" (31) after the war.

Students will probably embrace the optimistic answer in the preceding stanza—"true and brave" conduct in battle will lead to civic and social equality, "a land of just and equal laws / . . . A place where not a fettered slave / Shall ever clank his chain; / But where, without regard to caste, / Freedom and Truth shall reign" (24–29)—and perhaps even see it as an account of the actual results of the Civil War. However, questions aimed at eliciting information about historical facts with which many American students will be familiar—post–Civil War debt bondage and the long fight for full civil rights—can help them see the speaker's caution as realistic, even prescient. If time allows, newspaper accounts of attacks on black veterans in uniform as late as the mid–twentieth century could serve as reminders that black former soldiers "with arms in hand" (37) continued to be seen by some white Americans as an unacceptable threat to the established racial hierarchy. Depictions of slave rebels such as Denmark Vesey, Nat Turner, and John Brown's African American comrades could also illustrate both African Americans' desire for arms and European Americans' fear of armed former slaves. Even a relatively brief class discussion of Cary's and Clark's poems can sensitize students to the racial assumptions often implicit in Civil War–era writing about slavery, freedom, and African Americans' role (or lack thereof) in the fight.

If more time is available, analysis of additional texts and images can further illuminate the cultural context of Cary's, Clark's, and Boker's poems. The Union and Confederate versions of George F. Root's enormously popular song "Battle Cry of Freedom" (1862) provide further evidence of the degree to which both sides in the war embraced the ideal of freedom and offer an opportunity to explore their differing understandings of the concept. Root's call to "rally round the flag, boys" also exemplifies a nineteenth-century usage that hampers some students' ability to decode Cary's poem: the use of "boy" as a friendly form of address among adult males of equal status. Students have often heard that African American men were called "boy" by white men as a way of enforcing their subordinate status and, as a result, may have difficulty determining the race or age of the speakers in Cary's poem. Directing their attention to the composition date of "Battle Cry," which suggests that it, like "Song for Our Soldiers," was composed with white soldiers in mind, helps clear up this misunderstanding.[4]

Contemporary prose texts exemplifying the debate over African Americans' participation in the war also provide cultural context. Both the Library of Congress and the National Archives (*Teaching*) have extensive holdings tracing the history of the United States Colored Troops and often set digitized key texts in online exhibits and lesson plans. The digitized Frederick Douglass Papers at the Library of Congress is an especially rich resource; speeches such as "Men of Color, to Arms!" and "Why a Colored Man Should Enlist" reflect both Douglass's support for enlistment and his awareness that black men had good reason to be ambivalent about volunteering after two years of opposition to their participation. Harriet Jacobs's letters from Union-occupied Alexandria, Virginia, collected in Jean Fagan Yellin's *Harriet Jacobs Family Papers*, reveal a mixture of frustration at the delay in accepting African American volunteers, pride in their eventual achievements, and anger at the government's failure to treat them as equals to white soldiers in matters of pay, medical care, and eligibility for promotion to the rank of officer. Jacobs's 1 August 1864 speech at the presentation of a flag donated to L'Ouverture Hospital, with its description of the significance of African American soldiers' contributions to the war and its honor roll of the battles in which they valiantly fought and died—Fort Wagner, Fort Pillow, Plymouth—pairs particularly well with "Be Joyful!" and "The Black Regiment," which contain similar lists with similar function.[5]

Images can also play a role in an extended discussion. The classic "Am I Not a Man and Brother?" antislavery emblem and its female counterpart provide visual analogues for the white-initiated emancipation scenario in "Song for Our Soldiers," as do numerous representations of a standing Lincoln as the Great Emancipator juxtaposed with a kneeling or crouching former slave.[6] Kirk Savage reproduces and analyzes depictions of former slaves that suggest varying degrees of self-determination, including John Quincy Adams Ward's 1863 *Freedman* (53), Edmonia Lewis's 1868 *Forever Free* (63), and Randolph Rogers's 1870 *Emancipation* (86), and Celeste-Marie Bernier reproduces a woodcut depicting an armed Harriet Tubman in her role as a Union scout and discusses its significance (319–29). Kate Masur discusses images of contrabands, often depicted as unruly and in need of discipline, and also reproduces and analyzes a series of three paintings by Thomas Waterman Wood, later published as woodcuts in *Harper's Weekly*, tracing a black man's progression from contraband to soldier to disabled veteran ("'Rare Phenomenon'" 1077–78). Louis Kurz and Alexander Allison's 1890 print *Storming Fort Wagner*, which hangs in the hallway of Cedar Hill, Frederick Douglass's home in Washington, DC, suggests continuing cultural recognition of African American soldiers' contributions to the Civil War, as does Augustus Saint-Gaudens's 1897 memorialization of Robert Gould Shaw and the Massachusetts Fifty-Fourth. Ed Hamilton's 1998 sculpture *The Spirit of Freedom*, the centerpiece of the African American Civil War Memorial in Washington, DC, is a late-twentieth-century example of this still-evolving genre. Once students have become aware of the significance of such images, they may be able to discover additional examples in their immediate environment, especially if they live in the northeastern United States or in parts of the western United States settled before the Civil War.

Boker's "The Black Regiment" engages some of the same historical and thematic issues as "Song for Our Soldiers" and "Be Joyful!" while also providing opportunities for guiding students through more complex analysis of poetic form and literary language. Boker faces two challenges in lauding the bravery of African American troops: devising appropriate imagery to praise a regiment made up of dark-skinned soldiers in a culture that associates light with good and darkness with evil and picturing a disciplined grouping of black men for an audience more accustomed to comic depictions of lazy or pranksterish African Americans. For the most part, Boker succeeds in making countercultural associations by linking blackness and military order through the evocation of a gathering thunderstorm's power in stanza 1. The regiment's glittering polished weapons also ally its darkness with a complementary image of light: by 1863, lightning had become a cliché of wartime poetry.[7] In "The Black Regiment," as in Julia Ward Howe's "Battle Hymn of the Republic"—a text with which most American students are familiar—thunderstorm imagery allows the poet to suggest that the army is an agent of God's will. The suggestion is reinforced in stanza 4, where the "bondmen" (32) "driv[e] their lords like chaff" (37), invoking oft-repeated biblical imagery of God as a thresher separating the wheat (the saved) from the chaff (the damned)—for example, Psalms 1.4, Isaiah 5.24, Matthew 3.12.

At the same time, "The Black Regiment" occasionally employs images that seem perilously similar to those in comic, condescending depictions of African Americans in minstrel shows and cartoons. The lines "Down the long dusky line / Teeth gleam and eyeballs shine" (11, 12) in particular highlight features that served as key racial markers in nineteenth-century dramatic and visual representations. Students may or may not notice the stereotypical imagery in the poem and, if they do, may be reluctant to mention it. Political cartoons and other images exemplifying comic and more respectful depictions of African Americans, such as the images referenced and reproduced by Masur, can provide a frame of reference for examining possible tensions between the explicit message and what the imagery in the poem implies. In particular, students can be asked to reflect on whether the connections Boker creates between bright objects associated with racial stereotypes (teeth, eyeballs) and those associated with military might (bayonets, lightning bolts) are sufficient to support a new, heroic image of African Americans, or whether the stereotypical elements of the poem at least partly undermine its liberatory intent.[8]

Such reflections can be further enriched by consideration of Boker's 1862 "The Sword-Bearer," which exhibits an even more intriguing combination of condescension and admiration in its portrayal of a "little Negro" "page" (lines 13, 31) who rescues the sword of his "master" (15), George Upham Morris, a naval officer, from the wreck of the *Cumberland*.[9] "The Sword-Bearer" employs a shifting narrative voice. The beginning of the story is told from a distanced, apparently omniscient, perspective similar to that of "The Black Regiment," whereas in the closing scenes the narrator is revealed to be a participant-observer, a member of the crew inclined at ordinary times to see the servant's air of "pomp and curious pride" (25) as reason for laughter but compelled by circumstances to regard "the faithful negro lad" (43) in a more serious light. Even with this laudatory ending, some early verses in the poem—especially a reference to the sword-bearer's "sluggish brain" and dim understanding of the connection between the war and the fate of "his trampled race" (17–20)—coupled with the narrative's emphasis on the servant's determination to follow his master's orders (rather than on his loyalty to country or his determination to be free), seem to reinforce the idea of African Americans as a subordinate, dependent race, even as they also suggest the possession of qualities associated with good soldiers: loyalty, courage, willingness to follow orders to the death. Based on the evidence of these two poems, one could support several different arguments about Boker's attitude toward African Americans as soldiers: an evolution in thinking about their fitness for combat that in some ways parallels the national conversation (and the understanding of the sailor-narrator of "The Sword-Bearer"), a continuing tendency to invoke racial stereotypes that undermine the explicit intent of his poems, or, quite possibly, both.[10]

Tennyson's "The Charge of the Light Brigade," which encodes the European-derived cultural norms of order, bravery, and obedience by which Boker and many of his contemporaries judged African American soldiers, can provide additional context for discussion of Boker's poetry and its messages about African Americans' role in the war. As several critics have noted, "The Black Regiment" explicitly echoes Tennyson's enormously popular poem—frequently reprinted, reworked, and parodied in the United States during the Civil War years—in meter, imagery, and other poetic devices (e.g., Hack 211; Boker, "The Second Louisiana" n2). Such echoes support Boker's attempt to extend the respect for the English brigade embodied and reinforced by "The Charge of the Light Brigade" to an African American regiment that made a similarly deadly charge at Port Hudson. The middle of "The Black Regiment" effectively uses devices similar to those employed by Tennyson to portray both the determination of the former slaves to prove themselves worthy of their freedom and their bravery in battle. At the same time, Boker's final stanza, which, like Tennyson's, continues and concludes a pattern of repetition with variations, implicitly acknowledges the differences in the two units' situations in a way that students generally find easy to understand and sometimes even discover for themselves when asked to look for similarities and differences in the endings of the poems. Where Tennyson simply adjures his listeners to "honor the Light Brigade," a request with which he can confidently expect them to comply, Boker's admonitions to his audience, and especially to the white Union soldiers among them, acknowledge the possibility of continued prejudice even as he inveighs against it:

> O, to the living few,
> Soldiers, be just and true!
> Hail them as comrades tried;
> Fight with them side by side;
> Never in field or tent,
> Scorn the black regiment! (Lorang and Weir, lines 70–75)

Here the established rhythmic pattern of the poem works both with and against Boker's stated purpose, stressing the "never" in the penultimate line but also emphasizing the already strong "scorn," with its explosive initial consonants and snarling r. Even the earlier imperative "be just and true" suggests the possibility of its opposite. As the poem closes, the possibility of rejection hangs in the air despite the bravery and sacrifice dramatized in the earlier lines. Like Clark's "Be Joyful!," "The Black Regiment" must acknowledge that freedom and racial equality are works in progress, the outcome still uncertain.

Even a brief study of Civil War–era occasional poetry depicting African American soldiers will complicate students' understandings of the role of race in Civil War narratives of slavery and freedom. Since the poems are relatively obscure, they offer occasions for students to perform their own analysis with limited temptation or opportunity to look up "correct" interpretations in existing criticism. Thanks to the ongoing digitization of nineteenth-century periodicals and the appearance of related digital collections such as Elizabeth Lorang and R. J. Weir's, students can locate and analyze additional examples of the genre, thus expanding the body of evidence illustrating how Americans understood and sought to shape one another's understandings of the significance of race in the war. In addition to increasing students' understanding of nineteenth-century texts and their cultural contexts, such study can help students see twentieth- and twenty-first-century cultural productions, from movies such as *Glory* and *Lincoln* to poems such as Robert Lowell's "For the Union Dead" and Natasha Trethewey's "Native Guard," as part of an ongoing process of telling and retelling a story that remains open to multiple, sometimes conflicting, interpretations.

Notes

1. The earliest printing of "Song for Our Soldiers" I have found is in volume 5 of Frank Moore's *Rebellion Record*, which covers 1862. Given both Cary's and Moore's usual practice, an initial periodical appearance seems likely. Moore's placement of the poem suggests a date of July or August 1862—during debates over recruitment of African American soldiers reflected elsewhere in the volume but before the authorization of widespread recruiting in early 1863. For biographical information on Cary, see Fetterley and Pryse.

2. "Be Joyful!" appeared in the *Anglo-African* on 2 April 1864 and was later revised for Clark's collection *The Past, Present, and Future: In Prose and Poetry* (1867). There may be some biobibliographical confusion between "B. C. Clark, Sen." of York, Pennsylvania, author of *The Past, Present, and Future*, and B. C. Clark of Boston, Massachusetts, author of *A Plea for Hayti* (1853). Leslie Alexander identifies the latter, whose motives are avowedly more economic than ideological, as "Boston shipping tycoon Benjamin Cutler Clark" (70). *Literature Online* and several online poetry collections also assign the middle name Cutler to the author of *The Past, Present, and Future*. Whether or not this is correct, Clark of Pennsylvania has a distinct, less privileged voice. He identifies himself as the largely self-educated child of emancipated slaves (*Past* 7); Lorang and Weir, in a

biographical note grounded in primary research ("Be Joyful!" n1), add that he was a dyer, born in Maryland, who raised a large family in Pennsylvania and periodically published poems in African American newspapers.

3. "The Black Regiment" was written in response to an attack on Port Hudson on 27 May 1863 and first appeared under the title "The Second Louisiana" (based, Lorang and Weir suggest, on inaccurate early reports). Lorang and Weir record the poem's appearance in the *Christian Recorder* of 13 June 1863, followed quickly by reprintings in several other papers. Barrett and Miller record that it was also published by the Supervisory Committee for Recruiting Colored Regiments (112), but the publication date they provide—the date of the battle itself—seems unlikely. For biographical information about Boker, see Boker, "The Second Louisiana" n3; Barrett and Miller 377–78.

4. For more on "Battle Cry," see McWhirter, *Battle Hymns* or "Birth."

5. Yellin, *Harriet Jacobs Family Papers* 577–83 (pt. 8, doc. 21). For additional references by Jacobs to African American soldiers, see 468–72 (pt. 7, doc. 15), 519–20 (pt. 8, doc. 2), 558–64 (doc. 17), 609–11 (doc. 29), and 617–21 (doc. 33).

6. The antislavery emblems are pictured in Yellin, *Women* 4, 6; for Great Emancipator images, see Savage, chs. 3 and 4.

7. McWhirter reprints an 1862 satirical poem entitled "A Hint to Poets: Showing How to Make a War Song," which includes the line "God's lightning rifts the battle's gloom" and ends with embodied Truth hurling lightning followed by the words "And that will do—for all is done / When once the lightning's safely hurled" (*Battle Hymns* 32–33).

8. This problem persisted throughout the war. See a Chicago *Tribune* discussion of black soldiers' entry in Richmond quoted by Fincher (60).

9. "The Sword-Bearer" can in turn be compared with Backus's more straightforwardly admiring account in "The Black Hero of the Cumberland." Given the conventional relationship between captain and servant and the common issues of perception, expectation, and narrative perspective, "The Sword-Bearer" would also pair well with Melville's "Benito Cereno."

10. Boker's "Hymn of the Contrabands," similar in form to "Song for our Soldiers" and "Be Joyful!," provides an additional example of his depiction of black soldiers.

Jessica DeSpain

Women's Roles in Antislavery
and Civil War Literature

On 2 December 1863, approximately one year after the Emancipation
Proclamation went into effect, the nation celebrated the completion of
the Capitol's renovations by hoisting the *Statue of Freedom* onto a recently
completed iron dome. The event was accompanied by a thirty-five-gun
salute—one gun for each state in the Union then divided by civil war.
Standing atop an orbic pedestal representing the globe, sword in hand,
wearing a war helmet plumed with eagle feathers, Thomas Crawford's
Statue of Freedom used the female form as an emblem of the United States
government's plans for an imperialist future. It has long been a source
of fascination, as both object and symbol. In Louisa May Alcott's *Hospital Sketches*, her loosely autobiographical account of her time as a Civil
War nurse, the protagonist, Nurse Tribulation Periwinkle, goes to visit the
Capitol grounds and the *Statue of Freedom* one year before its placement
atop the dome, calling it the "statue of Liberty." Instead of noting the
statue's militant garb, Alcott describes *Freedom* as a proud mother who
rises above the mud and uncertainty of war to nurture a new equality:

> The statue of Liberty I recognized at once, for it had no pedestal as
> yet, but stood flat in the mud, with Young America most symbolically

making dirt pies, and chip forts, in its shadow. But high above the squabbling little throng and their petty plans, the sun shone full on Liberty's broad forehead, and, in her hand, some summer bird had built its nest. I accepted the good omen then, and on the first of January, the Emancipation Act gave the statue a nobler and more enduring pedestal than any marble or granite ever carved and quarried by human hands. ([ed. Fahs] 101)

Alcott's representation was one among a plethora of writings—including poems, essays, and articles—that referenced the statue as an iconic symbol that epitomized the authors' hopes and fears for the nation's future. Southern sympathizers, Unionists, and abolitionists easily bent the meaning of the statue for their own political purposes—everyone had a stake in *Freedom*.

I use the *Statue of Freedom* and the myriad literary works it inspired to engage students in a conversation about the evolution of gender identity leading up to and during the Civil War. In her work on feminized representations of the war, Alice Fahs indicates that literature during the period "was highly typological, tending to represent characters through a constellation of well-established conventions of portrayal" (*Imagined Civil War* 14). Women, especially mothers, were frequently described as objects of sentimentalized patriotism that "personalized the nation both north and south, [and] acted as connecting links between the private and the public realm" (122–23). Real women capitalized on this rhetoric to justify radical actions, including escaping from slavery, distributing petitions, and assuming professions as typesetters, nurses, and spies. This essay provides pedagogical methods for examining icons of womanhood alongside accounts of the lives and labors of actual women to consider how these women adapted and disrupted the typologies that Fahs identifies.

I use the *Statue of Freedom* as a touchstone in a 200-level topics course on American literature to 1865 that has a mix of beginning English majors and second-year students seeking to fulfill general education credits. (The series of readings and activities that I discuss can also be easily extended and adapted for a 400-level seminar on the American Civil War.) It is important in this class to anchor students' readings in a vibrant historical context that disrupts their tendency to make abstract textual analyses. Students are drawn to progress narratives that simplify the complexity of lived experience and lively political debate; this problem of simplification is particularly acute where discussions of gender are concerned. Because students often assume that women had little to no role in either the conflicts leading up to the war or the day-to-day actions of battle, the Civil War provides an opportunity for helping them develop a more historically grounded reading practice.

For the final unit of this topics course, I've selected excerpts from periodicals, popular fiction, transatlantic reprints, and newspaper accounts to show students how depictions of women's work were vital to both the war itself and the culture surrounding it. In addition to Alcott's *Hospital Sketches*, students read selections from the poems of Frances Ellen Watkins Harper, Harriet Beecher Stowe's *Uncle Tom's Cabin* (1852), Fanny Kemble's *Journal of a Residence on a Georgian Plantation in 1838–1839* (1863), Harriet Jacobs's *Incidents in the Life of a Slave Girl* (1861), Mary Boykin Miller Chesnut's *A Diary from Dixie* (1905), Sojourner Truth's speeches, and Wesley Bradshaw's *General Sherman's Indian Spy* (1865). When students put in a historical context accounts of women as slaves, domestics, reformers, war knitters, cross-dressing soldiers, and nurses, they begin to understand the complicated circles of influence in which women maneuvered during the nineteenth century.

The *Statue of Freedom* provides an entrée into these conversations because it epitomizes the usage of women's bodies and motherhood as symbols for national unity. For the first day of this final unit, students read *Hospital Sketches*, and I lead a hybrid lecture-discussion about the history of women as icons of the nation-state, the other works of art in the Capitol building, and the *Statue of Freedom*. The United States government's *Architect of the Capitol* Web site provides extensive background on the statue's construction and images of all three of Crawford's prototypes, as well as images of other Capitol artwork. I begin by showing an image of the completed *Statue of Freedom* and asking students to share their observations about its design. They often note that the Native American influences of the statue's headdress clash conspicuously with her flowing Roman robes. I then show them Samuel Jennings's painting *Liberty Displaying the Arts and Sciences* (1792), housed at the Library Company of Philadelphia and freely available online. In Jennings's painting Liberty is not a symbol of war but an abolitionist mother offering education to the grateful, supplicant freed slaves at her feet—a disturbing depiction of republican motherhood at work. This unit comes at the end of a course in which we discuss both gender and slavery from the early national period through the Civil War, with selections from Hannah Webster Foster's *The Coquette*, Catharine Maria Sedgwick's *Hope Leslie*, and James Fenimore Cooper's *The Last of the Mohicans*. Bringing in Jennings's painting allows us to contextualize the *Statue of Freedom* in the longer historical trajectory of the course.

After examining earlier representations of Liberty, we consider the Capitol's other artworks alongside Nurse Periwinkle's descriptions from *Hospital Sketches,* including the paintings *The Embarkation of the Pilgrims, The Baptism of Pocahontas,* and *Westward the Course of Empire Takes Its Way.* In contradistinction to the Capitol's warring maidens, Alcott imagines real women epitomized by the objects of their domestic labor, save for a few avid equestrians, artists, and writers:

> [W]hich was America and which Pocahontas was a mystery; for all affected much looseness of costume, dishevelment of hair, swords, arrows, lances, scales, and other ornaments quite *passé* with damsels of our day, whose effigies should go down to posterity armed with fans, crochet needles, riding whips, and parasols, with here and there one holding pen or pencil, rolling-pin or broom. ([ed. Fahs] 101)

I ask students to compare these iconic implements with Tribulation Periwinkle's labor. The nurse is torn between representing herself as a soldier on the battlefront or as a sentimental mother tending to the dying soldiers in Hurly-Burly House. Alcott's own debilitating illness as a result of exposure to disease and overwork in Washington suggests that performing the role of either womanly icon was too exhausting for her to sustain.

We then return to our examination of the statue, and I tell students about its history. *Freedom*'s story was a performance of compromise and political pandering that resulted in a confused set of symbolic referents that were irrevocably inflected by cultural conceptions of slavery and bodily ownership. Crawford initially imagined a rounded form in femininely draped robes with a crown of laurel and wheat. His earliest model held a sword in one hand, but in her other arm she cradled an olive branch representing peace. She stood on a simple pedestal surround by wreaths, suggesting a greater concern with sustaining the nation than with expanding an empire.[1] Two weeks later Crawford sent the project's director a photograph of a revised model. Crawford kept a sword and shield but removed the olive branch and therefore all representations of peace. He also added the globe as *Freedom*'s feet, asserting the nation's expansionist mission. His most radical decision, however, was to have *Freedom* don a liberty cap (the cap, also called a pileus, was worn by freed slaves in Rome to hide their shorn heads [Fryd, *Art* 185]). In earlier paintings, including Jennings's *Liberty Displaying the Arts and Sciences,* Liberty holds a pole with the liberty cap hanging on it; she is a proponent of liberty but does not herself need liberation.

When Jefferson Davis, then serving as secretary of war, saw Crawford's revision, he objected to the cap on the grounds that "its history renders it inappropriate to a people who were born free and would not be enslaved." Davis suggested that Liberty instead wear a helmet to indicate that "her conflict [is] over, her cause triumphant" (qtd. in Fryd, *Art* 193). In 1856, conflict was nowhere near over, but to appease Davis, Crawford realized he must avoid any allusion to slavery; he completed his final revision, giving the statue a helmet with an eagle's head and feathers reminiscent of a Native American headdress. Nevertheless, incidents surrounding the casting of the statue linked it directly with slavery. When the craftsman hired to oversee the work struck for higher wages, the government hired a slave named Philip Reid at $1.25 a day to finish the work (as a slave he was allowed to keep only the money he earned on Sundays).[2] Reid oversaw both the casting of the statue and its ascension to the dome. The finished piece was an amalgamation of America, Minerva, Pocahontas, and Liberty, suggesting imperial expansion, freedom at home, success in the arts and sciences, the suppression and extinction of Native American tribes, America as a civilizing force, and the country's irrepressible hunger for war—a great deal of symbolic freight for one woman's body to carry. The long story of *Freedom*'s design and construction shows students how women were used as a site for national debate and compromise concerning freedom and its entitlements. This lecture is followed by a class discussion of the statue, and students now pick up on the many amalgamations and contradictions at play in the design.

In the next class, I share quotations and images from Civil War–era periodicals that feature nurses, cross-dressing spies, women knitting for the war effort, and women departing from sons and lovers. We have less access to periodical databases at my university, so I collect resources in advance, but in a 400-level course students might be asked to hunt for their own examples of women's labor to share with the group. This activity complicates the categorization of women during the Civil War in descriptions of the statue.

I then put students in groups to consider one of the many periodical pieces from the period that address the statue's symbolism directly. Each group analyzes its periodical piece by looking for examples of how the statue was repurposed for political ends. The statue proved explosive during the time leading up to and succeeding the war. In popular periodicals, abolitionists attempted to claim *Freedom* as an omen of emancipation. Lincoln looked on the completion of the Capitol's renovation and the ceremony marking the statue's placement as a vindication of the Union's future. In southern-sympathizing publications, the statue represented northern oppression and its colonizing impulses. The student groups present their findings, and we use their reports to map how the statue was used to justify or represent an array of political positions.

As we move on to more extensive literary texts, we continue to identify gender typologies while searching for scenes that complicate them. In a minilecture, I introduce students to the criticism of Amy Kaplan, who explores the rhetorical sleight of hand that women reformers used to widen their influence and test their cultural limitations. In feminist criticism, the word *domestic* implies the private space of the home, but as Kaplan points out, the opposite of *domestic* is *foreign*. Such wordplay would have been useful for women who wanted to expand their influence beyond the parlor by framing themselves as the mothers not just of their own children but also of the nation on an international stage. Kaplan calls this strategy "manifest domesticity" ("Manifest Domesticity" 187).[3]

We discuss Kaplan's theory alongside scenes from the St. Clare's plantation in *Uncle Tom's Cabin*. Marie, the idle, vengeful plantation mistress; Little Eva, the idyllic child; Ophelia, the female philanthropist; Rosa, the tragic mulatta; and Dinah, the mammy, are illustrative of the positioning of gender roles in a complex social pattern. As students read, I ask them to draw a diagram that charts the interdependencies and hierarchies among these female characters. Students share their work during class discussion, and we develop a classwide model on the board. They are quick to note the types of women in Stowe's novel, but during our conversation I encourage them to see how the particularities of women's lives have resulted in the construction of those identities. We discuss, for example, how Marie's personality as a plantation mistress relies on Dinah's role as ideal mammy, but the general inefficacies of this plantation belie the fictions of southern gender identity as natural or ordained. I ask students to return to their diagram to explore how other icons of femininity interlock with one another and how the characters in Stowe's novel manipulate the social order through these interdependencies. The description of Dinah's kitchen is rife with examples.

During the next week, we see how these conscribed gender types are complicated in women's own accounts. We read poems and novels in which women struggle to articulate how their labor relates to the war. In

Lucy Larcom's poem "Weaving," the working-class speaker laments her role in the perpetuation of slavery while she works at her loom. We also read the variant versions of Sojourner Truth's speech delivered in 1851 at the Women's Convention in Akron, Ohio. Truth's words tie her identity directly to her labor, but the different versions of the speech indicate that editors wanted to frame her identity according to their own definitions of African American womanhood.

We then read selections from Kemble's *Journal of a Residence of a Georgian Plantation in 1838–1839*, a text that offers a transatlantic glimpse into the relation between slavery and white femininity. Kemble was a British actress who married a wealthy plantation owner during her American tour. Her indemnifying account of his plantation was not published until after the passage of the Emancipation Proclamation, when she felt impelled to encourage British support for the Union. At its best, her writing invokes the intricate linkages among institutionalized forms of gender, class, and racial oppression. At its worst, she casts herself as a heroine marooned on an uncivilized island who must endure the stupidity and uncleanliness of those around her. An actress, Kemble made a living through mimicry. She extends these skills to the page, creating her own stage out of the plantation and performing the roles of plantation mistress and manifest domestic to demonstrate their limitations for female empowerment. Her journal was excerpted and reprinted as a political pamphlet by the Ladies' London Emancipation Society (the publication was typeset by a team of female compositors at London's Victoria Press) and another pamphlet by the Union League of Philadelphia (a highly influential pro-Union gentleman's organization). We examine these pamphlets as a further illustration of how women's narratives were refigured for different political ends. The Ladies' London Emancipation Society pamphlet provides students with an example of how women's labor in Britain became metaphorically linked to slave labor in the United States. The Union League of Philadelphia pamphlet reprinted the famous silver albumen print of Private Gordon, a slave who escaped from his master and crossed enemy lines to join the Union army. The Union League pamphlet used Gordon's scarred back to illustrate Kemble's descriptions of plantation life for those in the North who refused to acknowledge the horrors of slavery.

Students read Kemble alongside excerpts from Chesnut's *A Diary from Dixie*, a firsthand account of a woman's life in the South during the war. Although there were women of all classes and occupations in the South, the plantation mistress became synonymous with the region. In

Tara Revisited, Catherine Clinton explains that the image of the pampered southern woman was essential to the region's identity: "Lush, conspicuous splendor was meant to hide the wrenching work necessary to maintain grandiose estates" (27). Chesnut presents students with an elite southern woman who defies expectations: she is mobile, politically active, and frequently torn in her allegiances, particularly in regard to the treatment of women as a result of slavery.

These selections pair well with Jacobs's *Incidents in the Life of a Slave Girl* and Harper's poem "An Appeal to My Countrywomen." Both African American authors reframe domestic tropes to argue for a slave's womanhood and right to freedom. Jacobs rejects the outcome of the tragic mulatta by outsmarting the sexual advances of her master, Dr. Flint, and she positions her grandmother not as a mammy but as an example of true womanhood. Both her narrative and Harper's poem demonstrate how African American writers found ways to recalibrate domestic femininity in order to influence nineteenth-century audiences.

Students finish the unit by reading Bradshaw's *General Sherman's Indian Spy,* an example of the ubiquitous dime novels produced during the war depicting a gender-bending woman who takes on the role of a spy or soldier. Wenonah, an Indian maiden who aids General Sherman in his march from Atlanta to Raleigh, may be the closest literary correlation to Crawford's design for the *Statue of Freedom.* The novel's frontispiece portrays her in similarly draped clothing with feathers in her hair and an eagle on the horizon. Because of her ambiguous sexuality and nationality, Wenonah has the ability to transcend the limits of race, class, and gender. Yet Wenonah, like the remnants of Native culture gracing Crawford's statue, becomes merely the exoticized other when she dies at the novel's end.

We return to the statue in our final class to discuss its contemporary importance. In 1993, Crawford's statue was placed in front of the Capitol's east facade for restoration. On the day that it was reinstalled, Rita Dove recited a commemorative poem "Lady Freedom among Us," which Janus Press later produced as a pop-up artist's book.[4] We listen to Dove, reading her poem, describe the statue as a bag lady with "oldfashioned sandals," "leaden skirts," "whiskers and heaped up trinkets" whom tourists try to avoid by "low[ering] their eyes and [cross]ing the street." Dove warns us not to pass by *Freedom:*

> don't think you can ever forget her
> don't even try
> she's not going to budge

no choice but to grant her space
crown her with sky
for she is one of the many
and she is each of us

Over a century after the statue's first commemorative installation, Dove's poem forces us to confront the full weight of history in the form of the *Statue of Freedom*. The poet values the statue's ability to withstand the climate of Washington: its pollution, its poverty, and its politics. On its high pedestal, this statue, so indicative of the war's central conflicts, including slavery, westward expansion, and women's rights, is easy to ignore. Ending the course with Dove's poem asks students to consider how we stand in relation to these weighty symbols of the past and in what ways they are still reclaimable for a national future.

Notes

1. For more on Crawford's changes to the statue, see Fryd, "Political Compromise." To learn more about how the statue worked in the larger context of the Capitol's renovations, see Wolanin; Gale; Hönnighausen; and Bruns.

2. More information about Reid, including a scan of his pay stub, can be found on the *Architect of the Capitol* Web site.

3. Kaplan's book *The Anarchy of Empire in the Making of U.S. Culture* provides a more extensive explanation of "manifest domesticity."

4. The University of Virginia developed a digital apparatus for interacting with the Janus text, available at www.lib.virginia.edu/etext/fourmill/DovLady.html.

Elizabeth Duquette

"Treasonable Sympathies": Affect and Allegiance in the Civil War

Abraham Lincoln's famous remark to Harriet Beecher Stowe—"So this is the little lady who made this big war"—may be apocryphal, but that certainly does not diminish the importance of Stowe's work for teaching the literature of the American Civil War (E. Wilson 3). Throughout *Uncle Tom's Cabin* (1852), Stowe demonstrates the many evils of slavery, appending to the end of the story a set of precepts to guide readers in their own antislavery efforts:

> There is one thing that every individual can do, they can see to it that *they feel right*. An atmosphere of sympathetic influence encircles every human being; and the man or woman who *feels* strongly, healthily, and justly on the great interests of humanity, is a constant benefactor to the human race. See, then, to your sympathies in this matter! (411)

According to Stowe, cultivating proper affects and directing them to worthy recipients could be both morally valuable and politically potent. In this belief she was not alone, for countless antebellum novels, sermons, and tracts argued that sympathy offered an important means of extending aid and comfort to sufferers, while also providing the basis for moral society and a form of political engagement (see Barnes; Stern, *Plight*).

Scholars have carefully documented the importance of sympathy—the ability to feel with or for others—across the antebellum period, detailing its central role in American literature and culture. But most studies of sympathy end before the start of the Civil War, and, as a result, the role of emotion in literature written during (and after) the conflict has been comparatively ignored. This is an unfortunate oversight for two key reasons. First, charting the status and shifting value of affect establishes important and often overlooked connections between ante- and postbellum literary traditions and practices. Second, conflicts between different kinds of affective bonds—family, region, state, and nation—are crucial to the discourse of allegiance and national belonging throughout the Civil War era. This second concern can be expressed pithily by recalling Stowe's phrase: what did it mean to "*feel right*" during the Civil War? At the beginning of the term, I pose this question to my students, and we return to it frequently as we move through the semester. The aim is to help students develop a greater understanding of the cultural construction of emotion, particularly its role in the ties we establish with people, groups, and nations.

The issue of sympathy's role during the Civil War is particularly important because it concerns as well the definition of national affiliation and sentiment. Misled by popular narratives, students often assume that allegiances were already determined at the start of hostilities in 1861, but the historical record reveals a more complicated picture. Virginia split, literally, over the question of allegiance, and Tennessee nearly followed; Maryland remained in the Union because of Lincoln's decisive action; and Kentucky, although a slave state, was neutral at the outset of the war and eventually petitioned the Union for protection. Poems like James R. Randall's "Maryland, My Maryland" (1861) and M. Jeff Thompson's "Price's Appeal to Missouri" (1861) can expose students to these complexities, letting them productively grapple with what Herman Melville would dub "the conflict of convictions" in a poem about the war's early months (*Battle-Pieces* [2001] 54–56). Also obscured by the standard division of North and South is the importance of the West during the conflict, a point that Richard Henry Stoddard addresses in an 1861 poem:

Men of the North and West
Wake in your might,

> Prepare, as the Rebels have done,
> For the fight;
> You cannot shrink from the test,
> Rise! Men of the North and West! (Barrett 47)

Like Randall and Thompson, Stoddard sets out to inspire strong emotions and, through them, secure allegiance and inspire action.

Although the issue is addressed in many different forums, the most direct treatment of the challenges associated with political sentiment may well be Nathaniel Hawthorne's July 1862 essay "Chiefly about War-Matters." Unpacking Hawthorne's nuanced reading of allegiance and sympathy can be revealing for students, who often overlook the affective complications associated with civil war. Describing a visit to Washington, DC, Hawthorne wonders "what proportion" of the people he meets, "soldiers or civilians, were true at heart to the Union, and what part were tainted, more or less, with treasonable sympathies and wishes" (61). Should we consider sentiments that never "blosso[m] into purpose" treasonous? Hawthorne reluctantly concludes that we must, a point on which I urge my students to pause. Would they want their thoughts or feelings on which they do not act to be judged? What does such a view imply about the connection between thought and action? Returning to the essay, we ponder the possibility that time and circumstance may have "converted" "honest people" into "traitors" (48):

> In the vast extent of our country,—too vast by far to be taken into one small human heart,—we inevitably limit to our own State, or, at farthest, to our own section, that sentiment of physical love for the soil. . . . If a man loves his own State, therefore, and is content to be ruined with her, let us shoot him, if we can, but allow him an honorable burial in the soil he fights for. (48–49)

It is reasonable for an honorable person to love his own state best, Hawthorne notes, and, given the "vast extent of our country," likely inevitable as well. If the state comes "nearest home to a man's feelings, and includes the altar and the heart," how can the national government compete? It "claims [a man's] devotion" but has little to secure allegiance beyond an "airy mode of law," lacking any "symbol" beyond the "flag" (48). According to Hawthorne, when claims on a person's allegiance conflict, it is easy enough to see why some might choose what is nearest to the heart, even if that counts as treason. What, I ask students, are the different claims on your allegiance? How do you determine which is most important? Were your home state to secede, would you support it? Hawthorne argues that during the Civil War "crowds of honest people" turned traitor "seem to themselves not merely innocent, but patriotic," dying "for a bad cause with as quiet a conscience as if it were the best." Would the reason (a good or bad cause) for secession matter to you, I continue, or would you follow your heart? In my experience, even those students who think the choice is obvious find this question difficult, and that difficulty gives them a new appreciation for the affective complexities of the Civil War. They read Hawthorne's conclusion—"thousands of warm-hearted, sympathetic, and impulsive persons . . . joined the Rebels, not from any real zeal for the cause, but because, between two conflicting loyalties, they chose that which necessarily lay nearest the heart"—with a new understanding of the political power and effects of emotion.

According to Hawthorne, "There never existed any other Government against which treason was so easy, and could defend itself by such plausible arguments as that of the United States" (48). Reading "Chiefly about War-Matters" alongside the definition of *treason* from the Constitution provides important contextual information for Hawthorne's assertion and additional ways for students to appreciate how feelings and politics merge. Article 3 specifies that "Treason against the United States shall consist only in levying War against them, or in adhering to their Enemies, giving them Aid and Comfort." Pausing on the possible meanings of "Aid and Comfort," particularly in the context of arguments like the one Stowe makes in *Uncle Tom's Cabin*, allows students to delve more deeply into Hawthorne's assertions. Is it reasonable to think that one might comfort an enemy by feeling for the enemy? Or that feeling for the enemy might put the nation in danger? "Chiefly about War-Matters" brings to the fore the rapid change in the cultural meaning of sympathy during the Civil War era. Sympathy's dangers derived directly from its former value—the ability to reveal the similarity between seemingly disparate persons and situations—now inappropriate politically and indicative of questionable judgment. Put differently, the "treasonable sympathies" that Hawthorne worries about were, for most people in the Union, a source of concern precisely because sympathy had been understood, merely a few years before, to be a powerful kind of political action. I cement these ideas for students by asking them to find a cartoon or poem about allegiance from the Civil War (*Harper's Weekly* is an excellent resource) and write a short response paper that details the representation of sympathy it offers.

The Civil War forced Americans in both the United States and the Confederate States of America to evaluate basic assumptions about what could or should unite individuals and join them as a people. Writers on each side attempted to explain what differentiated their nation and cause, seeking to define the specific basis of attachment that would motivate the sacrifices necessary for civil war. Here too emotion in general, and sympathy in particular, played a critical role. Union partisans were often suspicious of unruly emotions, regularly arguing that they were responsible for southern rebellion. In a characteristic poem, Oliver Wendell Holmes writes that "rash" South Carolina "has left us in passion and pride," underscoring the uncontrolled emotions of southern partisans (Barrett 54). In particularizing the bond to the Union, then, writers in the North rejected sympathy's uncertain attachments for a more abstract and thus more reliable definition of allegiance. Loyalty, they argued, was the better way to understand one's relation to the nation, because, as James Russell Lowell explained, loyalty had "its seat in the brain and not the blood" (213). Loyalty relied on the importance of right thinking, not right feeling, in the development of national and personal ties. Rather than an intimate attachment to home or hearth, loyal citizens celebrated the principles on which the Union was founded, even if some, like Hawthorne, complained they were too airy to inspire sacrifice and devotion ("Chiefly").

For Confederate supporters, the stakes were higher, as theirs was the new nation, but they had strong regional sentiments on which to build. Casting the North in the role of invaders and tyrants, comparing the Union to England, and arguing that their actions aligned them with the colonial patriots of 1776 were common strategies of Confederate nationalist rhetoric. In "The Stars and Bars" (1862), for example, the poet excoriates the Union flag, "once so prized" but "now so despised" as the "badge of tyranny and wrong," claiming that it is "[f]or home and altars" that the South "contend[s]," defending both against "violence" and "[w]asting, destruction" (Barrett 83–84).[1] Indeed, as the poem makes clear, where writers in the North tended to worry about indiscriminate emotionalism, southern partisans often sought to rouse the passions, adapting techniques associated with antebellum sympathy, to defend their nation and its actions.

Allegiance could be performed in many ways, and citizens in both nations were encouraged to make their affiliation easy to discern. For young men, martial heroism provided the most obvious (and desired) course of action, but Union and Confederate supporters articulated long lists of patriotic activities for men, women, and children unable to participate in battle. Given the wealth of material from the era available online, it can be instructive for students to search through newspapers and other periodicals to see the range of ways people of all ages were encouraged to act on their national commitment. Union material is more readily available, but there are also southern resources for students to consult; comparisons of Confederate and Union songs, sermons, poems, or cartoons can yield productive conversations about the surprising similarities yet pervasive differences among the texts.

Much of the material that addresses the issue of allegiance includes the representation of oaths, promises, and pledges. The Union relied heavily on loyalty oaths during, and after, the Civil War, but both sides were eager to secure allegiance by asking citizens to swear their fidelity. Oaths depend on the idea that words are powerful and binding, and it can be illuminating for students to consider to what extent this assumption is accurate by looking at the representations of promises, pledges, and oaths that appear regularly in stories from the period. Promises and oaths also introduce interesting temporal disruptions into narratives because their function is to fix the course of future events. A quick way to get students to see how oaths work is to ask them to recite the Pledge of Allegiance. Most students do not know that the pledge was written in 1892 by Francis Bellamy, who took his inspiration from the Civil War. Students who have read literature written during the war can find its influence in Bellamy's original text: "I pledge allegiance to my Flag and to the Republic for which it stands—one Nation indivisible—with Liberty and Justice for all" (Ellis 19). It is also useful to ask them to consider the moral or political obligations that are associated with the Pledge of Allegiance today; is it, for them, a binding promise? This is an easy way to remind students of the continuing relevance of the Civil War in American culture.

Discussions of affect, allegiance, and pledges can be complicated further by raising the question of choice. Hawthorne's emphasis on the role of "time and circumstance" in the determination of allegiance underscores a point that many of his contemporaries found difficult to navigate. They were eager to have citizens choose to support the nation, but at the same time they wanted to depict allegiance as so obvious as to be involuntary. Because both sides needed men to enlist, many stories and poems relied on female figures to represent the decision to support the nation: it was less risky to show women making a choice, particularly if the issue was presented through a courtship narrative. Lucy Larcom's "A Loyal Woman's No" (1863) provides an excellent example. In the poem, the young female speaker rejects a marriage proposal, explaining she cannot wed the suitor because he is "not man enough / To grasp [his] country's measure of a man" (727). Prizing "gain" over "the nation's need," he is unable to "hear the voices in the air"—"The morning chant of Liberty and Law!"—which call her to ascend the "heaven-smit summits" of Truth with "Heroes" and "martyrs" (727, 726). Although she admits that once she could have become lost "in the warm whirlpools of [his] voice," "[t]he sense of Evil, the stern cry of Right" has "steered [her] free" (726). Asking students to distinguish different kinds of emotion in the poem, to separate personal desire from national affection ("stern" but sustaining), can illuminate the complexities of the literature written during the war on the subject of right feelings.

"A Loyal Woman's No" appeared in the *Atlantic Monthly* in December 1863, along with a short work entitled "The Man without a Country." Published anonymously in the hope that it would be taken as a factual account, Edward Everett Hale's story shares with Larcom's poem a fundamental commitment to the representation of proper allegiance. Pairing these works provides the opportunity for students to think about how periodicals like the *Atlantic* worked to establish national affect. "The Man without a Country" begins during the Madison administration as Aaron Burr convinces a young officer to betray the United States; the plot is unsuccessful and the officer, Philip Nolan, is caught. In "a fit of frenzy" during his trial, Nolan adds insult to injury by condemning the nation (666). Nolan, the narrator explains, had grown up in the "West of those days"—the South of 1863—and so "to him 'United States' was scarcely a reality" (667). He is sentenced never to hear of his country again, and the story traces his growing realization of the deep privation this entails. Hale ends with Nolan's death, but not before showing that the prisoner has recreated an ideal version of the nation, now an object of ardent desire, which the narrator cannot mar with news of the Civil War. Combining seduction plot and rash oath, Hale's story includes many of the elements found in works about allegiance during the period.

Whereas most patriotic materials were produced for whites, black readers in the North were also encouraged to demonstrate their allegiance to the nation. African American activists seized on martial valor as a conduit to full citizenship, hoping that willingness to fight for the nation would earn them recognition *from* the nation. Speaking in 1862 to a Philadelphia audience, Frederick Douglass noted that "no man . . . has been able to cast the shadow of a doubt upon the loyalty and patriotism of the free colored people in this the hour of the nation's trial and danger" (Blight, *Frederick Douglass' Civil War* 153). Although the Union army was reluctant to grant African American soldiers the chance to demonstrate their bravery in battle, the association of Union allegiance and abolition by many activists offers yet another way for students to appreciate the concerns at stake in definitions of national belonging. How do we decide who belongs to a nation? Events in mid-July 1863—the New York draft riots and the assault on Fort Wagner by the Fifty-Fourth Massachusetts, a company of African American soldiers—were instrumental in changing Union sentiment and can be equally powerful for students today.

Examining the role of emotion during the war provides a means of establishing critical connections between the ante- and postbellum periods, too often seen as distinct rather than connected. One of the chief postbellum vehicles for establishing proper affective relationships was the reunion romance. Works with reunion plots appeared in several genres—novels, stories, and plays—and are consistently interested in the conversion of affect and the political implications of emotion. Although stories about the courtship of people from different sections of the United States antedate the Civil War, the sectional romance plot, or romance of reunion, became especially popular in the postwar years as a means of managing unruly emotions and affiliations.[2] John De Forest's *Miss Ravenel's Conversion from Secession to Loyalty* (1867) may be the most familiar of these works today, but it is only one of many (including a number by De Forest himself). On the page and on the stage, Americans in North and South alike appeared to relish representations of sectional division overcome by romantic attachment. Being flexible about what constitutes a novel in this genre, it is possible to expand the list in various directions and include works as diverse as Elizabeth Stuart Phelps's *The Gates Ajar* (1868), Albion Tourgée's *Bricks without Straw* (1880), Henry James's *The Bostonians* (1886), and Charles Chesnutt's *The Marrow of Tradition* (1901).[3] Taught together, these novels demonstrate the many ways that authors adapted the reunion formula to different elements of American culture, including the role of religion, the rise of realism, and the problems associated with race and racism. It is also possible to select a single novel to consider what happens to affect and sympathy in the postwar period. It has become common to locate sympathy's importance in the antebellum years, but, as these works make clear, the issues associated with sympathy are equally important after the Civil War, especially in the literary effort to imagine the nation as once again united by bonds of affection.

The reunion romance is often linked with the rise of plantation fiction, nostalgic depictions of the Old South peopled with happy slaves and noble planters. These stories were popular with late-nineteenth-century American readers, but their explicit racism makes them poor choices for students today. It can be useful, however, to teach a short story like Thomas Nelson Page's "Marse Chan" (1884) to help more sophisticated students see that the cultivation of particular affects can be reactionary as well as liberatory, a salutary reminder in our affect-saturated age. In my own teaching, I pair "Marse Chan" with Paul Laurence Dunbar's *The Fanatics* (1901). Dunbar is best known for his poetry, particularly the works he wrote in dialect, but he also penned several novels before his early death. *The Fanatics* details the loves and loyalties of residents of an Ohio town split between Union and Confederate supporters. The novel lingers almost obsessively on the challenges of allegiance as characters regularly consider how to adjudicate between competing and conflicting attachments. In one of the many passages considering the question, the narrator asks, "Is the love of country, which we call patriotism, a more commendable trait than filial affection and obedience, and can one deficient in the latter be fully capable of comprehending the former?" (131). This is a question students have encountered before, but Dunbar is writing for a different historical moment. What does it mean for an African American author to ask this question during the nadir of American race relations? How does a historical novel reframe an era's problems? One of the hallmarks of *The Fanatics* is that few characters have the kind of unqualified allegiance that was depicted as necessary during the war itself. While one young woman can boast that there "is no division" in her affections (11), most of Dunbar's characters struggle with their feelings. Why does Dunbar juxtapose the period's demand for "sharp divisions" with representations of the moral complexities that resulted (28)? Depending on the focus of the course, such questions can direct students to consider the representation of history or the ways that historical narrative can be used to provide a new perspective on current events. Because Dunbar is explicit that uncertainty about affective ties includes issues of racial loyalty, the novel can be profitably juxtaposed with short stories by Chesnutt ("The Sheriff's Children" or "The Wife of His Youth"), W. E. B. Du Bois's *The Souls of Black Folk*, or Booker T. Washington's *Up from Slavery*. *The Fanatics* concludes with the observation that regardless of affiliation, Union or Confederate, "[the people] were all fanatics" (314). The world created by and through fanatic devotion, as during Dunbar's Civil War, easily devolves into one where everyone, black or white, friend or foe, can be easily reduced to type or symbol. In the guise of reunion romance, *The Fanatics* attacks the structure of allegiance itself.

Many students in American classrooms take national belonging for granted; they have never had to make a choice between home and nation, and asking them to do so in a class on the Civil War gives them a more nuanced understanding of the challenges facing Americans on both sides of the Mason-Dixon line. Not only do these issues link thematically with antebellum literature, they can also provide a way for students to use their own experiences about national belonging to develop a better understanding of the challenges of civil war.

Notes

1. For a full overview of Confederate materials, see Hutchison, *Apples.*
2. Keely provides an excellent list of these novels.
3. On *The Gates Ajar* as a kind of reunion romance, see Duquette 85–99.

Part IV

Teaching Materials

Julia Stern

Teaching through Primary Source Documents

In the course of nearly ten years spent thinking and writing about Mary Chesnut's revised Civil War narrative, known in its edited entirety as *Mary Chesnut's Civil War*, I chronically worried about how to use the archives, those dedicated caches of papers and records pertaining to our objects of study and their historical contexts. When literary critics approached this other country, what things did they carry? I had no training in orthography or the study of penmanship, no guidance in explicating census records, and no instruction for how to approach the contents of personal letters in the context of public events. This essay takes my experience with primary sources as a case study for teaching students to use materials from special collections. I speak as an academic with no training in histories of the book, print, or material culture. Nonetheless, I have learned to love the archives in my own way, coming to see that no vintage document is decipherable without interpretation, textual exegesis, the very methods in which we literary scholars are steeped. In fact, this archive-a-phobe learned that her more than twenty years as a professional close reader opened the door into a once mystical-seeming domain.

I began with unpublished Chesnut family letters to ease myself into the archival waters. Formal properties of an early 1860s epistle from John

Manning, a former South Carolina governor, to Chesnut seemed to promise a backstory. Chesnut tells us in her manuscript that Governor Manning was known for his dazzling looks and flirtatious comportment. His handwriting provided corroboration: elegant to the point of flamboyance, with a dandy-like swagger, speaking to the man's notion of personality as performance and supporting Chesnut's humorous account of the vanities and the charms of her old family friend. Translating this find to the classroom, I ask my students to play handwriting expert, noting that while Governor Manning's paleography marks an extreme example even among the writing of elite, well-educated southern gentlemen, it sheds a fascinating light on our understanding of real-life actors in the past. This example affords students visceral appreciation of the materiality of a text as itself a repository of meanings.

Would that Manning's script were the norm of his class! One of the chief challenges to archival scholars, which had not occurred to me, is when handwriting central to their investigation proves indecipherable. That the most difficult hand with which I had to contend was Chesnut's own came as a blow; I could not have imagined that when I finally saw the manuscripts for her revised 1880s narrative, I would take one look at the fading brown ink and impossible scribbles and begin to weep. That I had read C. Vann Woodward's edition of Chesnut's narrative at least ten times over my decade of research and writing made it possible for me to work backward: I would decode a key word or an unusual combination of phrases, and the memory of the published version of the passage allowed me to decipher the details of the manuscript version. My slow success in this sort of reconstruction accustomed me to Chesnut's hand so that it became somewhat more manageable—though never immediately legible. I remind students that the reality of handwriting from past centuries often is difficult if not formidable; accordingly, one must use every tool in one's kit to coax it into focus.

On first confronting the fifty-four copybooks from the early 1880s that Chesnut left at her death and from which Woodward created *Mary Chesnut's Civil War*, I made a crucial decision. My task would be neither to double-check or reduplicate his multiyear labors with the manuscripts nor to reinsert the newspaper clippings and campaign artifacts that Chesnut had included in her notebooks and that Woodward had left out. When we work in the archives, often we are forced to determine what constitutes a text let alone choose the particular version of it to study. I focused on Woodward's edition because it afforded the widest range of Chesnut's expression available to readers 130 years after her death. I explain to my students that scholars encounter forks in the archival road as a matter of course; it is important to keep an open mind instead of assuming that there are correct and incorrect paths to follow.

Woodward decided to restrict his edition to writerly artifacts: most of the volume unfolds from Chesnut's 1880s revisions of the 1860s diaries, amplified by moments from the original 1860s text that offer far different views of a situation or tableau. For example, the racism that Chesnut came to express by the 1880s was in her original 1860s diaries far more tempered, muted, even absent. In his editorial apparatus, Woodward does not discuss the meaning of Chesnut's shift toward greater racial animosity; he allows readers to draw their own conclusions from his juxtaposition of the passages.

While Woodward remains silent at the level of judgment, I attempt to untangle just such contradictions and think about what they might say about Chesnut's racial ideology. I speculate that in the 1880s revisions, her hostility toward African Americans as a group was largely the consequence of her class position: white people, once the elite, experienced economic struggle and failure during Reconstruction. The going cultural fantasy of her genteelly impoverished milieu was that freed blacks were responsible for the joblessness and diminished circumstances of whites. Juxtaposing her 1860s passages with her 1880s revisions shows students some of the shifts that her writing and thinking underwent. It also allows them to contemplate racism in historical context rather than as an absolute.

This kind of reactionary double consciousness, however, is rare: the politics and perceptions of the 1880s reviser are generally congruent with those of the 1860s diarist. I make use of the passages Woodward highlights from the two different textual eras by his editorial bracketing system to talk to students about two strata of primary sources, first in a literary critical way, then against a cultural historical context. In the early 1860s diary jottings, Chesnut subtly affirmed that the black man could be educated out of the benighted state into which the white planter had sunk him. By the time of her 1880s revisions, she is bleakly influenced by the antiblack sentiment in post-Reconstruction South Carolina.[1]

Beyond the two strata of Chesnut documents (and sometimes three: in the late 1870s, she smoothed out the prose of a small portion of the 1860s narrative), I searched for other historical sources that might illuminate the literary patterning in what Woodward reconstituted in his masterful edition.[2] I came to believe that any archival document, rigorously questioned, could be unpacked and made to speak. So, what we might call the ambient artifacts that amplify and enrich Chesnut's revised narratives themselves become texts—material such as postwar account books and work rolls, affording information on former slaves who remained on the Chesnut plantation as free laborers; South Carolina census records for Kershaw County, which tracked inhabitants by domicile or plantation and by racial classification; South Carolina trial records, manumission decrees, reimbursements for emancipated slaves, and annuities granted to recently freed slaves for exceptional service.

I show my students how the shorthand used on census forms in the antebellum South (many of which are available online) affords an example of the challenges of reading archival documents: opaque expressions from the past may often elude tools for translation. The 1860 South Carolina census for Kershaw County, locale of Mulberry, the Chesnut plantation, is filled with potentially significant details—for example, the way the format registers enslaved versus free black people. My students, comparing the white and black populations, conclude that slaves outnumbered free people by a certain ratio. South Carolina, as a result of its geography and climate variations from coastal islands to upcountry farms, had a large number of slave plantations run by white overseers; the masters and their families were absentee, living in distant cities such as Charleston and Columbia, where the weather was less pernicious. Censuses mirrored these racially inflected population patterns.

Only by reading diacritically—comparatively—against the 1850 or 1870 census can my students and I consider why in certain districts in 1860 the three-part system of racial classification dropped B for black and came to divide its population into a binary M for mulatto and W for white. Obviously not all the black people had died off or departed. We know that racial mixing occurred across the South (and also in the North) from the seventeenth century on, but was it possible that all people of color in this community were of mixed heritage?

Having ventured into the realm of speculative close reading, which, ironically, the limited transparency of historical documents sometimes forces one to do, and helped both by the diacritical method I employed with the census and by the sort of literary exegesis in which English majors are trained, I have several thoughts on the meaning of this taxonomic transformation. I ask my students, What are the important details of this census accounting? Does any aspect of it stand out as abnormal? How would you tell a story about the change in classification? What would that story say over against what you know about the local culture? (These questions result from my e-mail exchange with Marion Chandler of the Santa Cruz Museum of Art and History.)

Thinking about how racial mixing was a crime in the eyes of southern law and paradoxically also a ubiquitous reality, I became fascinated by how white plantation mistresses experienced cross-racial contact. One of my favorite passages in Chesnut's revised narrative, both mysterious and haunting, seemed to defy explication. Then, while reading a secondary source on the history of slave uprisings, I was transported to Camden, South Carolina, where the Chesnuts lived, in 1816, nearly fifty years before the action of her narrative, when her mother-in-law was no more than forty. Chesnut describes the nearly ninety-year-old Mary Cox Chesnut, angelic, deaf, razor-sharp, and having an unusually keen sense of smell. On a summer night in 1861, at 2 a.m., old Mrs. Chesnut "smelled a smell" and insisted that the entire family circle, free and slave, ensconced for the summer six miles from Mulberry at the Sandy Hill Plantation, search the premises for traces of a blaze (*Mary Chesnut's Civil War* 77–78). Why, I wondered for years during my research for the project, was old Mrs. Chesnut so phobic about fire?

Historians long have understood that southern slave uprisings rarely involved firearms, which slaves were forbidden to use, unless they were able to steal guns and ammunition from their masters' holdings. House slaves, particularly cooks, were known to have poisoned the master's coffee or to have put ground glass in the mistress's food. In the passages surrounding her long and mesmerizing account of the murder of Betsy Witherspoon, a white septuagenarian and Chesnut's cousin, by her slaves, Chesnut details several assassination attempts.

But in *American Negro Slave Revolts*, Herbert Aptheker provides a compelling clue as to why old Mrs. Chesnut was terrified of fire. He recounts an event that took place seven years before Mary Boykin Chesnut was born and to which she never alluded in her revised narrative: the 1816 plot by a group of Camden slaves to rise on the Fourth of July, while the white community was celebrating the holiday. The conspirators planned to set fire to the homes of Camden's wealthiest citizens, drawing them away from the festivities on the village green to the other end of town. With the public space thus evacuated, the renegades would have access to the municipal arsenal and its scores of weapons, with which they planned to shoot their way out of Camden; they vowed to "rise and take the country" by arming fellow slaves along their way to "freedom" (142).[3]

The rebels' choice of date not only made tactical sense but also was politically symbolic. The Camden slave community knew as well as the whites for whom they toiled did that the promises of the Declaration of Independence had fallen woefully short of Jefferson's original vision, apart from his own complex record on slaveholding. As the conspiracy mounted, Scipio, a slave mason on the plantation of Colonel James Chesnut, Sr., became privy to the plot, apparently because it had originated among Camden's brick-working slaves. The record suggests that Scipio, for reasons unknown, wanted no part of the plan.

My information about his disruption of the conspiracy began with a telegraphic set of paragraphs in Aptheker's book, but it came to fruition in the South Carolina Department of Archives and History. Housed there were records for the trial of the eight slaves ultimately charged with conspiracy to murder Camden's white population. Five were hanged; three were sentenced to almost a decade in prison and then would be sold south. A few extant related documents indicated Scipio's role as informant against his slave peers. Mulberry's master mason apparently alerted James Chesnut to the fatal plans of the bricklayers. Law enforcement in the community staged a faux event on 2 July that would bring the conspirators together in a large field in Camden: clearing brush for an impromptu fox hunt. As the slaves gathered to do this work, they were arrested and taken to jail—Scipio included, because the officials wanted to protect him from being identified as the informant.

Filed with the trial records were several documents pertaining to the State of South Carolina's secret manumission of Scipio, in appreciation of his service in preventing the Fourth of July rebellion. The state compensated James Chesnut $1100 dollars for the loss of his slave, an enormous sum for even a young, healthy slave artisan in the early nineteenth century. Scipio appears to have stayed for the remainder of his life on what by 1820 would become Mulberry Plantation, according to evidence in the surviving material culture, visible in several remaining Chesnut homes, and through the Chesnut Williams family oral tradition. Christopher Daniels—a descendant of Chesnut's beloved sister Kate Miller Williams and her husband, David R. Williams, the nephew and surviving male heir of James Chesnut, Jr.—documents the building of the Mulberry great house. Assembled of red brick fabricated and fired on the premises, the home was erected between 1818 and 1820. Scipio, who would have been newly freed, apparently directed the brick making and the laying of the foundation for the three-story residence.

Additionally, Bloomsbury, the elder Chesnuts' Camden town home, was built on a foundation that historians have attributed to Scipio and his crew of Mulberry masons. These slaves apparently traveled from Mulberry to Camden to build the dwelling between 1849 and 1854, nearly forty years after the thwarted Fourth of July slave uprising. Their craftsmanship at mid-century suggests that Scipio not only stayed at Mulberry Plantation after his manumission in 1816 but also worked there for at least forty years alongside men who remained enslaved, into what was his sixth decade. James Chesnut, Sr., would have been approximately forty years old at the time of the foiled Camden Slave Rebellion; Scipio, archivists hypothesize, was in his early to mid twenties then.

A question that my students ask and that we may never know the answer to is why Scipio lived as a slave mason and supervised building projects when he had received from the state of South Carolina not only his freedom but an annuity of $50 a year in reward for his service in thwarting the revolt. Over the course of his adult lifetime, Scipio might have accrued more than $2500, approximately $53,000 in today's money, but could not have explained having such a large sum if he pretended to live as a slave.

Chesnut's revised narrative, focused exclusively on the years 1861–65, does not include Scipio the slave informant, but it does feature another bound Scipio, whom I hypothesize was the brick maker's son and namesake. Describing him in a passage dated one month after the Confederate surrender and using a classic Romantic racialist trope, Chesnut notes, "[H]e is six feet two, a black Hercules, and gentle as a dove" (*Mary Chesnut's Civil War* 815). Like the first Scipio, this one also protected the elder James Chesnut, this time from Yankee harassment and arrest when Mulberry fell to Sherman's march through the Carolinas in the winter and spring of 1865. A document entitled "Memories of Mulberry," self-published by Chesnut's granddaughter Esther Davis in the 1870s, detailed that in 1866, only months before his former master's death, this second Scipio attempted to buy a parcel of land on Mulberry and erect there a African Methodist Episcopal church for all the old colonel's freed people. I speculate that the second Scipio's resources came in part from what remained of the first Scipio's secret annuity. Instead of selling the land to his valet, the old colonel willed this small piece of his plantation to Mulberry's community of newly freed people.

How could someone choose slavery or the appearance of it over real and enduring freedom?, I ask my students. Here, the archive takes us only so far. In my book on Chesnut's narrative, *Mary Chesnut's Civil War Epic*, I suggest that Scipio's entire family and community remained slaves at Mulberry; to seek a life as a free black would have entailed forever leaving his Camden attachments (214). Many states, such as Virginia, mandated that freed slaves leave their home districts a certain number of days after manumission. Apparently, it was feared that in proximity the sweetness of liberty might become too attractive to the bound black community.

My archival discoveries would never have been made had I not noticed, reading closely, that old Mrs. Chesnut's fire phobia implied a great deal more than a slave family's making soap without tamping the ashes (Chesnut's explanation for the smell of smoke). The book on slave uprisings led me to the documents in the South Carolina Department of Archives and History. The smell seemed to lead back to a terrifying instance of slave rage and the possible end to the life of white privilege that she had enjoyed for more than eighty-five years. Pattern recognition, a staple of literary practice, allowed me to draw historical conclusions about the politics of fire and slavery during the Civil War.

I was intrigued by another African American who plays a crucial role in Chesnut's book: Molly, her sharp-witted, sardonic slave maid who accompanied the writer across the South as Chesnut's husband rose from an aide-de-camp to brigadier general. This young wife and mother, superb cook and ingenious, devoted companion, saw more of the daily workings of the Confederacy's political players than many a general did. Feminist critics have dismissed Molly's significance by calling her Chesnut's self-constructed foil or a fictionalized mouthpiece for the writer, a figure of comic relief in a narrative full of heartbreak and catastrophe. But what if we took seriously Molly's central place in Chesnut's adventures and searched for details of the woman behind the putative foil?

Several pieces of archival evidence helped me recover a sense of Molly's historical reality and complexity. Unlike even the most elite house slaves of the wartime South, Molly was lucky enough to be attached to a mistress who was committed to preserving her experience for future audiences. I direct students' attention to the rich anecdotes involving Molly's spatting with Laurence, the supercilious Chesnut slave valet, or her chaste frivolities at the ironing board with Anne, another Chesnut maid and Molly's fellow Methodist; I show students how these passages provide a textured description of slave culture as it unfolded on the road during wartime (*Mary Chesnut's Civil War* 432, 433, 457–58, 526). Chesnut's sociological insights reveal the way different slaves performed their relatively privileged status as talk of freedom moved to the front of their minds after 1863.

I share with students that I searched for archival traces of Molly, daunted by the scholarly doubters who had discounted her significance as a figure who sends up both bound blacks and white elites alike. But then I explain that as I was reading through Chesnut's postwar account book for the year 1878, sixteen years after the writer recorded Molly's proposal for a collaborative dairy business, I found an astonishing detail. A February entry, reading, "[W]ages for Molly, 3 dollars" (Account book), told me that Molly had in fact remained both at Mulberry and intimately attached to Chesnut. Laurence, on the other hand, is nowhere to be seen in Chesnut postwar records. Starting in 1864, Mary and James begin to speculate that Laurence is itching for freedom. After enduring several drunken episodes with the valet, Chesnut sends Laurence back to Mulberry for bad behavior, and at that point he disappears from the record. I point out to students that silence itself can be a text that must be read. How are we to understand Molly's proximity and Laurence's disappearance? Might we draw conclusions about the different kind of elite house slaves that were kept on at Mulberry and about their ideological as opposed to domestic commitments?

Molly made possible and endurable Chesnut's grueling wartime odyssey, transforming grimy, ghastly boardinghouse quarters into not only livable but comfortable domestic spaces, concocting delectable meals admired by President Jefferson Davis himself. The revising Chesnut records that Molly's culinary gifts were worthy of a trained French chef; from whatever ingredients were on hand, and informed by Chesnut's memories of eating haute cuisine as a senator's wife, the two would collaborate to magnificent effect.

Chesnut's 1878 account book shows that her total monthly earnings, beyond the leasing of Negro houses (former slave quarters) to the remaining Mulberry freed people for $144 a year, were only $12. It is not clear that General James ever again earned a legal fee. Meanwhile, as Chesnut's ongoing partner, Molly contributed vital labor to their business, and her daily wages added up to one quarter of Chesnut's monthly income, which, aside from the butter and eggs, comprised the profits from selling household stuffs, meat, and produce from Mulberry's smokehouses, kitchen gardens, and fields.

Numerous unpublished postwar letters from the Mulberry Plantation archives sent to Auntie Mary from her beloved "Sweet Williams," Kate's children, repeatedly included, in their closing salutations, "Send our love to Molly." Students who have studied slavery sometimes argue that such sentiments constitute white paternalism, the token nod to a devoted former slave by offspring of the once master class who are now removed to the North but still invested in fictive kinship (Patterson 62–65). I would assert, however, that the threads of Molly's life during and after the Civil War were tightly interwoven with Mary Chesnut and that their affective connection was real.

In late 2008, Martha Williams Daniels, family curator of the Mulberry archives, discovered and purchased at auction Chesnut's lost three-volume photograph album, to which the writer referred frequently in the revised narrative. The collection had disappeared in the 1930s, when warring Williams Chesnut heirs broke up and sold off pieces of the family estate. The current Williams descendants had for decades despaired of ever recovering the books. Martha's daughter, Marty Daniels, working with Barbara Mc-Carthy, spent the next two years cataloging the images, writing biographies of the three hundred sitters. Included were Lincoln and the reigning pope; all but six of the images were identifiable. Marty published the photography collection as the second part of a set; volume 1 was a reissue of *A Diary from Dixie*, the Avary-Martin 1905 edition of Chesnut's revised Civil War narrative (Daniels and McCarthy).

Soon after the Williams heirs purchased the albums, Marty invited me to Mulberry, and with great excitement she showed me one of the unidentified photographs. Its black female sitter is smartly attired in an elegant satin dress. The image was made in 1863, midwar, at Quimby's, Charleston's most elegant portrait studio. "It has to be Molly," Marty insisted. "Who else could it be? Chesnut wouldn't have had to caption this picture—everyone who knew the writer and her family also knew Molly. Look at her beautiful face, radiating intelligence and poise, juxtaposed with those huge, powerful hands. Who else could it be?"

The photograph is a study in paradox. A handsome twenty-something African American woman wears a beautiful striped satin dress covered from the waist by a full white or pale satin overskirt and topped by a translucent overjacket in darker fabric with a shawl draped over her left arm. She sports a white satin kerchief on her head, made of the same material as the overskirt, and large hoop earrings, perhaps the most African-inflected detail of her garb besides the head scarf. Below the neck, the ensemble telegraphs nothing of her unfree status: Sherman's army and the Emancipation Proclamation wouldn't reach South Carolina until the spring of 1865. All the while, Molly remained busy traveling among Richmond, Camden, and various small North Carolina towns as a refugee from, not in flight toward, the Yankees and freedom.

Students are fascinated that none of my colleagues in the archives had stories to tell me about the likenesses of slaves found in photograph albums of elite white nineteenth-century matrons. At most, they pointed to portraits of bound black nurses posing with infants and toddlers. That Mary Chesnut would have escorted or sent Molly to Quimby's studio for a portrait (for which she would have paid between $1 and $1.50, approximately $25 in 2012 money—hardly spare change) is remarkable. That this artifact has remained in her prized photograph collection is equally remarkable. I query my students over how we might use this primary source as a supplement for reading a relationship documented in a narrative that falls silent after representing 1865? As the portrait and its condition of production attest, theirs was a bond that flourished and was memorialized for decades. That in the middle of the war Chesnut invested in a studio carte de visite of Molly tells us something we didn't know before about this mistress and her maid. It also tells us about the magic to be found in the archives. As we bring primary source documents into our classrooms, encouraging a new form of close reading, it's vital to remind our students that imagination and analytic rigor together make the oldest documents new again. I also appeal to what I call the inner Nancy Drew in each of us: patience and even, at times, drudgery can yield field-transformative discoveries.

Notes

1. See *Mary Chesnut's Civil War* 208 (4 Oct. 1861), 256 (6 Dec. 1861). See also Stern, *Mary Chesnut's Civil War Epic* 268n11.

2. Not all historians were as thrilled with Woodward's edition as I, a literary scholar, had become: they criticized it for including alternative versions of 1880s scenes that Woodward found and correlated from Chesnut's diary jottings of 1861, 1864, and 1865, which still exist and have been edited by Woodward and Elisabeth Muhlenfeld: *The Private Mary Chesnut: The Unpublished Civil War Diaries.*

3. See the Records of the Court of Magistrates and Freeholders (Kershaw County), L28225, Trial Papers, 1802–61, held in the South Carolina Department of Archives and History.

Melissa J. Strong

Teaching with Images: Synthesizing the Civil War in Fact and Fiction

Cultural memory studies offers a particularly useful approach to Civil War literature, a genre that includes representations of the war in a variety of formats produced in a range of time periods and cultural contexts. That films set in the United States of the 1860s have enjoyed positive popular and critical reception since the late twentieth century shows the increasing importance Civil War memorial forms place on visual texts. Indeed, Hollywood movies may serve as a primary source of the information students have about the war.[1] The prevalence of Civil War films exemplifies the ever-growing dichotomy between history and memory, in which self-referential *lieux de mémoire* ("sites of memory") have replaced the reality of *milieux de mémoire* ("real environments of memory" [Nora 7]. The intrinsic link between media and cultural memory facilitates displacement of facts with fictionalized memories, memories in which authenticity of emotion or intent may trump historical accuracy. The result resonates deeply with audiences, and it possesses tremendous power in shaping collective memory (Erll 389).

Cultural or collective memory employs imagination to reconstruct the Civil War in the same way that Stephen Crane, who was born after the war's end, did in crafting a representation that turn-of-the-century readers interpreted as "real" (Fahs, "Civil War" 110). Memory is not fixed but constantly in flux and tied to the present, in contrast to the more stable, if flawed, "representation of the past" that history offers (Nora 8). Cultural memory emerges from the disconnect between history and memory.[2] Alice Fahs and Joan Waugh demonstrate that the memory of the Civil War is not fixed, observing that "each new generation has actively reinterpreted the Civil War to support its own ideological agendas" (Introduction 4).[3] Equally important, evolving cultural contexts shape memory over time and reflect changes in social attitudes, tastes, and even technology. We see this shaping in the commercial and critical success of the 1989 film *Glory* and the virtual disappearance of the battlefield tales that enjoyed wide readership during the nineteenth century. How can we pedagogically intervene and add a more nuanced historical understanding to popular cultural perceptions of the Civil War? I address this challenge in my classroom by pairing literary and visual texts. Moreover, I offer my students an assignment that is methodologically informed by cultural memory studies, new historicism, and best practices in teaching. This assignment also carefully accommodates different learning styles.

Civil War literature seems to have changed little when compared with the shifts in its portrayal in film. The Romantic revisionism of *Gone with the Wind* (1939) has given way to increasing emphasis on race and racial equality refracted through the lenses of whiteness and privilege in films such as *Glory* and *Lincoln* (2012).[4] Literature has remained more static, as the late twentieth century's reevaluation of the literary canon and the processes of canon formation did not yield tremendous changes in the canon of Civil War literature or the narrative it constructs. Contemporary anthologies like Bedford and Norton present Stephen Crane and other writers who recreate the Civil War and focus their attention on combat as the definitive voices of its literature. This approach leaves out of our accounts vast realms of Civil War experience and arguably contributes to slippage between fact and fiction. For example, college textbooks and curricula often continue to elide the Civil War experiences of women and people of color, many of whom actively played important roles. To address the gaps I perceived, and to call attention to the broader current cultural dissociation from the real war experiences of American citizens, I created a course at Northeastern State University (NSU) called The Civil War in Fact and Fiction. The organizing question of the course is, "What do we know about the Civil War, and how do we know it?" The course's foundational principles are that memory and history are not synonymous and that the stories we read and see about the Civil War shape and change our understandings of it.

My students analyze canonized texts but also examine a wider range of responses to and perspectives on the war. They think critically about, conduct research on, and compose versions of the real story of the Civil War. Historicizing texts yields good teaching moments. Reading Crane and Whitman alongside unfamiliar voices, such as Mary Livermore's, and authors whom students may not associate with Civil War writing, such as Louisa May Alcott, fosters a more complete understanding of the war's effect on American people and literature. Combining a variety of texts and genres also sheds light on how people and works of literature affected memories of the Civil War. Better understanding of the Civil War in turn helps achieve deeper understanding of "how freedom, citizenship, and nationhood have been and continue to be defined" and an awareness of the ever-changing role that war memories play in shaping these concepts (Fahs, "Civil War" 111).

The course combines occasional texts with twentieth-century and contemporary treatments of the war, from novels such as Geraldine Brooks's Pulitzer Prize–winning *March* (2006), Charles Frazier's *Cold Mountain* (1997), and E. L. Doctorow's *The March* (2005) to films such as *The Birth of a Nation* (1915), *Glory*, and *Gone with the Wind*. The fragmented, polyvocal perspectives in the novels of the late twentieth and early twenty-first centuries contrast with the first-person narration and urgent truth telling of nineteenth-century texts like Whitman's "The Wound-Dresser" (1867), Livermore's *My Story of the War* (1890), and Alcott's *Hospital Sketches* (1863). These texts often begin with a claim of authenticity such as an introduction from an authority figure, usually military, or a confirmation like "Nurse Periwinkle does exist . . . [and] she really did go to Washington" (Alcott, *Hospital Sketches* [ed. Jones] 18). The importance of veracity in these texts mirrors the emphasis on what Ann Fabian calls the "unvarnished truth" in accounts of prisoner-of-war experiences by John Ransom, T. H. Mann, Lieutenant A. C. Roach, and others (123). Brooks's *March*, *Cold Mountain*, and Doctorow's *The March* use multiple perspectives and alternating narrators to destabilize the certainty of earlier fiction and nonfiction eyewitness accounts. Shifts in voice undermine the sense of sanctioned unity that students might expect from historical accounts, even fictionalized ones. Whitman's constant shifts in voice and perspective set the precedent for contemporary Civil War texts, and their polyvocality suggests his claim to contain multitudes. At the same time, these texts incorporate stylistic and ideological features distinct to their cultural contexts. Connecting twentieth- and twenty-first-century texts to contemporary developments in artistic expression and thought, such as literary realism, poststructuralism, and postmodernism, helps students recognize that truth and reality are, as Pierre Nora suggests, evolving representations.

The Civil War in Fact and Fiction enrolls undergraduate and graduate students at NSU, mostly English majors and master's students. Nonmajors seeking general education units and American studies students fulfilling requirements in literature also take the course. The content attracts Civil War enthusiasts who range from history buffs to reenactors to Scarlett O'Hara aficionados. Many of the American studies students complete internships at area museums with Civil War holdings and connections, including the Murrell Home in Park Hill, Oklahoma, and the Broken Arrow Historical Society. The Civil War remains relevant to the lives of NSU students in ways both obvious, such as the Confederate flag's importance in regional identity, and complex, such as the citizenship dispute of the descendants of slaves owned by members of the Cherokee Nation.[5] NSU's main campus is headquartered in the same town as the Cherokee Nation of Oklahoma. Historic battlefields at Cabin Creek and Prairie Grove and the Confederate cemetery in Fayetteville, Arkansas, ensure that the Civil War maintains a physical presence in the area surrounding the university.

Local sites and connections to the war offer resources to students and help them relate the war to the past and present culture of the region. For instance, one student participated in the hundred-and-fiftieth-anniversary reenactment of the Battle of Pea Ridge, which took place approximately eighty-five miles from where NSU's main campus now is. Another student shared photographs of nineteenth-century cemeteries taken during her motorcycle trips through the region. The personal investment in the Civil War that people in the area might have raises questions about students' receptiveness to the course's organizing principle that truth and reality are evolving representations. Yet NSU students tend to reject the notion of a sole, definitive past. In my course, they demonstrate this sophistication by examining issues from different viewpoints, acknowledging that different viewpoints may coexist. One graduate student characterized class discussion as reflecting attitudes that conflicted, particularly on the topics of the Confederate flag and the depiction of slaves.

Students' familiarity with multifaceted television and Hollywood representations of historical events likely contribute to their open-mindedness. Other important factors are NSU's proximity to Cherokee Nation and

Muscogee (Creek) Nation and the K–12 curricula in the region. Students' own heritage—about twenty percent are American Indian or Alaskan Native—also plays a role. Many NSU students possess considerable knowledge of Cherokee history and culture. They also recognize that mainstream responses to indigenous people shift over time and rarely include native perspectives on history. Usually NSU students admit the complexity of historical events such as the Trail of Tears or Chief John Ross's treaty with the Confederacy. Of course, some desire strict adherence to a concrete sense of truth or a particular reality of the past. Students open to multiple perspectives can help their less flexible classmates consider issues from other angles.

The course, usually offered fully online, appeals to a range of students. NSU students increasingly choose online courses as more than eighty percent of undergraduates live off campus and many—twenty-nine percent of undergraduates, sixty-four percent of graduate students—enroll part-time, most often because they work. The online format makes the class accessible to students at all three NSU campuses, which serve a sizable geographic region: the Tahlequah main campus is sixty miles from the Tulsa metro campus in Broken Arrow and thirty miles from the Muskogee campus.

A visual text analysis assignment builds on class discussion of representations of the war in literature and film and the relation between the Civil War and cultural memory. Discussions for a fully online course take place through a software package or application for the management and delivery of learning content. They may include instant messaging or Web conferencing tools. Some of these tools offer archiving so that students may view or listen to recordings later. Asynchronous discussion has proved successful: students post written answers to questions posed by the instructor or other students and also write thoughtful responses to classmates' posts. In the visual text assignment, appropriate for both introductory surveys and upper-division seminars, students first research a visual text, such as an advertisement or a photograph, published between 1861 and 1865. Next, they prepare an analysis of the image that connects it to assigned material and course topics. Finally, they submit their analysis in a variety of ways, possibly in combination: an online presentation to their classmates, with embedded audio, uploaded to the course Web site; a written document, with the visual text, handed in to the instructor; a post to the discussion board; a post to a course blog. To promote further dialogue and synthesis of assigned readings with visual texts, I make part of the grade students' constructive comments on their classmates' work. The wealth of images available through online archives and digitized nineteenth-century periodicals, many of them with open access, gives students virtually endless options.

The visual text project engages students who learn best visually, those who are print-oriented, those who are interactive learners, and those who prefer hands-on activities. It can be incorporated easily into a face-to-face course. Retention of the assignment's online components in a traditional setting may offer benefits, since research indicates that students learn more effectively and retain more information in hybrid formats.[6] Moreover, asynchronous learning technologies such as discussion boards and blogs enhance student interaction with content, peers, and the instructor (Ishtaiwa and Abulibdeh 155–56). But what about students who prefer communicating in person or who wish to unplug? What of students who thrive in the structure of a physical classroom or students who lack the skills necessary for success in an online class? The visual text assignment's use of technology, and an online course in general, presents limitations for engaging learners who dislike or struggle with educational technology. Several strategies exist to assist this kind of learner. First, begin a fully online course by asking students to complete a self-assessment that evaluates their level of preparedness and addresses the myths and realities of online education.[7] Second, offer a variety of resources to support students. Most online-learning software applications have a "Help" section that an instructor can augment with course-specific features: discussion forums where students ask questions (anonymously or not), individual conferences or group office hours, video lectures, assistance from librarians.

The visual text assignment provides the opportunity to assess student comprehension of core concepts and texts and also a way to measure students' skills in research, close reading, writing, analysis, and synthesis. It privileges and measures the cognitive skills of application, analysis, synthesis, and evaluation. The research component can be customized and used as a means of introducing students to the university library, electronic databases, historical archives, and digital humanities. Students may need support such as an instructional session with a librarian or a list of resources for locating a visual text to complete this assignment. Reference and instructional librarians at my institution are eager to collaborate with faculty members on these kinds of projects.

Images can be used to explore Civil War facts and fictions—for example, the trope of the faithful woman who waits at home. Newspapers, magazines, and male-authored war literature popularized it. Henry Fleming in *The Red Badge of Courage* thinks often of a girl who "grew demure and sad at the sight of his blue and brass" as he heads off to war (Crane 5). Watching Henry's departure from her window, the girl epitomizes the ideal woman at wartime: emotionally supportive but passive. She also is identified with home by virtue of her remaining there and watching while safely contained in it. Idealized women, such as Henry's mother, provide aid from afar in manners consistent with their gender role. She knits Henry eight pairs of socks so he will be "jest as warm and comf'able as anybody in the army" and directs him to send the socks home to her when they get holes so she "kin dern 'em" (4). Faithful, idealized women cannot participate in the war themselves. Cursing the war by "dern[ing]" is the only action available to Henry's mother.

Charles S. Reinhart's illustration "The Floral Tribute to the Nation's Dead" reinforces the memorialization of men as primary actors and of women as performing supporting roles. The image appeared in *Harper's Weekly* in 1870 and can be viewed at harpweek.com, the open-access online index for *Harper's Weekly*. It depicts women as the principal mourners. As in Crane's novel, men fight and sacrifice while women wait and sympathize from the safe, feminized space of the home front. The women in the *Harper's* illustration perform the demure sadness of Henry Fleming's girl through their downcast eyes, bowed heads, and physical arrangement around the focal point of the memorial to "our dead heroes." The monument looming over them aligns with the conventional characterization in Civil War literature of men's roles as vital and actively engaged and women's as auxiliary or passive. Even the lone male figure in the image, a white-bearded man likely too old to have served in the war, takes a prominent, dynamic position by supporting the female mourner who leans on his arm.

Representations of mortally wounded soldiers provide another way to examine the intersection of written and visual texts. Memoirs such as Livermore's often rework the sentimental novel's deathbed salvation scene by having devout women nurses orchestrate the conversions of male patients. Jane E. Schultz observes that nurses' roles in these scenes, which appeared in many women's Civil War narratives, "illustrated the female caregiver's moral influence over truant soldiers" (*Women* 79). Livermore's *My Story of the War* features a nurse praying over a dying soldier so effectively that the man dies peacefully, infused with a divine grace that shows itself in the "most heavenly smile" on his face (210). The accompanying illustration by F. O. C. Darley portrays the nurse bending over the soldier's bed like an angel as the ward master; another nurse looks on while light radiates on them from an invisible source.[8] The shadows shrouding the rest of the ward give the impression that the celestial light comes at the intercession of the nurse.

Darley's image evokes an 1853 lithograph depicting the death of Eva, the child martyr of *Uncle Tom's Cabin*. Exploring connections between "The Dying Soldier" and Louisa Corbaux's illustration of Eva's death reveals how cultural attitudes and popular artistic styles inform modes of expression. Eva, like the soldier, looks serene even as those at her deathbed convey anguish. Her fair hair and light-colored garments and bed linens render her the brightest point in the image. Goodness and purity seem to emanate from her.[9] Such stylized representations of death stand out to contemporary audiences familiar with media violence and the frank treatment of death in memorial forms like the film *Saving Private Ryan* (1998). Students find that Civil War images of mortality like Darley's "The Dying Soldier" and Reinhart's "The Floral Tribute to the Nation's Dead" form a stark contrast to photographs captured by Mathew Brady and others during the 1860s. Like the eyewitness writers of his era, Brady recorded the war because "he felt he was acting as the nation's historian . . . [and] contributing toward building a record of the war's events" (Sullivan 7).

An undated image of Confederate dead in Fredericksburg, Virginia, attributed to Brady's team of photographers, demonstrates the objective viewpoint of his pioneering photojournalistic style.[10] The man in the foreground is splayed in an awkward position, not a relaxed and peaceful one. The munitions scattered around the scene suggest haste and chaos, not the serenity of "Eva's Farewell" and "The Dying Solider." Instead of conveying noble sacrifice, as in "The Floral Tribute," or promising a spiritual reward as the dying soldier's recompense, this image raises questions about the cost of war and is consonant with the realistic portrayal of the death of John in *Hospital Sketches*. Alcott candidly and unsparingly documents John's agonizing decline: "[H]e slowly breathed his life away" in "distressful gasps" while the other patients looked on helplessly ([Redpath] 63). The scene offers none of the comforts of *My Story of the War*'s deathbed conversion, itself modeled on Stowe's influential modulation of Eva's untimely death with heavenly visions. The narrative voice of Alcott's Nurse Tribulation Periwinkle records the horrible reality of what she sees, like Brady's camera. John's last words are not a trite contrivance to reassure the living but a request for an open window: "For God's sake, give me air!" (57).

To promote connections between students' readings of visual texts and the course's focus on the tensions between fact and fiction, I ask students to consider a series of study questions, such as, How does a particular image engage with concepts like sacrifice, freedom, citizenship, and nationhood? How do the images question or corroborate accounts of the war we have studied in class? What role do memory and imagination play in an image's reconstruction of the war's events? Students also may evaluate the similarities and differences between the images they chose and those chosen by their classmates. We conclude the assignment by discussing the inescapability of the filter that always distances representation from Nora's "real environments of memory."

The core concepts of the course help students recognize that all representations of the past are representations, whether written or visual, fiction or nonfiction, ornate or frank, romanticized or realistic. Brady's photographs and Ken Burns's 1990 documentary may seem more true and real when compared with the melodrama of Darley's illustration and Selznick's *Gone with the Wind*. Yet Brady's staff members took many of the images attributed to Brady, and some of these were posed.[11] Despite his technical skill and interest in documenting history, he "sought action to advance his career" (Widmer). Burns's *The Civil War* draws heavily on Brady's work and imbues his photographs with authenticity by placing them alongside primary sources like letters, diaries, and newspaper articles and secondary sources from well-known historians. These examples demonstrate how history functions as an imperfect "representation of the past" and how texts participate in the recording and shaping of history and cultural memory (Nora 8). Students show knowledge of these concepts by relating Civil War photographs of questionable authenticity to fake or altered images from the more recent past, such as the photoshopped picture of Sarah Palin wearing an American flag bikini and the widely circulated version of John Filo's Pulitzer Prize–winning photograph of the Kent State shootings that airbrushed out the pole behind Mary Ann Vecchio. They recognize that image alteration is not new, existing before the advent of software programs that make easy the simulation and modification of images. Students become aware that even documents known to be false contain messages that shape public opinion.

Ironically, Civil War photographs like Mathew Brady's are more accessible today than they were during the war thanks to digital humanities initiatives and online archives. Software also helps us spot fakery, embellishment, and the artist's agenda. Because photographs were not published in newspapers and magazines during the war—the technology did not yet exist—and it was impossible to take clear pictures of moving subjects,[12] war photographs frequently were adapted as wood engravings for reproduction in *Harper's*, *Frank Leslie's Illustrated Newspaper*, and other periodicals. An 1863 image from *Frank Leslie's* by J. F. E. Hillen depicting the Battle of Chickamauga, "The War in Georgia," demonstrates the way artists could use their imaginations to invent scenes they did not witness or to mute the brutality of the battlefield.[13] Mountains dwarf the fighting of distant soldiers to provide a comforting image of stability amid the confusion of battle. The image uses a wide focus that makes soldiers seem smaller and farther away, depersonalizing their suffering and literally diminishing them. No man's face is clearly rendered; more important, much of the chaos is obscured by the artist's rendering of gunpowder smoke.

Analyzing images like these and learning about the various technical and interpretive methods writers and artists have used to represent and remember the Civil War demonstrate the tensions between history and cultural memory. Digital humanities offer a unique medium for connecting diverse visual and written texts and examining the unity of canonical records, literary and historical. The emphasis in digital humanities on applying media and technology to enduring and emerging questions in many disciplines fosters better understanding of the relation among different forms of communication and knowledge of the Civil War. Students can easily access and compare representations of and responses to the war from the nineteenth century to the present. Observing changes in modes of remembrance helps them recognize history as constantly evolving and memory as malleable. Technology and electronic resources foster discovery of the shifting boundary between fact and fiction and allow students to see that what once was accepted as true later proves false, and vice versa. The Library of Congress's "The Case of the Moved Body" makes it possible to compare versions of Alexander Gardner's staged photos of a Confederate soldier (Beeghley). Twenty-first-century scholars confirm events in Loreta Janeta Velazquez's account of fighting as a Confederate soldier while disguised as a man, authenticating a text widely considered fictionalized since its 1875 publication.[14] Introducing students to a greater variety of perspectives, which are now more accessible than ever, offers a way to move toward an understanding of the Civil War that, informed by awareness of cultural memory, is more complex.

Completing the visual text analysis assignment allows students to better understand the literature of the Civil War as well as the cultural contexts in which writers created these works. For example, one student characterized a photograph from the Burns Civil War series that was originally published in August 1865 as a staged, idealized image designed to comfort and appeal to Americans who did not participate in the war. The student interpreted the photograph of patients in Ward K of Armory Square Hospital as a sanitized image that hides the filth and pain, which are depicted explicitly in a hospital scene in Brooks's novel *March* (204). Another student, finding an advertisement seeking a hundred colored men to form an army regiment, noted that *The Red Badge of Courage* makes no mention of the formation of colored regiments, which led the class to do further research on the role of African American soldiers in the Civil War and an analysis of their omission from many canonical narratives.

In recognizing what Stuart McConnell terms the geography of Civil War memory, we expand our understanding beyond the purview of a monolithic official narrative or discrete and disconnected versions, such as Union and Confederate (249). This expansion poses the risk that the combination of multiple visions could obscure the ideological, political, and moral stakes of the war. Instructors should be sensitive to this danger and address it by ensuring that students do not lose sight of the war's key causes and results. The benefits of rethinking the geography of Civil War memory, however, outweigh the risks. The process prepares teachers and students to think critically about how historians, writers, artists, and filmmakers since the 1860s have shaped our knowledge of the past and to answer the question, "What do we know about the Civil War, and how do we know it?" The rise of commercial entertainment and its place of prominence in contemporary United States culture make television and film the means by which most Americans remember the Civil War and create a popular correlation between memory and entertainment (264). Disney World features the Hall of the Presidents, and HBO's *John Adams* (2008) won more awards than any miniseries in television history. The Civil War has received and likely will continue to receive similar attention. Through teaching the literature of the Civil War we address gaps in cultural memory and the literary canon. Reading Civil War texts of the nineteenth, twentieth, and twenty-first centuries alongside historical images engages different learning styles and promotes collaborative learning and critical thinking about the content and sources of our knowledge of the war.

Notes

1. Stuart McConnell argued in 2004 that "more people have seen a single fictional Civil War film, *Gone with the Wind*, than have read the works of all professional Civil War historians combined" (259). David O. Selznick's 1939 epic may seem a bit outmoded today, but McConnell makes an important and enduring point regarding the power of visual texts, including popular film.

2. Pierre Nora designates the disconnect "historiographical consciousness" (9). Maurice Halbwachs, Jann Assmann, and Richard Terdiman all develop this concept and define it as collective memory or cultural memory.

3. Fahs and Waugh point out that symbols of the war remain "deeply meaningful" in contemporary United States politics, particularly the politics of race, and that representations and references such as the Confederate flag constitute methods of inclusion and exclusion (1).

4. In a *New York Times* op-ed piece, Kate Masur called *Lincoln* "disappointing," since "African-American characters do almost nothing but passively wait for white men to liberate them" ("In Spielberg's *Lincoln*"). *Django Unchained* (2012), which remakes the antebellum years, affords its title character more autonomy but also generated criticism. Spike Lee, for instance, dismissed the film as "disrespectful" (qtd. in Ryzik).

5. According to Todd Hembree, the Cherokee Nation attorney general, tribal membership is "not a race-based situation. It is an identity" (qtd. in Murphy). Excluding the freedmen's descendants represents the tribe's sovereign right to determine citizenship (Murphy). Celia E. Naylor argues that "slaveowning and non-slaveowning Cherokees benefited from the unpaid labor and services of enslaved people," who "influenced the Cherokee Nation's development and survival as a sovereign nation" even though most did not own slaves.

6. See, for example, Boyle et al.; Dziuban et al. Lisa Gonzales and Devin Vodicka identify "four standard models of blended learning that have been proven to meet student academic needs and provide flexibility with instructional settings" (8).

7. *Illinois Online Network* and *Minnesota State Colleges and Universities Online*, for example, offer resources such as the self-assessment "Is Online Learning Right for You?," which lists factors for students to consider before taking an online course, such as the need for basic computer skills, a high-speed Internet connection, self-motivation, and the ability to express oneself in writing.

8. This illustration, entitled "The Dying Soldier," is available online at The Civil War in Art: Teaching and Learning through Chicago Collections.

9. Corbaux's illustration "Eva's Farewell," appeared in the 1853 Stannard and Dixon edition of *Uncle Tom's Cabin*. The image can be viewed through the British Museum's online collection. Joseph Boggs Beale designed a similar image

in 1881 for the C. W. Briggs Company's magic lantern production of *Uncle Tom's Cabin*, "Eva's Dying Farewell." It can be accessed through the University of Virginia's multimedia archive Uncle Tom's Cabin *and American Culture*.

10. The National Archives maintains *The Civil War as Photographed by Mathew Brady*, where this image and others can be viewed. The image discussed here is "Confederate Dead behind a Stone Wall at Fredericksburg, VA."

11. Both William A. Frassanito and Frederic Ray have revealed that Civil War photographs were staged, posed, and manipulated. Frassanito questions the authenticity of two images taken following the Battle of Bull Run in 1861 because they depict the same group of men. He writes, "Someone apparently told the soldiers to pretend they were fighting in the one view, and then instructed them to pretend they were dead in the other" (*Antietam* 31–32). Alexander Gardner, a photographer who worked for Brady, rearranged the corpse of a "rebel sharpshooter" in a series of images with shifting locations, positions, and props (Ray).

12. George Sullivan observes that photographs were not widely used in newspapers until the 1880s (34).

13. This illustration appears in *Frank Leslie's Illustrated Civil War*, edited by Louis Shepheard Moat. It can be viewed online at the *Library of Congress* Web site.

14. See Blanton and Cook 97; Alemán; and *Rebel*. These works suggest that the disruption of gender roles, national borders, and identity in Velazquez's *The Woman in Battle* may have contributed to its reception as a fabrication.

Kathleen Diffley

Recollecting the Civil War through Nineteenth-Century Periodicals

It used to be that approaching the experience of civil crisis through the pages of early magazines was just doomed. Not only was the subject of Civil War literature a nonstarter in most English departments but there was also a genuine concern about access to nineteenth-century periodicals. Even in the large state university where I teach, a goodly number of the literary monthlies and weekly newsmagazines held by the library were available only in out-of-the-way places. Some had been relocated to off-site storage, some shelved in basement facilities with erratic delivery, and some assigned to Special Collections with reduced hours (forget weekends). Students weren't allowed into the Special Collections periodicals cage down several floors, which meant no browsing, no dawdling, no startling discoveries. It was tough to find out what Herman Melville's first audiences might have been reading before *Battle-Pieces and Aspects of the War* was published, and overscheduled undergraduates weren't likely to spare an hour for Special Collections and *Harper's New Monthly Magazine*, where poems like his "Gettysburg" and "The March to the Sea" first appeared amid travel narratives, scientific essays, celebrity portraits, local tours, and natural history sketches that were worth noticing. Despite the culture of books, which still persists in most of our classrooms,

211

nineteenth-century readers in parlors and camps, hospital wards and prison cells, actually stayed tuned to magazine pages in ways that even English majors have long neglected.

During the Civil War and its immediate aftermath, periodicals fed a hunger for firsthand accounts, for pictures in prose or engraving, and for the stories that would linger, enough to create what Alice Fahs has called "a print memory of the war" (*Imagined Civil War* 30). In our own era of redefining what counts and reprinting less familiar texts for classroom use, putting together a syllabus that draws on the fiction and drama, poetry and songs, photographs and memoirs of the 1860s has become a cinch, and so has the shiver of rediscovering the war's imagined narratives. Yet culturally attentive methodologies and newly affordable editions have also opened a can of worms for an English department's close readers. The selective omissions in newly available texts are at once inevitable and disquieting, enough to tax the literary habit of exegesis when it proves tricky to read closely what isn't there, what has remained unremembered—for example, contemporary discussions of female volunteers and midwar emancipation, debates about class frictions and the war in the West. When recovered texts are taught for the unexpected details they include, it becomes all the harder to credit what still gets left out.

Fortunately, primary research in nineteenth-century periodicals offers a deft pedagogical alternative, and not simply because the earlier and sometimes less revised work by writers like Melville and John W. De Forest, Louisa May Alcott and Frederick Douglass, also appeared in contemporary periodical pages. Since nineteenth-century magazines were decidedly various, in both their mounting numbers and their hodgepodge contents, they offer a revealing corrective to the more isolated trade in books that often passes as "print memory" but shouldn't, because Fahs's term encompasses so much more. In fact, teaching the Civil War through the lens of magazines can enable a more comprehensive recovery of the crisis years and their aftermath in at least three ways. For one thing, magazines provide their own written contexts for how Civil War accounts were once read and could be read again. For another, magazines were generally founded in urban areas, which means that investigating city demographics can shed light on what even periodicals have stunted, rearranged, or selectively promoted, generally to suit the editorial agendas that students can profile expeditiously. Finally, the polemical engagements of a contentious magazine marketplace often led to the buried traces of rebuttal in literary texts, where they lurk as a pattern that points to social fears. From contexts to filters to hidden signs, periodicals provide ways to track print memory without neglecting its silent gaps.

Taking magazines themselves as sites of production also enables a classroom shift to a process of discovery and correction that can augment almost any syllabus. Indeed, choosing literary texts as the basis for classroom discussion and then shifting to periodical investigations adds primary research expeditiously and creatively. Quite a few of my students, graduate and undergraduate, have taken to the brash appeal of weeklies and monthlies, women's periodicals and religious organs, illustrated newsmagazines and reform vehicles. In this essay, I want to focus mostly on Civil War Cultures, a graduate seminar that I have taught more than once, but almost any survey course that grazes the Civil War can provide an opportunity for introducing undergraduates to nineteenth-century magazines. Even at the most budget-challenged institutions, instructors with an eye to the Internet's growing archive (and a healthy appreciation for its selective priorities) can slip in periodical research and thereby change classroom dynamics overnight.

Twenty years ago, when I first taught a nineteenth-century survey on my way to Civil War Cultures, there was just a week given to researching battlefield illustrations. In an era without electronic access, graduate students had to get their hands on issues of New York's *Harper's Weekly* or Richmond's *Southern Illustrated News*, even if that meant lugging huge folio reprints off top shelves or peering at microfilm rolls in dark cubicles, where copying costs ran high. These days, both extended searches and unexpected revelations are common, because hundreds of periodicals have become digitized, word-searchable, a clickety-click away. So many full runs are available online at freely accessible sites like the *Making of America* libraries at Michigan and Cornell, as well as subscription databases like the *American Periodical Series* and *HarpWeek*, that even underclassmen in, say, Hawthorne and His Contemporaries or Literature and Culture of Nineteenth-Century America can arrive at edgy new readings of Melville's war poetry or Douglass's *The Heroic Slave* in no time. Of course, the heaping possibilities of primary research can also bewilder psych undergrads or theater studies majors, not to mention English doctoral students, unless help is provided—with clustered readings, research queries, pivotal paragraphs, classroom tricks, and conference papers or scholarly essays at term's end.

Whatever written work becomes the basis for course grading, periodical research most often thrives when a syllabus clusters eight to ten texts in groups, the number depending on how many papers seem appropriate. In Civil War Cultures, I have favored textual pairs. Before anyone goes to the stacks or spends an afternoon at the keyboard, we first discuss Melville's *Battle-Pieces* with Alcott's *Hospital Sketches*, or the battlefield scenes of De Forest's *Miss Ravenel's Conversion from Secession to Loyalty* with the unnerving plates of Alexander Gardner's *Photographic Sketch Book of the Civil War*, or the continuing appeal of Harriet Beecher Stowe's *Uncle Tom's Cabin* on the stage (shorter! more arresting!) with Rebecca Harding Davis's *Waiting for the Verdict* or, if time allows, with a postbellum slave narrative like Sam Aleckson's "Before the War and after the Union: An Autobiography," recently unearthed and reprinted in *I Belong to South Carolina*. Selected chapters of James M. McPherson's *Battle Cry of Freedom* ground literary endeavor in the war's theaters and events, while scholarly commentary and student presentations from Fahs's *The Imagined Civil War* or, just as usefully, from Elizabeth McHenry on the black press in *Forgotten Readers*, Joshua Brown on illustrating the war in *Beyond the Lines*, or David Blight on the politics of cultural memory in *Race and Reunion* help make discussion more adventurous.

My syllabus arcs are small because responses of roughly five pages regularly supplement our literary focus with an appetite for data, so that the play of a text is caught up in the play of ambient culture. On paper, at least in four brief reading responses, that intersection has worked best in reverse order: instead of taking one of the paired texts as a given and a wide-ranging search of periodicals as the stuff of a report, students after discussion begin with primary research and then bring their findings to bear by returning to a single text with new eyes. How does coverage of a particular battle or military figure jibe with Melville's irregular stanzas, especially given the "disruption" Timothy Sweet sees even in his rhymes (*Traces* 172)? Where do the collaboration and friction between wartime surgeons and ward nurses, what Jane Schultz describes as their "web of relations" ("Embattled Care" 105), help orient Alcott's episodic structure? What types of spaces were African Americans seen to occupy in illustrated periodicals after emancipation was proclaimed on 1 January 1863? How, then, does Gardner's "What Do I Want, John Henry?" (plate 27) or "A Burial Party" (plate 94) become more provocative, more recognizably what Elizabeth Young calls "alternative representations of racial hierarchy and rebellion" (56)? Returning to a paired text in a reading response makes renewing class discussion that much more productive each day such short papers are due, especially when a syllabus is organized around contrasting texts that set enthusiastic researchers at odds.

If clustering texts is best planned in advance, initiating research queries is best done in the classroom, where genuine curiosity can jump-start primary research. Post two or three more developed queries on a course Web site, and interested students can choose one, all thanks to a classroom maneuver that becomes second nature. At least once a week as conversation concludes, I ask what everyone wants to know more about, especially given the unpredictable torque of the day's discussion. When we finished our class on Davis's *Waiting for the Verdict*, which was serialized in New York's *Galaxy* during 1867, three questions immediately surfaced: How was miscegenation treated in magazines of the 1860s? How were surgeons and new medical developments described? And what about contemporary perceptions of Philadelphia, where much of Davis's novel was set? Three shared bursts of curiosity, and I had an hour or so of work cut out for me—namely, turning quick questions into extended research queries like the following, a query that incorporates contemporary events, suggests search tactics, and invites specific returns to the text at hand:

> How was miscegenation treated by the popular press? This was a particular issue during the late 1860s, when Reconstruction amendments to the Constitution were being debated and issues like abolition, federal jurisdiction, and voting rights were discussed with some heat. But "miscegenation" as a term? You might try searching "amalgamation" instead. You might also try focusing on a newsmagazine like *Harper's Weekly*, especially when you can search illustrations and thus the political cartoons on each issue's final page. Alternately, "octoroon" or "mulat*" (to catch *mulatto* and its variations) could turn up stories in more literary magazines via the *American Periodical Series*, the *Making of America* Web sites at Cornell and Michigan, or (say) weeklies like the African Methodist Episcopal Church's *Christian Recorder*, available from *Accessible Archives*. Does one or more of these databases make it easier to understand the otherwise pallid Garrick Randolph or the "yellow" Dr. Broderip, the sharp disdain of Margaret Conrad or the education of young Ross?

Developed into paragraphs like this one, research queries can orient investigations, save search time, and, if reasonably well conceived and posted within twenty-four hours, keep follow-up discussions from sheer welter. Mind you, none of my nudges have kept anyone from other search terms and other choices among Davis's troubling scenes. But posted queries have generally streamlined searches and thus made more time for student thought. Just as significant, favoring two or three research queries as prompts has ensured that a later discussion of completed reading responses will also favor two or three specific concerns born of shared curiosity.

Candidly, shared curiosity can also lead to zilch, at least in the hour or so that new cultural historians have for searching. Sometimes they grab a less promising database, like *African American Newspapers*, for probing mixed-race marriages when antebellum fugitives heading north were more intent on emancipation. Sometimes hasty search terms are too current or too close to subject headings for digitized word searching: "mixed race" and "African American" really don't track well across nineteenth-century periodicals. Even when a database is intelligently chosen and search terms are shrewdly lifted from texts discussed, a serious search may not uncover much data. After all, there's no guarantee that classroom curiosity about miscegenation or hospital reconfiguration or even wartime Philadelphia was shared by magazine editors and contributors during the 1860s and 1870s. After about half an hour of fruitless searching, it's time to reword or combine queries; adjustments are fine as long as discoveries can be part of the same upcoming conversation in class. Alternatively, there's always another query on the same text, or the other paired text with posted queries of its own. Whatever students decide to do, it's important for them to discover something worth speculating about after a rueful acknowledgment of time wasted. Reading responses or short papers are informal enough to allow for a brief lament—hopefully on the way to boffo success in another quarter.

For anyone undertaking primary research, the next task after collecting periodical data is to renew literary purpose. Over the years, I have found that such paragraphs are most useful when they conclude with a textual question that research has inspired. For example, if Stowe's Little Eva inherits heaven on the wings of a dove in one dramatist's final tableau, does Topsy inherit the earth and control of the broom, thereby becoming the rambunctious agent of social change? Naturally such questions can materialize only after students have selected their research query, completed their periodical search, made three to five tantalizing selections, and drafted a paragraph worth posting on the course Web site. After those postings accumulate the night before cultural context gets discussed, a one-class workshop on simple but pivotal paragraphs can reveal who's lost in the archives, who's found something unexpected, and who's already formulating a crackerjack question for the paper's remaining pages. Iron out those differing results in small groups, and everyone has a shot at the thrill of discovery, maybe even a revised question so incisive that papers will be a kick to read.

This workshop is often as ad hoc as the paragraphs that students post. But the transition from periodical research to textual reengagement can nonetheless be specific, especially as students reconsider the broad questions about character or plot or the author's point that they first concocted. What patterns turn up in their three to five selections? What now seems peculiar enough in the pages we read together to raise a question worth asking? Concentrating on that pivot in class also separates heaped data from renewed close reading, while quietly confirming that everyone got the archival work finished and there's still time to solve problems. With an emphasis on steady progress, it pays to make pivotal paragraphs informal ("I was surprised to find that . . ."), even if quirky phrasing spills into the upcoming paper, because it's better to lurch into an idea worth pursuing than to aim for a safe focus and safer prose. Better to tumble into something that's not easy to explain, something that might intrigue everyone else, including me. So undergrads will toy with, say, unreported backstories, copycat revolts, and the tug of Christian principles in Douglass's *Heroic Slave*, while grad students may return to Davis's *Waiting for the Verdict* with an abstract's greater care, as Blake Bronson-Bartlett recently did in brooding on Negro doctor scandals that cropped up in Philadelphia's *Medical and Surgical Reporter, Christian Recorder,* and *Saturday Evening Post.* Struck by the manner in which that city "acts upon Broderip's body, the way it allows him to be white and then allows him to be black," Bronson-Bartlett ventured early on into Philadelphia's "unconscious, from the hospitalesque suburbs to the carnivalesque urban ghetto, where Broderip becomes a 'black doctor' and returns with the vaccine he will propose to the nation." Heady stuff in a simple paragraph.

Moderating discussions of periodical research can be heady as well, not at all the sensible examination of syllabus texts that everybody brings to class. For two consecutive brainstorming sessions, first on pivotal paragraphs and then on completed responses, everybody brings something different. As a result, discussion can fly off in fifteen, twenty, twenty-five different directions without classroom tricks. The key I've found is to focus on the process of discovery and correction. In the workshop on pivotal paragraphs, that's best done in groups, particularly when organizational zeal, searching genius, and time management skills vary. Some undergraduates have trouble pulling a paragraph together, some founder on search terms, and some just start late. The easiest way to enable trim pivots is to write your own paragraph and post it. Then group discussions aren't about what that paragraph looks like but about how that paragraph can look better, how a striking new question can invite textual return and closer reading. Because the pivot brings the syllabus back into focus, I prefer to organize posted paragraphs and then classroom groups by text: everybody working on Melville's *Battle-Pieces* works together. But when undergrads are hesitant about sharing hard-won discoveries and incisive questions with aimless classmates, an easy alternative is to create random groups by counting off around the room, no matter who's working on what. Theft is then less of a worry and questions sharpen, especially when I visit.

For me, the preview of discoveries in pivotal paragraphs is exhilarating, but it's also a reminder of pending sprawl, the spill of data that might make completed responses messy. When those are discussed in the next class, it pays to focus on process with questions about searching. "Who found three to five usable selections in under an hour? How did you do it?" Since most students are busting to talk about their keyboard magic, a few will always volunteer, and they are the likeliest to reopen discussion of paired texts just as economically. Asking about how everyone settled on research queries, search terms, and specific databases takes only a few minutes and can tease out other comments ("Me too," "I saw that!") while demonstrating which texts and queries really caught fire. If there is a moment when the tug of periodical fare is keen, this is it. For undergraduates, the result is research euphoria, while graduate students recognize a brisk way to detail cultural ambience. In Civil War Cultures, it has also been easy to get from the report of discovery to the more settled project of correction. "What looked significant about all that when you returned to *Hospital Sketches*?" That's the literary pivot this discussion should take as well.

Four five-page responses throughout the term may be enough writing for any class. Still, there's an available summa in a semester essay or conference paper, ten to twelve pages based on a shorter response already completed. This substantive undertaking allows students to move beyond initial discoveries and into more thoughtful speculation about a significant piece of literature as well as the culturally laden magazines of its period and the manner in which a text comments on its historical moment. At twice the length, this more robust paper should add at least five more magazine selections to corroborate earlier findings and at least five scholarly sources to reveal an ongoing professional conversation while encouraging an original contribution. Here, particularly, it's important to profile each periodical source with information on typical contents, editors, publication site, dates of appearance, and editorial agenda. No periodical offers uncontested truth; every periodical aims for a market niche, sometimes as the official organ of an institution, society, or church. Reckoning with different editorial priorities as well as different scholarly conversations can lead to a more astute issue or a counterintuitive turn, which a shorter response only tickled.

For honors courses or graduate seminars, ambitious research essays of twenty to twenty-five pages can begin with an even broader sample: at least ten periodical selections and at least ten secondary sources. Out of the intersection of wider periodical debate and more scholarly commentary, a knottier cultural problem may emerge, particularly when a single text can be seen addressing the recurring debates that periodicals once championed. Bronson-Bartlett combined queries to investigate Philadelphia as a wartime medical center with a preference for hospital redesign, specifically for the sequential wards that in his hands operated like sovereign states reorganized along a national corridor. Six months after completing that essay, he had a conference paper for the American Literature Association convention, a paper so successful that the Rebecca Harding Davis Society invited him to organize his own session the following year. And why not, when he could write in his seminar essay, "The ambiguities of Dr. Broderip's environment have been transformed into a system of sanitary surfaces, racially coded and ready to co-exist, separate and never equal"? A mulatto slave recast as a white doctor and then a black soldier, Dr. Broderip becomes the image of a reconstruction that fails.

Ultimately, periodical discoveries can cast unusual light on familiar textual developments and bring into focus scenes, stanzas, or images that otherwise get lost. Not only does that make classroom discussions more engaging, especially for quieter students who happen to be keyboard wizards, but also hours of grading can become riveting. Better yet, the trim periodical archive that an English major brings to rereading, say, Douglass's *The Heroic Slave* can produce a crackerjack writing sample for grad school applications or a sizzling personal statement for law school. Graduate students in their turn take periodical research skills to seminars on

Whitman or Dickinson, Native literatures or gender studies, comps articles or dissertation chapters, conference talks or book proposals. In the flash these days of instant periodical access, thanks to Internet Web sites and subscription databases, print memory expands exponentially and the clamor of civil crisis is reanimated, a boon to the Civil War dead stirred anew and to a continued reckoning that is forever under way.

Timothy Sweet

Teaching with Contemporary Anthologies

In a conventional one-semester survey of American literature that goes from the beginnings to 1865, we can hope to devote two weeks at most to the Civil War. Yet two weeks is enough to organize a substantial array of primary materials in terms of three framing questions: How do the materials approach the issue of slavery? How do they imagine nationhood? How do they address the violence of the war?

Since a Civil War unit will likely come at the end of this semester, the course will probably already have addressed the first and second of these questions, and possibly the third in a general way. For example, Frederick Douglass's 1845 *Narrative* and Herman Melville's "Benito Cereno" anticipate the linkage of the second and third questions in raising the question of the role of violence in antislavery action. Regarding the question that concerns nationhood, perhaps the syllabus has included some texts on state formation or community identity, such as the Mayflower Compact from William Bradford's *Of Plymouth Plantation*, John Winthrop's "Model of Christian Charity," the Declaration of Independence, or the *Federalist Papers*. William Lloyd Garrison's preface to Douglass's *Narrative* also addresses the question of nationhood: "No Union with Slaveholders!" (*Norton Anthology* [ed. Levine and Krupat] 1180).

The unit is organized chronologically to focus first on the political turbulence of 1859–60 and then on the war itself. The readings are:

Week 1

Herman Melville, "The Portent," "Apathy and Enthusiasm"
South Carolina Declaration of Secession
Mississippi Declaration of Secession
Henry Timrod, "Ethnogenesis"
Abraham Lincoln, First Inaugural Address
Walt Whitman, "Beat! Beat! Drums!"
"Scenes on the Battlefield of Antietam," *Harper's Weekly*, 18 Oct. 1862
Battlefield photographs from Antietam
Melville, "The March into Virginia," "A Utilitarian View of the Monitor's Fight," "Shiloh," "The House-top"
Emily Dickinson, "It feels a shame to be Alive"

Week 2

Whitman, "Cavalry Crossing a Ford," "Vigil Strange I Kept on the Field One Night," "A March in the Ranks Hard-Prest," "A Sight in Camp in the Daybreak," "As Toilsome I Wander'd Virginia's Woods," "The Wound-Dresser," "Reconciliation," "As I Lay with My Head in Your Lap, Camerado"
Gettysburg photographs from Gardner's *Photographic Sketch Book of the War*
Abraham Lincoln, Gettysburg Address, Second Inaugural Address
Whitman, "When Lilacs Last in the Dooryard Bloom'd"

Most standard anthologies of American literature include Lincoln's Gettysburg Address and Second Inaugural Address. The First Inaugural, although it is not regularly anthologized, is worth adding. Supplementing the anthology with one or two Confederate states' declarations of secession is an efficient way of providing historical context on motivations for the war.[1] Most anthologies include selections from Melville's *Battle-Pieces* and Whitman's *Drum-Taps*. While many of Dickinson's frequently anthologized poems seem to respond to the war, I suggest using a seldom anthologized poem that speaks more directly to the framing question about violence.[2] Confederate poets are not regularly anthologized, so the inclusion of someone like Timrod will require supplementation. Standard anthologies never include contemporary short fiction about the war itself, though a substantial amount was published during the war (see Diffley). Including an example, however, would require more time than the two-week unit I describe here.

Any of the three framing questions could be adapted as a short in-class writing exercise to prepare students for group work or class discussion. I suggest particular points for discussion as I work through the readings below; most of these could be used as writing prompts. If you assign a short paper at this point in the semester, any of the framing questions could be used as a topic from which to develop a thesis. Or they could be adapted as essay exam questions. If your exam covers only the Secession and Civil War unit, you might devise questions such as:

Analyze how at least four writers, including Abraham Lincoln, frame the violence of the Civil War in the attempt to make it meaningful. Draw some comparisons to the photographs and engravings we viewed in class.

Compare and contrast ideas of nationhood given by at least four texts.

Compare and contrast how at least four writers, including Abraham Lincoln, address or fail to address the issue of slavery in writing about secession or the Civil War.

If the exam covers more than the Civil War unit, the framing questions about slavery and nationhood could easily be adapted to look back to earlier readings. The framing question about violence in a more general form, such as, What are the roles and limits of violence in securing liberty?, could provide an exam question that reaches back as far as the colonial and revolutionary periods.

The unit begins with Melville's poem on John Brown's execution, "The Portent." You might start the discussion with the political turmoil leading up to the war, lecturing briefly on Brown's 1859 raid on the federal armory at Harpers Ferry, and then asking the class, "Was John Brown a terrorist?" Brown's raid brings together the framing questions regarding slavery and violence. The connection between them will recede from view as the syllabus moves on to battlefield materials, so it is worth emphasizing here. The figure of Brown's beard as a "meteor" of the war may (with some prompting) remind students of the Puritan typological or emblematic habit of mind, which interprets worldly events as portents or messages from God—but notice that God is absent and "the future veils its face."[3] Those who can afford to spend more time here may assign Ralph Waldo Emerson's "John Brown" or Henry David Thoreau's "A Plea for Captain John Brown," noting especially how Thoreau squarely addresses the question of violence in antislavery action.

Southern states' declarations of secession help keep the focus on the framing question of slavery and provide context for Lincoln's First Inaugural Address. A time line running from the spring and summer 1860 Republican and Democratic nominating conventions through the April 1861 bombardment of Fort Sumter will help students locate the declarations as responses to Lincoln's election in November 1860, and Lincoln's First Inaugural Address in turn as a response to the declarations. Several intertwined issues are at stake in these materials: slavery, the legacy of the Revolutionary War, national identity, and the linkage of nation to physical environment.

South Carolina's declaration is important because it comes first, because it claims the authority of Revolutionary War patriotism by putting secession in line with the Declaration of Independence, and because it cites the election of Lincoln, "whose opinions and purposes are hostile to slavery," as the precipitating cause ("Declaration" [South Carolina]). Mississippi's declaration announces the primary issue in its second sentence: "Our position is thoroughly identified with the institution of slavery—the greatest material interest of the world." Some students may be surprised at how directly the southern states expressed their commitment to preserving slavery. This commitment could spark discussion about the current symbolism of the Confederate flag.

Mississippi's declaration is also interesting for its environmental account of the slave economy, in the claim that certain staple crops are "peculiar" to a subtropical climate in which only "the black race" is adapted to labor ("Declaration" [Mississippi]). This environmental theme is developed in Timrod's poem "Ethnogenesis," with its memorable, paradoxical image of cotton fields ready for harvest as "the snow of southern summers" and its concluding vision of the Confederacy shaping the Atlantic world economy like the "genial streams" of the Gulf current (Barrett and Miller 313, 315).

Like South Carolina's declaration, Timrod marshals Revolutionary War history to legitimate the cause. Whereas the declarations emphasize the sovereignty of the individual states, his poem attempts, as the title indicates, to forge a national identity. This sense of national unity contrasts with the generational division depicted in Melville's "Apathy and Enthusiasm," a seldom anthologized early poem in the chronologically organized *Battle-Pieces* volume, and compares with the prowar energy of Whitman's "Beat! Beat! Drums!," an early poem in *Drum-Taps*. If Timrod extends the declarations' imagination of nationhood and elaborates their environmental themes, he nevertheless eliminates slavery entirely from the southern pastoral landscape: at most, there is a claim that the southern system gives "life, and home, and health" to the "poor and humble" (Barrett and Miller 314). It does not take much prompting for students to compare the euphemistic or elided treatment of slavery here with the accounts given in Douglass's *Narrative* or Stowe's *Uncle Tom's Cabin*.

In the light of the declarations of secession and Timrod's imagination of an agrarian southern nation exerting global influence, Lincoln's rhetorical goal of conciliation in the First Inaugural Address appears more pointed. Lincoln advances several figures or ideas of nationhood and links the question of nationhood to slavery.[4] It is important to point out that poems and presidential addresses do different kinds of cultural work and to discuss the different kinds of authority that each claims. However, given that Timrod's "Ethnogenesis" was written specifically to commemorate the first meeting of the Confederate Congress, it may be attempting to claim political authority as well. Lincoln's rejection of the metaphor of divorce for secession, because different parts of the country cannot "go out of the presence, and beyond the reach of each other" (*Speeches* 222), accords with South Carolina's insistence that "a geographical line has been drawn across the Union" with the election of 1860 ("Declaration" [South Carolina]). During class discussion, you might turn to an excerpt from Mary Chesnut's Civil War diary that uses the metaphor Lincoln rejects: "We separated because of incompatibility of temper. We divorced, North and South, because we hated each other so. If we could only separate—a 'séparation à l'agréable,' as the French say it, and not a horrid fight after divorce" (*Norton Anthology* [Levine and Krupat] 1310). Given the date, it is possible that Chesnut was alluding to Lincoln's speech. Finally, Lincoln's invocation of providential history ("the Almighty Ruler of nations" [*Speeches* 223]), in which students may hear again echoes, resonates with the third stanza of "Ethnogenesis," in which Timrod identifies the Confederacy as God's chosen nation. Despite the professed goals of the speech, Lincoln cannot help but follow the logic of secession in dividing the United States into two nations, slave and free. However, he concludes with a complex metaphor of union that appeals to a common history: "The mystic chords of memory, streching [sic] from every battle-field, and patriot grave, to every living heart and hearthstone, all over this broad land, will yet swell with the chorus of Union, when again touched, as surely they will be, by the better angels of our nature" (224).

Students may notice a contrast between the secessionists' forthright embrace of slavery and Lincoln's very cautious handling of the topic— despite earlier antislavery speeches such as the sometimes anthologized "House Divided" Speech from his 1858 senatorial campaign. A point of comparison might be Melville's and Whitman's handling of slavery. Whereas Whitman largely avoids the issue, Melville does address it in a few of the poems in *Battle-Pieces*. None of these is regularly anthologized, however, except for his poem on the New York City draft riots of 1863, "The House-top." If time permits, this poem might provide an occasion to discuss different views held by different groups regarding the link between slavery and the war (*Norton Anthology* [ed. Levine and Krupat] 1585).[5]

Considerations of slavery and nationhood recede from images and texts that focus primarily on the battlefield and the casualties of war. A brief presentation of battlefield photographs is an effective way to introduce the theme of the violence of the war. Students will need to know that visual reportage consisted primarily of woodblock engravings taken from drawings or photographs. It is easy enough to put together a *PowerPoint* presentation using images from the *HarpWeek* database and other Internet sources. Engravings taken from artists' drawings show live action but minimize deaths and wounds. Engravings taken from battlefield photographs use various framing devices to create meaning.[6] For example, a two-page layout in the 18 October 1862 issue of *Harper's Weekly* organizes Alexander Gardner's photographs of corpses on the Antietam battlefield around the picturesque image of the bridge, which dominates the visual field. Sometimes the framing devices were already present in the photographs. By the time the photographer got to the field, the dead had already been arranged in an orderly fashion for burial, as in Gardner's photograph of corpses arranged in a chevron.[7] One photograph includes a pensive observer at the scene. Moving back and forth between magazine layout and photograph, students can ponder the problem of giving meaning to death in war.

That meaning can be pursued in Melville's, Dickinson's, and Whitman's poems. Several of Melville's thematize disillusionment. "The March into Virginia" tells the story of raw recruits who imagine war as both bucolic—a "berrying party, pleasure-wooed"—and heroic—a chance for "glory . . . lasting in belaureled story." However, many of these innocent youths "die, experienced"; they "[p]erish, enlightened by the vollied glare" (*Norton Anthology* [ed. Levine and Krupat] 1584). "A Utilitarian View of the Monitor's Fight" also concerns disillusionment, though of a different sort: if "passion" is replaced by mechanistic "calculations," "War's made less grand than Peace" (Barrett and Miller 276). The nostalgia evident here for traditional warfare cuts against the criticism of war proposed by "The March into Virginia." In "The March," Melville's deadly pun on the "berrying" party may be especially evident to students who have just seen the battlefield photographs. You might ask of Melville's pun on "enlightened," what kind of enlightenment comes in the moment of death? Here, students may point to some lines from "Shiloh":

> . . . dying foemen mingled there—
> Foemen at morn, but friends at eve—
> Fame or country least their care:
> What like a bullet can undeceive! (*Norton Anthology* [ed. Levine and Krupat] 1585)

These lines return the discussion explicitly to the framing questions about slavery and nationhood. How do these dying soldiers imagine nationhood? "Shiloh" might be compared with a more sentimental treatment of the reconciliation-in-death theme such as that of J. Augustine Signaigo's poem "On the Heights of Mission Ridge" (Barrett and Miller 120).

Dickinson's "It feels a shame to be Alive" seems to counter Melville's skepticism. While Dickinson wrote a large number of poems in response to the war, this one is clearly organized around one of the most common tropes used to make sense of its violence: sacrifice.[8] The soldier "put away / What little of Him we—possessed / In Pawn for Liberty" (Barrett and Miller 356). "Liberty" has many associations in a patriotic context, but students who have recently read abolitionist literature and the southern states' declarations of secession will probably identify the emancipation of slaves as the word's primary reference. How is slavery connected to the poem's "we"? In subsequent stanzas, Dickinson develops the trope of sacrifice to reveal its economic structure:

> The price is great—Sublimely paid—
> Do we deserve—a Thing—
> That lives—like Dollars—must be piled
> Before we may obtain?

Anticipating the calculus of blood that forms the conclusion of Lincoln's Second Inaugural address, her explicit comparison of "lives" to "Dollars" asks the question of sufficient worth. Whatever students may make of the calculus, they should come to see that for Dickinson and her contemporaries it was understood in theological terms. If some students miss the allusion of the next line—the "Enormous Pearl" referring to the "pearl of great price" from Matthew 13.45–46—most will notice how the characterization of the soldiers as "Saviors" evokes Christ's sacrifice. This characterization transcends the economic structure of the trope of sacrifice developed in the previous two stanzas. Yet in this transcendence, the figure seems to carry national, political meaning: Christ died to redeem humankind from original sin, so contemporary readers of Dickinson would have understood her as suggesting that the soldiers' sacrifice redeems the nation from its original sin of slavery. Students may recall Thoreau's characterization of John Brown as one "who offered himself to be the saviour of four millions of [slaves]" (*Norton Anthology* [ed. Levine and Krupat] 1168). A discussion question might focus on the language of sacrifice in the contemporary United States discourse on war.

Students who compare Dickinson's and Whitman's use of Christian symbolism will have a better grasp of the ideological work of the trope of sacrifice. In Whitman's "A Sight in Camp in the Daybreak," this symbolism is both more overt than Dickinson's and less transactional: "Young man I think I know you—I think this face is the face of the Christ himself, / Dead and divine and brother of all, and here again he lies" (1398). It is not at all clear whether this soldier-Christ has died for anything, has accomplished anything with his death. Elaborating this question is a line from "The Wound-Dresser," in which the noncombatant speaker says, "poor boy! I never knew you / Yet I think I could not refuse this moment to die for you, if that would save you" (1400). Put in the subjunctive mood, the trope of sacrifice offers not a hypothetical transaction but a means of organizing, in the speaker's interior monologue, the emotions of grief, horror, and empathy.[9] Note the absence of national reference in Whitman's battlefield poems such as "Cavalry Crossing a Ford," "Vigil Strange," and "A March in the Ranks Hard-Prest." Students may assume that these poems describe the experience of the Union soldier. But some may know that the "guidon flags" of many Confederate regiments were also "Scarlet and blue and snowy white" (1396 ["Cavalry"]).

Whitman provides a more graphic account of the results of violence than any other writer, especially in "A March in the Ranks" and "The

Wound-Dresser." Indeed, the survey course up to this point has probably included few such depictions. At most, such moments would have
been the episode from J. Hector St. John de Crèvecœur's *Letters from an
American Farmer* in which Farmer James sees a caged slave hung from a
tree and left to die, and some episodes from Douglass's 1845 *Narrative*
such as the whipping of Aunt Hester and the fight with the slave breaker
Covey. Yet the violence in Whitman's poems remains dissociated from the
problem of slavery. If students are asked what the experience of the war
was like for the speakers of his dramatic monologues, one of the answers
may be affectional bonding between soldiers. Often eroticized, this bonding finally takes on political meaning in "Reconciliation": the abstract discourse of the opening lines—"war," "deeds of carnage," "sisters Death
and Night"—morphs into a fantasy in which the speaker imagines kissing
the corpse of "my enemy" (*Norton Anthology* [ed. Levine and Krupat]
1401). The class may already have discussed the importance of homo-
eroticism for Whitman's poetic project, may have considered, for example,
the "Live Oak with Moss" sequence from the 1850s, which was broken
up and integrated into the *Calamus* section of the 1860 *Leaves of Grass*
(1380–82).[10] The deployment of homoerotic imagery in *Drum-Taps* provides an occasion to revisit, or to open for the first time, the question of
Whitman's vision of nationhood. In ignoring slavery in favor of white
male bonding, his Civil War poems seem to illustrate the thesis of David
Blight's *Race and Reunion*, according to which the reconciliation of white
veterans eclipsed the war's emancipationist promise.

Lincoln's Gettysburg Address and Second Inaugural Address reinstate
the connections among the framing questions concerning slavery, nationhood, and violence. If time permits, you might want to contextualize the
occasion of the Gettysburg Address by showing a couple of battlefield
photographs from Gettysburg and giving a brief account of the establishment of this first national cemetery, which formally marked the segregation of Union and Confederate dead in separate interments.[11] The
Gettysburg sequence from Gardner's *Photographic Sketch Book of the War*
(1866) provides an opportunity to illustrate how reportage constructed
the meaning of the war's violence.[12] That the *Sketch Book* was produced
after the war as a historiographic document (see Lee and Young) could
open the question of Lincoln's framing of the war with an eye toward the
historical record. Gardner supplies captions, such as "A Harvest of Death"
and "Home of a Rebel Sharpshooter," as well as narrative and descriptive
texts to endow the images of corpses with meaning. The texts focus on

the question of nationhood, using geographic and political references to differentiate Union from Confederate soldiers even though he captioned the images of corpses arbitrarily.[13] None of Gardner's lengthy captions mentions slavery. Although Lincoln does not explicitly mention slavery in the Gettysburg Address, students will likely identify allusions to it in the opening and closing sentences: "dedicated to the proposition that all men are created equal" and "a new birth of freedom" (*Norton Anthology* [ed. Levine and Krupat] 738). They should also be able to recognize the trope of sacrifice ("gave the last full measure of devotion") and link it to Lincoln's political language ("shall not have died in vain"). Consider this question for discussion: Given the occasion and his rhetorical purpose, why didn't he mention slavery?

By contrast, Lincoln devotes over half of his Second Inaugural Address to the problem of slavery, identifying it as "the cause of the war" (739). His rhetoric links slavery, nationhood, and violence. Asking students to focus on any one of these framing questions, perhaps in a short piece of in-class writing, will probably draw attention to the other two. Lincoln's reference to "the providence of God" (739) may remind students of Puritan providential history—for example, William Bradford's account of the Pequot massacre or Mary Rowlandson's account of both individual and national experience during King Philip's War (for Bradford and for Rowlandson, see *Norton Anthology* [ed. Franklin, Gura, and Krupat] 134–35, 236–67, resp.). Students may find that the calculus of violence that Lincoln introduces—"until every drop of blood drawn with the lash, shall be paid by another drawn with the sword"—recalls some graphic imagery from abolitionist literature ([ed. Levine and Krupat] 740). At the time of Lincoln's second inauguration (4 Mar. 1865), the issue of the war was not in doubt. Thus the calculus of blood is meant both to justify the continued prosecution of the war and to provide a larger historical explanation. Some close reading is in order here, for the ledger will balance in this exchange only if the blood drawn by the sword is that of slaveholders or their representatives. But what about the violence suffered by Union soldiers, some of whom were themselves former slaves: did they too represent the slaveholders? Lincoln's closing paragraph suggests that the answer is, somehow, yes. For he asks his auditors "to bind up the nation's wounds"—and the "nation" here must include the conquered Confederacy (740). Thus in his brilliant ambiguity the object of the war's violence could be both white and black, northern and southern, general and particular, national and local.

If by this point in the unit the class sessions lag behind the schedule of readings, the complex linkages developed in Lincoln's Second Inaugural among the three framing questions will provide an apt conclusion to the unit. But if time remains, students may pursue these questions into Whitman's pastoral elegy for Lincoln, "When Lilacs Last in the Dooryard Bloom'd." Students may observe that slavery is nowhere mentioned and that Whitman addresses the violence of the war only late in the poem, in stanza 15, even then seeing it "askant." Thus in the immediate aftermath of the war, one of the framing questions, concerning slavery, has already receded from view while another, concerning violence, appears in altered perspective. If, in the poet's vision, the dead "were fully at rest, they suffer'd not," yet "the living remain'd and suffer'd . . . / And the armies that remain'd suffer'd," what political prospect does the post-war future hold (*Norton Anthology* [vol. B] 1408)? Given the poem's varied landscape imagery, brought into focus by the journey of Lincoln's coffin across the continent from Washington, DC, to Springfield, Illinois (a northerly route through Pennsylvania, New York, Ohio, and Indiana), as well as its symbolization of Lincoln as a "western" star, you might ask, what is the poem's national vision? Can this vision extend beyond the individual poet's experience of mourning the death of President Lincoln?[14]

Notes

1. Declarations issued and other Confederate state papers are available online through the Avalon Project of the Yale Law School Lillian Goldman Law Library (http://avalon.law.yale.edu/subject_menus/csapage.asp).

2. In this essay, I cite the eighth edition of the *Norton Anthology* if the text is printed there. The *Bedford Anthology* (2nd ed.) contains less of Whitman, Melville, and Lincoln than do the Norton, Heath (7th ed.), and Pearson (9th ed.) anthologies, though the Bedford is the only one to print the Dickinson poem I discuss here. A good source for supplemental texts, including popular verse, is Barrett and Miller.

3. On Melville's historiographic project, see Sweet, *Traces* 165–200; Griffin 65–93.

4. For a brief account of Lincoln's sense of nationhood, see Sweet, "Lincoln."

5. A full understanding of this poem requires historical context, some of which is supplied by the anthology's footnotes. A question might be: Given the stance toward war evident in Melville's others poems, is Melville the speaker of this poem?

6. Although not all college libraries can afford *HarpWeek*, many images from *Harper's Weekly* can be retrieved through online image searches. A good,

searchable source for photographs is the Civil War Glass Negatives and Related Prints collection in the *Library of Congress Prints and Photographs Online Catalog* (www.loc.gov/pictures/collection/cwp/). To locate drawings, search the *Harp-Week* database or directly search notable artists such as Winslow Homer or Alfred Waud. A good print collection is Katz and Virga.

7. On Gardner's visual rhetoric, see Sweet, *Traces* 120–37; Lee and Young.

8. On Dickinson and the Civil War, see Wolosky; Miller 147–75.

9. On the trope of sacrifice in *Drum-Taps*, see Sweet, *Traces* 24–37.

10. On homoerotic desire in *Drum-Taps* and postwar editions of *Leaves of Grass*, see Moon 210–22.

11. On the establishment of the first national cemetery at Gettysburg, see Faust 71–73, 99–100.

12. The Cornell University Library provides a useful site devoted to the *Sketch Book*, digitizing the title page and thirty images and captions and providing background information on each (*Gardner's Photographic Sketch Book*).

13. Gardner photographed one set of corpses from different angles and, in the *Sketch Book*, labeled one such photograph as depicting Confederate dead and another as depicting Union dead. See Frassanito, *Gettysburg* 222–28.

14. For a brilliant reading of this elegy's generative possibilities, see Cavitch 233–85.

Jess Roberts

Teaching with Historical Anthologies

The sheer number of poems published and of poets who published them during the American Civil War would seem to make it as difficult as it is imperative to teach Civil War poetry. How do you choose which texts to teach when there is so much material? How do you teach the poems to students in ways that make visible the world that produced them? How do you help students engage meaningfully with poems that lack the ambivalence and eccentricities that they have likely been trained to value as defining characteristics of poetry?

Frank Moore's *The Rebellion Record* has given me one way to answer these questions and meet these challenges. Both a resource from which to draw and a text in its own right, *The Rebellion Record* is an impressive compendium of documents that contains hundreds of poems published as the war unfolded. Reading Moore's *Record* in a Civil War class or in a unit on Civil War literature in a survey class enables students to encounter poetry in a print context familiar to nineteenth-century Americans and productively familiar and unfamiliar to our students: an anthology. It helps students see and comprehend aspects of the Civil War print culture and poetry's place in that culture even as it equips students to be more canny readers of anthologies in general.

A Very Brief Description of Frank Moore's *The Rebellion Record*

Known to literary scholars mainly because of Herman Melville's use of it, *The Rebellion Record* began its life in print as a weekly circular shortly after the war started and grew quickly into a more permanent and expansive document. In volumes that ran between six and seven hundred pages and would ultimately total twelve, Moore, the editor, set out to give the war "a digested and systematic shape" by excerpting accounts of events from daily newspapers in both the North and South, publishing military documents from Union and Confederate forces, and printing "poetry, incidents and rumors" that first appeared in local, regional, and national newspapers.[1] In order to "[sift] fact from fiction and rumor" and "[present] the poetical and picturesque aspects . . . separate from the graver and more important documents" (Preface iii), Moore divided each volume into three sections: "Diary of Events," "Documents and Narratives," and "Poetry, Incidents, Rumors, Etc." Each section adheres to its own internal pagination, and many (though not all) of the documents included in second and third sections are listed in section-specific tables of contents that appear in the beginning of each volume.

In the pages of the *Record*, the poems are interspersed among the "rumors," "incidents," and whatever might fall in the category "et cetera." In the table of contents, the poems are listed individually by title, whereas those of "Incidents, Rumors, Etc." are identified as an undifferentiated, unpaginated block. The number of poems is high in the first two volumes (187 in vol. 1, 124 in vol. 2) but tapers off thereafter, ceasing completely by volume 10. Moore would mine the archive of poems he created in the *Record* for later anthologies, such as the Red, White, and Blue Series, which included the alliterative *Lyrics of Loyalty*, *Songs of Soldiers*, and *Personal and Political Ballads* and their companion, *Rebel Rhymes and Rhapsodies*—all published in 1864. These anthologies are wonderful repositories of popular verse, but I tend not to use them to teach Civil War poetry because they do not require students to recognize and reckon with many of the aspects of the print culture, which the *Record* insistently and effectively does.

Practical Matters and Classroom Strategies

My objectives in teaching poems by way of the *Record* are to expose my students to the type of poetry that filled the columns of newspapers, magazines, and contemporary anthologies; to embed those poems and others in the print culture that produced them and through which they circulated; to help students think about how the context of a poem influences what and how the poem means; and to model reading strategies that take their cues from the poems themselves. The *Record* helps me do as much by not only providing students with the texts of individual poems but also enabling—even requiring—them to see the poems as things that lived in and traveled by way of particular print contexts.

My students encounter poems in the pages of the *Record* in two different kinds of classes: either thematically or generically oriented classes that cluster popular and canonical poems or classes devoted to the *Record* as text in its own right. The thematically oriented classes are fairly typical. For instance, the students might read a cluster of call-to-arms poems from the first volume of the *Record* alongside poems from Whitman's *Drum-Taps* and Melville's *Battle-Pieces and Aspects of the War* that either share formal strategies (e.g., the imperative mood) or address themselves to the early days and events of the war. So Whitman's "Beat! Beat! Drums!" and "1861" might find themselves taught alongside George Boker's "Ad Poetas," the anonymously printed "Southrons!," and C. G. Leland's "Northmen, Come Out!," among others. This teaching of more popular poetry alongside the poetry of Whitman and Melville is hardly novel and might be easily accomplished without the *Record*. What I find, though, is that by providing my students with the popular poems as they appear in the *Record*—that is, providing them not just with the words that constitute the poems but also with those words embedded in the pages of Moore's anthology—the students begin to see the poems differently and experience how the poems' place of publication might shape how the poems are read.

The pages of the *Record* look different from those of most books my students tend to use in their classes, and that difference makes them aware of the page as a thing and of its layout as potentially significant and historically specific. In single-author collections like Whitman's and Melville's or even in the pages of Moore's other anthologies, the poems that appear are often surrounded by white space. The white space doesn't make them any less a product of nineteenth-century print culture, but it does make it less likely that students will recognize them as such. By contrast, the poems in the *Record* often appear in a crowd of text. The columns are tight, the font small; prose often frames and sometimes intrudes on sequences of poems; the year is emblazoned on the top of every alternate page; the original place of publication is often found at the foot of each poem; and so on. These visual differences help students see the document as something that has been assembled in a particular historical moment.

Though the syllabus provides the title of a poem and, when appropriate, the author, I no longer circle or draw an arrow to the poem on the page of the *Record*; students must find it. It is not all that difficult to find a poem, but I have found that students are more apt to notice the page if they must search it. The pages can be pedagogically useful because they make visible an important, though easily overlooked, historical fact: that the *Record* and the poems it transmits were made possible by a much larger culture of print.

The characteristics and consequences of the print culture of the Civil War era come into sharper focus in classes devoted to the *Record*, where we think of Moore's anthology as a text in its own right. For this class, I ask the students to read between fifteen and twenty consecutive pages from one volume, usually the second. Though the number of pages is somewhat arbitrary, it should be great enough so that the students will have to confront the challenges of reading an anthology of this sort. As I am reminded whenever I teach it, the *Record* is not easy to read—for them and for me—because it is made up of so many parts that can take on, in any one reading, so many different relationships to one another. But this difficulty is what makes the text such an effective pedagogical tool: the students become aware of their reading methods when those methods stop working.

My focus in this class is on reading poems in relation to the nonpoetic texts that surround them and on considering how the context Moore creates in and by way of his anthology makes meaning. The idea that context determines meaning may seem painfully obvious, but in my experience it is both easily overlooked and wonderfully teachable. The *Record* is effective in teaching the contextual nature of meaning precisely because the context in which the poems appear is not of my making. When I select and cluster the poems we read, I am creating a context; even if my selection is dutifully representative of poems that Civil War Americans were reading, my selection is still made with the benefits and limitations of hindsight. It is therefore a modern context. Moore's anthology is, in contrast, a print context that a nineteenth-century American made and in which nineteenth-century Americans read. Recognizing as much helps students come to see the making of context as not just the work of professors thinking about the past from the vantage point of the present or about literature from the vantage point of a classroom.

That is not to say that print context is the only thing that determines meaning or that Moore, in assembling his anthology, definitively fixed the meaning of the texts included in the *Record*. The hodgepodge nature of the *Record* encourages readers to dip into its pages at random. That very randomess creates fields of meaning and associations, and this idea guides my organization of our class discussion.

My approach to the *Record* in this class is simple. The text itself operates by way of accumulation and juxtaposition and so invites comparative reading. I tell my students that our goal is to arrive at a complex and interesting interpretation that results from comparing two texts that appear in a page we've read. Given the way the *Record* itself invites dipping—reading this, then that—rather than continuous reading, I don't require that the two texts be contiguous or obviously related to each other. I choose one of the texts (always a poem) and allow students to choose the other.

Giving them that choice is both energizing and unnerving. It is unnerving because if I am true to my word, they could choose anything. They could choose, for instance, the battle summary from the *New Orleans Picayune* that presents the opposing sides as though they were involved in a horse race ("Jeff. Davis enters colt *Confederate*, ridden by *Beauregard* . . . Abe Lincoln enters bl. g. *Union*, ridden by *Scott*" [*Rebellion Record* 2: 15 (poetry sec.)]). But my giving up this control energizes the class. Not only do they see me willingly experience the discomfort of not knowing exactly what will anchor the discussion and so where it will go (the kind of discomfort that they experience daily); they also see me think on my feet and meet interpretive challenges as they come. Though such uncertainty may occur in any discussion, I find that the students and I are particularly aware of it in this kind of exercise. They see the sometimes messy but importantly replicable process of idea making at work. In the end, I can say and they can see that we have made something in our time together that didn't exist before.

What does this teaching look like on the ground? The last time I taught the *Record* in this way, we began by reading a poem I selected entitled "It Grows Very Dark, Mother—Very Dark," by a person identified as Z. R. Prefaced by an epigraph taken from the *Cincinnati Gazette* and made up of seven six-line stanzas, each of which takes as its refrain some variation on the title, the poem stages a soldier's dying as his comrades look on in the midst of battle, "[t]hough the balls flew thick around them." The dying soldier's delirium allows the poem to juxtapose the peace of home (embodied by his hallucinated mother) with the violence of the battlefield (signified by his death). In an interesting grammatical turn, the poem, much of which is narrated in the past tense, addresses the living soldiers in the imperative mood: "Bend down closely comrades" and then, once he has died, "Gather round him, soldiers, gather, fold his hands and close his eyes." The poem ends with yet another wounded soldier commanding, "[F]ight on, comrades, speedily avenge our death!" before he too dies, thus leaving "two sad mothers [to] say, 'It has grown dark, ah! *very* dark'" (11).

When I asked the students to select the other element of our comparison, they did not choose another poem or prose piece that addressed the deaths of soldiers, nor did they select another text that juxtaposed the home front and battlefront, even though our brief initial discussion of "It Grows Very Dark" might have prompted them to do so. Instead, they selected a short piece that appeared under the heading "What the Rebels Said They Carried," an account, attributed to the *Memphis Argus,* of the Confederate army's having ransacked the Union army's provisions after the rout at Bull Run. The Confederate soldiers allegedly found their way to a "large table spread with a sumptuous dinner" that General McDowell had left in haste. The final paragraph includes a description of the "sad havoc" the soldiers "commenced" upon the "delicious drinkables" and a toast of thanks offered by one "sprightly officer" to "the gouty old Scott." It ends both with the men "vociferously" cheering the toaster and having a moment of derisive silence for "the great man's memory" as they drink his wine (7).

After brief discussions of each piece independent of the other, several students pointed out that both seemed invested in producing and presenting a spectacle. In the poem, men stand and watch one of their number as he dies, delirious though comforted in some way by that delirium. In the short prose piece, men stand and watch one of their number as he toasts the defeated McDowell with McDowell's own wine. In both cases, the spectacle has an internal audience (the one in the text) and an external audience (the one of the *Record*). The differences between the two audiences struck the students as significant. In both pieces, of course, the internal audience is an audience of soldiers, one presumably Union, the other certainly Confederate. (The students noted the only evidence we have of the sectional affiliation of the dying soldier in the poem is the identification of his home as in Ohio and the particular newspaper that printed the poem.) The external audience for both pieces, readers of the *Record*, would generally have been Northerners with strong Union sympathies. Whereas the poem seems interested in diminishing the distance between the internal and external audiences through a shared experience, a shared sentiment, and the grammatical turn to the imperative (thus addressing the soldiers and the readers at once), the prose piece in that particular print context widens the gap between the internal and external audiences, accentuating not what they share but what divides them. What for the internal audience was a display of power and wit was for the external audience a show of disrespect and unseemliness, all the more keen for the lost lives, such as the one in the poem, that this display indirectly demeans.

Though our focus in the discussion was initially narrow—our eyes were fixed on two specific texts—the juxtaposition of them helped us consider issues of audience and allegiance, spectatorship and context, that created a critical and conceptual landscape in which to read the other poems in the pages of the *Record*. At the students' urging, we went on to consider issues of spectacle and war in the poetic representations of and reflections on the civilian audience at the First Battle of Bull Run.

I judge the success of classes like this by the dynamism of the ideas that the students generate and the degree to which we can make interesting connections between that idea and some of the poems that were not one of the elements of that comparison. That day was a success, but it is not one I will seek to repeat with those two texts. Its success had everything to do with the students' ability to choose and my willingness not to insist that the discussion take a particular tack. I doubt that I will ever again teach those two texts alongside each other. Next time, a new group of students will choose something else, and so the idea that we generate will be different. In the *Record*, options abound.

I don't do this particular exercise with students on the first day of class or even in the first few weeks. In order for it to work, I have to create a space in which the students are willing to participate and collaborate. I have to show them that their participation matters, and more and more I have to show them how to participate. This need may strike those of us who have grown up in the humanities as surprising: how could someone not know how to contribute to a discussion? But I find increasingly that my students are willing but unsure how exactly to contribute. I used to read their silence as a form of resistance, but as time passed, I learned that it was the product of confusion.

In cultivating meaningful, collaborative class discussions, it is particularly helpful to give students time to think before they speak. I ask them to
write in class: writing engages their minds and produces language they can
draw on when I ask them (often by name) to share their thoughts. Writing
can mean simply generating a list of observations, responding to an open-
ended question, or composing an imitation of one sort or another. The
prompts generate thought and give students a sense of the different kinds
of things they might offer up in discussion. I always write with them, to
give visible evidence that we are in the process of creating together, and
I have found that my own in-class writing consistently provides me with
new insights. In-class writing also enforces a period of productive silence
in which students can gather their thoughts. The experience teaches them
that silence is a part of discussion rather than its antithesis.

To be sure, this approach does not always work. Some students con-
fuse intellectual rigor with the pedagogy of lecturing and so resist and
dismiss collaboration. I find that it helps to talk to them early and explicitly about their resistance, because many are unaware of it. I try not to be
defensive in such encounters. Instead I prompt them to analyze logically
their notion of how learning happens and what rigor looks like. As I indicated earlier, I often find that students I originally thought were resistant
just didn't know how to participate. These students tend to have spent a
great deal of time in classes where they are not asked to speak and simply
don't have the strategies, initially, to engage. Such reflection—particularly
after they have seen the amazing things that can happen in a discussion—
may give them the strategies they need to participate, and acquiring that
ability can be quite animating.

Advantages and Disadvantages

Relying on the *Record* has its limits. Teaching pages from one volume
means teaching no more than a slice of popular poetry printed in a particular time period and so risks presenting as representative of the war
what was true only of a few months. The context of the *Record* amplifies
the poems' similarities to one another rather than their differences. Clearly
a Union document, the *Record* gives short shrift to Confederate poetry,
though it does include it. Moore claims to "aim" at "impartiality" but
concludes his preface with a description of the war as "the most extraordinary and unjustifiable conspiracy and rebellion which the world has ever
witnessed" (iv). That bias shows itself in other ways as well—for instance,

in the framing commentary about some Confederate verse and prose, in the sometimes disproportionate number of "rumors" drawn from the Confederate press, in the very title of the volumes. But I have found that his bias is part of what makes the *Record* an effective teaching tool. Students see it at work because it is so visible and easily identifiable.

One practical benefit of Moore's *Record*, which is available in many libraries in hard copies and online, is that it is inexpensively accessed. Modern anthologies can be expensive. Importantly, the *Record* offers an inexpensive alternative to modern anthologies that has considerable pedagogical benefits. That said, it might be best used in conjunction with a modern anthology like Faith Barrett and Cristanne Miller's *"Words for the Hour"*: it would give students visual insight into the print culture that *"Words for the Hour"* makes an effort to represent.

In the end, the most compelling and enduring consequence of teaching Moore's *Record* may have little to do with the Civil War or poetry but a great deal to do with anthologies in general. It makes clear that it was assembled according to a particular way of understanding the value of literature and the nature of the "rebellion." His agenda is so clear that students can see his principle of selection at work and so discuss the fact and implications of his editorial choices. That discussion prepares them to see other modern anthologies as likewise assembled according to a particular way of understanding literature or according to a particular organizing idea. Reading the *Record* might just change how students think not only about a thing called Civil War poetry but also about how the anthologies they use in their other classes shape their understanding of historical periods, literary genres, and national literatures.

I experienced this change as an undergraduate. For a research project, Bill Spengemann sent me to the library in search of every extant anthology of nineteenth-century American poetry. The books were many and heavy. Though late-twentieth-century anthologies were not particularly interesting to me at the time, the anthologies assembled and published in or quite near the nineteenth century struck me with the force of revelation. The making of the thing called American poetry was, I realized, just that—an act of making—and it was ongoing. The anthologies as material objects announced to me their status as historical documents and helped me understand that they and the versions of American poetry that they offered were products of a particular set of institutions. These things seem obvious to me now, and I am quite sure that I had professors who said as much in class. Yet those ideas were hopelessly abstract until I found myself looking at the pages of anthologies like Edmund Stedman's *An American Anthology* (1900). After that, I never thought about anthologies in the same way again. If my students' experiences are like my own, working with anthologies like Moore's *Record* will help them know intellectually and experientially that all anthologies are made things, organized by and representative of particular ways of thinking about the texts they assemble.

Note

1. Of the twelve volumes of Moore's *Record*, one was a supplement to volume 1, published in 1861. For slightly fuller historical accounts of the *Record*, see Greenspan 410–12; Fahs, *Imagined Civil War* 51–53.

Susan M. Ryan

Using Digital Archives

Students interested in the Civil War encounter no shortage of modern interpretations and reinterpretations of its battles, key figures, and consequences. Indeed, a search for "American Civil War" on *Google Books* yields 1.5 million results, while a similar search in the academic database *America: History and Life* produces over 36,000. This superabundance, however textured and multiperspectival in the aggregate, can have a disabling effect on undergraduates' academic inquiries insofar as the war's exhaustive, and perhaps exhausting, secondary corpus leaves students with the impression that everything one might say about the era has already seen print. While versions of this anxiety erupt whenever students attempt to incorporate published scholarship into their own writing, I have found the problem to be especially acute in courses on the Civil War.

Like many of my colleagues in and beyond American literary studies, I respond to this challenge by directing students, at least in part, to primary texts—texts that provide a mix of the familiar and the obscure—in order to train their attention on specific moments, representations, and interventions rather than on overarching explanatory narratives. Extensive use of primary sources, especially from the era's wide range of periodicals, brings thematic richness to a course on the literature of the Civil War, conveying to students a sense of the chaotic quality of the times, including journalists' and politicians' misguided predictions that the war would be brief and commentators' disparate interpretations of events that we may now believe we comprehend clearly. Such sources also insist that students pay attention to the ways in which the war shaped broader cultural phenomena without necessarily controlling or delimiting them. A newspaper might have covered a recent battle in detail, but it reported other news as well—and printed poetry, opinion pieces, advertisements, and so on—reminding us that civilian life continued even as the nation was riveted by the violence of armed conflict. Popular magazines, too, though designed to offer escapist entertainment, nevertheless incorporated war stories into their fictional offerings. A broad, synchronic look at wartime print culture, and at personal writings and other manuscript sources, allows students to read the war differently, and perhaps more independently, even as they attend to such often studied works as Lincoln's speeches or Whitman's poems.

Reorienting students toward lesser-known primary sources also shapes their research and writing processes in productive ways. Most obviously, this approach encourages inductive thinking, as students encountering unfamiliar documents must examine what the texts actually say and consider the kinds of claims or interpretive moves they support. In the process, students will abandon some of their presuppositions about the conflict, its participants, and its commentators. Teaching them to locate and use primary sources that speak to their particular research interests opens up a range of interpretive possibilities grounded in texts that are not so shopworn, that haven't been thoroughly mined by scholars and popular historians. No one would deny the importance, both historical and rhetorical, of the Gettysburg Address—but politicians, ministers, and other public figures offered myriad speeches memorializing the war dead, many of which have received little sustained analysis. Immersion in primary sources also requires attention to both context and scale. As students move from individual texts to their larger print or manuscript contexts (the rest of the page, magazine issue, or diary; analogous or contradictory treatments of the issues at hand in contemporaneous sources), they learn a great deal about situating their findings within meaningful circumstances and discursive networks.

Although these interrelated pedagogical goals can be pursued through paper or digital archives (or a combination of the two), in this essay I focus on digital sources, for a number of reasons. First, digital archives change the terms of student access in ways well worth considering. One need not be located near a library with extensive 1860s (paper) holdings in order to adopt these teaching strategies, so geography matters much less than it did even ten or fifteen years ago. Digital access is far from perfectly democratic—high-speed Internet access and computers with reasonably fast processors are essential, and many of the most extensive digital databases are available only by paid subscription, at prices that many college and university libraries cannot afford. Still, much of what I suggest can be accomplished through open-access sources such as the *Making of America* Web sites (sponsored by Cornell University and the University of Michigan), the Library of Congress's digital resources, and the University of North Carolina's digital collection titled *Documenting the American South*. Using digital texts, whether proprietary or open, fundamentally changes the speed and ease of access to primary documents, as students do not need to travel physically to archives, sign in, request materials, and await their delivery. Primary research can happen in an all-hours study lounge, a dormitory room, a coffeeshop—even in class. Further, keyword searching, though it presents problems of its own, does much to decrease the time that elapses between conceiving a question and accessing specific documents that might begin to address it. Immersion in digital databases, given the near-immediate access they provide, can make the 1860s seem less remote, with effects both salubrious and risky. That is, such immersion can enhance students' engagement with course materials, even as it offers a sometimes misleading illusion of similarity between the 1860s and our own cultural moment.

Whatever the costs and benefits of (perceived) familiarity, the relative convenience of digital archives allows us to reformulate questions and reframe classroom debates in productive ways. For instance, we no longer have to rely exclusively on the editor's introduction to a particular literary text for information on its reception; we can supplement and complicate that account with a survey of original reviews, including those that appeared in less widely circulating sources. There is an ever-present risk, of course, that what is easy may become facile, as students, accustomed to quick results, assume that the first document they locate represents a widely shared point of view when in fact it's idiosyncratic—or, worse, assume that there's nothing available on a particular topic because the first set of search terms used yielded zero results. Our responsibility as instructors is to use these missteps as teaching opportunities. That is, we have to push our students to read as widely as possible in order to develop a sense of which documents are representative and which are not and to attempt several different searching strategies before giving up. Even more foundationally, we have to guide them toward the kinds of databases that will allow them to do credible primary research in nineteenth-century materials. In order to forestall their habitual reliance on familiar search engines (e.g., *Google*) and reference resources (e.g., *Wikipedia*), I require that they use specific databases such as *American Periodicals* or *Documenting the American South*, and I schedule at least a couple of class meetings in a computer lab so that they can establish familiarity with these databases in a structured context (i.e., with a specific, bounded research assignment to be conducted on site, the results of which are shared by a brief response paper or an informal presentation during a subsequent class meeting).

The exigencies of digital research can have positive effects. For instance, the vast amount of material now available reinforces the importance of narrowing one's questions in order to avoid a deluge of unassimilable text—a quick keyword search in class for, say, "Lincoln" or "Jefferson Davis" makes the point obvious. Noting the difficulties that result, we discuss various ways of getting to a more focused and manageable set of documents. Incorporating digital databases into course work offers students an opportunity to become skilled at navigating many user interfaces, and they move toward greater accuracy and specificity by refining their search terms, narrowing their date ranges, and adding other limiting elements. Indeed, a productive tension often emerges among representational modes, as adeptness with Boolean operators and other aspects of search syntax both requires and reinforces a familiarity with mid-nineteenth-century vocabularies, styles of address, and even typographic quirks.

Digital archives cannot entirely displace paper-based research and archiving. Some documents of great interest will not be digitized in our lifetimes, and even those that are available electronically exist in formats that may prove cumbersome, even unusable, as technologies change. Too, the browsing that paper texts encourage has important implications for intellectual projects and for cognition itself. The associativeness, serendipity, and (sometimes) linearity of reading on paper are substantively altered in the move to digital research, even as the materiality of the text is diminished if not entirely lost in most digital forums. In the classroom strategies and assignments that follow, I offer digital research methods as supplements to the other kinds of reading and research that we—and our students—will continue to do.[1]

John Brown: From Traitor to Union Saint

My course on the Civil War and American culture begins with John Brown, whose 1859 execution Herman Melville termed a "portent" of the conflict to come.[2] In exploring the aftermath of Brown's raid, we read and discuss Melville's poem about Brown's hanging, Thoreau's "A Plea for Captain John Brown," Franny Nudelman's chapter "The Blood of Millions" from her book *John Brown's Body* (2004), and versions of the Union marching song "John Brown's Body."[3] Students are typically perplexed by Brown's transformation from enemy of the state to Union martyr: when one reads forward from his attack on a federal armory and subsequent capture, it's difficult to see how he could be recuperated, indeed sanctified, so rapidly. Magazine and newspaper accounts that were published in the fall of 1859 help us to understand this trajectory.

To start the conversation on Brown's prewar, postcapture status, I bring to students' attention a piece that appeared in the 28 October 1859 issue of the *Liberator.* This unsigned editorial, probably by William Lloyd Garrison, begins with an ambivalence that has surprised my students. Knowing little about Garrison's pacifism, they expect the longest-running abolitionist newspaper in the nation to defend Brown unequivocally. Instead, the piece calls Brown's effort "well-intended but sadly misguided" and, a bit further on, "wild and futile" ("Tragedy"). But it then drifts toward praise of Brown's character and excoriation of his enemies. "In vain," the author intones, "will the sanguinary tyrants of the South, and their Northern minions, seek to cover [Brown] with infamy." The piece ends with a warning for those seeking Brown's execution: "It will be a terribly losing day for all Slavedom when John Brown and his associates are brought to the gallows. It will be sowing seed broadcast for a harvest of retribution. Their blood will cry trumpet-tongued from the ground. . . ." The article thus prefigures a broader movement in the North from discomfort with Brown's violent methods to their embrace, even as it ends with a plea for southern repentance—"O that they might avoid all this"— that struggles for congruence with the paper's nonviolent principles.

In addition to this oddly prescient piece, I ask students to locate and analyze, in a brief written response and in class discussion, other interventions, ranging from ostensibly objective reports of the attack and its aftermath to relentless condemnations of Brown's actions and ideologies.[4] Beyond what these articles can tell us about the responses to Brown himself, they effectively introduce students to nineteenth-century periodicals as a matrix of genres. Class members typically remark on the visual density of the printed page, the limited use of illustration, the preponderance of quoted letters purportedly sent by eyewitnesses, and the unfamiliar typographic conventions (my own favorite is the little pointing finger). Students are also struck by the pseudo-up-to-the minute reportage of the events at Harpers Ferry in articles that seem to serve as the CNN bottom-of-the-television-screen ticker of their day but that in fact performed an immediacy that was literally impossible, given the time lags and constraints inherent in the medium. One piece, which appeared in the *Liberator* just over a week before the editorial mentioned above, uses a breathless present tense in reporting the various stages of the raid and capture, with section headings labeled according to the location, date, and time of day of the events to be conveyed—details that seem inconsequential in that the article appeared several days later. Another report, appearing in the New York–based *Independent*, recounts events in the past tense but closes with a paragraph titled "Latest," which begins, "The latest intelligence by telegraph, which comes to us just as we go to press, mentions that Capt. Brown's house has been thoroughly searched, and that letters have been found from various individuals at the North . . ."—including Frederick Douglass and Gerrit Smith ("Riot"). Students note the continuities with our own crisis news delivery systems—the reporting of unsubstantiated details, the invocation of the latest technologies for conveying up-to-the-minute developments, et cetera—but they must also think carefully about what it would be like to receive almost all such information in print rather than on screen and through text rather than through photographs, voice, or video.

This exercise also encourages students to complicate their notions of sectional ideologies vis-à-vis slavery. They expect to encounter admiration for Brown in abolitionist sources and excoriation of him in the South. What's surprising is how harshly his actions were judged in many northern venues and how measured, even ambivalent, a source like the *Liberator* was in the immediate aftermath of his capture. The varied responses to Brown abundantly demonstrate that the North was divided over the slavery question and that even abolitionists did not agree about reformist methods (e.g., violence, nonviolence, political action, moral suasion). If this context makes Thoreau's "Plea" seem more politically risky than it otherwise might, it also makes the North appear far less keen on a war to end slavery than many students initially suppose.

Melville's *Battle-Pieces*

Digital archives can inform the study of more self-consciously literary texts as well. Melville's poem "The House-top: A Night Piece," one of a handful in *Battle-Pieces* that train readers' attention on the northern home front, recounts a sleepless New Yorker's musings on the city's infamous draft riots, which took place in July 1863. When I teach this poem, I talk about the stunning violence of those days and nights, emphasizing that, according to historians' accounts, many of those killed or injured were African American men and many of the perpetrators, either in fact or in public perception, were working-class Irish immigrants. With this context in mind, students often comment on the poem's erasure of the riot's victims and foregrounding of the poem's speaker, a privileged, or at least not immediately threatened, citizen contemplating relatively distant urban unrest. When I taught my Civil War class in the spring of 2011, a student's remark prompted an especially illuminating investigation. Pointing to passages in the poem that characterized the riot's perpetrators as "ship-rats" and "rats of the wharves" (lines 11 and 12), the student said that she found the poem's anti-Irish racism troubling. Others disagreed, asserting that the poem was classist and nativist—especially in its invocation of the "priestly spells" that had "late held hearts in awe" (13)—but not racist. These counterclaims were animated by two investments, one theoretical and the other experiential. First, their proponents argued that to call any negative identity-based representation racist had the effect of diluting the term's force; second, as several students noted, their own Irish ethnicity had never exposed them to racial injustice. The charge simply did not make sense to them.

This debate provided an opportunity to address the shifting historical contingencies of United States racial categories and attributions and specifically the complex set of cultural transformations that allowed the Irish, over time, to "become white," in the historian Noel Ignatiev's formulation. Attention to digitally accessible primary sources can do much to contextualize the poem's rendering of the Irish. Derogation of the Irish took many forms in the mid-nineteenth-century United States. Among the most egregious were political cartoons that called into question Irish intelligence, patriotism, and fitness for citizenship, often by establishing visual and discursive analogies with African Americans, whose abject status was then a cultural commonplace. (Michael O'Malley of George Mason University has collected several such images on his Web site—for example,

The Chairman of the Hanging Committee; others can be accessed through *Google Images* or other search engines.) Articles in newspapers and magazines yielded less stark but still derisive representations, including pieces on the perceived crisis in domestic service that excoriated Irish "helps" for their lack of skill and their antiauthoritarian attitudes (just as mainstream culture, both North and South, ridiculed the supposed ineptitude and pretensions of slaves engaged in domestic service). An article that appeared in the *Liberator* in 1862 noted that Southerners preferred to use Irish laborers in especially hazardous settings. The author, Joseph Brennan of Louisville, Kentucky, quotes an ostensibly representative slaveholder, who remarks, "Every negro man I own is worth from twelve to fifteen hundred dollars. Let one of them die, that money is dead loss. Let an Irishman die, I lose nothing—not one cent. There is another to take his place next day, and glad of the chance." While the individual cited most obviously advances the dubious proslavery argument that slaves were protected from physical harm by their market value, he also likens the Irish to African American slaves by ranking them a step lower—they experience what slaves would experience if not for the self-interest of their owners.

These homologies between Irish immigrants and African Americans both free and enslaved tell only part of the story. As Melville's poem suggests and any number of periodical pieces affirm, representations of the Irish were infused with Protestant America's deep suspicion of Roman Catholicism, which was not a typical feature of antiblack racism. Web sites that specifically address anti-Irish prejudice tend to present the most extreme examples, whereas a broader keyword search (here *American Periodicals* is especially useful) yields more varied and nuanced representations. For instance, when students are asked to investigate newspaper coverage of the Irish in America, they are often surprised by the extent to which journalists dwelled on the prosaic details of immigration: articles attend to the numbers of Irish nationals arriving on particular ships; to reports of disease, especially cholera, among passengers; and to the implications, both positive and negative, of new arrivals for various labor markets. Students find, then, both commonality and divergence in the ways mainstream print media represented African Americans and Irish immigrants. This range of representations complicates their understanding of Melville's poem, even as the poem elides the complex intergroup encounters that underlay the riots themselves.

Melville's narrative poem "Donelson," also from *Battle-Pieces*, allows us to examine more directly how a literary text might adapt, reconfigure, and comment on the era's periodical print culture. The poem begins in an unnamed northern locale, with an anxious crowd "pelted by sleet" gathering around a bulletin board to read the "latest news from West or South" (lines 6 and 10). An especially tall bystander is asked to read aloud and obliges, with the paper's supposed contents appearing in italics. The poem proceeds in this mode across several wet days, the journalistic narrative alternating with a more immediate verse rendering of the home front scene. I invite students to consider Melville's minute attention to the materiality of news and news-seeking—to the townspeople waiting for the next issue to be posted and the paper itself "washed by the storm" until it grew "every shade of a streaky blue" (lines 41, 42). The mock ventriloquizing of newspaper accounts belies the care with which Melville has converted journalistic into poetic language (replete with rhyme, syntactic inversion, and elevated diction). The poem's uses of the tropes and gestures of newspaper war reporting can best be understood in conversation with actual periodical coverage of the Union victory at Fort Donelson, which was covered extensively in the northern press, especially the New York *Herald*. Again, it makes sense to ask students to locate a range of articles in order to investigate this intersection. One way to structure their research is to divide the class into groups, each responsible for investigating the coverage that appeared in a particular source or in the papers of a particular city. Alternatively, I might ask groups or individuals to look at and report to the class on specific elements of the battle's coverage, such as the representation of the enemy, the degree to which the fighting is sensationalized or sanitized, and the journalist's narrative choices and style. These sources help us to assess what happens—aesthetically, affectively, and persuasively—when news is converted into poetry, and they enable us to consider in what sense the news has a poetics of its own, with practices and exigencies that might inform our reading not just of Melville but also of many other topical poems.

Digital Archives and Writing Assignments

I often find it useful to assign a relatively brief (four-to-five-page) essay that invites students to investigate how the literary texts they're reading for class were initially received and evaluated. Reviews and printed commentary on the book and author obviously figure prominently, but I also ask students to look at publishers' advertisements and, if available, readers' comments in digitally accessible journals and letters. These inquiries yield important insights into mid-nineteenth-century book marketing and evaluative criteria, even as they provide opportunities for refining research skills. In a small or medium-sized class, students can present their findings informally. In a large class, I might assign a group of students to research the reception of a particular text and make a more formal presentation.

The vagaries of keyword searching are especially present in these projects. For example, students learn that they have to search for "Miss Alcott" as well as "Louisa May Alcott" or for "Mrs. Child" or "L. M. Child" or "L. Maria Child" as well as the now-more-familiar "Lydia Maria Child." The names of male authors tend to appear in fewer variations, though even here students might find "Mr. Whitman" rather than "Walt Whitman." Proper names are not the only complicating factors; early in their research, students sometimes use "review" as a keyword, not realizing that nineteenth-century book reviews often did not use that term to describe themselves.[5] Similarly, "reception" is an apt term for this avenue of inquiry, but it's not terribly useful as a search term; in nineteenth-century documents, it typically yields references to formal social events rather than instances of critical response.

Though many literary texts could form the basis of this assignment, Whitman's *Drum-Taps* (1865) and Elizabeth Stuart Phelps's *The Gates Ajar* (1868) work especially well. Responses to the former, many of which allude to the poet's scandalous reputation, allow students to analyze first-hand the much discussed moral recuperation of Whitman through his writings on the war, which lent him a patriotic gravitas in part by fore-grounding his service in Union hospital wards. For readers accustomed to thinking of him as the century's sexual and poetic outlaw, this reception history offers insights into his cultivation—perhaps even exploitation—of a perceived common ground with others who had suffered through the war. Investigating Phelps's reception helps students steeped in a modernist or postmodernist literary aesthetic to understand the terms on which readers embraced her unabashedly sentimental and spiritualist narrative. In both cases, 1860s reviews acquaint students with the Victorian era's imbrication of literary value and authorial character, an evaluative matrix that our own cultural moment both resurrects and derides.

My Civil War course includes a substantial research and writing project that students develop and revise across the second half of the semester. A key feature of the assignment is that the final essay must incorporate primary sources drawn from digital archives. Students are welcome to explore print sources as well, but I want the research project to reinforce and extend the work we do throughout the term with digital databases and research methods. Many students elect to locate and analyze texts that allow them to establish some sort of context for a more-or-less canonical work they've chosen to analyze; others use little-known sources as their objects of analysis. In either case, they discover early on that they have to refine their research questions lest they be overwhelmed by the vastness of the archive.

My students have brought tremendous creativity and diligence to these projects, immersing themselves in nineteenth-century materials while incorporating their own long-standing interests. One student, a self-described cooking enthusiast, took advantage of the fact that the *American Periodicals* database allows users to search for recipes; her essay on food in the Civil War used published recipes—alongside material from personal diaries and broader commentary on food availability and wartime cooking practices—to analyze food's unifying and divisive effects. A premedical student used periodicals, advertisements, and diaries to examine the cultural resonances of widespread wartime amputations, with particular attention to the multivalent social meanings of artificial limbs. Other students took more overtly literary approaches, investigating the gendering of patriotic responsibility in wartime children's literature, much of which appeared in periodical form, or establishing a meaningful context for Melville's "The Swamp Angel" by analyzing journalistic accounts of the siege of Charleston, where the newly developed long-distance gun referenced in the poem's title was famously used. The range of possible projects in a course like this one is immense. In future semesters, I hope to encourage students to make more extensive use of soldiers' memoirs and home front diaries (beyond that of the ubiquitous Mary Chesnut), to look more carefully at responses to the conflict in African American periodicals, and to exploit the keyword search function in the *Wright American Fiction* database in order to investigate how popular fiction during and after the war reformulated its key themes. I expect that my own obsession with nineteenth-century periodical cultures will continue to inform their projects as well.

The expansiveness and multivocality of digitally available sources have the potential to do important pedagogical work, evoking in students (and in their instructors, no doubt) what we might call a productive bewilderment. Our students, understandably, try to make sense of history in part by collapsing its complications, but reading 1860s periodicals and other primary documents will disabuse them of those enabling simplifications, including the tendency to overstate intrasectional unity or to overlook the abundance of cultural production that was not immediately or obviously about the war. Any serious engagement with primary sources requires an openness to uncertainty, complexity, nuance, and contradiction—and yet a successful interpretive essay has to find a way to navigate, if not tame, that chaos. As teachers, we need to give students the tools with which to approach both challenges.

Notes

1. These strategies are geared toward upper-level undergraduates, though they could be adapted for students at other levels.

2. "The Portent," a meditation on Brown's execution, is the opening poem in Melville's *Battle-Pieces*.

3. The Library of Congress Web site includes an undated song sheet and a choral performance of "John Brown's Body," recorded in 2003 (http://www.loc .gov/teachers/lyrical/songs/john_brown.html). Other versions, including one by Pete Seeger, are available on *YouTube* and elsewhere.

4. To ensure breadth of representation, I ask some students to investigate mainstream, widely circulating sources and others to look specifically at African American, abolitionist, and southern periodicals (e.g., *DeBow's* and the *Southern Literary Messenger*, both of which commented on Brown). Because John Brown is a commonly occurring proper name in the United States, students have to find other ways to delimit their searches—narrowing date ranges or including other terms like "Harpers Ferry" (usually written as "Harper's Ferry" in 1859) or "Osawatomie" (sometimes spelled "Ossawatomie"), a town in Kansas with which Brown was closely associated.

5. The *American Periodicals* database allows users to search by document type (e.g., reviews, obituaries, letters to the editor). Though useful, this function sometimes filters out material a researcher might want, like commentary on a book or author in an article that is not strictly speaking a book review.

Rebecca Entel

Civil War Literature and First-Year Writing Instruction

As part of the First-Year Experience program at a liberal arts college, I teach a writing course called Literary Responses to War. All first-year students take a seminar and a writing course; the courses are mutually reinforcing, introducing them to academic honesty, critical reading, information literacy, and writing both in a discipline and across the curriculum. One of my primary goals is for them to take ownership of their writing, making choices according to their selected purpose and a defined audience rather than trying to guess what their professor wants. My course description reads:

> Walt Whitman said of the Civil War that the "real war will never get in the books." What versions of war, then, do get in books? This course will expose students to different artistic responses to war and the critical skills necessary to analyze them. Course discussions will consider the limitations of representation and documentation, the intersections of public and private life, and the uses of art. We will ask such questions as, How can trauma be documented? How do authors represent the unspeakable? What is the purpose of a personal account versus a documentary about the "whole" war? Students will hone their skills in analyzing both primary and secondary sources. They will engage in

several different types of academic writing and will conduct their own research projects. Because this is a writing course, significant time will be spent on the writing process, with a focus on revision.

This description suggests a split between the content-based portion of the course about literature and what students will do as writers. I find that the literature of the American Civil War helps solder this split.

Civil War literature introduces students to literary study and academic writing by teaching them about the mediation involved in translating war experience into war literature. Of course war literature is not, despite many students' initial assumptions, a documentary record of what happened. Authors' rhetorical decisions may be influenced by publication context or audience and may be limited by the medium of language. The nursing narratives of Louisa May Alcott and Walt Whitman lead students to investigate the limits of language in representing war experience as well as the relation between rhetorical choice and audience expectation. Moreover, because both these writers revised their narratives—from diaries and letters to later published versions—the narratives show students that writing is a mediated product constructed with specific audiences in mind. Ultimately, by recognizing the processes of formation involved in the texts they read, students make more informed choices as writers. As readers of Civil War literature, they learn how literature may be transformed by historical events; as writers, they learn to make appropriate choices based on audience, convention, and intention. They learn to view literature, and therefore their own writing, as the artful execution of rhetorical purpose rather than as the unmediated presentation of neutral content.

Many students come into this class expecting to learn about military history or at least to learn about what happened from soldiers' eyewitness accounts. My first job, then, is to get them to question the categories of war writing and war experience, to separate what happened from how it is represented or not represented. On the first day of class, students discuss Whitman's famous statement that the "real war will never get in the books" (*Portable Walt Whitman* 555). This discussion leads them to revise their expectations about transparency as well as their assumptions about authenticity.

Students brainstorm about what Whitman's statement might mean: Why can't the real war get into the books, and what does Whitman mean by "real"? They discuss the reasons gaps may form between what happened and what is written: from witnesses not surviving to failures of traumatic memory to the fact that the writer may not have been an eyewitness but is imagining the experiences. Students' assumption that the most authentic writing is the most unmediated begins to emerge. Considering the implications of that idea, we are able to move from a discussion of the more logistical impediments to writing about war to a discussion of the limits of language. We discuss why not everything can be written down in language and the fact that writing imposes an order on experience: war is chaotic and exceeds explanation, while narrative is ordered and formal. Students also think about how war prompts some writers to seek new forms of expression.

Whitman's paradoxical claim about war books in his own war book remains at the heart of the class's work as we delve into literary responses to war. I ask my students why we are studying war in an English class and particularly in a writing class. How, for example, does writing need to change to accommodate a topic like Civil War? This discussion is informed by students' reading of Kate McLoughlin's "War and Words" (in *The Cambridge Companion to War Writing*), a comprehensive survey of how the real wars have not got into the books—the ways "war defeats language" (17). McLoughlin reminds her readers that "*not* finding the words for war—or at least claiming not to find them—may . . . be the most potent technique for conveying its magnitude" (22). We begin the course on war writing, then, by specifically looking for what is not conveyed and what the texts cannot do. Whitman's and Alcott's texts help us explore these issues.

Louisa May Alcott's "Unities"

Both Alcott and Whitman faced not only entirely new experiences in the war but also the challenge of how to represent them. I offer students some background on the status of women's nursing in the nineteenth century as well as the publication history of *Hospital Sketches* so they can understand the popularity of the book, the import of its being published during the war, and the genre of nursing narratives it initiated.

Alice Fahs's accessible historical introduction to the Bedford edition of *Hospital Sketches* (from the Bedford Series in History and Culture) informs students about Alcott's family and political background, women's contributions to the war effort, and hospital life; it also orients them to what Alcott fictionalized and how her narrative compares with what we know historically (about the author and about war hospitals). For students who want to pursue this line of inquiry in a research paper, I recommend Jane Schultz's comprehensive *Women at the Front*. Students are quick to point out discrepancies between what they learn about Alcott and the war hospitals and what her narrator, Tribulation Periwinkle, tells them, which gives them the critical distance they need to assess the author's choices in representing her nursing experience.

Alcott's representation was influenced by readers' hunger for war news but also by their anxieties about female war nurses. How does she mitigate her audience's discomfort about single women leaving home to interact, often intimately, with men? If war writing is most authentic when most immediate, why does she fictionalize her story and pack the text with literary devices, most prominently metaphors and allusions? These two issues are related in the text, as she translates her war experience into a story suited to her audience's sense of the familiar. *Hospital Sketches* presents unfamiliar experiences in familiar terms; that is, Alcott familiarizes those aspects of her story that might be controversial or difficult for her readers. My class focuses on her use of metaphor for this purpose. She uses metaphor as a "narrative safety valve," in Schultz's terms, to ease her readers' anxieties ("Embattled Care" 108). For example, Alcott compares volunteering as a nurse to leaving her parents' home as a new bride or enlisting as a soldier as a young man. Such metaphors invite nineteenth-century audiences to accept a woman's somewhat controversial act and to understand women's contributions as war experience. By interrogating her metaphors, students see how war texts reflect social and literary convention, and they ultimately understand the relation between rhetorical choice and audience expectation.

I begin by explaining the predominant theory of metaphor in Alcott's time, as an explanatory device comparing A, something unfamiliar, to B, something familiar.[1] Students then offer their own comparisons. Their A—the unfamiliar experience analogous to Alcott's nursing experience—is "Starting college," since they are all in their first semester. I write, "Starting college is like . . . ," on the board and give them a few minutes to complete the sentence. Each student reads aloud his or her B, and I take notes on the board. Students are immediately able to see patterns emerge: some comparisons express fear and uncertainty, some freedom; some are funny, some serious; some draw on specific cultural references meaningful only to a certain audience. This brief exercise prepares us to analyze Alcott's metaphors and illuminates what that analysis might tell us about her text.

Students, interrogating the metaphors in *Hospital Sketches*, can identify when Alcott makes claims for women's war efforts, when she placates readers' anxieties about women who serve as nurses, and when she is uncertain about the meaning of what she encounters. From the opening pages of *Hospital Sketches,* she compares the decision to nurse with enlisting in the Union army. The chapter title "Obtaining Supplies" sets the tone, of course, and Tribulation Periwinkle insists that she "could do the work, was offered a place, and accepted it, promising not to desert, but stand ready to march on Washington at an hour's notice." She tells her family, "I've enlisted!," and she "turned military at once, called [her] dinner [her] rations, saluted all new comers, and ordered a dress parade" ([ed. Fahs] 54, 55). She even asks her readers' cooperation in buying into this metaphor: she "shouldered [her] knapsack—it was only a traveling bag, but do let [her] preserve the unities" (55)—a wink to readers that students can parse for an understanding of the craftedness of this war account.

When Tribulation arrives at the hospital, students note, her confidence begins to seem like naïveté, and her faltering metaphors reflect her shock. When asked to bathe a number of patients on her first day, she responds, "If she had requested me to shave them all, or dance a hornpipe on the stove funnel, I should have been less staggered; but to scrub some dozen lords of creation at a moment's notice, was really—really—" (72). As her footing as a nurse becomes more sure, students note that she describes her interactions with soldiers through maternal images. Her patients "took the performance like sleepy children, leaning their tired heads against [her] as [she] worked" (72), and she develops "a womanly pride in their regard, a motherly affection for them all" (80). Fahs's introductory remarks on accepted nineteenth-century gender roles support students' analyses of why Alcott would describe the patients as childlike and the nurses as maternal.

Although my students begin looking for patterns of how the individual metaphors can accrue into an argument, the conversation opens up when we find that the metaphors are not so neatly categorized, when the unfamiliar remains strange to Nurse Tribulation. Students are drawn particularly to descriptions of amputees: "he resembled a dripping merman, suffering from the loss of a fin" (74) and "a one-legged phantom . . . balancing himself on one leg, like a meditative stork"—"What to do with the creature [she] didn't know" (84). Such descriptions illustrate that uncertainty and the newness of the war experience cannot be completely assuaged through language. Through this more complex lens, we revisit our earlier discussion of Alcott's comparisons meant to calm her audience's anxieties, and students discuss how metaphor may also defamiliarize the ordinary.

Introducing students to various historical contexts also shows them how Alcott's narrative was shaped by a particular audience's (and a particular genre's) expectations. For example, in *The Imagined Civil War*, Fahs offers a cogent close reading of the death of the soldier-patient John in the context of nineteenth-century conceptions of the sentimental and meaningful death. Her reading complements Whitman's focus in *Specimen Days* on deaths that are not commemorated. Sharing contemporary reviews of *Hospital Sketches* (collected in Beverly Clark's *Louisa May Alcott*) can also reveal how the book was defined as a war text in its own time.

Another salient topic for *Hospital Sketches* is Alcott's depiction of African Americans. Both Fahs's and Schultz's books give accounts of the history of *contraband* in the hospital and discuss the issues of race that Alcott does not directly confront. Providing information about blackface minstrelsy helps students understand Alcott's depictions of African American characters, described by Mary Capello as "blacks in blackface" (76), as well as Nurse Tribulation's comment that she "passed colored people, looking as if they had come out of a picture book, or off the stage" (67). Such information contextualizes Alcott's stereotypical depictions of African Americans (e.g., animalistic descriptions and the exaggerated rendering of dialect). When students recognize that these depictions are mediated by contemporary literary conventions, such as sentimentalism and minstrelsy, they are alerted to the many ways a writer crafts a narrative of lived experience.

All these discussions show *Hospital Sketches* to be both a historical and a rhetorical document—but they also allow students to discuss, as writers, the act of addressing a specific audience. In this course, my students are to assume that the audience for their papers is their classmates, that is, readers have read the primary text and know about the class's preliminary discussions. The writing challenge is both to use the familiar in a strategic way (e.g., avoiding plot summary and using shared knowledge as a grounding) and to present the unfamiliar in a strategic way (e.g., adding something new to the scholarly conversation and presenting it clearly). Our focus on metaphors in relation to audience also reminds students that there is room for creativity in academic writing to convey tone and to connote.

Walt Whitman and the "Unknown"

While Alcott familiarizes the strange, Whitman hopes "the melange's lackings and wants of connection [in his work will] take care of themselves"

(*Portable Walt Whitman* 463). Offering a pose of unmediated writing, he both attempts to document all aspects of the war and to undermine that documentation by continually reminding readers of what remains unknown. He deviates from standard grammar to reflect the disorderliness of his subject matter, illustrating to students how even sentence structure can reflect content and how some content will not fit into conventional forms. *Specimen Days* is challenging for first-year students on both a micro and macro level, as they strive to put all the disparate pieces and unwieldy sentences into a coherent whole. I find it helpful to begin with a discussion of Whitman's deliberate dismissal of coherence for this particular mélange.

I pair *The Portable Walt Whitman*'s well-chosen excerpt of *Specimen Days* with relevant poems such as "The Wound-Dresser." In addition, Michael Warner's introduction to *The Portable Walt Whitman* explains clearly some important elements of Whitman's style, particularly his use of free verse and the long Whitmanian line, in the context of nineteenth-century poetry.

Understanding Whitman's war writing involves interrogating a central tension: Whitman is known for his voluminous lines and encyclopedic lists—his seeming belief that the world can be described and that those descriptions can be collected; yet, in this sprawling, seemingly encyclopedic book, he insists that "the real war will never get in the books," and the book itself points to incompletion. After discussing Warner's introduction about the poetic line and Whitman's impulse to catalog, students gloss the title of *Specimen Days*. We look at the *OED* entry for *specimen*, which includes some of the more obvious definitions (something experimental, something typical of a larger group) but also the obsolete definition "a brief and incomplete account of something in writing; a rough draught or outline."

We turn to the opening section of the text, "A Happy Hour's Command," in which Whitman claims that most of the book was scribbled on the spot, in the moment of war, creating the "most spontaneous, fragmentary book ever printed"; his notebooks are even covered with blood, because he carried them in the war hospital, and he instructs readers that in this fragmented, "blood-smutch'd" book he has refrained from revising any of his wartime notes (464). We also consider his letter to the editor, James Redpath (the letter is included in the edition's notes), that focuses on the marketability of authentic war texts and provides evidence that Whitman did in fact revise his text. He is crafting immediacy for this book, and we brainstorm about why he would do so.

We talk through sections of the book that lean toward one extreme or the other: Whitman's encyclopedic impulse and his emphasis on incompleteness. Students at first view the book as encyclopedic, perhaps because of its length and dense prose, but more and more they notice elements that are less certain. The echo of Whitman's famous quotation from the first day of class helps raise the importance of this idea for them, so they pay special attention to the final sections of the book, where the quotation occurs, to see where Whitman leaves his readers. The book ends with the unknown, the unwritten: "Think how much, and of importance, will be—how much, civic and military, has already been—buried in the grave, in eternal darkness" (556).

We ultimately cannot separate Whitman's uncertainty from the style of his prose. Because this is a writing class, students focus on sentence-level issues as both close readers of literature and as budding academic writers learning to control their prose. Most first-year students find Whitman's prose difficult, and we assess why through our discussion of the penultimate chapter, "The Million Dead, Too, Summ'd Up." This section is a hodgepodge of casualty statistics from the War Department and reminders of what remains uncountable. The title suggests the summarizing impulse of the Whitmanian catalog, but the prose style, in which one paragraph is a single sentence and another is entirely in parentheses, offers an opportunity for students to investigate how punctuation may reflect, reinforce, or contradict content. The paragraph-long sentence is a great example of how Whitman uses punctuation to jumble, misdirect, and open up the sentence rather than to order, direct, and help the reader come to a clear conclusion:

> And everywhere among these countless graves—everywhere in the many soldier Cemeteries of the Nation, (there are now, I believe, over seventy of them)—as at the time in the vast trenches, the depositories of slain, Northern and Southern, after the great battles—not only were the scathing trail passed those years, but radiating since in all the peaceful quarters of gravestones, singly or in masses, to thousands or tens of thousands, the significant word *Unknown*. (554)

Students work in small groups to experiment with rewriting this passage. I allow them to cut as much as they like and to add or remove punctuation. (They will have already had a minilesson on how to employ varying levels of emphasis with dashes, commas, and parentheses, all of which are relevant to Whitman's writing. They can see how Whitman is breaking the rules.) They untangle the paragraph's dashes, commas, and parentheses to identify the main statement Whitman is making, and they talk about why this main statement needs untangling in the first place. What does this form have to do with summarizing an ultimately uncountable group of unnamed corpses? Students get a challenging grammar lesson trying to sift out the many partial sentences in Whitman's rushing prose, but they also see that his tone is lost when his writing is cleaned up and ordered. We are able, then, to consider whether Whitman wrote these unwieldy sentences to convey uncertainty. We also have a broader discussion about how students, as writers, may use punctuation and sentence structure in connection with—not separate from—the content they want to convey.

Writing Assignments

Students have written papers about such varied topics as Alcott's depictions of African Americans, her use of metaphor, and the claims she makes for nurses in relation to the war effort; they have written about Whitman's wide-ranging definition of war experience, how he presents similar material differently in poetry and prose, and how the form of his work relates to the content. Their writing assignments are not designed to be only content-based analyses of texts. They are also charged with revising an early draft into a final paper that will be more than twice as long and must include four scholarly secondary sources. As students work on these final papers—the revision process includes large-group class workshops in which other students read and comment on their work—they are engaging with many of the writing issues they have learned from studying Alcott and Whitman. They must define their audience and make writing choices in relation to that audience's expectations and knowledge, and they must think carefully about how to create emphasis, clarity, and tone. The nursing narratives of Alcott and Whitman, presented in their historical-literary contexts, help student writers tackle these sophisticated issues of audience, rhetorical purpose, and the translation of ideas into a specific genre of writing.

Note
1. I base this framework on the work of Hugh Blair, the Scottish rhetorician whose theory of metaphor, in which an unfamiliar principal is explored through a familiar accessory, was the main influence on nineteenth-century American rhetoric handbooks and rhetorical instruction.

Part V

Resources

These resources are meant to supplement the materials provided in the list of works cited. An asterisk designates an open access source.

Reference Guides

American Civil War Music and Resources: Performing Arts Encyclopedia at the Library of Congress. Lib. of Congress, 11 Nov. 2013. Web. 12 Aug. 2015. <http://www.loc.gov/performingarts/civilwar/>.

Boatner, Mark. *Civil War Dictionary.* New York: Random, 1989. Print.

Civil War Washington. Ed. Susan C. Lawrence, Kenneth M. Price, and Kenneth J. Winkle. Center for Digital Research in the Humanities. U of Nebraska, Lincoln, n.d. Web. 12 Aug. 2015. <http://civilwardc.org/>.

The Complete Civil War on DVD-ROM. Oliver Computing, n.d. Web. 12 Aug. 2015. <http://www.civilwaramerica.com/>.

Eicher, David J. *Civil War Battlefields: A Touring Guide.* Dallas: Taylor Trade, 2005. Print.

Good, Timothy S., ed. *We Saw Lincoln Shot: One Hundred Eyewitness Accounts.* Jackson: UP of Mississippi, 1995. Print.

Luvas, Jay, and Harold W. Nelson. *Guide to the Battle of Gettysburg.* Lawrence: UP of Kansas, 1986. Print.

McClure, Alexander Kelly, ed. *The Annals of the Civil War: Written by Leading Participants North and South.* New York: Da Capo, 1994. Print.

McLoughlin, Kate, ed. *Cambridge Companion to War Writing.* New York: Cambridge UP, 2009. Print.

Parrish, T. Michael, and Robert M. Willingham, Jr. *Confederate Imprints: A Bibliography of Southern Publications from Secession to Surrender.* Austin: Jenkins, 1987. Print.

Wells, Jonathan Daniel. *A House Divided: The Civil War and Nineteenth-Century America.* New York: Routledge, 2012. Print. Companion Web site: www.routledge.com/cw/wells-9780415998703/.

Woodworth, Steven E. *Beneath a Northern Sky: A Short History of the Gettysburg Campaign.* Wilmington: Scholarly Resources, 2003. Print.

General Studies

Aaron, Daniel. *The Unwritten War: American Writers and the Civil War.* Madison: U of Wisconsin P, 1987. Print.

The Abolitionists. Dir. Rob Rapley. PBS, 2013. DVD.

Barrish, Philip J. *The Cambridge Introduction to American Literary Realism.* New York: Cambridge UP, 2011. Print.

The Center for Civil War Research at the University of Mississippi. Center for Civil War Research, n.d. Web. 12 Aug. 2015. <http://www.civilwarcenter.olemiss.edu>.

The Civil War. National Park Service, U.S. Department of the Interior, 20 July 2015. Web. 12 Aug. 2015. <www.nps.gov/civilwar/index.htm>.

Civil War and Reconstruction, 1861–1877. Gilder Lehrman Inst. of Amer. History, n.d. Web. 12 Aug. 2015. <http://www.gilderlehrman.org/history-by-era/civil-war-and-reconstruction-1861-1877>.

Cullen, Jim. *The Civil War in Popular Culture*. Washington: Smithsonian, 1996. Print.

Disunion. Opinionator. New York Times. New York Times, n.d. Web. 12 Aug. 2015. <http://opinionator.blogs.nytimes.com/category/disunion/>.

Garvey, Ellen Gruber. "Anonymity, Authorship, and Recirculation: a Civil War Episode." *Book History* 9 (2006): 159–78. Print.

Kagan, Neil, ed. *Eyewitness to the Civil War: The Complete History from Secession to Reconstruction*. Monterey: National Geographic, 2007. Print.

Kaufman, Will. *The Civil War in American Culture*. Ed. Simon Newman and Carol R. Smith. Edinburgh: Edinburgh UP, 2006. Print.

Mott, Frank Luther. *A History of American Magazines*. 5 vols. Cambridge: Harvard UP, 1957. Print.

Potter, David J. *The Impending Crisis, 1848–1861*. New York: Harper, 1976. Print.

Roberts, Jessica Forbes. "*E Pluribus Unum*: Conventions, Imperatives, and the Poetic Call-to-Arms in Frank Moore's *Rebellion Record*." *ESQ: A Journal of the American Renaissance* 54.1–4 (2008): 171–98. Print.

War and Peace Studies Caucus. Amer. Studies Assn., 18 Jan. 2014. Web. 12 Aug. 2015. <http://www.theasa.net/caucus_war_and_peace_studies/>.

Warner, Michael. "What like a Bullet Can Undeceive?" *Public Culture* 15 (2003): 41–54. Print.

Anthologies, Readers, and Document Collections

Abraham Lincoln Online: Libraries and Museums with Abraham Lincoln Collections. Abraham Lincoln Online, n.d. Web. 12 Aug. 2015. <http://www.abrahamlincolnonline.org/lincoln/resource/library.htm>.

Abraham Lincoln Papers at the Library of Congress. Lib. of Congress, 1 Mar. 2002. Web. 14 Aug. 2015. <http://memory.loc.gov/ammem/alhtml/malhome.html>.

American Broadsides and Ephemera, Series I: 1760–1900. Readex, n.d. Web. 12 Aug. 2015.

American Pamphlets, Series 1, 1820–1922: From the New-York Historical Society. Readex, n.d. Web. 12 Aug. 2015. <http://www.readex.com/content/american-pamphlets-series-1-1820-1922-new-york-historical-society>.

American Periodical Series Online. ProQuest, n.d. Web. 12 Aug. 2015. <http://www.proquest.com/en-US/catalogs/databases/detail/aps.shtml>.

Belasco, Susan, and Linck Johnson, eds. *The Bedford Anthology of American Literature*. Vol. 1. Boston: St. Martin's, 2008. Print.

Born in Slavery: Slave Narratives from the Federal Writers' Project, 1936–1938. Lib. of Congress, 23 Mar. 2001. Web. 12 Aug. 2015. <http://memory.loc.gov/ammem/snhtml/snhome.html>.

Browne, Francis F., ed. *Bugle-Echoes: A Collection of the Poems of the Civil War Northern and Southern*. New York: White, Stokes, and Allen, 1886. Print.

Capps, Claudius Meade, ed. *The Blue and the Gray: The Best Poems of the Civil War*. Boston: Humphries, 1943. Print.

Civil War Resources. VMI Archives. Virginia Military Inst., n.d. Web. 12 Aug. 2015. <http://www.vmi.edu/Archives/Civil_War/Civil_War_Resources_Home/>.

Crawford, Richard, ed. *The Civil War Songbook*. New York: Dover, 1977. Print.

Confederate States of America: Documents. The Avalon Project: Documents in Law, History, and Diplomacy. Lillian Goldman Law Lib., n.d. Web. 12 Aug. 2015. <http://avalon.law.yale.edu/subject_menus/csapage.asp>.

Divided and United: The Songs of the Civil War. ATO Records. Audio CD. 2 discs.

Divided and United: The Songs of the Civil War Reimagined. NPR, 25 Nov. 2013. Web. 12 Aug. 2015. <http://www.npr.org/2013/11/25/247161677/divided-united-songs-of-the-civil-war-reimagined>.

Documenting the American South. Univ. Lib., U of North Carolina, Chapel Hill, 12 Aug. 2015. Web. 12 Aug. 2015. <http://docsouth.unc.edu/>.

Early American Newspapers Series 1, 1690–1976. Readex, n.d. Web. 12 Aug. 2015. <http://www.readex.com/content/early-american-newspapers-1690-1922-series>.

Harper's Weekly: 1857–1912. Alexander Street, n.d. Web. 12 Aug. 2015. <http://alexanderstreet.com/products/harpers-weekly-1857-1912>.

Hayward, General William H. *Camp Songs for the Soldier and Poems of Leisure Moments.* Baltimore: H. A. Robinson, 1864. Print.

Historical Newspapers. ProQuest, n.d. Web. 14 Aug. 2015.

Lauter, Paul, et al., ed. *The Heath Anthology of American Literature.* 6th ed. Vol. B. Belmont: Wadsworth, 2009. Print.

Lincoln Logarithms: Finding Meaning in Sermons. Emory Libs., n.d. Web. 14 Aug. 2015. <http://disc.library.emory.edu/lincoln/>.
    Uses four text analysis tools to examine fifty-seven full text sermons given on the occasion of Lincoln's assassination.

Loewen, James W., and Edward H. Sebesta, eds. *The Confederate and Neo-Confederate Reader: The "Great Truth" about the "Lost Cause."* Jackson: UP of Mississippi, 2010. Print.

*Lorang, Elizabeth, and R. J. Weir, eds. "Will Not These Days Be by Thy Poets Sung": Poems of the Anglo-African and National Anti-slavery Standard, 1863–1864. *Scholarly Editing* 34 (2013): n. pag. Center for Digital Research in the Humanities, U of Nebraska, Lincoln, n.d. Web. 14 Aug. 2015. <http://www.scholarlyediting.org/2013/editions/intro.cwnewspaperpoetry.html>.

Making of America. Cornell U Lib., n.d. Web. 14 Aug. 2015. <http://ebooks.library.cornell.edu/m/moa/>.

Marius, Richard, and Keith W. Frome, eds. *Columbia Book of Civil War Poetry: From Whitman to Walcott.* New York: Columbia UP, 1994. Print.

Mason, Emily V., ed. *The Southern Poems of the War.* Baltimore: J. Murphy, 1867. Print.

McMichael, George, et al., ed. *Anthology of American Literature.* 10th ed. Vol. 1. New York: Longman, 2010. Print.

Moore, Frank, ed. *The Civil War in Song and Story, 1860–65.* New York: P. F. Collier, 1889. Print.

———. *Lyrics of Loyalty.* New York: George P. Putnam, 1864. Print. Available through the *HathiTrust Digital Library.*

———. *Personal and Political Ballads.* New York: George P. Putnam, 1864. Print. Available through the *HathiTrust Digital Library.*

———. *Rebel Rhymes and Rhapsodies.* New York: George P. Putnam, 1864. Print. Available through *Google Books.*

————. *Songs of the Soldiers.* New York: George P. Putnam, 1864. Print. Available through the *HathiTrust Digital Library.*

A Newspaper Perspective. Accessible Archives, n.d. Web. 12 Aug. 2015. Part 1 of *The Civil War Collection.*

Parks, Edd Winfield. *Southern Poets: Representative Selections.* New York: Amer., 1936. Print.

Shepperson, William G., ed. *War Songs of the South.* Richmond: West and Johnston, 1862. Print.

Simms, William Gilmore, ed. *War Poetry of the South.* New York: Richardson and Company, 1867. Print.

Steinmetz, Lee, ed. *The Poetry of the American Civil War.* East Lansing: Michigan State UP, 1991. Print.

**Wright American Fiction.* Indiana U, n.d. Web. 14 Aug. 2015. <http://www.letrs.indiana.edu/web/w/wright2/>.

Visual Materials

**Civil War Era Collection.* Gettysburg Coll., n.d. Web. 14 Aug. 2015. <gettysburg.cdmhost.com/cdm/landingpage/collection/p4016coll2>.

**Nineteenth-Century Advertising.* HarpWeek, n.d. Web. 14 Aug. 2015. <advertising.harpweek.com>.

Visual Culture of the American Civil War. Amer. Social History Productions, n.d. Web. 14 Aug. 2015. <http://civilwar.picturinghistory.gc.cuny.edu/>.

Photography

**Civil War Glass Negatives and Related Prints.* Prints and Photographs Online Catalog. Lib. of Congress, n.d. Web. 14 Aug. 2015. <www.loc.gov/pictures/collection/cwp>.

*"Cornell University Library's Seven Millionth Volume: *Gardner's Photographic Sketch Book of the War.*" Cornell U Lib., Division of Rare and Manuscript Collections. Web. <http://rmc.library.cornell.edu/7milVol/index.html>.

**Daguerreotypes. Prints and Photographs Online Catalog.* Lib. of Congress, n.d. Web. 14 Aug. 2015. <memory.loc.gov/ammem/daghtml/daghome.html>.

Images of the American Civil War: Photographs, Posters and Ephemera. Alexander Street, n.d. Web. 14 Aug. 2015. < http://alexanderstreet.com/products/images-american-civil-war>.

National Historical Society Photographic Portrait of the Civil War. New York: Black Dog; Leventhal, 1997. Print.

Lossing, Benson J. *Mathew Brady's Illustrated History of the Civil War.* New York: Gramercy, 1994. Print.

**Pictorial Americana.* Lib. of Congress, 2 Dec. 2014. Web. 15 Aug. 2015. <www.loc.gov/rr/print/list/picamer/toc.html>.

**Pictures of the Civil War. National Archives.* U.S. Natl. Archives and Records Administration. Web. <www.archives.gov/research/military/civil-war/photos/index.html>.

Teaching with Documents: The Civil War as Photographed by Mathew Brady. National Archives U.S. National Archives and Records Administration, n.d. Web. 15 Aug. 2015. <www.archives.gov/education/lessons/brady-photos>.
Watts, Jennifer, curator. *A Strange and Fearful Interest: Death, Mourning, and Memory in the American Civil War.* Huntington Lib., n.d. Web. 15 Aug. 2015. <http://huntington.org/civilwar/about.htm>.

Art, Illustrations, and Sketches

The Civil War and American Art. Smithsonian Inst., n.d. Web. 15 Aug. 2015. <americanart.si.edu/exhibitions/online/art_civil_war>.
Frank Leslie's Illustrated Civil War. Ed. Louis Shepherd Moat. Jackson: UP of Missouri, 1992. Print.
Harvey, Eleanor Jones. *The Civil War and American Art.* Washington: Smithsonian Inst.; Yale UP, 2012. Print.
The Lines Are Drawn: Political Cartoons of the Civil War. Ed. Kristen M. Smith. Athens: Hill Street, 1999. Print.
Patriotism through the Mail: Image Gallery Essay: Civil War Envelopes. Wisconsin Historical Soc., n.d. Web. 15 Aug. 2015. <http://www.wisconsinhistory.org/whi/feature/envelopes/>.
Sketches for Frank Leslie's Illustrated Newspaper. New York Public Lib., n.d. Web. 15 Aug. 2015. <digitalgallery.nypl.org/nypldigital/dgkeysearchresult.cfm?parent_id=1880878>.
Timeline: The Civil War and American Art. Smithsonian Inst., n.d. Web. 15 Aug. 2015. <http://americanart.si.edu/exhibitions/online/civilwar_timeline/>.

Sculpture and Monuments

Brown, Thomas. *The Public Art of Civil War Commemoration.* Bedford–St. Martin's, 2004. Print.
"The Corner-Stone of the Capitol." *Saturday Evening Post* 8 June 1861. *Illustrated Civil War Newspapers and Magazines.* HarpWeek, n.d. Web. 15 Aug. 2015. <http://www.lincolnandthecivilwar.com>.
"Crawford, the Sculptor." *Southern Literary Messenger* 30.6 (1860): 455–66. *American Periodical Series Online.* Web. 15 Aug. 2015.
"Dome of the Capitol at Washington." *Scientific American* 13 Dec. 1862: 373. *American Periodical Series Online.* Web. 15 Aug. 2015.
"Freedom and the Fourth of July." *Southern Illustrated News* 20 Jun. 1863. *Illustrated Civil War Newspapers and Magazines.* HarpWeek, n.d. Web. 15 Aug. 2015. <http://www.lincolnandthecivilwar.com>.
"Lyrics of Freedom." *Liberator* 15 Jan. 1864: 12a. *Illustrated Civil War Newspapers and Magazines.* HarpWeek, n.d. Web. 15 Aug. 2015. <http://www.lincolnandthecivilwar.com>.
"Matters and Things in Washington." *Frank Leslie's Illustrated Newspaper* 13 Dec. 1862: 179. *Illustrated Civil War Newspapers and Magazines.* HarpWeek, n.d. Web. 15 Aug. 2015. <http://www.lincolnandthecivilwar.com>.

"The New Dome at the Capitol." *Christian Recorder* 20 Dec. 1862. *Illustrated Civil War Newspapers and Magazines.* HarpWeek, n.d. Web. 15 Aug. 2015. <http://www.lincolnandthecivilwar.com>.

"The Right of Interference." *Index* 10 July 1862: 170–71. *Illustrated Civil War Newspapers and Magazines.* HarpWeek, n.d. Web. 15 Aug. 2015. <http://www.lincolnandthecivilwar.com>.

Statue of Freedom. The *Architect of the Capitol* Web site (www.aoc.gov/) is the best source for primary documents pertaining to Phillip Reid, the slave who completed the statue's casting.

"The Statue of Freedom." *Liberator* 1 Jan. 1864: 4d. *Illustrated Civil War Newspapers and Magazines.* HarpWeek, n.d. Web. 15 Aug. 2015. <http://www.lincolnandthecivilwar.com>.

"The Statue of Liberty in the Capitol." *Old Guard* 4.12 (1866): 764. *Illustrated Civil War Newspapers and Magazines.* HarpWeek, n.d. Web. 15 Aug. 2015. <http://www.lincolnandthecivilwar.com>.

Recommended Print Editions

Alcott, Louisa May. *Hospital Sketches.* Ed. Alice Fahs. Boston: Bedford–St. Martin's, 2004.

Brown, William Wells. *Clotel.* New York: Modern Lib., 2000.
    The authoritative digital edition, edited by Christopher Mulvey, is published by the University of Virginia Press (http://rotunda.upress.virginia.edu:8080/clotel/).

———. *The Works of William Wells Brown: Using His "Strong, Manly Voice."* Ed. Paula Garrett and Hollis Robbins. New York: Oxford UP, 2006.

Crane, Stephen. *The Red Badge of Courage.* New York: Norton, 1994.

Dickinson, Emily. *The Poems of Emily Dickinson.* Ed. R. W. Franklin. Cambridge: Harvard UP, 1998.

Douglass, Frederick. *The Life and Writings of Frederick Douglass.* 5 vols. Ed. Philip S. Foner. New York: Intl., 1950–75.

———. *Narrative of the Life of Frederick Douglass.* Ed. William L. Andrews and William S. McFeely. New York: Norton, 1997.

Emerson, Ralph Waldo. *The Complete Works of Ralph Waldo Emerson.* Ed. Edward Waldo Emerson. 12 vols. 1903–04. Rpt. New York: AMS, 1968. Available online at http://quod.lib.umich.edu/e/emerson/.

Harper, Frances. *A Brighter Coming Day: A Frances Ellen Watkins Harper Reader.* New York: Feminist, 1990.

Hawthorne, Nathaniel. *The Centenary Edition of the Works of Nathaniel Hawthorne.* Ed. William Charvat et al. 23 vols. Columbus: Ohio State UP, 1962–97.

Higginson, Thomas Wentworth. Army Life in a Black Regiment *and Other Writings.* New York: Penguin, 1997.

———. *The Complete Civil War Journal and Selected Letters of Thomas Wentworth Higginson.* Ed. Christopher Looby. Chicago: U of Chicago P, 2000.

Horton, George Moses. *Naked Genius.* Chapel Hill: Chapel Hill Historical Soc., 1982. Photofacsimile of the original 1865 edition.

Howe, Julia Ward. *Later Lyrics.* Boston: J. E. Tilton, 1866.

Jacobs, Harriet. *Incidents in the Life of a Slave Girl: Written by Herself.* Ed. Jean Fagan Yellin. Cambridge: Harvard UP, 1994.

Melville, Herman. *Battle-Pieces and Aspects of the War.* Ed. Lee Rust Brown. New York: Da Capo, 1995. Photofacsimile of the original 1866 edition.

Piatt, Sarah. *Palace-Burner: The Selected Poetry of Sarah Piatt.* Ed. Paula Bernat Bennett. Urbana: U of Illinois P, 2001.

Stowe, Harriet Beecher. *Uncle Tom's Cabin; or, Life among the Lowly.* New York: Norton, 2010. Print.

Timrod, Henry. *The Collected Poems of Henry Timrod.* Ed. Edd Winfield Parks and Aileen Wells Parks. Athens: U of Georgia P, 1965.

Whitman, Walt. *Civil War Poetry and Prose.* New York: Dover, 1995.

Additional Resources for Specific Authors and Texts

Louisa May Alcott's Hospital Sketches

Alcott, Louisa May. *Alternative Alcott.* Ed. Elaine Showalter. New Brunswick: Rutgers UP, 1997. Print.

———. *Selected Letters of Louisa May Alcott.* Ed. Joel Myerson and Daniel Shealy. Athens: U of Georgia P, 1995. Print.

Contemporary Reviews: Louisa May Alcott. Ed. Beverly Lyon Clark. New York: Cambridge UP, 2004. Print.

Laffrado, Laura. "'How Could You Leave Me Alone When the Room Was Full of Men?': Gender and Self-Representation in Louisa May Alcott's *Hospital Sketches.*" *ESQ: A Journal of the American Renaissance* 48.1–2 (2002): 71–95. *ProQuest.* Web. 8 May 2013.

William Wells Brown's Clotell

Chaney, Michael A. *Fugitive Vision: Slave Image and Black Identity in Antebellum Narrative.* Bloomington: Indiana UP, 2009. Print.

Farrison, William Edward. *William Wells Brown: Author and Reformer.* Chicago: U of Chicago P, 1969. Print.

Mulvey, Christopher. Introduction. *Clotel, by William Wells Brown: An Electronic Scholarly Edition.* Univ. of Virginia, n.d. Web. 21 May 2013. <http://www.upress.virginia.edu/rotunda/>.

Raimon, Eve Allegra. *The "Tragic Mulatta" Revisited: Race and Nationalism in Nineteenth-Century Antislavery Fiction.* Piscataway: Rutgers UP, 2004. Print.

Stadler, Gustavus. *Troubling Minds: The Cultural Politics of Genius in the United States, 1840–1890.* Minneapolis: U of Minnesota P, 2006. Print.

Emily Dickinson's War Poetry

Emily Dickinson Archive. Edickinson.org, n.d. Web. 15 Aug. 2015. <http://www.edickinson.org>.

Friedlander, Benjamin. "Emily Dickinson and the Battle of Ball's Bluff." *PMLA* 124.5 (2009): 1582–99. Print.

Richards, Eliza. "Correspondent Lines: Poetry, Journalism, and the U.S. Civil War." *ESQ: A Journal of the American Renaissance* 54.1–4 (2008): 145–70. Print.

Frederick Douglass

Blight, David. *Frederick Douglass' Civil War: Keeping Faith in Jubilee*. Baton Rouge: Louisiana State UP, 1991. Print.

Douglass, Frederick. *The Frederick Douglass Papers: Series 1: Speeches, Debates, and Interviews*. 5 vols. Ed. John W. Blassingame et al. New Haven: Yale UP, 1979–92. Print.

———. *The Frederick Douglass Papers at the Library of Congress*. Lib. of Congress, n.d. Web. 15 Aug. 2015. <http://www.loc.gov/collection/frederick-douglass-papers/about-this-collection/>.

Ralph Waldo Emerson's Civil War Writings

Emerson, Ralph Waldo. *The Journals and Miscellaneous Notebooks of Ralph Waldo Emerson*. Ed. William H. Gilman, Ralph H. Orth, et al. Vol. 15 (1860–66). Cambridge: Harvard UP, 1960–82. Print.

Richardson, Robert D., Jr. *Emerson: The Mind on Fire*. Berkeley: U of California P, 1995. Print.

Nathaniel Hawthorne's Civil War Writings

Hawthorne, Nathaniel. "Chiefly about War-Matters." *Atlantic Monthly* July 1862: 43–61. Print.

Mellow, James R. *Nathaniel Hawthorne in His Times*. Boston: Houghton, 1980. Print.

Reynolds, Larry J. *Devils and Rebels: The Making of Hawthorne's Damned Politics*. Ann Arbor: U of Michigan P, 2008. Print.

Fanny Kemble's *Journal of a Residence on a Georgian Plantation, 1838–39*

Clinton, Catherine. *Fanny Kemble's Civil Wars*. New York: Simon, 2000. Print.

Rev. of *Journal of a Residence on a Georgian Plantation, 1838–1839*, by Frances Anne Kemble. *British Quarterly Review* 38.75 (1863): 244. *ProQuest British Periodical Collections I and II*. Web. 15 Aug. 2015.

Rev. of *Journal of a Residence on a Georgian Plantation, 1838–1839*, by Frances Anne Kemble. *New York Times* 27 July 1863. *ProQuest Historical Newspapers*. Web. 15 Aug. 2015.

Rev. of *Journal of a Residence on a Georgian Plantation, 1838–1839*, by Frances Anne Kemble. *Athenaeum* 3016 (1863): 737. *ProQuest British Periodical Collections I and II*. Web. 15 Aug. 2015.

Rev. of *Journal of a Residence on a Georgian Plantation, 1838–1839*, by Frances Anne Kemble. *The Rose, the Shamrock, and the Thistle* 3.16 (1863): 438. *ProQuest British Periodical Collections I and II*. Web. 15 Aug. 2015.

"Miss Kemble's 'Georgia.'" Rev. of *Journal of a Residence on a Georgian Plantation, 1838–1839*, by Frances Anne Kemble. *Littell's Living Age* 4 July 1863: 25. *American Periodical Series Online.* Web. 15 Aug. 2015.

Abraham Lincoln's Writings and Speeches

Samuels, Shirley, ed. *The Cambridge Companion to Abraham Lincoln.* Cambridge: Cambridge UP, 2011. Print.
> See especially the essays by Faith Barrett, Stephen Cushman, Timothy Sweet, Harold Bush, and Anne Norton.

Herman Melville's War Poetry

Garner, Stanton. *The Civil War World of Herman Melville.* Lawrence: UP of Kansas, 1993. Print.

Harriet Beecher Stowe's Uncle Tom's Cabin

*Railton, Stephen, dir. Uncle Tom's Cabin *and American Culture: A Multi-media Archive.* Railton; U of Virginia, n.d. Web. 17 Aug. 2015. <http://utc.iath.virginia.edu/>.
*Uncle Tom's Cabin *in the National Era.* Harriet Beecher Stowe Center, n.d. Web. 17 Aug. 2015. <http://nationalera.wordpress.com/>.

Walt Whitman's War Writings

Cavitch, Max. *American Elegy: The Poetry of Mourning from the Puritans to Whitman.* Minneapolis: U of Minnesota P, 2007.
> See chapter 6, on Whitman's "Lilacs," pp. 233–85.

Davis, Robert Leigh. *Whitman and the Romance of Medicine.* Berkeley: U of California P, 1997. Print.
The Walt Whitman Archive. Ed. Ed Folsom and Kenneth M. Price. Center for Digital Research in the Humanities, U of Nebraska, Lincoln, n.d. Web. 17 Aug. 2015. <http://www.whitmanarchive.org>.
*"Wound Dresser: Civil War Carnage." *Revising Himself: Walt Whitman and Leaves of Grass.* Lib. of Congress. Web. 16 Aug. 2010. <www.loc.gov/exhib­its/treasures/whitman-wounddresser.html>.

Autobiographies and Diaries

Primary

The American Civil War: Letters and Diaries. Alexander Street, n.d. Web. 17 Aug. 2015. <http://alexanderstreet.com/products/american-civil-war-letters-and -diaries>.
Bacot, Ada W. *A Confederate Nurse: The Diary of Ada W. Bacot, 1860–1863.* Ed. Jean V. Berlin. Columbia: U of South Carolina P, 1994. Print.

Breckinridge, Lucy. *Lucy Breckinridge of Grove Hill: The Journal of a Virginia Girl, 1862–1864.* Ed. Mary D. Robertson. Columbia: U of South Carolina P, 1994. Print.

Buck, Lucy Rebecca. *Shadows on My Heart: The Civil War Diary of Lucy Rebecca Buck of Virginia.* Ed. Elizabeth R. Baer. Athens: U of Georgia P, 2012. Print.

Burge, Dolly Lunt. *The Diary of Dolly Lunt Burge.* Ed. Christine Jacobson Carter. Athens: U of Georgia P, 1997. Print.

Chesnut, Mary. *Mary Chesnut's Diary.* Ed. Catherine Clinton. New York: Penguin, 2011. Print.

Clemson, Floride. *A Rebel Came Home.* Ed. Charles M. McGee, Jr., and Earnest M. Lander, Jr. Columbia: U of South Carolina P, 1961. Print.

Cumming, Kate. *Kate: The Journal of a Confederate Nurse.* Ed. Richard Barksdale Harwell. Baton Rouge: Louisiana State UP, 1959. Print.

Edmondston, Catherine Ann Devereux. *"Journal of a Secesh Lady": The Diary of Catherine Ann Devereux Edmondston, 1860–1866.* Ed. Beth G. Crabtree and James W. Patton. Raleigh: Division of Archives and History, Dept. of Cultural Resources, 1979. Print.

Folwell, William Watts. "Civil War Diary, 1862–64." U of Minnesota Archives. Box 11. MS.

Green, Anna Maria. *The Journal of a Milledgeville Girl, 1861–1867.* Ed. James C. Bonner. Athens: U of Georgia P, 1964. Print.

Heyward, Pauline DeCaradeuc. *A Confederate Lady Comes of Age: The Journal of Pauline DeCaradeuc Heyward, 1863–1888.* Ed. Mary D. Robertson. Columbia: U of South Carolina P, 1991. Print.

Holmes, Emma. *The Diary of Miss Emma Holmes, 1861–1866.* Ed. John F. Marszalek. Baton Rouge: Louisiana State UP, 1979. Print.

House, Ellen Renshaw. *A Very Violent Rebel: The Civil War Diary of Ellen Renshaw House.* Ed. Daniel E. Sutherland. Knoxville: U of Tennessee P, 1996. Print.

Jervey, Susan Ravenel, and Charlotte St. J. Ravenel. *Two Diaries from Middle St. John's, Berkeley, South Carolina, February–May, 1865.* Ed. Yates Snowden. Pinepolis: St. John's Hunting Club, 1921. Print.

LeConte, Emma. *When the World Ended: The Diary of Emma LeConte.* Ed. Earl Schenck Miers. Lincoln: U of Nebraska P, 1987. Print.

Lomax, Elizabeth Lindsay. *Leaves from an Old Washington Diary, 1854–1863.* Ed. Lindsay Lomax Wood. Mount Vernon: Golden Eagle, 1943. Print.

McDonald, Cornelia. *A Diary with Reminiscences of the War and Refugee Life in the Shenandoah Valley, 1860–1865.* Ed. Hunter McDonald. Nashville: Cullom, 1934. Print.

McDowell, Amanda. *Fiddles in the Cumberlands.* Ed. Lela McDowell Blankenship. New York: Smith, 1943. Print.

*Mosler, Henry. *Henry Mosler's Civil War Diary.* Smithsonian Inst., n.d. Web. 17 Aug. 2015. <http://civilwardiary.aaa.si.edu/diary.html>.

North American Women's Letters and Diaries. Alexander Street, n.d. Web. 17 Aug. 2015. <http://alexanderstreet.com/products/north-american-womens-letters-and-diaries>.

Seixas, Eleanor Cohen. "The Diary of Eleanor Cohen Seixas: Columbia, South

Carolina, 1865–1866." *Private Pages: Diaries of American Women, 1830s–1970s.* Ed. Penelope Franklin. New York: Ballantine, 1986. 303–23. Print.

Secondary

Benstock, Shari, ed. *The Private Self: Theory and Practice of Women's Autobiographical Writings.* Chapel Hill: U of North Carolina P, 1988. Print.

Bunkers, Suzanne L., and Cynthia A. Huff, eds. *Inscribing the Daily: Critical Essays on Women's Diaries.* Amherst: U of Massachusetts P, 1996. Print.

Culley, Margo, ed. *A Day at a Time: The Diary Literature of American Women from 1764 to the Present.* New York: Feminist, 1985. Print.

Franklin, Penelope, ed. *Private Pages: Diaries of American Women, 1830s–1970s.* New York: Ballantine, 1986. Print.

Hampsten, Elizabeth. *"Read This Only to Yourself": The Private Writings of Midwestern Women, 1880–1910.* Bloomington: Indiana UP, 1982. Print.

Heilbrun, Carolyn G. *Writing a Woman's Life.* New York: Norton, 1988. Print.

Hogan, Rebecca. "Engendered Autobiographies: The Diary as a Feminine Form." *Autobiography and Questions of Gender.* Spec. issue of *Prose Studies* 14.2 (1991): 95–107. Print.

Jelinek, Estelle C. "Introduction: Women's Autobiography and the Male Tradition." *Women's Autobiography: Essays in Criticism.* Ed. Jelinek. Bloomington: Indiana UP, 1980. 1–20. Print.

Kadar, Marlene. "Coming to Terms: Life Writing—From Genre to Critical Practice." *Essays on Life Writing.* Ed. Kadar. Toronto: U of Toronto P, 1992. 3–16. Print.

Kagle, Steven E. *American Diary Literature, 1620–1799.* Boston: Twanye, 1979. Print.

———. *Late Nineteenth-Century American Diary Literature.* Boston: Twayne, 1988. Print.

Lejeune, Philippe. "How Do Diaries End?" *Biography: An Interdisciplinary Quarterly* 24.1 (2001): 99–113. Print.

———. *On Diary.* Ed. Jeremy Popkin and Julie Rak. Trans. Katharine Durnin. Honolulu: Center for Biographical Research, U of Hawai'i, 2009. Print.

Miller, Nancy K. *But Enough about Me: Why We Read Other People's Lives.* New York: Columbia UP, 2002. Print.

Moffatt, Mary Jane. Foreword. *Revelations: Diaries of Women.* Ed. Moffat and Charlotte Painter. New York: Vintage, 1974. 3–12. Print.

Olney, James, ed. *Autobiography: Essays Theoretical and Critical.* Princeton: Princeton UP, 1980. Print.

———. *Memory and Narrative: The Weave of Life-Writing.* Chicago: U of Chicago P, 1998. Print.

Scheffler, Judith. "'Uncommon, Bad, and Dangerous': Personal Narratives of Imprisoned Confederate Women, 1861–1865." *Women's Life-Writing: Finding Voice, Building Community.* Ed. Linda S. Coleman. Bowling Green: Bowling Green State U Popular P, 1997. 119–38. Print.

Schultz, Jane Ellen. "Mute Fury: Southern Women's Diaries of Sherman's March to the Sea, 1864–1865." *Arms and the Woman: War, Gender, and Literary Rep-*

resentation. Ed. Helen Cooper, Adrienne Munich, and Susan Squier. Chapel Hill: U of North Carolina P, 1989. 59–79. Print.

Smith, Sidonie. "Performativity, Autobiographical Practice, Resistance." *a/b: Auto/Biography Studies* 10.1 (1995): 17–33. Print.

———. "Resisting the Gaze of Embodiment: Women's Autobiography in the Nineteenth Century." *American Women's Autobiography: Fea(s)ts of Memory.* Ed. Margo Culley. Madison: U of Wisconsin P, 1992. 75–110. Print.

Smith, Sidonie, and Julia Watson., eds. *Women, Autobiography, Theory: A Reader.* Madison: U of Wisconsin P, 1998. Print.

Dime Novels

Collections

* The American Women's Dime Novel Project: Dime Novels for Women, 1870–1920. George Mason U, n.d. Web. 17 Aug. 2015. <http://chnm.gmu.edu/dimenovels/>.

* Dime Novels. American Treasures of the Library of Congress. Lib. of Congress, n.d. Web. 17 Aug. 2015. <http://www.loc.gov/exhibits/treasures/tri015.html>.

* Dime Novels and Penny Dreadfuls. Stanford U, n.d. Web. 17 Aug. 2015. <http://www-sul.stanford.edu/depts/dp/pennies/home.html>.

* Street and Smith Dime Novel Covers. Syracuse U Libs., n.d. Web. 17 Aug. 2015. <http://library.syr.edu/find/scrc/collections/diglib/streetsmith.php>.

Teaching Recommendations

Incidents of American Camp Life. 1862. Internet Archive. Web. 17 Aug. 2015. <http://archive.org/details/incidentsofameri00dawl>.

Kaser, David. *Books and Libraries in Camp and Battle: The Civil War Experience.* Westport: Greenwood, 1984. Print. Contributions in Librarianship and Information Science 48.

Kaser lists the titles that soldiers recorded reading:

> Lever, Charles. *The Confessions of Con Cregan: The Irish Gil Blas.* 1860. *Internet Archive.* Web. 17 Aug. 2015. <http://archive.org/details/confessionsconc01unkngoog>.
>
> ———. *Jack Hinton; or, The Guardsman.* 1845. *Internet Archive.* Web. 17 Aug. 2015. <http://archive.org/details/15041607.2496.emory.edu>.
>
> Sumner, Albert W. *The Sea Lark: or, The Quadroon of Louisiana: A Thrilling Tale of the Land and Sea.* 1850. *HathiTrust Digital Library.* Web. 17 Aug. 2015. <http://catalog.hathitrust.org/Record/009184660>.
>
> Victor, Frances Fuller. *The Far West; or, The Beauty of Willard's Mill.* 1862. *Internet Archive.* Web. 17 Aug. 2015. <http://archive.org/details/04297674.1621.emory.edu>.

Kaser claims the following Confederate novels were popular with Union soldiers:

"Dollie" and "Mollie." *Our Own Heroes: A Thrilling Narrative.* 1863. *Internet Archive.* Web. 17 Aug. 2015. <http://archive.org/details/our ownheroesthri01atla>.

[Evans, Augusta J.]. *Macaria; or, Altars of Sacrifice.* 1864. *Internet Archive.* Web. 17 Aug. 2015. <http://archive.org/details/macariaoraltarso00 evan>.
The novel was dedicated "To the Army of the Southern Confederacy, who have delivered the South from despotism."

Herndon, Mary E. *Louise Elton: or, Things Seen and Heard.* 1853. *Wright American Fiction, 1851–75.* Indiana U, n.d. Web. 17 Aug. 2015. <http:// www.letrs.indiana.edu/cgi/t/text/text-idx?c=wright2;idno=wright2 -1178>.
The novel was dedicated to Jefferson Davis.

Versions of the Susan Brownlow story:

"Miss Brownlow." *Harper's Weekly* 21 Dec. 1861: 805. *U Penn Online Books.* Web. 31 July 2013.
This piece popularized the story of the valiant daughter of Parson Brownlow, who was the staunchly Unionist Tennessee editor of the *Knoxville Whig.* She protected the Union flag.

Reynolds, Major W. D. *Miss Martha Brownlow; or, The Heroine of Tennessee.* Philadelphia: Barclay and Co., 1863. *Internet Archive.* Web. 20 July 2013. <http://archive.org/details/missmarthabrownl00reyn>.

Victor, M. V. *The Unionist's Daughter: A Tale of the Rebellion of Tennessee.* New York: Beadle and Company, 1862. *Internet Archive.* Web. 25 July 2013. <http://archive.org/details/unionistsdaughte00vict>.

Walker, Celia. "Susan Brownlow." *Shades of Gray and Blue.* Vanderbilt U Libs., n.d. Web. 1 Aug. 2013.

Special Topics

Transnational Perspectives on the Civil War

Bonner, Robert, Sarah Cornell, Don Doyle, Niels Eichhorn, Andre Fleche, and David Prior. "Teaching the American Civil War in Global Contexts." Round-table discussion. *Journal of the Civil War Era* 5.1 (2015): 97–125. Print.

Briggs, Laura. *Reproducing Empire: Race, Sex, Science, and U.S. Imperialism in Puerto Rico.* Berkeley: U of California P, 2002. Print. Amer. Crossroads 11.

"British Philanthropy and American Slavery: An Affectionate Response to the Ladies of England, Etc., from the Ladies of the Southern United States. . . ." *DeBow's Review and Industrial Resources, Statistics, . . .* 19 (1853): 258. *Pro-Quest American Periodical Series Online.* Web. 18 Aug. 2015.

Dubois, Laurent. *Avengers of the New World: The Story of the Haitian Revolution.* Cambridge: Belknap–Harvard UP, 2004. Print.

Foreign Relations of the United States. University of Wisconsin Digital Collections Center. U of Wisconsin, n.d. Web. 18 Aug. 2015. <http://uwdc.library.wisc .edu/collections/FRUS>.

Official documentary historical record of major United States foreign policy decisions that have been declassified and edited for publication. It begins with the administration of Abraham Lincoln in 1861.

Jones, Howard. *Blue and Gray Diplomacy: A History of Union and Confederate Foreign Relations.* Chapel Hill: U of North Carolina P, 2010. Print. Littlefield History of the Civil War Era Ser.

Ladies' London Emancipation Society, *The Essence of Slavery,* not yet available online, but a photocopy can be purchased from the New York Historical Society. Articles about the female team of compositors who printed the pamphlet:

Faithfull, Emily. "Women Compositors." *English Woman's Journal* 8.1 (1862): 39. *Google Books.* Web. 18 Aug. 2015.

Frawley, Mariah. "Feminism, Format and Emily Faithfull's Victoria Press Publications." *Nineteenth-Century Feminisms* 1 (1999): 39–63. Print.

Lueck, Beth L., Brigitte Bailey, and Lucinda L. Damon-Bach. *Transatlantic Women: Nineteenth-Century American Women Writers and Great Britain.* Durham: New Hampshire UP, 2012. Print. Becoming Modern: New Nineteenth-Century Studies.

May, Robert E. "Reconsidering Antebellum US Women's History: Gender, Filibustering, and America's Quest for Empire." *American Quarterly* 57.4 (2005): 1155–88. Print.

Mays, Kelly J. "Slaves in Heaven, Laborers in Hell: Chartist Poets' Ambivalent Identification with the (Black) Slave." *Victorian Poetry* 39.2 (2001): 136–62. Print.

McFadden, Margaret. *Golden Cables of Sympathy: The Transatlantic Sources of Nineteenth-Century Feminism.* Lexington: Kentucky UP, 1999. Print.

Midgley, Clare. *Women against Slavery: The British Campaigns, 1780–1870.* London: Routledge, 1992. Print.

Pickens, Lucy Petaway Holcombe. *The Free Flag of Cuba: The Lost Novel of Lucy Halcombe Pickens.* Ed. Georganne B. Burton and Orville Vernon Burton. Baton Rouge: Louisiana State UP, 2002. Print.

Ripley, Eliza. *From Flag to Flag: A Woman's Adventures and Experiences in the South during the War, in Mexico, and in Cuba.* 1889. *Documenting the American South.* U of North Carolina, 9 Nov. 1998. Web. 18 Aug. 2015.

Ruiz de Burton, María. *Who Would Have Thought It?* Philadelphia: J. B. Lippincott, 1872. Print.

Streeby, Shelley. *American Sensations: Class, Empire, and the Production of Popular Culture.* Berkeley: U of California P, 2002. Print.

Velazquez, Loreta Janeta. *The Woman in Battle: The Civil War Narrative of Loreta Velazquez, Cuban Woman and Confederate Soldier.* Ed. Jesse Alemán. Madison: U of Wisconsin P, 2003. Print.

"The Women of Great Britain to the Women of America." *National Era* 30 Dec. 1852: 210. *ProQuest American Periodical Series Online.* Web. 18 Aug. 2015.

War and Gender

Carnes, Mark C. *Secret Ritual and Manhood in Victorian America.* New Haven: Yale UP, 1989. Print.

Chapman, Mary, and Glenn Hendler. *Sentimental Men: Masculinity and the Politics of Affect in American Culture*. Berkeley: U of California P, 1999. Print.

Clawson, Mary Ann. *Constructing Brotherhood: Class, Gender, and Fraternalism*. Princeton: Princeton UP, 1989. Print.

Clinton, Catherine, ed. *Half Sisters of History: Southern Women and the American Past*. Durham: Duke UP, 1994. Print.

———. *The Plantation Mistress: Woman's World in the Old South*. New York: Pantheon, 1982. Print.

Clinton, Catherine, and Nina Silber, eds. *Battle Scars: Gender and Sexuality in the American Civil War*. New York: Oxford UP, 2006. Print.

———, eds. *Divided Houses: Gender and the Civil War*. New York: Oxford UP, 1992. Print.

Cobbe, Frances Power. "What Shall We Do with Our Old Maids?" *Prose by Victorian Women: An Anthology*. Ed. Andrea Broomfield and Sally Ledger. Oxford: Taylor, 1996. 231–60. Print.

Dumenil, Lynn. *Freemasonry and American Culture, 1880–1930*. Princeton: Princeton UP, 1984. Print.

Faust, Drew Gilpin. *Mothers of Invention: Women of the Slaveholding South in the American Civil War*. Chapel Hill: U of North Carolina P, 1996. Print.

Forgie, George B. *Patricide in the House Divided: A Psychological Interpretation of Lincoln and His Age*. New York: Norton, 1979. Print.

Fox-Genovese, Elizabeth, and Eugene D. Genovese. *The Mind of the Master Class: History and Faith in the Southern Slaveholder's Worldview*. Cambridge: Cambridge UP, 2005. Print.

Friedman, Jean E. *The Enclosed Garden: Women and Community in the Evangelical South*. Chapel Hill: U of North Carolina P, 1985. Print.

Greg, W. R. "Why Are Women Redundant?" *National Review* 14 (1862): 434–60. *British Periodicals Collections I and II*. Web. 18 Aug. 2015.

Kete, Mary Louise. *Sentimental Collaborations: Mourning and Middle-Class Identity in Nineteenth-Century America*. Durham: Duke UP, 2000. Print.

King, Wilma. "The Mistress and Her Maids: White and Black Women in a Louisiana Household, 1858–1868." *Discovering the Women in Slavery: Emancipating Perspectives on the American Past*. Ed. Patricia Morton. Athens: U of Georgia P, 1996. 82–106. Print.

Macdonald, Anne. *No Idle Hands: The Social History of American Knitting*. New York: Random, 2010. *Google Books*. Web. 18 Aug. 2015.

McCurry, Stephanie. "Producing Dependence: Women, Work, and the Yeoman Households in Low-Country South Carolina." *Neither Lady nor Slave: Working Women in the Old South*. Ed. Susanna Delfino and Michele Gillespie. Chapel Hill: U of North Carolina P, 2002. 55–71. Print.

McPherson, Tara. *Reconstructing Dixie: Race, Gender, and Nostalgia in the Imagined South*. Durham: Duke UP, 2003. Print.

Merish, Lori. "Sentimental Consumption: Harriet Beecher Stowe and the Aesthetics of Middle-Class Ownership." *American Literary History* 8 (1996): 1–33. Print.

Rable, George C. *Civil Wars: Women and the Crisis of Southern Nationalism*. Urbana: U of Illinois P, 1989. Print.

Stauffer, John. "Embattled Manhood and New England Writers, 1860–1870."
Clinton and Silber, *Battle Scars* 120–39.

Whites, LeeAnn. *The Civil War as a Crisis in Gender: Augusta, Georgia, 1860–1890.* Athens: U of Georgia P, 1995. Print.

Nursing, Injury, and Medicine

Brochett, L. P., and Mary Vaughn. *Women's Work in the Civil War: A Record of Heroism, Patriotism, and Patience.* 1867. *Project Gutenberg.* Web. 18 Aug. 2015.

Freemon, Frank R. *Microbes and Minie Balls: An Annotated Bibliography of Civil War Medicine.* London: Associated UPs, 1993. Print.
   Lists primary and secondary sources, arranged by author and with descriptions of each work. Includes index.

* *National Museum of Health and Medicine.* Nat'l. Museum of Health and Medicine, 1 Aug. 2015. Web. 18 Apr. 2016. <http://www.medicalmuseum.mil>.

* *Nursing History Research Resources.* Amer. Assn. for the History of Nursing, n.d. Web. 9 Dec. 2015. <http://www.aahn.org/resource.html>.

Smith, Adelaide W. *Reminiscences of an Army Nurse during the Civil War.* New York: Greaves, 1911. Print.

United States Sanitary Commission. *The Sanitary Commission of the United States Army: A Succinct Narrative of Its Works and Purposes.* New York: Arno, 1972. Print.

Wormeley, Katharine Prescott. *The United States Sanitary Commission: A Sketch of Its Purpose and Its Work.* 1863. *Internet Archive.* Web. 18 Aug. 2015.

Regions

Ayers, Edward L., et al. *All over the Map: Rethinking American Regions.* Baltimore: Johns Hopkins UP, 1996. Print.

Bassett, John E., ed. *Defining Southern Literature: Perspectives and Assessments, 1831–1952.* Madison: Fairleigh Dickinson UP, 1997. Print.

Crow, Charles L., ed. *A Companion to the Regional Literatures of America.* Malden: Blackwell, 2003. Print.

Fetterley, Judith, and Marjorie Pryse. *Writing out of Place: Regionalism, Women, and American Literary Culture.* Urbana: U of Illinois P, 2003. Print.

Race

**Africana and Black History. New York Public Library Digital Collections.* New York Public Lib., n.d. Web. 18 Aug. 2015. <digitalgallery.nypl.org/nypldigital /explore/dgexplore.cfm?topic=culture&collection_list=AfricanaBlackHistory &col_id=147>.

African American Newspapers. Accessible Archives. Accessible Archives, n.d. Web. 18 Aug. 2015. <http://www.accessible-archives.com/collections/african -american-newspapers/>.

African American Newspapers, 1827–1998. Readex. NewsBank, n.d. Web. 18 Aug. 2015. <http://www.readex.com/content/african-american-newspapers-1827 -1998>.

African American Periodicals, 1825–1995. Readex. NewsBank, n.d. Web. 18 Aug. 2015. <http://www.readex.com/content/african-american-periodicals-1825 -1995>.

Alcott, Louisa May. *On Race, Sex, and Slavery.* Ed. Sarah Elbert. Boston: Northeastern UP, 1997. Print.

Chalmers, David M. *Hooded Americanism: The History of the Ku Klux Klan.* Chicago: Quadrangle, 1968. Print.

Chester County USCT Index. Chester County Pennsylvania. Chester County, n.d. Web. 18 Aug. 2015. <http://www.chesco.org/index.aspx?NID=2273>. An attempt to document all African American soldiers and sailors from Chester County, PA, who served in the Civil War.

Foner, Eric. *Reconstruction: America's Unfinished Revolution, 1863–1877.* San Francisco: Harper, 1988. Print.

Franklin, John Hope. *From Slavery to Freedom: A History of Negro Americans.* 1956. New York: Knopf, 1968. Print.

Freedmen and Southern Society Project. Freedman and Southern Soc. Project, 21 May 2014. Web. 18 Aug. 2015. <www.freedmen.umd.edu>.

Goodman, Paul. *Of One Blood: Abolitionism and the Origins of Racial Equality.* Berkeley: U of California P, 1998. Print.

Litwack, Leon F. *North of Slavery: The Negro in the Free States, 1790–1860.* Chicago: U of Chicago P, 1961. Print.

MacLean, Nancy. *Behind the Mask of Chivalry: The Making of the Second Ku Klux Klan.* New York: Oxford UP, 1994. Print.

Mayer, Henry. *All on Fire: William Lloyd Garrison and the Abolition of Slavery.* New York. St. Martin's, 1998. Print.

Oates, Stephen B. *To Purge This Land with Blood: A Biography of John Brown.* Amherst: U of Massachusetts P, 1984. Print.

Ownby, Ted, ed. *Black and White Cultural Interaction in the Antebellum South.* Jackson: UP of Mississippi, 1993. Print.

Reynolds, David. *John Brown, Abolitionist: The Man Who Killed Slavery, Sparked the Civil War, and Seeded Civil Rights.* New York: Knopf, 2005. Print.

Scartoons: Racial Satire and the Civil War. U of Virginia, n.d. Web. 18 Aug. 2015. <xroads.virginia.edu/~cap/scartoons/cartoons.html>.

Sterling, Dorothy, ed. *We Are Your Sisters: Black Women in the Nineteenth Century.* New York: Norton, 1984. Print.

Sundquist, Eric J. *To Wake the Nations: Race in the Making of American Literature.* Cambridge: Belknap–Harvard UP, 1993. Print.

The Views of Judge Woodward and Bishop Hopkins on Negro Slavery at the South, Illustrated from the Journal of a Residence on a Georgian Plantation *by Mrs. Frances Anne Kemble. Internet Archive.* Web. 18 Aug. 2015. Jessica DeSpain mentions that Private Gordon's silver albumen print was reproduced on the cover of the Union League Pamphlet. Images of Gordon first appeared in *Harper's Weekly.* Fahs discusses the images in *The Imagined*

Civil War, but she does not mention that Gordon's pictures were accompanied by a horrifying account of a slave mistress who tortured her slaves, originating from the same area from which Gordon fled. See "The Typical Negro." *Harper's Weekly.* 4 Jul. 1863. 0429ad-0430a. *HarpWeek.*

Wiebe, Robert H. *The Search for Order, 1877–1920.* New York: Hill, 1967. Print.

Willis, Deborah, and Barbara Krauthamer. *Envisioning Emancipation: Black Americans and the End of Slavery.* Philadelphia: Temple UP, 2013. Print.

Woodward, C. Vann. *Reunion and Reaction: The Compromise of 1877 and the End of Reconstruction.* Boston: Little, 1951. Print.

Performance and Reenactment

Horwitz, Tony. *Confederates in the Attic: Dispatches from the Unfinished Civil War.* New York: Vintage, 1999. Print.

Kaufmann, Will. *The Civil War in American Culture.* Edinburgh: Edinburgh UP, 2006. Print.

Masur, Louis P. "Lincoln at the Movies." *Chronicle of Higher Education.* Chronicle of Higher Educ., 26 Nov. 2012. Web. 15 Dec. 2013. <http://chronicle.com/article/Lincoln-at-the-Movies/135880/?cid=cr&utm_source=cr&utm_medium=en>.

Nemerov, Alexander. *Acting in the Night: Macbeth and the Places of the Civil War.* Berkeley: U of California P, 2010. Print.

Schneider, Rebecca. *Performing Remains: Art and War in Times of Theatrical Reenactment.* London: Routledge, 2011. Print.

Notes on Contributors

Faith Barrett is associate professor of English at Duquesne University. She is the author of *To Fight Aloud Is Very Brave: American Poetry and the Civil War*. With Cristanne Miller she coedited *"Words for the Hour": A New Anthology of American Civil War Poetry*.

Alex W. Black is assistant professor of English at Hobart and William Smith Colleges. His first book is a study of the print and performance cultures of the nineteenth-century antislavery movement in the United States. His work has appeared in *American Quarterly* and *J19: The Journal of Nineteenth-Century Americanists*.

Colleen Glenney Boggs is professor of English at Dartmouth College. She is the author of *Transnationalism and American Literature: Literary Translation, 1773–1892* (2007) and *Animalia Americana: Animal Representations and Biopolitical Subjectivity* (2013). She is working on a monograph tentatively entitled "Civil War Substitutes: How the Military Draft Changed American Literature."

Allison E. Carey is associate professor of English at Marshall University and teaches courses in American literature and English education. Her current research focuses on digital pedagogy, dime novels, and the Civil War.

Tess Chakkalakal is associate professor of Africana studies and English at Bowdoin College. Her most recent books are *Jim Crow, Literature, and the Legacy of Sutton E. Griggs* and *Novel Bondage: Slavery, Marriage, and Freedom in Nineteenth-Century America*.

Matthew R. Davis has recently completed a book-length project entitled "Fratricidal Nation: Rethinking Brotherhood in Nineteenth-Century American Literature and Culture." He is an instructor of English at Cuesta College. His work has appeared in *ESQ: A Journal of the American Renaissance*, *Science as Culture*, *Mississippi Quarterly*, and *Contemporary Justice Review*.

Jessica DeSpain is associate professor of English language and literature at Southern Illinois University, Edwardsville. She is the author of *Nineteenth-Century Transatlantic Reprinting and the Embodied Book* and the lead editor of *The Wide, Wide World Digital Edition*.

Kathleen Diffley is associate professor of English at the University of Iowa. She is the author of *Where My Heart Is Turning Ever: Civil War Stories and Constitutional Reform* and the editor of *To Live and Die: Collected Stories of the Civil War, 1861–1876*.

Elizabeth Duquette is an associate professor in the Department of English at Gettysburg College. She is the author of *Loyal Subjects: Bonds of Nation, Race, and Allegiance in Nineteenth-Century America* and a coeditor of *Elizabeth Stuart Phelps: Selected Tales, Essays, and Poems.*

Rebecca Entel is associate professor of English and creative writing at Cornell College, where she also directs the Center for the Literary Arts. She is the author of articles on Louisa May Alcott in *American Periodicals* and the forthcoming *Arts and Culture of the American Civil War* and of many works of fiction.

Ian Finseth is associate professor of English at the University of North Texas. He is the author of *Shades of Green: Visions of Nature in the Literature of American Slavery, 1770–1860* and the editor of *The American Civil War: A Literary and Historical Anthology.*

Christopher Hager is associate professor of English at Trinity College in Hartford, Connecticut. He is the author of *Word by Word: Emancipation and the Act of Writing.*

Coleman Hutchison is an associate professor of English at the University of Texas at Austin. He is the author of *Apples and Ashes: Literature, Nationalism, and the Confederate States of America*; a coauthor, with Karen Gocsik, of *Writing about American Literature*; and the editor of *A History of American Civil War Literature.*

Shawn Jones is lead counselor at Portland Christian High School. Previously he served as academic dean and professor of biblical studies at Cascade College, a branch of Oklahoma Christian University.

Wiebke Omnus Klumpenhower completed her PhD on twentieth-century southern United States women's writing at the Université de Montreal. She was assistant professor of English literature at Keimyung University in Daegu, South Korea, between 2009 and 2013.

Dana McMichael is associate professor of language and literature at Abilene Christian University and serves as the director of graduate studies in English. She is the author of *How Confederate Women Created New Self-Identities as the Civil War Progressed: A Study of Their Diaries* (2008).

Larry J. Reynolds is University Distinguished Professor and Thomas Franklin Mayo Professor of Liberal Arts at Texas A&M University. He is the author of *Devils and Rebels: The Making of Hawthorne's Damned Politics* and *Righteous Violence: Revolution, Slavery, and the American Renaissance.*

Jess Roberts is an associate professor of English at Albion College. Her recent work includes articles on the nineteenth-century poet Sarah Piatt, in *The Cambridge Companion to Nineteenth-Century American Poetry* and *Oxford Bibliographies.*

Susan M. Ryan is associate professor of English at the University of Louisville. She is the author of *The Grammar of Good Intentions: Race and the Antebellum Culture of Benevolence* (2003) and *The Moral Economies of American Authorship: Reputation, Scandal, and the Nineteenth-Century Literary Marketplace* (2016).

Catherine E. Saunders is a term associate professor of English at George Mason University. She studies the literature of the American abolitionist movement and is currently writing about Harriet Jacobs's dispatches from Civil War–era Alexandria and the antislavery novels of Emily Clemens Pearson.

William Steele is associate professor of English in the Department of Language and Literature at Oklahoma Christian University in Edmond, OK. His manuscript "Who's on First and Everywhere Else: Baseball and Identity in W. P. Kinsella's Fiction" is under contract for publication by McFarland.

Julia Stern is Herman and Beulah Pearce Miller Research Professor in Literature, Charles Deering McCormick Professor of Teaching Excellence, and professor of English and American studies at Northwestern University. She is the author of *The Plight of Feeling: Sympathy and Dissent in the Early American Novel* (1997) and *Mary Chesnut's Civil War Epic* (2010).

Melissa J. Strong is associate professor of English at Northeastern State University. Her work has appeared in *Americana: The Journal of American Popular Culture, 1900 to the Present* and the anthology *Women and Work: The Labors of Self-Fashioning*.

Timothy Sweet is Eberly Family Distinguished Professor of American Literature at West Virginia University. He is the author of *Traces of War: Poetry Photography, and the Crisis of the Union* and *American Georgics: Economy and Environment in Early American Literature*.

Darren T. Williamson is the preaching minister for the Keizer Church of Christ, Oregon, and adjunct instructor of history and religious studies at George Fox University. He is the author of articles on early modern history.

Michael Ziser is associate professor of English and codirector of the Environments and Societies Research Initiative at the University of California, Davis. He is the author of *Environmental Practice and Early American Literature* (2013).

Works Cited

Aaron, Daniel. *The Unwritten War: The Impact of the Civil War*. New York: Knopf, 1973. Print.

The Abolitionists. Dir. Rob Rapley. PBS, 2013. DVD.

"An Act Authorizing a Grant to the State of California of the Yo-Semite Valley, and of the Land Embracing the Mariposa Big Tree Grove." *American Memory*. Lib. of Congress, n.d. Web. 28 July 2015. Pub. L. 159. 13 Stat. 325. June 1864.

Alcott, Louisa May. *Hospital Sketches*. Boston: J. Redpath, 1863. Print.

———. *Hospital Sketches*. Ed. Bessie Z. Jones. Cambridge: Belknap–Harvard UP, 1960. Print.

———. *Hospital Sketches*. Ed. Alice Fahs. New York: St. Martin's, 2003. Print. Bedford Ser. in History and Culture.

———. "My Contraband." Hospital Sketches *and* Camp and Fireside Stories. Boston: Roberts Brothers, 1869. 169–97. Print.

———. "My Contraband." *Alternative Alcott*. Ed. Elaine Showalter. New Brunswick: Rutgers UP, 1988. 74–94. Print.

Alemán, Jesse. "Authenticity, Autobiography, and Identity: *The Woman in Battle* as Civil War Narrative." Velazquez ix–xl.

Alexander, Leslie M. "'The Black Republic': The Influence of the Haitian Revolution on Northern Black Political Consciousness, 1816–1862." *African Americans and the Haitian Revolution: Selected Essays and Historical Documents*. Ed. Maurice Jackson and Jacqueline Bacon. New York: Routledge, 2010. 57–79. Print.

American Speeches: Political Oratory from Patrick Henry to Barack Obama. 2 vols. Ed. Ted Widmer. New York: Lib. of Amer., 2011. Print.

Anderson, Benedict. *Imagined Communities: Reflections on the Origin and Spread of Nationalism*. Rev. ed. New York: Verso, 1991. Print.

Andrews, Eliza Frances. *The War-time Journal of a Georgia Girl*. New York: Appleton, 1908. Print.

Andrews, Matthew Page. Introduction. *The Poems of James Ryder Randall*. Ed. Andrews. New York: Tandy-Thomas, 1910. 1–36. Print.

Aptheker, Herbert. *American Negro Slave Revolts*. 1943. 50th anniversary ed. New York: International, 1993. Print.

Ash, Stephen V. *Firebrand of Liberty: The Story of Two Black Regiments That Changed the Course of the Civil War*. New York: Norton, 2008. Print.

Assmann, Jan. *Cultural Memory and Early Civilization: Writing, Remembrance, and Political Imagination*. Cambridge: Cambridge UP, 2011. Print.

Backus, E. M. "The Black Hero of the Cumberland." Lorang and Weir.

Barnes, Elizabeth. *States of Sympathy*. New York: Columbia UP, 1997. Print.

Barrett, Faith. *To Fight Aloud Is Very Brave: American Poetry and the Civil War*. Amherst: U of Massachusetts P, 2012. Print.

Barrett, Faith, and Cristanne Miller, eds. *"Words for the Hour": A New Anthology of American Civil War Poetry.* Amherst: U of Massachusetts P, 2005. Print.

Barrish, Philip J. *The Cambridge Introduction to American Literary Realism.* New York: Cambridge UP, 2011. Print.

Battles and Leaders of the Civil War. eHistory. Ohio State U Dept. of History, n.d. Web. 24 July 2015.

Beale, Joseph Boggs, illus. "Eva's Dying Farewell." *UTC as Magic Lantern Show. Uncle Tom's Cabin and American Culture.* Stephen Railton; U of Virginia, n.d. Web. 6 Aug. 2015.

Bedford Anthology of American Literature. 2nd ed. Vols. 1 and 2. Ed. Susan Belasco and Linck Johnson. Boston: Bedford–St. Martin's, 2013. Print.

Beeghley, Jim. "'The Case of the Moved Body' at the Library of Congress." *Penn Live.* PA Media Group, 21 June 2013. Web. 6 Aug. 2015. <http://blog.pennlive.com/gettysburg-150/2013/06/the_case_of_the_moved_body_and.html>.

Bell, Andrew McIlwaine. *Mosquito Soldiers: Malaria, Yellow Fever, and the Course of the American Civil War.* Baton Rouge: Louisiana State UP, 2010. Print.

Berger, John. "Photographs of Agony." *About Looking.* New York: Vintage, 1991. 41–44. Print.

Bergland, Renée. "The Eagle's Eye: Dickinson's View of Battle." Smith and Loeffelholz 133–56.

Berlin, Ira, et al. *Freedom: A Documentary History of Emancipation, 1861–1867.* Cambridge: Cambridge UP, 1982. Black Military Experience.

Bernier, Celeste-Marie. *Characters of Blood: Black Heroism in the Transatlantic Imagination.* Charlottesville: U of Virginia P, 2012. Print.

Bierce, Ambrose. *Tales of Soldiers and Civilians.* San Francisco: E. L. G. Steele, 1891. Print.

———. "What I Saw of Shiloh." *The Ambrose Bierce Project.* Ed Craig A. Warren. Ambrose Bierce Project, n.d. Web. 30 July 2015.

The Birth of a Nation. Dir. D. W. Griffith. 1915. Inspired Studio, 2001. DVD.

Blair, Hugh. *Lectures on Rhetoric and Belles Lettres.* 1819. Ed. Charlotte Downey. Delmar: Scholars' Facsims. and Rpts., 1993. Print.

Blanton, DeAnne, and Lauren Cook. *They Fought like Demons: Women Soldiers in the Civil War.* New York: Vintage, 2003. Print.

Blight, David. *Frederick Douglass' Civil War: Keeping Faith in Jubilee.* Baton Rouge: Louisiana State UP, 1991. Print.

———. *Race and Reunion: The Civil War in American Memory.* Cambridge: Belknap–Harvard UP, 2002. Print.

Blodgett, Harriet. *Centuries of Female Days: Englishwomen's Private Diaries.* New Brunswick: Rutgers UP, 1988. Print.

Boggs, Colleen Glenney. *Transnationalism and American Literature: Literary Translation, 1773–1892.* Routledge, 2007. Print.

———. "A War of Words." *New York Times.* New York Times, 2 Oct. 2012. Web. 28 Apr. 2015. Opinionator ser.

Boker, George Henry. "The Black Regiment." Barrett and Miller 112–14.

———. "Hymn of the Contrabands." Lorang and Weir.

———. "The Second Louisiana." Lorang and Weir.

———. "The Sword-Bearer." Barrett and Miller 78–80.

"Books for Camp and Home." Advertisement. *American Literary Gazette and Publishers' Circular* 1 Mar. 1864: 318. *HathiTrust Digital Library.* HathiTrust, n.d. Web. 19 Nov. 2015.

Boritt, Gabor. *The Gettysburg Gospel: The Lincoln Speech That Nobody Knows.* New York: Simon, 2006. Print.

Boyle, Tom, et al. "Using Blended Learning to Improve Student Success Rates in Learning to Program." *Journal of Educational Media* 28.2–3 (2003): 165–78. Print.

Bradshaw, Wesley. *General Sherman's Indian Spy.* Philadelphia: C. W. Alexander, 1865. *Wright American Fiction, 1851–1875.* Indiana U, n.d. Web. 1 May 2013.

Brady, Lisa M. *War upon the Land: Military Strategy and the Transformation of Southern Landscapes during the American Civil War.* Athens: U of Georgia P, 2012. Print.

Brady, Mathew. "Confederate Dead behind a Stone Wall at Fredericksburg, VA." *Teaching with Documents: The Civil War As Photographed by Mathew Brady. National Archives.* U.S. Natl. Archives and Records Administration, n.d. Web. 28 Apr. 2015.

Brennan, Joseph F. "Slavery, and Its Characteristics: No. I." *Liberator* 12 Sept. 1862: 148. Print.

Brodhead, Richard H. *Cultures of Letters: Scenes of Reading and Writing in Nineteenth-Century America.* Chicago: U of Chicago P, 1993. Print.

Bronson-Bartlett, Blake. "The 'Doubly Perplexing' Doctor Broderip: Rebecca Harding Davis's *Waiting for the Verdict* and Medical Reform during the Civil War." Amer. Lit. Assn. Twenty-First Annual Conf. on Amer. Lit. Hyatt Regency San Francisco. 27 May 2010. Address.

Brooks, Geraldine. *March.* New York: Viking, 2005. Print.

Brown, John. "An 'Idea of Things in Kansas': John Brown's 1857 New England Speech." Ed. Kark Gridley. *Kansas History: A Journal of the Central Plains* 27.1–2 (2004): 76–85. Print.

Brown, Joshua. *Beyond the Lines: Pictorial Reporting, Everyday Life, and the Crisis of Gilded Age America.* Berkeley: U of California P, 2006. Print.

Brown, William Wells. *Clotel; or, The President's Daughter: A Narrative of Slave Life in the United States.* 1853. New York: Collier, 1970. Print.

———. *Clotelle: A Tale of the Southern States.* Boston: James Redpath, 1864. *Project Gutenberg.* Web. 15 Feb. 2013.

———. *Clotelle: A Tale of the Southern States.* Boston: James Redpath, 1864. Ed. Christopher Mulvey. *Rotunda.* U of Virginia P, n.d. Web. 21 May 2013. <http://www.upress.virginia.edu/rotunda/>.

———. *The Negro in the American Rebellion: His Heroism and Fidelity.* Athens: Ohio UP, 2003. Print.

Browne, C. A. *The Story of Our National Ballads.* New York: Crowell, 1918. Print.

Bruns, Roger. "The Embodiment of Freedom." *American History Illustrated* 28.4 (1993): 46–51. *Academic Search Complete.* Web. 1 May 2013.

Buck, Lucy Rebecca. *Sad Earth, Sweet Heaven: The Diary of Lucy Rebecca Buck during the War between the States.* Ed. William P. Buck. Birmingham: Cornerstone, 1973. Print.

Burns, Ken, dir. *The Civil War.* PBS, 28 Sept. 2004. DVD.

Butler, Benjamin. "General Orders, No. 28 (15 May 1862)." *The War of the Rebellion: A Compilation of the Official Records of the Union and Confederate Armies.* Ser. 1, vol. 15. Washington: GPO, 1886. 426. Print.

Butos, Cynthia. "Louisa May Alcott." *The Heath Anthology of American Literature.* Ed. Paul Lauter. *Wadsworth Cengage Learning Online Study Center.* Cengage Learning, n.d. Web. 31 July 2015.

Capello, Mary. "'Looking about Me with All My Eyes': Censored Viewing, Carnival, and Louisa May Alcott's *Hospital Sketches.*" *Arizona Quarterly* 50.3 (1994): 59–88. Print.

Capper, Charles, and Conrad Edick Wright, eds. *Transient and Permanent: The Transcendentalist Movement and Its Contexts.* Boston: Massashusetts Historical Soc., 1999. Print.

Cary, Alice. "Song for our Soldiers." Moore, *Rebellion Record* 47.

Castagna, JoAnn E. "Maum Guinea." *Encyclopedia of the American Civil War: A Political, Social, and Military History.* Santa Barbara: ABC-CLIO, 2000. *Credo Reference.* Web. 3 May 2013.

Cavitch, Max. *American Elegy: The Poetry of Mourning from the Puritans to Walt Whitman.* Minneapolis: U of Minnesota P, 2007. Print.

Chesnut, Mary Boykin Miller. Account book for 1878. Williams-Chesnut-Manning Collection, Caroliniana Lib., U of South Carolina, Columbia. MS.

———. *A Diary from Dixie.* Ed. Myrta Lockett Avery and Isabella Martin. New York: Appleton, 1905. Print.

———. *Mary Chesnut's Civil War.* Ed. C. Vann Woodward. New Haven: Yale UP, 1981. Print.

———. *The Private Mary Chesnut: The Unpublished Civil War Diaries.* Ed. C. Vann Woodward and Elisabeth Muhlenfeld. New York: Oxford UP, 1984. Print.

Chesnutt, Charles. "Cicely's Dream." *Conjure Tales and Stories of the Color Line.* Ed. William L. Andrews. New York: Penguin, 2000. 170–87. Print.

———. *The Conjure Woman.* Boston: Houghton, 1899. Print.

Clark, B. C. [of Boston]. *A Plea for Hayti.* 3rd ed. Boston: Eastburn's, 1853. *Hathi Trust Digital Library.* Web. 27 May 2013.

Clark, B. C. [of York]. "Be Joyful!" Lorang and Weir.

———. *The Past, Present, and Future: In Prose and Poetry.* Toronto: Adam, Stevenson, Co., 1867. *Internet Archive.* Web. 27 May 2013.

Clark, Beverly Lyon, ed. *Louisa May Alcott: The Contemporary Reviews.* New York: Cambridge UP, 2004. Print.

Clinton, Catherine. *Tara Revisited: Women, War, and the Plantation Legend.* New York: Abbeville, 1995. Print.

Cohen, Lara Langer. Rev. of *Clotel, by William Wells Brown: An Electronic Scholarly Edition* [ed. Mulvey]. *African American Review* 43 (2009): 749–51. Print.

Conforti, Joseph A. "Regional Identity and New England Landscapes." Harrison and Judd 17–36.

Connery, Thomas B. *Journalism and Realism: Rendering American Life.* Evanston: Northwestern UP, 2011. Print.

Corbaux, Louisa, illus. "Eva's Farewell." *The Annotated* Uncle Tom's Cabin. By

Harriet Beecher Stowe. Ed. Henry Louis Gates, Jr. New York: Norton, 2007. 305. Print.

Crane, Stephen. *Great Short Works of Stephen Crane.* New York: Harper, 2009. Print.

———. *The Red Badge of Courage.* New York: Dover, 1990. Print.

Culley, Margo. Introduction. *A Day at a Time: The Diary Literature of American Women from 1764 to the Present.* Ed. Culley. New York: Feminist, 1985. 3–26. Print.

Daniels, Christopher. "Colonel James Chesnut, II: His Life and Economic Circumstance." MA thesis. U of Colorado, 1995. Print.

Daniels, Martha, and Barbara McCarthy, eds. *Mary Chesnut's Illustrated Diary: Mulberry Edition.* 2 vols. Columbia: Pelican, 2011. Print.

Darley, F. O. C., illus. "The Dying Soldier." *My Story of the War.* By Mary Livermore. Hartford: A.D. Worthington and Co., 1890. 211. Print.

Davis, Arthur. Introduction. W. Brown, *Clotel* [1970] vii–xvi.

Davis, Donald Edward. *Where There Are Mountains: An Environmental History of the Southern Appalachians.* Athens: U of Georgia P, 2003. Print.

Davis, Esther. "Memories of Mulberry." Appendix to Daniels.

Davis, Rebecca Harding. "David Gaunt." Harris and Cadwallader 24–84.

———. "Ellen." Harris and Cadwallader 211–35.

———. "John Lamar." Harris and Cadwallader 1–23.

———. *Waiting for the Verdict.* 1867. Ed. Donald Dingledine. Albany: NCUP, 1995. Print.

Davison, Gideon M. *The Fashionable Tour: A Guide to Travellers Visiting the Middle and Northern States and the Provinces of Canada.* Saratoga Springs: G. M. Davison, 1822. Print.

"Dawley's Camp and Fireside Library." Advertisement. *Harper's Weekly* 12 Mar. 1864: 176. *The Online Books Page.* U of Penn, n.d. Web. 9 June 2013.

"Declaration of the Immediate Causes Which Induce and Justify the Secession of South Carolina from the Federal Union." *The Avalon Project: Documents in Law, History, and Diplomacy.* Lillian Goldman Law Lib., Yale Law School, n.d. Web. 28 Apr. 2015. <http://avalon.law.yale.edu/19th_century/csa_scarsec.asp>.

"Declaration of the Immediate Causes Which Induce and Justify the Secession of the State of Mississippi from the Federal Union." *The Avalon Project: Documents in Law, History, and Diplomacy.* Lillian Goldman Law Lib., Yale Law School, n.d. Web. 28 Apr. 2015. <http://avalon.law.yale.edu/19th_century/csa_missec.asp>.

De Forest, John W. *Miss Ravenel's Conversion from Secession to Loyalty.* 1867. Ed. Gary Scharnhorst. New York: Penguin, 2000. Print.

Delany, Martin. *Blake; or, The Huts of America.* Boston: Beacon, 1970. Print.

Denning, Michael. *Mechanic Accents: Dime Novels and Working-Class Culture in America.* 2nd rev. ed. Brooklyn: Verso, 1998. Print.

Dicey, Edward. "Nathaniel Hawthorne." *Macmillan's Magazine* 10 (July 1864): 241–46. Print.

Dickinson, Anna. *What Answer?* Boston: Ticknor and Fields, 1868. Print.

Dickinson, Emily. *The Poems of Emily Dickinson.* Ed. R. W. Franklin. Cambridge: Belknap–Harvard UP, 1998. Print.

Diffley, Kathleen, ed. *To Live and to Die: Collected Stories of the Civil War, 1861–1876.* Durham: Duke UP, 2002. Print.

———. *Where My Heart Is Turning Ever.* Athens: U of Georgia P, 1992. Print.

Dimock, Wai Chee. *Through Other Continents: American Literature across Deep Time.* Princeton: Princeton UP, 2006. Print.

Dixon, Edward. *The Terrible Mysteries of the Ku-Klux-Klan.* Upper Saddle River: Literature, 1970. Print.

Dixon, Thomas, Jr. *The Clansman: An Historical Romance of the Ku Klux Klan.* 1905. *Project Gutenberg.* Project Gutenberg, 9 Aug. 2008. Web. 1 Aug. 2015.

Django Unchained. Dir. Quentin Tarantino. Weinstein; Columbia Pictures, 2012. Film.

Doctorow, E. L. *The March.* New York: Random, 2005. Print.

Douglass, Frederick. *Autobiographies.* New York: Lib. of Amer., 1994. Print.

———. *Douglass' Monthly* May 1861: n pag. New York Heritage Digital Collections, n.d. Web. 5 Nov. 2015.

———. "Men of Color, to Arms!" Frederick Douglass Papers at the Library of Congress, n.d. Web. 25 Feb. 2013.

———. *Narrative of the Life of Frederick Douglass, an American Slave, Written by Himself. The Norton Anthology of American Literature.* Ed. Nina Baym. 6th ed. Vol. B. New York: Norton, 2003. 2032–97. Print.

———. "West India Emancipation, Speech Delivered at Canandaigua, New York, August 3, 1857." *Frederick Douglass: Selected Speeches and Writings.* Ed. Philip S. Foner. Abr. and adapt. Yuval Taylor. Chicago: Hill, 1999. 358–68. Print.

———. "Why a Colored Man Should Enlist." Frederick Douglass Papers at the Library of Congress, n.d. Web. 25 Feb. 2013.

Dove, Rita. "Lady Freedom among Us." *American Studies at the University of Virginia.* U of Virginia Lib. Electronic Text Center, n.d. Web. 1 May 2013.

duCille, Ann. "Where in the World Is William Wells Brown? Thomas Jefferson, Sally Hemings, and the DNA of African-American Literary History." *American Literary History* 12 (2000): 443–62. Print.

Dunbar, Paul Laurence. *The Fanatics.* New York: Dodd, 1901. Print.

Duquette, Elizabeth. *Loyal Subjects: Bonds of Nation, Race, and Allegiance in Nineteenth-Century America.* New Brunswick: Rutgers UP, 2010. Print.

Dwight, Theodore. *The Northern Traveller.* New York: J. P. Haven, 1841. Print.

Dziuban, Charles D., et al. "Blended Learning." *Center for Applied Research Bulletin.* Educause, 30 Mar. 2004. Web. 6 Aug. 2015.

Eakin, Paul John. *Living Autobiographically: How We Create Identity in Narrative.* Ithaca: Cornell UP, 2008. Print.

East, Charles. Introduction. Morgan xv–xli.

Eicher, David J. The Longest Night: A Military History of the Civil War. New York: Simon, 2001. Print.

Elbert, Sarah. Introduction. *Louisa May Alcott on Race, Sex, and Slavery.* By Louisa May Alcott. Boston: Northeastern UP, 1997. ix–lx. Print.

Elkins, Stanley M. *Slavery: A Problem in American Institutional and Intellectual Life.* Rev. 3rd ed. Chicago: U of Chicago P, 1976. Print.

Ellis, Richard J. *To the Flag: The Unlikely History of the Pledge of Allegiance.* Lawrence: U of Kansas P, 2005. Print.

Ellison, Ralph. *Invisible Man*. New York: Vintage, 1995. Print.

Emerson, Ralph Waldo. *The Complete Works of Ralph Waldo Emerson*. Ed. Edward Waldo Emerson. 12 vols. 1903–04. Rpt. New York: AMS, 1968. Print.

———. *Emerson's Antislavery Writings*. Ed. Len Gougeon and Joel Myerson. New Haven: Yale UP, 1995. Print.

———. "Hymn: Sung at the Completion of the Concord Monument, April 19, 1836." *Collected Poems and Translations*. New York: Lib. of Amer., 1974. 125. Print.

———. *The Journals and Miscellaneous Notebooks of Ralph Waldo Emerson*. Ed. William H. Gilman et al. 16 vols. Cambridge: Belknap–Harvard UP, 1960–82. Print.

Erll, Astrid. "Literature, Film, and the Mediality of Cultural Memory." *A Companion to Cultural Media Studies*. Ed. Erll and Ansgar Nünning. Trans. Sara B. Young. Berlin: de Gruyter, 2010. 389–98. Print.

Evans, Augusta Jane. *Macaria; or, Altars of Sacrifice*. Richmond: West and Johnston, 1864. Print.

Fabian, Ann. *The Unvarnished Truth: Personal Narratives in Nineteenth-Century America*. Berkeley: U of California P, 2000. Print.

Fahs, Alice. "The Civil War in American Culture." *A Companion to American Cultural History*. Ed. Karen Halttunen. Hoboken: Wiley, 2008. 110–24. Print.

———. *The Imagined Civil War: Popular Literature of the North and South, 1861–1865*. Chapel Hill: U of North Carolina P, 2001. Print.

———. Introduction. Alcott, *Hospital Sketches* [ed. Fahs] 1–49.

Fahs, Alice, and Joan Waugh. Introduction. Fahs and Waugh, *Memory* 1–4.

———, eds. *The Memory of the Civil War in American Culture*. Chapel Hill: U of North Carolina P, 2004. Print.

Farrison, William Edward. *William Wells Brown: Author and Reformer*. Chicago: U of Chicago P, 1969. Print. Negro Amer. Biographies and Autobiographies.

Faust, Drew Gilpin. *This Republic of Suffering: Death and the American Civil War*. New York: Vintage, 2009.

Fetterley, Judith, and Marjorie Pryse. "Alice Cary: 1820–1871." *Legacy* 1.1 (1984): 1–3. *JSTOR*. Web. 21 Feb. 2013.

Fiege, Mark. *The Republic of Nature: An Environmental History of the United States*. Seattle: U of Washington P, 2012. Print.

Fincher, Jack. "The Hard Fight Was Getting into the Fight at All." *Smithsonian* 21.7 (1990): 46–60. *EBSCOhost*. Web. 28 Feb. 2013.

Finseth, Ian Frederick, ed. *The American Civil War: An Anthology of Essential Writings*. New York: Routledge, 2006. Print.

———. *Shades of Green: Visions of Nature in the Literature of American Slavery, 1770–1860*. Athens: U of Georgia P, 2009. Print.

FitzHugh, George. *Cannibals All!; or, Slaves without Masters*. 1857. *Internet Archive*. Internet Archive, 3 July 2008. Web. 28 July 2015.

Foreman, P. Gabrielle. "Sentimental Abolition in Douglass's Decade: Revision, Erotic Conversion, and the Politics of Witnessing in *The Heroic Slave* and *My Bondage and My Freedom*." *Sentimental Men: Masculinity and the Politics of Affect in American Culture*. Ed. Mary Chapman and Glenn Hendler. Berkeley: U of California P, 1999. 149–62. Print.

Fothergill, Robert A. *Private Chronicles: A Study of English Diaries.* London: Oxford UP, 1974. Print.

Foucault, Michel. "What Is an Author?" *The Critical Tradition: Classic Texts and Contemporary Trends.* 2nd ed. Ed. David H. Richter. Boston: Bedford, 1998. 890–900. Print.

Fox-Genovese, Elizabeth. *Within the Plantation Household: Black and White Women of the Old South.* Chapel Hill: U of North Carolina P, 1988. Print.

Franklin, John Hope. *A Southern Odyssey: Travelers in the Antebellum North.* Baton Rouge: Louisiana State UP, 1975. Print.

Frassanito, William. *Antietam: The Photographic Legacy of America's Bloodiest Day.* New York: Scribner's, 1978. Print.

———. *Early Photography at Gettysburg.* Gettysburg: Thomas, 1995. Print.

———. *Gettysburg: A Journey in Time.* New York: Scribner's, 1975. Print.

Frazier, Charles. *Cold Mountain.* New York: Grove, 1997. Print.

Freeman, David B. *Carved in Stone: The History of Stone Mountain.* Macon: Mercer UP, 1997. Print.

Freire, Paulo. *Pedagogy of the Oppressed.* Trans. Myra Bergman Ramos. New York: Continuum, 1986. Print.

Friedlander, Benjamin. "Emily Dickinson and the Battle of Ball's Bluff." *PMLA* 124.5 (2009): 1582–99. Print.

Friedman, Susan Stanford. "Women's Autobiographical Selves: Theory and Practice." *The Private Self: Theory and Practice of Women's Autobiographical Writings.* Ed. Shari Benstock. Chapel Hill: U of North Carolina P, 1988. 34–62. Print.

Fryd, Vivien Green. *Art and Empire: The Politics of Ethnicity in the United States Capitol, 1815–1860.* New Haven: Yale UP, 1992. Print.

———. "Political Compromise in Public Art." *Critical Issues in Public Art: Content, Context, and Controversy.* Ed. Harriet F. Senie and Sally Webster. New York: Harper, 1992. 105–114. Print.

Fuller, Randall. *From Battlefields Rising: How the Civil War Transformed American Literature.* New York: Oxford UP, 2011. Print.

Gale, Robert L. *Thomas Crawford: American Sculptor.* Pittsburgh: U of Pittsburgh P, 1964. Print.

Gallagher, Gary W. *Two Witnesses at Gettysburg: The Personal Accounts of Whitelaw Reid and A. J. L. Fremantle.* St. James: Brandywine, 1994. Print.

Galt, William. *William Galt Cadet Notebook.* Virginia Military Inst. Archives, n.d. Web. 28 Apr. 2015. < http://digitalcollections.vmi.edu/cdm/ref/collection/p15821coll11/id/2012>.

Gardner's Photographic Sketch Book of the War. Cornell U Lib., Division of Rare and Manuscript Collections, n.d. Web. 28 Apr. 2015. <http://rmc.library.cornell.edu/7milVol/index.html>.

Garvey, T. Gregory, ed. *The Emerson Dilemma: Essays on Emerson and Social Reform.* Athens: U of Georgia P, 2001. Print.

Gilroy, Paul. *The Black Atlantic: Modernity and Double Consciousness.* Cambridge: Harvard UP, 1993. Print.

Glazener, Nancy. *Reading for Realism: The History of a U.S. Literary Institution, 1850–1910.* Durham: Duke UP, 1997. Print.

Glory. Dir. Edward Zwick. Tristar Pictures, 1989. Film.

Gone with the Wind. Webarchive.org, n.d. Web. 21 July 2015. Script.

Gonzales, Lisa, and Devin Vodicka. "Blended Learning: A Disruption That Has Found Its Time." *Leadership* 42.2 (2012): 8–10. *ERIC*. Web. 28 Apr. 2015.

Gougeon, Len. *Virtue's Hero: Emerson, Antislavery, and Reform*. Athens: U of Georgia P, 1990. Print.

Grant, Ulysses S. *Papers of Ulysses S. Grant*. Vol. 9. Ed. John Y. Simon. Carbondale: Southern Illinois UP, 1982. Print.

———. *Personal Memoirs of U. S. Grant*. New York: Charles L. Webster and Co., 1885. Print.

Gray, Thomas R., publisher. *The Confessions of Nat Turner, the Leader of the Late Insurrection in Southampton, Va.* 1831. *Documenting the American South*. U Lib., U of North Carolina, Chapel Hill, 13 Apr. 2016. Web.

Greenspan, Ezra. *George Palmer Putnam*. University Park: Penn State UP, 2000. Print.

Griffin, Martin. *Ashes of the Mind: War and Memory in Northern Literature, 1865–1900*. Amherst: U of Massachusetts P, 2009. Print.

Grimké, Charlotte Forten. *The Journals of Charlotte Forten Grimké*. Ed. Brenda Stevenson. New York: Oxford UP, 1988. Print.

Guelzo, Allen C. *Lincoln's Emancipation Proclamation: The End of Slavery in America*. New York: Simon, 2004. Print.

Hack, Daniel. "Wild Charges: The Afro-Haitian 'Charge of the Light Brigade.'" *Victorian Studies* 54.2 (2012): 199–225. *Project Muse*. Web. 21 Feb. 2013.

Hager, Christopher. *Word by Word: Emancipation and the Act of Writing*. Cambridge: Harvard UP, 2013. Print.

Hager, Christopher, and Cody Marrs. "Against 1865: Reperiodizing the Nineteenth Century." *J19: The Journal of Nineteenth-Century Americanists* 1.2 (2013): 259–84. Print.

Halbwachs, Maurice. *On Collective Memory*. Trans. Lewis A. Corser. Chicago: U of Chicago P, 1992. Print.

Hale, Edward Everett. "The Man without a Country." *Atlantic Monthly* Dec. 1863: 665–80. Print.

Hamilton, Ed. *The Spirit of Freedom*. 1998. African American Civil War Memorial, Washington DC. Bronze sculpture.

Harper, Frances Ellen Watkins. "An Appeal to My Countrywomen." Barrett and Miller 300–02.

———. *Iola Leroy; or, Shadows Uplifted*. Ed. and introd. Hollis Robbins. New York: Penguin, 2010. Print.

Harris, Sharon M., and Robin L. Cadwallader, eds. *Rebecca Harding Davis's Stories of the Civil War Era: Selected Writings from the Borderlands*. Athens: U of Georgia P, 2009. Print.

Harrison, Blake, and Richard W. Judd, eds. *A Landscape History of New England*. Cambridge: MIT P, 2011. Print.

Harvey, Charles M. "The Dime Novel in American Life." *Atlantic Monthly* July 1907: 37–45. *Electronic Text Center*. U of Virginia Lib., n.d. Web. 10 Mar. 2013.

Harwood, W. S. "Secret Societies in America." *North American Review* May 1897: 617–24. Print.

Hawthorne, Nathaniel. *The Centenary Edition of the Works of Nathaniel Hawthorne.* Ed. William Charvat et al. 23 vols. Columbus: Ohio State UP, 1962–97. Print.

———. "Chiefly about War-Matters." *Atlantic Monthly* July 1862: 43–61. Print.

Hedrick, Joan. *Harriet Beecher Stowe: A Life.* New York: Oxford UP, 1994. Print.

Helper, Hinton Rowan. *The Impending Crisis of the South: How to Meet It. Documenting the American South.* Univ. Lib., U of North Carolina, Chapel Hill, 4 Apr. 2001. Web. 28 July 2015.

Henkin, David M. *The Postal Age: The Emergence of Modern Communications in Nineteenth-Century America.* Chicago: U of Chicago P, 2007. Print.

Hentz, Caroline Lee. *The Planter's Northern Bride.* Philadelphia: T. B. Peterson, 1854. Print.

Higginson, Thomas Wentworth. Army Life in a Black Regiment *and Other Writings.* New York: Penguin, 1997. Print.

———. *The Complete Civil War Journal and Selected Letters of Thomas Wentworth Higginson.* Ed. Christopher Looby. Chicago: U of Chicago P, 2000. Print.

Hofstadter, Richard. *The American Political Tradition and the Men Who Made It.* New York: Knopf, 1973. Print.

Holmes, Emma. *The Diary of Miss Emma Holmes, 1861–1866.* Ed. John F. Marszalek. Baton Rouge: Louisiana State UP, 1979. Print.

Hönnighausen, Lothar. "Washington D.C. and the National Myth." *Interdisciplinary Approaches.* Ed. Hönnighausen and Andreas Falke. Tubingen: Francke, 1993. 43–58. Print.

Hopkins, Cyril G. *The Story of the Soil, from the Basis of Absolute Science and Real Life.* Boston: Badger, 1911. Print.

Horton, George Moses. *The Black Bard of North Carolina: George Moses Horton and His Poetry.* Ed. Joan Sherman. Chapel Hill: U of North Carolina P, 1997. Print.

Horwitz, Tony. *Confederates in the Attic: Dispatches from the Unfinished Civil War.* New York: Vintage, 1999. Print.

Howe, Daniel Walker. *What Hath God Wrought: The Transformation of America, 1815–1848.* New York: Oxford UP, 2007. Print.

Howe, Julia Ward. "Battle Hymn of the Republic." Barrett and Miller 75.

———. "Reminiscences of Julia Ward Howe." *Atlantic Monthly* May 1899: 701–12. UNZ.org, n.d. Web. 30 Apr. 2015.

Huddleston, John. *Killing Ground: Photographs of the Civil War and the Changing American Landscape.* Baltimore: Johns Hopkins UP, 2002. Print.

Hutchison, Coleman. *Apples and Ashes: Literature, Nationalism, and the Confederate States of America.* Athens: U of Georgia P, 2012. Print.

———. "'Eastern Exiles': Dickinson, Whiggery, and War." *Emily Dickinson Journal* 13.2 (2004): 1–26. Print.

Hyun In-taek. "The Present State of the Relationship between North and South Korea and Future of the Korean Peninsula." Smith Hall, Keimyung U, Daegu, South Korea. 12 Oct. 2010. Address.

I Belong to South Carolina: South Carolina Slave Narratives. Ed. Susanna Ashton. Columbia: U of South Carolina P, 2010. Print.

Ifill, Gwen. "The 1992 Campaign: New York; Clinton Admits Experiment with Marijuana in 1960s." *New York Times.* New York Times, 30 Mar. 1992. Web. 21 July 2015.

Ignatiev, Noel. *How the Irish Became White.* New York: Routledge, 1995. Print.

Ishtaiwa, Fawi Fayez, and Enas Said Abulibdeh. "The Impact of Asynchronous e-Learning Tools on Interaction and Learning in a Blended Course." *International Journal of Instructional Media* 39.2 (2012): 141–59. Web. 28 Apr. 2015.

Is Online Learning Right for You? Minnesota State Colls. and Univs., n.d. Web. 6 Aug. 2015.

Jackson, Leon. "The Black Bard and the Black Market." *The Business of Letters: Authorial Economies in Antebellum America.* Stanford: Stanford UP, 2008. 53–88. Print.

Jackson, Virginia. *Dickinson's Misery: A Theory of Lyric Reading.* Princeton: Princeton UP, 2005. Print.

Jacobs, Harriet. *Incidents in the Life of a Slave Girl: Written by Herself. Slave Narratives.* Ed. William L. Andrews, E. Maynard Adams, and Henry Louis Gates, Jr. New York: Lib. of Amer., 2000. 743–948. Print.

James, Henry. *Hawthorne.* 1879. Ithaca: Cornell UP, 1997. Print.

Jarrett, Gene. *Deans and Truants: Race and Realism in African American Literature.* Philadelphia: U of Pennsylvania P, 2007. Print.

Jefferson, Thomas. *Notes on the State of Virginia.* Ed. Frank Shuffelton. New York: Penguin, 1999. Print.

Jelinek, Estelle C. *The Tradition of Women's Autobiography: From Antiquity to the Present.* Boston: Twayne, 1986. Print.

Johannsen, Albert. *The House of Beadle and Adams and Its Dime and Nickel Novels.* Vol. 1. Norman: U of Oklahoma P, 1950. Print.

———. *The House of Beadle and Adams and Its Dime and Nickel Novels: The Story of a Vanished Literature.* Northern Illinois U Libs., 12 Jan. 2010. Web. 25 Jan. 2013. <http://www.ulib.niu.edu/badndp/bibindex.html>.

John Brown's Body. Boston: Oliver Ditson, 1861. Print.

Johnson, Walter. *River of Dark Dreams: Slavery and Empire in the Cotton Kingdom.* Cambridge: Belknap–Harvard UP, 2013. Print.

Kagle, Steven, and Lorenza Gramegna. "Rewriting Her Life: Fictionalization and the Use of Fictional Models in early American Women's Diaries." *Inscribing the Daily: Critical Essays on Women's Diaries.* Ed. Suzanne L. Bunkers and Cynthia A. Huff. Amherst: U of Massachusetts P, 1996. 38–55. Print.

Kaplan, Amy. *The Anarchy of Empire in the Making of U.S. Culture.* Cambridge: Harvard UP, 2005. Print.

———. "Manifest Domesticity." *No More Separate Spheres! A Next Wave American Studies Reader.* Ed. Cathy N. Davidson and Jessamyn Hatcher. Durham: Duke UP, 2002. 183–208. Print.

———. "Nation, Region, and Empire." *Columbia History of the American Novel.* Ed. Emory Elliott. New York: Columbia UP, 1991. 240–66. Print.

Kaser, David. *Books and Libraries in Camp and Battle: The Civil War Experience.*

Westport: Greenwood, 1984. Print. Contributions in Librarianship and Information Science 48.

Katz, Harry L., and Vincent Virga, eds. *Civil War Sketch Book: Drawings from the Battlefront.* New York: Norton, 2012. Print.

Keely, Karen. "Marriage Plots and National Reunion: The Trope of Romantic Reconciliation in Postbellum Literature." *Mississippi Quarterly* 51.4 (1998): 621–48. Print.

Kemble, Frances Anne. *Journal of a Residence on a Georgian Plantation in 1838–1839.* New York: Harper Brothers, 1863. *Google Books.* Web. 1 May 2013.

Kennedy, John Pendleton. *Swallow Barn; or, A Sojourn in the Old Dominion, in Two Volumes. Documenting the American South.* Univ. Lib., U of North Carolina, Chapel Hill, n.d. Web. 29 July 2015.

Kim, Dong In. "Bare Hills." *Korean Short Stories.* Trans. Myoung-Hee Hong. Seoul: Il Ji Sa, 1975. 7–16. Print.

Kirby, Jack Temple. *Mockingbird Song: Ecological Landscape of the South.* Raleigh: U of North Carolina P, 2008. Print.

Kurz, Louis, and Alexander Allison. *Storming Fort Wagner.* c. 1890. Lithograph. Chicago: Kurz and Allison Art Publishers. *Library of Congress Prints and Photographs Online Catalog.* Lib. of Congress, n.d. Web. 4 June 2013.

Larcom, Lucy. "A Loyal Woman's No." *Atlantic Monthly* Dec. 1863: 726–27. Print.

———. "Weaving." Barrett and Miller 86–88.

Lee, Anthony W., and Elizabeth Young. *On* Gardner's Photographic Sketch Book of the Civil War. Berkeley: U of California P., 2007. Print.

Lee, Maurice. "Writing through the War: Melville and Dickinson after the Renaissance." *PMLA* 115 (2000): 1124–28. Print.

Levine, Robert S. *Dislocating Race and Nation: Episodes in Nineteenth-Century American Literary Nationalism.* Chapel Hill: U of North Carolina P, 2008. Print.

Limon, John. *Writing after War: American War Fiction from Realism to Postmodernism.* New York: Oxford UP, 1994. Print.

Lincoln. Dir. Steven Spielberg. Touchstone Pictures, 2012. Film.

Lincoln, Abraham. "Address Delivered at the Dedication of the Cemetery at Gettysburg, November 19, 1863." *Great Speeches: Abraham Lincoln.* New York: Dover, 1991. 104. Print.

———. *The Collected Works of Abraham Lincoln.* Ed. Roy P. Basler. 9 vols. New Brunswick: Rutgers UP, 1953. Print.

———. *The Gettysburg Address.* Abraham Lincoln Online, n.d. Web. 10 Nov. 2015.

———. *Speeches and Writings, 1859–1865.* New York: Lib. of Amer., 1989. Print.

Linenthal, Edward. *Sacred Ground: Americans and Their Battlefields.* Carbondale: U of Illinois P, 1991. Print.

Livermore, Mary. *My Story of the War.* 1889. *Internet Archive.* Internet Archive, 14 Feb. 2011. Web. 6 Aug. 2015.

Long, Alecia P. "(Mis)Remembering General Order No. 28: Benjamin Butler, the Woman Order, and Historical Memory." *Occupied Women: Gender, Military Occupation, and the American Civil War.* Ed. LeeAnn Whites and Long. Baton Rouge: Louisiana State UP, 2009. 17–32. Print.

Longfellow, Henry Wadsworth. "The Cumberland." *Poetical Works of Henry Wadsworth Longfellow: Author's Complete Edition*. London: George Routledge and Sons, 1872. 592–93. Print.

Looby, Christopher. "Introduction: A Literary Colonel." Higginson, *Complete Civil War Journal* 1–32.

Lorang, Elizabeth, and R. J. Weir, eds. "'Will Not These Days Be by Thy Poets Sung': Poems of the *Anglo-African and National Anti-slavery Standard*, 1863–1864." *Scholarly Editing* 34 (2013): n. pag. Web. 26 Apr. 2015.

Lowell, James Russell. *The Writings of James Russell Lowell*. Vol. 5. Cambridge: Riverside, 1890. Print.

Lowell, Robert. "For the Union Dead." Life Studies *and* For the Union Dead. New York: Farrar, 2007. 63–65. Print.

Lyell, Charles. *A Second Visit to the United States of North America*. 2 vols. New York: Harper, 1849. Print.

———. *Travels in North America*. 2 vols. New York: Wiley and Putnam, 1845. Print.

Marien, Mary Warner. *Photography and Its Critics: A Cultural History, 1839–1900*. Cambridge: Cambridge UP, 1997. Print.

Marsh, George Perkins. *Man and Nature; or, Physical Geography as Modified by Human Action*. New York: Charles Scribner, 1864. Print.

Masur, Kate. "In Spielberg's *Lincoln*, Passive Black Characters." *New York Times*. New York Times, 12. Nov. 2012. Web. 30 Apr. 2015.

———. "'A Rare Phenomenon of Philological Vegetation': The Word 'Contraband' and the Meanings of Emancipation in the United States." *Journal of American History* 93.4 (2007): 1050–84. *Oxford Journals*. Web. 10 Aug. 2011.

McCarthy, Cormac. *Blood Meridian; or, The Evening Redness in the West*. New York: Vintage, 1992. Print.

McConnell, Stuart. "The Geography of Memory." Fahs and Waugh, *Memory* 258–66.

McHenry, Elizabeth. *Forgotten Readers: Recovering the Lost History of African American Literary Societies*. Durham: Duke UP, 2002. Print.

McKivigan, John. *Forgotten Firebrand: James Redpath and the Making of Nineteenth-Century America*. Ithaca: Cornell UP, 2008. Print.

McLoughlin, Kate. "War and Words." *Cambridge Companion to War Writing*. Ed. McLoughlin. New York: Cambridge UP, 2009. 15–24. Print.

McMichael, Dana. *How Confederate Women Created New Self-Identities as the Civil War Progressed: A Study of Their Diaries*. Lewiston: Mellen, 2008. Print.

McPherson, James M. *Battle Cry of Freedom: The Civil War Era*. 2nd ed. New York: Oxford UP, 2003. Print.

———. *For Cause and Comrades: Why Men Fought in the Civil War*. Oxford: Oxford UP, 1998. Print.

McWhirter, Christian. *Battle Hymns: The Power and Popularity of Music in the Civil War*. Chapel Hill: U of North Carolina P, 2012. Print.

———. "Birth of the 'Battle Cry.'" *New York Times*. New York Times, 27 July 2012. Web. 25 Feb. 2013. Disunion.

McWilliams, John. "Lexington, Concord, and the 'Hinge of the Future.'" *American Literary History* 5.1 (1993): 1–29. Print.

Melville, Herman. *Battle-Pieces and Aspects of the War*. New York: Harper, 1866. Print.

———. *Battle-Pieces and Aspects of the War*. Amherst: Prometheus, 2001. Print.

———. "Benito Cereno." *The Piazza Tales*. New York: Dix, 1956. 109–270. *Google Books*. Web. 5 June 2013.

———. "Donelson." Melville, *Published Poems* 23–36.

———. "The House-top: A Night Piece." Melville, *Published Poems* 64.

———. *Mardi, and a Voyage Thither*. New York: Harper and Brothers, 1849. Print.

———. "The Portent." Melville, *Published Poems* 5.

———. *Published Poems: Battle-Pieces [and]* John Marr *[and]* Timoleon. Ed. Robert C. Ryan et al. Evanston: Northwestern UP; Chicago: Newberry Lib., 2009. Print.

———. "Shiloh." Melville, *Published Poems* 46.

———. "A Utilitarian View of the Monitor's Fight." *Battle-Pieces and Aspects of the War*. Ed. Sidney Kaplan. Amherst: U of Massachusetts P, 1972. 42. Print.

Menand, Louis. *The Metaphysical Club: A Story of Ideas in America*. New York: Macmillan, 2001. Print.

Miller, Cristanne. *Reading in Time: Emily Dickinson in the Nineteenth Century*. Amherst: U of Massachusetts P, 2012. Print.

Mitchell, Margaret. *Gone with the Wind*. New York: Scribner's, 2007. Print.

Mitchell, Reid. *Civil War Soldiers*. New York: Penguin, 1997. Print.

Moon, Michael. *Disseminating Whitman: Revision and Corporeality in* Leaves of Grass. Cambridge: Harvard UP, 1991. Print.

Moore, Frank. *Anecdotes, Poetry, and Incidents of the War: North and South, 1860–1865*. *Internet Archive*. Internet Archive, 17 June 2008. Web. 30 July 2015.

———. Preface. Moore, *Rebellion Record* 1: iii–iv.

———, ed. *The Rebellion Record: A Diary of American Events, with Documents, Narratives, Illustrative Incidents, Poetry et Cetera*. Vol. 1. New York: Putnam, 1861. Print.

———, ed. *Rebellion Record: A Diary of American Events*. Vol. 5. New York: G. P. Putnam, 1863. *Google Books*. Web. 4 June 2013.

Morgan, Sarah. *The Civil War Diary of Sarah Morgan*. Ed. Charles East. Athens: U of Georgia P, 1991. Print.

Morton, Samuel George. *Crania Americana; or, A Comparative View of the Skulls of Various Aboriginal Nations of North and South America: To Which Is Prefixed an Essay on the Varieties of the Human Species*. Philadelphia: J. Dobson, 1839. *Internet Archive*. Internet Archive, 9 June 2011. Web. 10 Sept. 2012.

Muench, David, and Michael B. Ballard. *Landscapes of Battle: The Civil War*. Jackson: UP of Mississippi, 1988. Print.

Murphy, Sean. "Cherokee Freedmen Controversy: Court Lets Slaves' Descendants Sue Cherokee Chief." *Huffington Post*. Huffington Post, 14 Dec. 2012. Web. 30 Apr. 2015. HuffPost Blackvoices.

Myer, J. C. *Sketches on a Tour through the Northern and Eastern States*. Harrisonburg: Wartmann, 1849. Print.

"My Maryland." *Harper's Weekly* 11 Oct. 1862: 0642a. Harpweek, n.d. Web. 14 Oct. 2015.

Nat Turner: A Troublesome Property. Dir. Charles Burnett. California Newsreel, 2002. DVD.

Naylor, Celia E. "History Lost in the Cherokee Freedmen Controversy." *First Peoples: New Directions in Indigenous Studies*. U of Arizona P, U of Minnesota P, U of North Carolina P, and Oregon State UP, 5 Oct. 2011. Web. 30 Apr. 2015. Blog.

Nelson, Megan Kate. *Ruin Nation: Destruction and the American Civil War*. Athens: U of Georgia P, 2012. Print.

Newkirk, Thomas. *The Art of Slow Reading: Six Time-Honored Practices for Engagement*. Portsmouth: Heinemann, 2012. Print.

Noll, Mark A. *The Civil War as a Theological Crisis*. Chapel Hill: U of North Carolina P, 2006. Print.

Nora, Pierre. "Between Memory and History: *Les Lieux de Mémoire*." Trans. Marc Roudebush. *Representations* 26.1 (1989): 7–24. Web. 30 Apr. 2015.

Northup, Solomon. *Twelve Years a Slave*. Auburn: Derby and Miller, 1853. Print.

Norton Anthology of American Literature. Ed. Nina Baym. New York: Norton, 2011. Print.

Norton Anthology of American Literature. Vol. A: Beginnings to 1820. 8th ed. Ed. Wayne Franklin, Philip F. Gura, and Arnold Krupat. New York: Norton, 2012. Print.

Norton Anthology of American Literature. Vol. B: 1820–65. 8th ed. Ed. Robert S. Levine and Arnold Krupat. New York: Norton, 2012. Print.

Nudelman, Franny. "The Blood of Millions: *John Brown's Body*, Public Violence, and Political Community." *John Brown's Body: Slavery, Violence, and the Culture of War*. Chapel Hill: U of North Carolina P, 2004. 14–39. Print.

Olmsted, Frederick Law. *The California Frontier, 1863–1865*. Ed. Victoria Post Ranney. Baltimore: Johns Hopkins UP, 1990. Print. Vol. 5 of *The Papers of Frederick Law Olmsted*.

———. *The Cotton Kingdom*. New York: Mason Brothers, 1861. Print.

———. "Preliminary Report upon the Yosemite and Big Tree Grove." Olmsted, *California Frontier* 488–516.

Olney, James. *Metaphors of Self*. Princeton: Princeton UP, 1972. Print.

O'Malley, Michael. "Alien Menace." *Nineteenth-Century Modules. Exploring US History*. George Mason U, Aug. 2004. Web. 23 May 2016. <http://chnm .gmu.edu/exploring/19thcentury/alienmenace/>.

Packer, Barbara. "The Transcendentalists." *Prose Writing, 1820–1865*. Ed. Sacvan Bercovitch. Cambridge: Cambridge UP, 1995. 329–604. Print. Vol. 2 of *The Cambridge History of American Literature*.

Page, Thomas Nelson. "Marse Chan: A Tale of Old Virginia." *Century* 27.6 (1884): 932–42. Print.

Parker, Theodore. "Of Justice and the Conscience." *Ten Sermons of Religion*. Boston: Crosby, Nichols, and Co., 1853. 66–101. Print.

Patterson, Orlando. *Slavery and Social Death*. Cambridge: Harvard UP, 1982. Print.

Pearson, Elizabeth Ware, ed. *Letters from Port Royal: Written at the Time of the Civil War*. Boston: W. B. Clarke, 1906. Print.

Peck, William Henry. *The M'Donalds; or, The Ashes of Southern Homes: A Tale of Sherman's March.* New York: Metropolitan Record Office, 1867. Print.

Perry, Nora. "Mrs. F.'s Waiting Maid." Diffley, *To Live* 103–15.

Pettigrew, William S. Letter to Charles L. Pettigrew, 7 June 1862. Folder 254 of the Pettigrew Family Papers 592. *Southern Historical Collection.* Wilson Lib., U of North Carolina, Chapel Hill, 7 June 2012. Web. 29 Apr. 2013. <http://www.lib.unc.edu/blogs/civilwar/index.php/2012/06/07/7-june-1862/>.

Phelps, Elizabeth Stuart. *The Gates Ajar.* Boston: Fields, Osgood, 1868. Print.

Pitts, Reginald. "'Let Us Desert This Friendless Place': George Moses Horton in Philadelphia—1866." *Journal of Negro History* 80.4 (1995): 145–56. Print.

Pratt, Lloyd. *Archives of American Time.* Philadelphia: U of Pennsylvania P, 2010. Print.

Price, Kenneth M. "Editing Whitman in the Digital Age." *The Walt Whitman Archive.* Whitman Archive, 30 July 2012. Web. 29 Mar. 2013.

Randall, James Ryder. "My Maryland." Barrett and Miller 49–51.

Ray, Frederic. "The Case of the Rearranged Corpse." *Civil War Times* 3.6 (1961): 19. Web.

Rebel: Loreta Velazquez, Secret Soldier of the American Civil War. Dir. Maria Agui Carter. PBS, 2013. DVD.

"Rebel Cruelty." *Harper's Weekly* 18 June 1864: 387. Print.

Redkey, Edwin S. ed., *A Grand Army of Black Men: Letters from African-American Soldiers in the Union Army, 1861–1865.* Cambridge: Cambridge UP, 1992. Print.

Regosin, Elizabeth A., and Donald R. Shaffer. *Voices of Emancipation: Understanding Slavery, the Civil War, and Reconstruction through the U.S. Pension Bureau Files.* New York: New York UP, 2008. Print.

Reinhart, Charles S. "The Floral Tribute to the Nation's Dead." *Harper's Weekly* 4 June 1870. *HarpWeek.* Harpweek, n.d. Web. 30 Apr. 2015.

Renker, Elizabeth. *Strike through the Mask: Herman Melville and the Scene of Writing.* Baltimore: Johns Hopkins UP, 1996. Print.

Renza, Louis A. "The Veto of the Imagination: A Theory of Autobiography." *Autobiography Essays Theoretical and Critical.* Ed. James Olney. Princeton: Princeton UP, 1980. 268–95. Print.

Reynolds, Larry J. *Righteous Violence: Revolution, Slavery, and the American Renaissance.* Athens: U of Georgia P, 2011. Print.

Rhodes, Elisha Hunt. *All for the Union: The Civil War Diary and Letters of Elisha Hunt Rhodes.* Ed. Robert Hunt Rhodes. New York: Vintage, 1992. Print.

Richards, Eliza. "'How News Must Feel When Traveling': Dickinson and Civil War Media." Smith and Loeffelholz 157–79.

"The Riot at Harper's Ferry." *Independent* [New York] 20 Oct. 1859: 1. Print.

Robillard, Douglas, ed. *The Poems of Herman Melville.* Kent: Kent State UP, 2000. Print.

Rogers, Seth. "Letters of Dr. Seth Rogers, 1862, 1863." *Proceedings of the Massachusetts Historical Society* 43.1 (1910): 337–98. Print.

Rohrbach, Augusta. *Truth Stranger than Fiction: Race, Realism, and the U.S. Literary Marketplace.* New York: Palgrave, 2002. Print.

Rosen, Hannah. *Terror in the Heart of Freedom: Citizenship, Sexual Violence, and the Meaning of Race in the Postemancipation South.* Chapel Hill: U of North Carolina P, 2009. Print.

Ruby, Jay. *Secure the Shadow: Death and Photography in America.* Cambridge: MIT P, 1995. Print.

Ruffin, Edmund. *An Essay on Calcareous Manures.* Petersburg: J. W. Campbell, 1832. Print.

———. *Nature's Management: Writings on Landscape and Reform, 1822–1859.* Ed. Jack Temple Kirby. Athens: U of Georgia P, 2006. Print.

Ruiz de Burton, María. *Who Would Have Thought It?* Philadelphia: J. B. Lippincott, 1872. Print.

Ryden, Kent C. "The Handselled Globe: Natural Systems, Cultural Process, and the Formation of the New England Landscape." Harrison and Judd 37–50.

Ryzik, Melena. "Spike Lee Goes after *Django Unchained.*" *New York Times.* New York Times, 25 Dec. 2012. Web. 30 Apr. 2015. ArtsBeat: The Culture at Large.

Sachs, Aaron. *Arcadian America: The Death and Life of an American Environmental Tradition.* New Haven: Yale UP, 2013. Print.

Saint-Gaudens, Augustus. *Robert Gould Shaw Memorial.* 1897. Boston Common, Boston. Bronze sculpture.

Samuels, Shirley, ed. *Cambridge Companion to Abraham Lincoln.* Cambridge: Cambridge UP, 2012. Print.

Sanborne, Geoffrey. "People Will Pay to Hear the Drama." *African American Review* 45.1–2 (2012): 65–82. Print.

Savage, Kirk. *Standing Soldiers, Kneeling Slaves: Race, War, and Monument in Nineteenth-Century America.* Princeton: Princeton UP, 1997. Print.

Scharnhorst, Gary. Introduction. De Forest ix–xxxv.

Schultz, Jane E. "Embattled Care: Narrative Authority in Louisa May Alcott's *Hospital Sketches.*" *Legacy* 9.2 (1992): 104–18. Print.

———. *Women at the Front: Hospital Workers in Civil War America.* Chapel Hill: U of North Carolina P, 2007. Print.

Shaara, Michael. *The Killer Angels.* Philadelphia: McKay, 1974. Print.

Sherman, Joan. Introduction. Horton 1–46.

Shi, David E. *Facing Facts: Realism in American Thought and Culture, 1850–1920.* New York: Oxford UP, 1995. Print.

Silber, Nina. *The Romance of Reunion: Northerners and the South, 1861–1900.* Chapel Hill: U of North Carolina P, 1993. Print.

Simmons, Michael K. "Maum Guinea; or, A Dime Novelist Looks at Abolition." *Journal of Popular Culture* 10 (1976): 81–87. Print.

Simms, William Gilmore. *The Sack and Destruction of the City of Columbia, South Carolina.* Columbia: Power Press of Daily Phoenix, 1865. Print.

———. *The Sword and the Distaff.* Philadelphia: Lippincott, 1852. Print.

———. *The Yemassee.* Ed. Joseph V. Ridgely. New Haven: New Coll. and UP, 1964. Print.

Slotkin, Richard. *No Quarter: The Battle of the Crater, 1864.* New York: Random, 2009. Print.

———. "'What Shall Men Remember?': Recent Work on the Civil War." *American Literary History* 3.1 (1991): 120–35. Print.

Smith, Diane Monroe. *Fanny and Joshua: The Enigmatic Lives of Frances Caroline Adams and Joshua Lawrence Chamberlain*. Gettysburg: Thomas, 1999. Print.

Smith, John David. Introduction. W. Brown, *Negro* xv–xliii.

Smith, Martha Nell, and Mary Loeffelholz, eds. *A Companion to Emily Dickinson*. Oxford: Blackwell, 2008. Print.

Smith, Sidonie. *Subjectivity, Identity, and the Body: Women's Autobiographical Practices in the Twentieth Century*. Bloomington: Indiana UP, 1993. Print.

Smith, Sidonie, and Julia Watson. *Reading Autobiography: A Guide for Interpreting Life Narratives*. 2nd ed. Minneapolis: U of Minnesota P, 2010. Print.

Sontag, Susan. *Regarding the Pain of Others*. New York: Farrar, 2003. Print.

"Specimen." *The Oxford English Dictionary*. Oxford UP, n.d. Web. 7 Dec. 2015.

St. Armand, Barton Levi. *Emily Dickinson and Her Culture: The Soul's Society*. Cambridge: Cambridge UP, 1984. Print.

Stern, Julia A. *Mary Chesnut's Civil War Epic*. Chicago: U of Chicago P, 2010. Print.

———. *The Plight of Feeling: Sympathy and Dissent in the Early American Novel*. Chicago: U of Chicago P, 1997. Print.

Still, William. Introduction. Harper, *Iola Leroy* 5–6.

St. John de Crèvecœur, J. Hector. *Letters from an American Farmer*. Hypertexts. U of Virginia, n.d. Web. 28 July 2015.

Stokes, Mason. *The Color of Sex: Whiteness, Heterosexuality, and the Fictions of White Supremacy*. Durham: Duke UP, 2001. Print.

Stone, Kate. *Brokenburn: The Journal of Kate Stone, 1861–1868*. Ed. John Q. Anderson. Baton Rouge: Louisiana State UP, 1995. Print.

Storey, Deborah. "Civil War Expert Ed Bearss to Speak in Huntsville on September 13." *AL.com*. Alabama Media Group, 13 Aug. 2012. Web. 5 Sept. 2014.

Stowe, Harriet Beecher. *Uncle Tom's Cabin; or, Life among the Lowly*. New York: Norton, 2010. Print.

Stutler, Boyd. "John Brown's Body." *Civil War History* 4 (1958): 251–61. Print.

Sullivan, George. *In the Wake of Battle: The Civil War Images of Mathew Brady*. New York: Prestel, 2004. Print.

Sundquist, Eric J. "Slavery, Revolution, and the American Renaissance." *The American Renaissance Reconsidered*. Ed. Walter Benn Michaels and Donald E. Pease. Baltimore: Johns Hopkins UP, 1985. 1–33. Print.

Sweet, Timothy. "Lincoln and the Natural Nation." Samuels 72–90.

———. *Traces of War: Poetry, Photography, and the Crisis of the Union*. Baltimore: Johns Hopkins UP, 1990. Print.

Tagg, John. *The Disciplinary Frame: Photographic Truths and the Capture of Meaning*. Minneapolis: U of Minnesota P, 2009. Print.

Taylor, Susie King. *Reminiscences of My Life in Camp: An African American Woman's Civil War Memoir*. Athens: U of Georgia P, 2006. Print.

Teaching with Documents: Black Soldiers in the Civil War. National Archives. U.S. Natl. Archives and Records Administration, n.d. Web. 25 Feb. 2013.

Tennyson, Alfred. "The Charge of the Light Brigade." *Selected Poems*. London: Penguin, 2007. 215–16. Print. Penguin Classics.

Terdiman, Richard. *Present Past: Modernity and the Memory Crisis.* Ithaca: Cornell UP, 1993. Print.

Thompson, G. R. *Reading the American Novel, 1865–1914.* Malden: Wiley, 2012. Print.

Thompson, William. *Major Jones's Sketches of Travel.* Philadelphia: T. B. Peterson, 1848. Print.

Thoreau, Henry David. "Slavery in Massachusetts." *Reform Papers.* Ed. Wendell Glick. Princeton: Princeton UP, 1973. 91–109. Print.

Tourgée, Albion W. "The South as a Field for Fiction." *Forum* 6 (1888): 404–13. Print.

Towne, Laura M. *Letters and Diary of Laura M. Towne: Written from the Sea Islands of South Carolina, 1862–1864.* Ed. Rupert Sargent Holland. Cambridge: Riverside, 1912. Print.

Trachtenberg, Alan. *Reading American Photographs: Images as History, Mathew Brady to Walker Evans.* New York: Hill, 1989. Print.

"Tragedy at Harper's Ferry." *Liberator* 28 Oct. 1859: 170. Print.

Trelease, Allen W. *White Terror: The Ku Klux Klan Conspiracy and Southern Reconstruction.*

Trethewey, Natasha. "Native Guard." *Native Guard.* Boston: Houghton, 2007. 25–30. Print.

Trowbridge, John. "The Field of Gettysburg." *Atlantic Monthly* Nov. 1865: 616–25. Print.

———. "The Wilderness." *Atlantic Monthly* Jan. 1866: 39–47. Print.

Truth, Sojourner. "Sojourner Truth's Speeches and Commentary." *Sojourner Truth Institute.* Sojourner Truth Inst., n.d. Web. 1 May 2013.

Turner, Nat. The Confessions of Nat Turner *and Related Documents.* Ed. Kenneth S. Greenberg. New York: Bedford–St. Martin's, 1996. Print. Bedford Ser. in History and Culture.

Twain, Mark. *Life on the Mississippi. Mississippi Writings.* New York: Lib. of Amer., 1982. 217–616. Print.

Velazquez, Loreta Janeta. *The Woman in Battle: The Civil War Narrative of Loreta Velazquez, Cuban Woman and Confederate Soldier.* Ed. Jesse Alemán. Madison: U of Wisconsin P, 2003. Print.

Verne, Jules. *The Mysterious Island.* Trans. Stephen W. White. 1874. Philadelphia: Evening Telegraph Rpt., 1876. Print.

Victor, Metta V. *Maum Guinea, and Her Plantation "Children"; or, Holiday-Week on a Louisiana Estate: A Slave Romance.* New York: Beadle and Company, 1861. *Google Books.* Web. 20 Nov. 2010.

Von Frank, Albert J. *The Trials of Anthony York Burns: Freedom and Slavery in Emerson's Boston.* Cambridge: Harvard UP, 1998. Print.

Wade, Wyn Craig. *The Fiery Cross: The Ku Klux Klan in America.* New York: Oxford UP, 1998. Print.

Walker, David. *David Walker's Appeal, in Four Articles: Together with a Preamble, to the Coloured Citizens of the World, but in Particular, and Very Expressly, to Those of the United States of America.* New York: Hill, 1995. Print.

War and Peace Studies Caucus Main Page. Amer. Studies Assn., n.d. Web. 25 Apr. 2015. <http://www.theasa.net/caucus_war_and_peace_studies/>.

Ward, Geoffrey, Ric Burns, and Ken Burns. *The Civil War*. New York: Vintage, 1994. Print.

Warner, Michael. Introduction. Whitman, *Portable Walt Whitman* xi–xxxvii.

Warren, Kenneth. *Black and White Strangers: Race and American Literary Realism*. Chicago: U of Chicago P, 1993. Print.

Weaver, Raymond. Introduction. *Uncle Tom's Cabin: or, Life among the Lowly*. By Harriet Beecher Stowe. New York: Modern Lib., 1948. vii–xx. Print.

Welter, Barbara. *Dimity Convictions: The American Woman in the Nineteenth Century*. Columbus: Ohio State UP, 1976. Print.

White, Garland. "Black Chaplain to the Secretaries of War and State." Berlin et al. 141.

———. "Garland H. White to Edwin M. Stanton." *From Slavery to Freedom*. 28–29. Gilder Lehrman Inst. of Amer. History, n.d. Web. 13 Apr. 2016. <https://www.gilderlehrman.org/sites/all/themes/gli/panels/civilwar150/Civil%20War%20Reader%204%20(single-page%20version).pdf>.

———. "An Interesting Letter from the 28th U.S.C.T." *Christian Recorder* 21 Oct. 1865: 1. Print.

Whitman, Walt. *Complete Poetry and Collected Prose*. Ed. Justin Kaplan. Washington: Lib. of Amer., 1982. Print.

———. *Drum-Taps*. New York: Peter Eckler, 1865. Print.

———. *Poetry and Prose*. New York: Lib. of Amer., 1996. Print.

———. *Portable Walt Whitman*. Ed. Michael Warner. New York: Penguin, 2004. Print.

———. *Specimen Days*. Whitman, *Portable Walt Whitman* 387–640. Excerpt.

Whittier, John Greenleaf. *"The Panorama," and Other Poems*. 1856. *Internet Archive*. Internet Archive, 10 Nov. 2006. Web. 29 July 2015.

Widmer, Ted. "The All-Seeing Eye." *New York Times*. New York Times, 25 July 2011. Web. 25 Oct. 2013.

Wiggins, William H. "From Galveston to Washington: Charting Juneteenth's Freedom Trail." *Jubilation! African American Celebrations in the Southeast*. Ed. Wiggins and Douglas DeNatale. Columbia: U of South Carolina P, 1993. 61–67. Print.

Wills, Gary. *Lincoln at Gettysburg: The Words That Remade America*. New York: Simon, 1992. Print.

Wilson, Anthony. *Shadow and Shelter: The Swamp in Southern Culture*. Jackson: UP of Mississippi, 2006. Print.

Wilson, Edmund. *Patriotic Gore: Studies in the Literature of the American Civil War*. 1962. New York: Norton, 1994. Print.

Wilson, Ivy G. "Rhetorically Lincoln: Abraham Lincoln and Oratorical Culture." Samuels 8–21.

Wolanin, Barbara A. "Miegs the Art Patron." *Montgomery C. Meigs and the Building of the Nation's Capital*. Ed. William C. Dickinson et. al. Athens: Ohio UP, 2001. 133–65. Print.

Wolosky, Shira. *Emily Dickinson: A Voice of War*. New Haven: Yale UP, 1984. Print.

Wonham, Henry B. *Playing the Races: Ethnic Caricature and American Literary Realism*. New York: Oxford UP, 2004. Print.

Woodward, C. Vann, ed. *Mary Chesnut's Civil War*. New Haven: Yale UP, 1981. Print.

Wright, Chris. *Korea: Its History and Culture*. Seoul: Jungmunsa Munhwa, 1994. Print.

Yellin, Jean Fagan, ed. *The Harriet Jacobs Family Papers*. Chapel Hill: U of North Carolina P, 2008. Print.

———. *Women and Sisters: The Antislavery Feminists in American Culture*. New Haven: Yale UP, 1989. Print.

Young, Elizabeth. "Verbal Battlefields." *On Alexander Gardner's* Photographic Sketch Book of the Civil War. Berkeley: U of California P, 2007. 52–94. Print.

Young, Louis Gourdin. Letter to William Pettigrew, 2 June 1862. Folder 254 of the Pettigrew Family Papers 592. *Southern Historical Collection*. Wilson Lib., U of North Carolina, Chapel Hill, n.d. Web. 29 Apr. 2013. <http://www.lib.unc.edu/blogs/civilwar/index.php/2012/06/02/2-june-1862/>.

Z. R. "It Grows Very Dark, Mother—Very Dark." Moore, *Rebellion Record* 2: 10–11.

Index

Aaron, Daniel, 2, 52n1
Abulibdeh, Enas Said, 203
Alcott, Louisa May, 2, 9, 88, 132, 147–50,
  152, 155nn1–2, 165–68, 200, 205,
  212, 214, 252, 256–60, 263
Aldrich, Thomas Bailey, 50
Aleckson, Sam, 214
Alemán, Jesse, 210n14
Alexander, Leslie, 163n2
Allison, Alexander, 160
Anderson, Benedict, 154
Andrews, Eliza Frances, 106, 108
Andrews, Matthew Page, 5, 19n1
Anne (Chesnut slave), 194
Aptheker, Herbert, 191, 192
Ash, Stephen V., 120n3
Assmann, Jann, 209n2
Austin, Mary, 51

Backus, E. M., 164n9
Baker, Obadiah Ethelbert, 75
Ballard, Michael B., 144
Balzac, Honoré de, 46, 47
Barnard, George, 79
Barnes, Elizabeth, 175
Barrett, Faith, 3, 5, 8, 9, 11, 78, 80n5,
  115, 117, 164n3, 176, 178, 224–25,
  227, 231n2, 241
Barrish, Phillip J., 52n1
Baym, Nina, 148
Beale, Joseph Boggs, 209n9
Bearss, Ed, 66
Beauregard, P. T. G., 48, 49, 237
Beeghley, Jim, 207
Bell, Andrew McIlwaine, 141
Bellamy, Francis, 179
Benson, Richard, 33
Berger, John, 127
Bergland, Renée, 80n5
Berlin, Ira, 100
Bernier, Celeste-Marie, 159
Bierce, Ambrose, 48, 142
Black, Alex W., 8, 9, 13
Blair, Hugh, 263n1
Blanton, DeAnne, 210n14
Blight, David, 143, 181, 214, 229

Blodgett, Harriet, 103
Boker, George Henry, 156, 158, 160–62,
  164 (nn 3, 10), 235
Booth, John Wilkes, 6
Borglum, Gutzom, 144
Boritt, Gabor, 113, 114, 115, 119
Boyle, Tom, 209n6
Bradford, William, 221, 230
Bradshaw, Wesley, 167, 172
Brady, Lisa M., 141, 142
Brady, Mathew, 205–07, 210n11
Braugher, Andre, 33
Brennan, Joseph, 250
Broderick, Matthew, 33
Brodhead, Richard H., 49–50, 51
Bronson-Bartlett, Blake, 217, 219
Brooks, Geraldine, 200, 208
Brown, John, 23, 24, 28–30, 59–61, 64,
  73–74, 79, 140, 158, 223–24, 228,
  247–48, 254nn 2–4
Brown, Joshua, 214
Brown, William Wells, 35, 37–40, 42,
  84–86, 88, 90n3
Browne, C. A., 74
Bruner, Peter, 110n7
Bruns, Roger, 173n1
Buck, Lucy, 110n5
Burnett, Charles, 25
Burns, Anthony, 24, 28
Burns, Ken, 24, 61–62, 206, 208
Burns, Ric, 61–62
Burroughs, Edgar Rice, 142
Butler, Benjamin, 12, 97–98
Butos, Cynthia, 155n2

Capello, Mary, 260
Capper, Charles, 32n2
Carey, Allison E., 9, 12, 17
Cary, Alice, 156–58, 163n1
Casares, Oscar, 51
Castagna, JoAnn E., 84, 88, 89, 90
Cavitch, Max, 232n14
Chakkalakal, Tess, 9, 10
Chamberlain, Joshua Lawrence, 62–63
Chandler, Marion, 191
Chesnut, James, Jr., 192, 195

Chesnut, James, Sr., 192, 193
Chesnut, Mary Boykin Miller, 5, 105–08,
  110nn5–6, 167, 171–72, 187–97,
  197n2, 225, 253
Chesnut, Mary Cox, 191, 194
Chesnutt, Charles, 14, 51, 133–34, 144,
  181, 182
Child, Lydia Maria, 107, 252
Childs, Rhoda Ann, 99–100
Chopin, Kate, 51, 128, 129
Clark, Benjamin, 156–58, 163, 163n2
Clark, Beverly, 260
Clarke, James Freeman, 74
Clinton, Catherine, 172
Clinton, William Jefferson, 103
Cohen, Lara Langer, 89
Conforti, Joseph A., 137
Connery, Thomas B., 134n2
Cook, Lauren, 210n14
Cooke, John Esten, 50
Cooper, James Fenimore, 167
Corbaux, Louisa, 205, 209n9
Crane, Hart, 97
Crane, Stephen, 3, 14, 48, 52, 130–31,
  142, 198, 199, 200, 204
Crawford, Thomas, 14, 165, 167–69, 172,
  173n1
Crèvecœur, J. Hector St. John de, 137, 229
Culley, Margo, 103, 108
Curry, J. L. M., 48

Daniels, Christopher, 192
Daniels, Martha Williams, 196
Daniels, Marty, 196
Darley, F. O. C., 205, 206
Davis, Arthur, 88
Davis, Donald Edward, 137
Davis, Esther, 193
Davis, Jefferson, 77, 113, 143, 144, 169,
  195, 237, 246
Davis, Matthew R., 9, 14
Davis, Rebecca Harding, 92, 132, 214,
  215–16, 217, 219
Davison, Gideon Minor, 139
De Forest, John W., 47–49, 129–30, 141,
  181, 212, 214
Delany, Martin, 140
Denning, Michael, 90n1
DeSpain, Jessica, 9, 14, 17
Dicey, Edward, 32
Dickinson, Anna E., 35, 39–42
Dickinson, Austin, 75

Dickinson, Emily, 2, 8–9, 74–76, 118,
  220, 222, 226–28, 231n2, 232n8
Diffley, Kathleen, 9, 15, 98, 141, 223
Dimock, Wai Chee, 44
Dixon, Edward H., 147, 150–53
Dixon, Thomas, 147, 153–53, 155n3
Doctorow, E. L., 200
Douglas, Stephen A., 112
Douglass, Frederick, 25, 28, 35, 56, 77,
  101, 109, 116, 119, 140, 159, 160,
  180, 212, 213, 217, 219, 221, 225,
  229, 248
Dove, Rita, 172–73
Du Bois, W. E. B., 182
duCille, Ann, 88
Dunbar, Paul Laurence, 51, 132, 182
Duquette, Elizabeth, 9, 14, 16, 183n3
Dwight, Theodore, 139
Dziuban, Charles D., 209n6

Eakin, Paul John, 110n3
East, Charles, 108
Edmonds, Sarah Emma, 132
Eicher, David J., 135
Elbert, Sarah, 149
Elkins, Stanley M., 32n1
Ellis, Richard J., 179
Ellison, Ralph, 34
Emerson, Ralph Waldo, 23, 24, 26–32,
  114, 117, 224
Emmett, Dan, 77
Entel, Rebecca, 9, 16
Erll, Astrid, 198
Euclid, 109
Evans, Augusta Jane, 48–49
Everett, Edward, 113–14

Fabian, Ann, 200
Fahs, Alice, 3, 6, 80n3, 81, 87, 89, 166,
  168, 199, 200, 209n3, 212, 214,
  242n1, 257, 259, 260
Farrison, William Edward, 88
Faulkner, William, 52
Faust, Drew Gilpin, 34, 232n11
Fetterley, Judith, 163n1
Fiege, Mark, 137, 141
Fields, James, 155n1
Filo, John, 206
Fincher, Jack, 164n8
Finseth, Ian, 3, 9, 13, 114, 140
FitzHugh, George, 139
Flaubert, Gustave, 46–47

Foreman, P. Gabrielle, 86
Foster, Hannah Webster, 167
Fothergill, Robert A., 103
Foucault, Michel, 110n2
Fox-Genovese, Elizabeth, 107
Franklin, John Hope, 139
Franklin, Ralph W., 80n6
Franklin, Wayne, 230
Frassanito, William A., 144, 210n11,
    232n13
Frazier, Charles, 142, 200
Freire, Paulo, 110n8
Freeman, David B., 144
Freeman, Morgan, 33
Fremantle, A. J. L., 60, 63, 64
Frey, James, 110n3
Friedlander, Benjamin, 80n5
Friedman, Susan, 106
Fryd, Vivien Green, 168, 169, 173n1
Fuller, Randall, 52n1

Gage, Frances Dana Barker, 119
Gale, Robert L., 173n1
Gallagher, Gary W., 60, 61, 63, 65
Galt, William, 5
Gardner, Alexander, 79, 127, 207,
    210n11, 214, 222, 226, 229–30, 232
    (nn 7, 12, 13)
Garland, Hamlin, 51, 128
Garrison, William Lloyd, 16, 25, 27, 28,
    64, 221, 247
Garvey, T. Gregory, 32n2
Gilroy, Paul, 16
Glazener, Nancy, 134n2
Gonzales, Lisa, 209n6
Gougeon, Len, 32n2
Gramegna, Lorenza, 103
Granger, Gordon, 119
Grant, Ulysses S., 35, 42, 128, 135, 136,
    141, 142, 144n2
Gray, Thomas, 25
Greenspan, Ezra, 242n1
Griffith, D. W., 153
Grimké, Angelina 107
Grimké, Charlotte Forten, 119
Guelzo, Allen C., 118, 120n2
Gura, Philip F., 230

Hack, Daniel, 162
Hager, Christopher, 9, 12, 44, 47, 100n1
Halbwachs, Maurice, 209n2
Hale, Edward Everett, 180

Hale, Sarah Josepha, 50
Hamilton, Ed, 160
Harper, Frances Ellen Watkins, 35, 39,
    41–42, 77, 167, 172
Harvey, Charles M., 82, 88, 90
Harwood, W. S., 146
Hawthorne, Nathaniel, 8, 23–24, 29–32,
    46–47, 141, 176–79, 213
Hayne, Paul Hamilton, 50
Hedrick, Joan, 1
Helper, Hinton Rowan, 139
Hembree, Todd, 209n5
Hemings, Sally, 88
Henkin, David M., 91
Hentz, Caroline Lee, 50, 51, 141
Hicks, Thomas Holliday, 5
Higginson, Thomas Wentworth, 9, 34–35,
    36–39, 42, 77, 100, 118–19
Hillen, J. F. E., 207
Hofstadter, Richard, 116
Holmes, Emma, 108
Holmes, Oliver Wendell, 5, 19n1, 178
Homer, Winslow, 232n6
Hong Myoung-hee, 57
Hönnighausen, Lothar, 173n1
Hopkins, Cyril, 144
Horton, George Moses, 76–78, 80nn7–8
Horwitz, Tony, 144
Howe, Daniel Walker, 138
Howe, Julia Ward, 71, 73–75, 80n4, 160
Howells, William Dean, 47, 97, 124
Huddleston, John, 144
Hunter, David, 117
Hutchison, Coleman, 8, 10, 17, 48, 49,
    80n5, 183n1
Hyun In-taek, 55

Ifill, Gwen, 103
Ishtaiwa, Fawi Fayez, 203

Jackson, Leon, 80n7
Jackson, Mattie, 110n7, 132
Jackson, "Stonewall," 144
Jackson, Virginia, 80n2, 114
Jacobs, Harriet, 100, 101, 110n7, 159,
    164n5, 167, 172
James, Henry, 45–47, 123, 124, 129, 181
Jarrett, Gene, 131
Jefferson, Thomas, 88, 101, 109, 192
Jelinek, Estelle, 104–05
Jennings, Samuel, 167–68
Jewett, Sarah Orne, 51

Johannsen, Albert, 82
Johnson, Walter, 137
Jones, Bessie Z., 200
Jones, Shawn, 11

Kagle, Steven, 103
Kaplan, Amy, 50, 51, 170, 173n3
Kaser, David, 82, 89
Katz, Harry J., 232n6
Keely, Karen, 183n2
Kemble, Fanny (Frances Anne), 17, 167, 171
Kenan, Randall, 51
Kennedy, John Pendleton, 141
Kim Dong-in, 57
King, Martin Luther, Jr., 119
Kirby, Jack Temple, 137
Kirstein, Lincoln, 33
Klumpenhower, Wiebke Omnus, 9, 11, 17
Krupat, Arnold, 113, 221, 225, 226, 227, 228, 229, 230
Kurz, Louis, 160

Lanier, Sidney, 50
Larcom, Lucy, 171, 179–80
Laurence (Chesnut slave), 194, 195
LeConte, Emma, 110n5
Lee, Anthony W., 229, 232n7
Lee, Maurice, 80n5
Lee, Robert E., 6, 60, 61–62, 144
Lee, Spike, 209n4
Leland, C. G., 235
Levine, Robert S., 43, 52, 113, 221, 225, 226, 227, 228, 229, 230
Lewis, Edmonia, 159
Limon, John, 134nn1–2
Lincoln, Abraham, 1, 6, 9, 13, 31, 33, 35, 38–39, 42, 56, 60, 62, 65, 76, 79, 88, 93–94, 111–18, 135, 159, 170, 174–75, 196, 222–26, 228–31, 231n2 4, 237, 244, 246
Linenthal, Edward, 144
Livermore, Mary, 200, 204
Long, Alecia P., 97
Longfellow, Henry Wadsworth, 79, 128–29
Longstreet, Augustus Baldwin, 50, 51, 62
Looby, Christopher, 36
Lorang, Elizabeth, 162, 163, 163–64nn2–3
Lowell, James Russell, 178

Lowell, Robert, 51, 163
Lyell, Charles, 138

Mann, T. H., 200
Manning, John, 187–88
Marien, Mary Warner, 125
Marrs, Cody, 44, 47
Marsh, George Perkins, 138
Masur, Kate, 159, 161, 209n4
Marx, Karl, 31
McCarthy, Barbara, 196
McCarthy, Cormac, 142
McClellan, George, 31
McConnell, Stuart, 208, 209n1
McDowell, Irvin, 238
McHenry, Elizabeth, 214
McKivigan, John, 82, 83, 84
McLoughlin, Kate, 257
McMichael, Dana, 12, 18, 109n
McPherson, James M., 5, 6, 75, 214
McWilliams, John, 26
McWhirter, Christian, 164 (nn 4, 7)
Meade, George, 62
Melville, Herman, 2, 14, 48, 78–80, 80n1, 92, 97, 128–30, 140–41, 164n9, 175, 211, 212, 213, 214, 218, 221, 222–23, 225–27, 231 (nn 2–3, 5), 234–35, 247, 249–51, 253, 254n2
Menand, Louis, 52n1
Miller, Cristanne, 3, 5, 78, 80 (nn 2, 5), 115, 117, 164n3, 224–25, 227, 231n2, 232n8, 241
Mitchell, Margaret, 142
Mitchell, Reid, 75
Moat, Louis Shepheard, 210n13
Molly (Chesnut slave), 194–97
Moon, Michael, 232n10
Moore, Frank, 79, 146, 163n1, 233–37, 240–42, 242n1
Morgan, Sarah, 108
Morton, Samuel George, 85, 90
Muench, David, 144
Muhlenfeld, Elisabeth, 110n6, 197n2
Mulvey, Christopher, 88
Murphy, Sean, 209n5
Myer, J. C., 139

Naylor, Celia E., 209n5
Nelson, Megan Kate, 141
Newkirk, Thomas, 95
Noll, Mark A., 62

Nora, Pierre, 198, 199, 201, 206, 209n2
Northup, Solomon, 138, 140
Nudelman, Franny, 247

O'Brien, Tim, 48
O'Connor, Flannery, 51
Olmsted, Frederick Law, 136, 138–39
Olney, James, 103
O'Malley, Michael, 249
O'Sullivan, Timothy, 127

Packer, Barbara, 32n2
Page, Thomas Nelson, 182
Palin, Sarah, 206
Parker, Theodore, 133
Patterson, Orlando, 196
Payne, Daniel Alexander, 62
Peabody, Elizabeth, 29
Pearson, Elizabeth Ware, 118
Peck, William Henry, 142, 143
Perry, Nora, 92
Pettigrew, James Johnston, 96
Phelps, Elizabeth Stuart, 128, 181, 252
Pitts, Reginald, 80n8
Poe, Edgar Allan, 50
Pound, Ezra, 97
Pratt, Lloyd, 44
Price, Kenneth M., 67
Private Gordon, 171
Pryse, Marjorie, 163n1

Randall, James Ryder, 5, 6, 19, 175–76
Ransom, John, 200
Rapley, Rob, 25
Ray, Frederic, 210n11
Raymond, Jon, 51
Read, Thomas Buchanan, 79
Redkey, Edwin S., 94
Redpath, James, 82, 84, 88–89, 205, 261
Reekie, John, 127Regosin, Elizabeth A.,
    99, 100n3
Reid, Philip, 169, 173n2
Reid, Whitelaw, 60–61, 63
Reinhart, Charles S., 204, 205
Renker, Elizabeth, 97
Renza, Louis, 110n2
Reynolds, Larry J., 8, 10, 16, 28
Rhodes, Elisha Hunt, 75
Rice, John H., 62
Rivers, Prince, 118
Roach, A. C., 200

Roberts, Jess, 15
Rogers, Randolph, 159
Rogers, Seth, 118
Rohrbach, Augusta, 131
Root, George F., 158
Rosen, Hannah, 100n4
Ross, John, 202
Rowlandson, Mary, 230
Ruby, Jay, 125
Ruffin, Edmund, 138
Ruiz de Burton, María Amparo, 17, 142
Ryan, Susan M., 9, 15
Ryden, Kent C., 137
Ryzik, Melena, 209n4

Sachs, Aaron, 141
Saint-Gaudens, Augustus, 34, 160
Sanborne, Geoffrey, 39
Saunders, Catherine E., 14, 16
Savage, Kirk, 159, 164n6
Scharnhorst, Gary, 47
Schultz, Jane E., 204, 214, 257, 258, 260
Scipio (Chesnut slave, father), 192–93
Scipio (Chesnut slave, son), 193
Scott, Walter, 6, 16
Sedgwick, Catherine Maria, 167
Seeger, Pete, 254n3
Selznick, David O., 206, 209n1
Seward, William H., 93–94, 150
Shaw, Robert Gould, 33, 41–42, 160
Shaara, Michael, 142
Shaffer, Donald R., 99, 100n3
Sherman, Joan, 80n7
Sherman, William Tecumseh, 82, 136,
    141–42, 144n2, 167, 172, 193, 196
Shi, David E., 123, 134n2
Signaigo, J. Augustine, 227
Sigourney, Lydia H., 50
Silber, Nina, 47
Simmons, Michael K., 88
Simms, William Gilmore, 50, 78, 101,
    141, 143
Slotkin, Richard, 1, 144n1
Smith, Diane Monroe, 63
Smith, Gerrit, 248
Smith, John David, 38
Smith, Sidonie, 103–04, 110n8
Sontag, Susan, 127
Spengemann, William, 241
Spielberg, Steven, 209n4
Stader, Douglas, 19n1

Stanton, Edwin, 93, 94
St. Armand, Barton Levi, 80n5
Stearns, Frazar, 75
Stedman, Edmund, 242
Steele, William, 11
Stephens, Alexander, 113
Stern, Julia A., 9, 15, 175, 197n1
Still, William, 41
St. John de Crèvecœur, J. Hector, 137, 229
Stoddard, Richard Henry, 175–76
Stokes, Mason, 90
Stone, Kate, 98, 107–08
Storey, Deborah, 66
Stowe, Harriet Beecher, 1, 56–57, 101, 140–41, 167, 170, 174–75, 177, 205, 214, 216, 225
Strong, Melissa J., 9, 15
Stutler, Boyd, 74
Sullivan, George, 205, 210n12
Sumner, Charles, 24, 28, 106
Sundquist, Eric J., 25
Sutton, Robert, 118–19
Sweet, Timothy, 9, 15, 214, 231nn3–4, 232 (nn 7, 9)

Tagg, John, 125
Taylor, Bayard, 115–17
Taylor, Susie King, 118
Tennyson, Alfred, 17, 157, 162
Terdiman, Richard, 209n2
Thompson, G. R., 134n2
Thompson, John R., 50
Thompson, M. Jeff, 175–76
Thompson, William Tappan, 139
Thoreau, Henry David, 28, 140, 224, 228, 247, 248
Timrod, Henry, 50, 78, 222, 223, 224–25
Toombs, Robert, 93
Tourgée, Albion W., 10, 43, 45, 51–52, 181
Toussaint-Louverture, François-Dominique, 27
Towne, Laura M., 120n4
Trachtenberg, Alan, 125
Trelease, Allen W., 150, 151
Trethewey, Natasha, 51, 163
Trowbridge, John, 79
Truth, Sojourner, 167, 171
Tubman, Harriet, 159

Tucker, Nathaniel Beverly, 27
Turner, Nat, 25–26, 38, 64, 86–87, 140, 158
Twain, Mark, 6, 16, 51, 123, 128, 132

Vecchio, Mary Ann, 206
Velazquez, Loreta Janeta, 128, 207, 210n14
Verne, Jule, 142
Vesey, Denmark, 38, 64, 158
Victor, Metta V., 17, 84, 85–87, 88, 89–90
Virga, Vincent, 232n6
Vodicka, Devin, 209n6
Von Frank, Albert J., 32n2

Wade, Wyn Craig, 150
Walker, David, 109
Ward, Geoffrey, 61–62
Ward, John Quincy Adams, 159
Warner, Michael, 261
Warren, Kenneth, 131
Washington, Booker T., 182
Washington, Denzel, 33
Watkins, Samuel, 128
Watson, Julia, 103–04
Waud, Alfred, 232n6
Waugh, Joan, 199, 209n3
Wedgwood, Josiah, 147
Weir, R. J., 162, 163, 163–64nn2–3
Welter, Barbara, 108
Wheatley, Phyllis, 109
White, Garland, 92–94, 100n1
Whitman, Walt, 2, 3, 8, 12, 63, 67, 91, 100, 128, 200, 220, 222, 225–26, 228–29, 231, 231n2, 235, 244, 252, 255–57, 260–63
Whittier, John Greenleaf, 140
Widmer, Ted, 206
Wiggins, William H., 119
Williams, David R., 192
Williams, Kate Miller, 192, 195
Williamson, Darren T., 11, 16
Wills, Gary, 113
Wilson, Edmund, 36, 47–48, 52n1, 71, 73, 80n1, 97, 174
Wilson, Ivy G., 119
Winthrop, John, 221
Wolanin, Barbara A., 173n1
Wolosky, Shira, 2, 80n5, 232n8

Wonham, Henry B., 131
Woo Min-hee, 57
Wood, Thomas Waterman, 159
Woodward, C. Vann, 106, 110n6,
    188–89, 197n2
Wright, Chris, 56
Wright, Conrad Edick, 32n2

Yellin, Jean Fagan, 107, 159, 164nn5–6
Young, Elizabeth, 214, 229, 232n7
Young, Louis Gourdin, 96

Ziser, Michael, 14
Zola, Emile, 46–47
Z. R., 237

Teaching the Literatures of the American Civil War. Ed. Colleen Glenney Boggs. 2016.

Teaching Human Rights in Literary and Cultural Studies. Ed. Alexandra Schultheis Moore and Elizabeth Swanson Goldberg. 2015.

Teaching the Latin American Boom. Ed. Lucille Kerr and Alejandro Herrero-Olaizola. 2015.

Teaching Early Modern English Literature from the Archives. Ed. Heidi Brayman Hackel and Ian Frederick Moulton. 2015.

Teaching Anglophone Caribbean Literature. Ed. Supriya M. Nair. 2012.

Teaching Film. Ed. Lucy Fischer and Patrice Petro. 2012.

Teaching Seventeenth- and Eighteenth-Century French Women Writers. Ed. Faith E. Beasley. 2011.

Teaching French Women Writers of the Renaissance and Reformation. Ed. Colette H. Winn. 2011.

Teaching Law and Literature. Ed. Austin Sarat, Cathrine O. Frank, and Matthew Anderson. 2011.

Teaching British Women Playwrights of the Restoration and Eighteenth Century. Ed. Bonnie Nelson and Catherine Burroughs. 2010.

Teaching Narrative Theory. Ed. David Herman, Brian McHale, and James Phelan. 2010.

Teaching Early Modern English Prose. Ed. Susannah Brietz Monta and Margaret W. Ferguson. 2010.

Teaching Italian American Literature, Film, and Popular Culture. Ed. Edvige Giunta and Kathleen Zamboni McCormick. 2010.

Teaching the Graphic Novel. Ed. Stephen E. Tabachnick. 2009.

Teaching Literature and Language Online. Ed. Ian Lancashire. 2009.

Teaching the African Novel. Ed. Gaurav Desai. 2009.

Teaching World Literature. Ed. David Damrosch. 2009.

Teaching North American Environmental Literature. Ed. Laird Christensen, Mark C. Long, and Fred Waage. 2008.

Teaching Life Writing Texts. Ed. Miriam Fuchs and Craig Howes. 2007.

Teaching Nineteenth-Century American Poetry. Ed. Paula Bernat Bennett, Karen L. Kilcup, and Philipp Schweighauser. 2007.

Teaching Representations of the Spanish Civil War. Ed. Noël Valis. 2006.

Teaching the Representation of the Holocaust. Ed. Marianne Hirsch and Irene Kacandes. 2004.

Teaching Tudor and Stuart Women Writers. Ed. Susanne Woods and Margaret P. Hannay. 2000.

Teaching Literature and Medicine. Ed. Anne Hunsaker Hawkins and Marilyn Chandler McEntyre. 2000.

Teaching the Literatures of Early America. Ed. Carla Mulford. 1999.

Teaching Shakespeare through Performance. Ed. Milla C. Riggio. 1999.

Teaching Oral Traditions. Ed. John Miles Foley. 1998.

Teaching Contemporary Theory to Undergraduates. Ed. Dianne F. Sadoff and William E. Cain. 1994.

Teaching Children's Literature: Issues, Pedagogy, Resources. Ed. Glenn Edward Sadler. 1992.

Teaching Literature and Other Arts. Ed. Jean-Pierre Barricelli, Joseph Gibaldi, and Estella Lauter. 1990.

New Methods in College Writing Programs: Theories in Practice. Ed. Paul Connolly and Teresa Vilardi. 1986.

School-College Collaborative Programs in English. Ed. Ron Fortune. 1986.

Teaching Environmental Literature: Materials, Methods, Resources. Ed. Frederick O. Waage. 1985.

Part-Time Academic Employment in the Humanities: A Sourcebook for Just Policy. Ed. Elizabeth M. Wallace. 1984.

Film Study in the Undergraduate Curriculum. Ed. Barry K. Grant. 1983.

The Teaching Apprentice Program in Language and Literature. Ed. Joseph Gibaldi and James V. Mirollo. 1981.

Options for Undergraduate Foreign Language Programs: Four-Year and Two-Year Colleges. Ed. Renate A. Schulz. 1979.

Options for the Teaching of English: Freshman Composition. Ed. Jasper P. Neel. 1978.

Options for the Teaching of English: The Undergraduate Curriculum. Ed. Elizabeth Wooten Cowan. 1975.